*The Documentary Conscience*

# The Documentary Conscience
## A Casebook in Film Making

Alan Rosenthal

University of California Press
Berkeley • Los Angeles • London

*Library of Congress Cataloging in Publication Data*

Main entry under title:

The Documentary conscience.
   Includes bibliographical references and index.
   1. Moving–pictures, Documentary—History and
criticism. I. Rosenthal, Alan, 1936–
PN1995.9.D6D55      791.43'53      79–64487
ISBN 0-520-03932-7
ISBN 0-520-04022-8 pbk.

*University of California Press*
*Berkeley and Los Angeles, California*

*University of California Press, Ltd.*
*London, England*

*© 1980 by*
*The Regents of the University of California*

*Printed in the United States of America*

*1 2 3 4 5 6 7 8 9*

*For Miki, Gil and Tal*

# Contents

## Acknowledgments

First my thanks to all those film libraries and distributors who let me burrow through their files and see film after film. I would, on this score, like to thank in particular Bill Sloan of the Donnell Film Library and Gary Crowdus of Tricontinental Films who not only took immense trouble to find the films I needed, but who were also prepared to lay on facilities at a moment's notice. I would also like to express my gratitude to Jeremy Isaacs and Jerome Kuehl for giving me free access to all "The World at War" films and other gems from the Thames Television library.

Thanks are also due to the Faculty of Social Sciences of the Hebrew University who supported the research over two years, and to Debra Carton, Barbara Eisman, and Birta Edwards who did all the typing.

For illustrations I would like to acknowledge my debt to Anomaly Films, Emile de Antonio, the BBC, Cabin Creek Films, Richard Cohen, Jill Godmilow and Rocky Mountain Productions, the Kartemquin Collective, Maysles Films, Inc., the National Film Board of Canada, New Day Films, AO Films, Will Roberts, and the late Robert Vas.

I am of course deeply grateful to all the film makers appearing in this book for giving so much of their time and help. During our meetings and talks I think we developed a number of warm friendships which I hope will deepen with the years. This pleasure and delight is, however, touched with sadness because of the sudden death of Robert Vas whose friendship I had only just begun to know.

Many people helped with this book, but four people, above all others guided my steps and made absolutely invaluable contributions. The first was Patricia Erens who turned up obscure articles, bombarded me with suggestions, taught me a great deal about women and films and conducted two absolutely essential interviews for me—one with Jerry Blumenthal and Jennifer Rohrer and the other with Will Roberts.

My second guide was Colin Young, Director of the British National Film School, who went through the manuscript with a fine-toothed comb, provoking, stimulating and challenging my loose thinking. Another valued mentor was my old friend and teacher Professor Henry

*Acknowledgments*

Breitrose of Stanford University who discussed the concept of the book with me at the start and made excellent suggestions after reading the draft introduction.

My last guiding light was Ernest Callenbach who once again gave me unflagging editorial help and supporting enthusiasm along every inch of the way. To all four my thanks and gratitude.

This book is about documentary in the seventies and the extraordinary vitality it maintains today. It is a book about two passions—
the love of the medium and the exploration of its techniques and possibilities. And it is also about the peculiar passions and dedications of
documentary film makers whose outlooks vary but who share a common social concern.

Who are these people? They are film makers who believe that in one
way or another film can and should be used as a tool, some would even
say a weapon, for social change. They work in vastly different ways,
but all believe that the function of the documentary is to clarify choices,
interpret history and promote human understanding. They believe film
should provide a revelation of human dignity. Many of them—even
some who work in large broadcasting organizations—believe film should
be embattled.

This book explores who these people are, the choices they make and
what moves them and drives them. Often the drive is relentless and
compulsive. It was this inner drive that kept Barbara Kopple and Hart
Perry filming under the guns of the scabs in *Harlan County USA*. It
was this peculiar madness that made Abe Osheroff leave his work as
a carpenter, go to Spain, and risk arrest by the Franco police to say
something about the Spanish Civil War and fascism.

The actions and beliefs of these people made them produce certain
kinds of films. Some might call them committed documentaries. Others
would use the word concerned. Many of these films, unfortunately,
have not been given the public recognition which is their due. Thus
an overall objective of this book is to remedy that situation by pointing
out and proclaiming their worth.

Another and more specific aim is to look at these films in diverse
ways which will help us understand more fully the whole film making
process. I want to look at the working methods and production problems of these films from financing and fund raising through restrictions
such as censorship and personal pressures, to the other hundred and
one problems that beset the film maker on the way. The first question
is *how*.

A further specific aim is to ask *why*. The book probes why the films
were made. It examines the background of the film maker and his or

her view of society. It asks questions about the function of film and about the extent to which film can really effect social change. And it asks what happens to the film maker in the process of filming.

Such matters are delicate, personal, and too seldom discussed. Often the documentarist is seen as a teacher and moralist to the world, but what are the changes taking place within the film maker? After shooting *The Gift of Endless Dreams* Tom Haydon came away with a softer view of British imperialism. John Pett's work on "The World at War" drew him closer to his father and deepened his understanding of war's brutality. For Sue McConachy, researching a film not only brought about strange meetings but also occasioned some severe ethical crises.

Finally, the book aims to re-examine certain general documentary questions: the situation of the freelance film maker, the position of the networks both as sponsors and as end users of documentary, and the mood of documentary today. Related areas for discussion arise from my own personal interests, such as the way documentary treats history and the place of ethics and responsibility in these kinds of films.

In asking the above questions and in shaping the book I have tried to keep two different types of readers in mind. I hope that film makers—students or veterans—who want to hear and learn more of the practical and theoretical problems which have faced others in the field will gain information which will be useful and applicable to their own work.

My other audience is the general reader, since the fate of documentary film making and distribution is a matter that affects the political health of the entire society, and thus concerns us all—even people who may think "documentary" means only films on lions or polar bears.

This book consists of a series of case studies. Like my previous book *The New Documentary in Action*, it elicits information about the making of particular films through discussing them with the film maker. This kind of study is now fairly common for other mass media; Edward Jay Epstein's *News from Nowhere* is one of the better examples. Among feature films the classic study is still Lillian Ross's book on the making of *The Red Badge of Courage*, which has now been joined by a number of "quickies": *The Jaws Log* and other paperbacks on the making of *2001*, *Brewster McCloud*, *The Exorcist*, and *Star Wars*.

Unfortunately the documentary case study is still rare. This is sad not just because the films are important but because the processes and problems they involve are often more intricate and interesting than those of the feature. Recently some pioneering efforts have been made in this case study area by magazines including *Jump Cut*, *Cineaste*, and

*Film Library Quarterly*. These magazines, however, have only touched the fringe and the area still remains understudied and overlooked.

Most of the case studies in this book try to follow a film from initial idea to release print and to examine the decision-making process along the way. Some of the interviews go further and delve into problems of distribution. Many of the interviews discuss the ultimate use of the film among both large audiences and small groups. In some of the interviews I have tried to probe the effects of the monopoly power of network transmission. Not all the interviews are meant to be comprehensive. Thus Ellen Hovde restricts herself to the editing of *Grey Gardens* while Jeremy Sandford gives the writer's view on *Edna, the Inebriate Woman*.

While many documentarists operate independently, important work in documentary is also done in a series format for broadcast, and to cope with the complexities of production involved I wanted to examine such a series in depth, from the multiple viewpoints of the different participants. I was very lucky in getting the cooperation of the team that produced "The World at War." Over forty production personnel worked on this series. In the end I chose to interview the associate producer Jerome Kuehl, director John Pett, and researchers Raye Farr and Sue McConachy. Taken together their interviews give an excellent vantage point for understanding how a complex series is put together from start to finish.

Many different considerations guided selection of the book's contents. I wanted films that would describe and illustrate the challenges and concerns of films today, from the obvious and traditional social problems to more recent issues such as the women's movement. And given my interest in process and the "nitty gritty" of film making it was imperative to include a range of work that would illustrate the varied methods and techniques of documentary in the seventies.

What is fascinating, of course, is to follow the frequent sheer divergence of approach. Thus while George Stoney and others will sometimes change a film according to a subject's comments, Jill Godmilow is adamant about refusing editing rights to others. Morton Silverstein works hand in hand with his editor. *Grey Gardens* was edited by Ellen Hovde and Muffie Meyers with the Maysles brothers standing almost completely aside. On the question of whether to use commentary, Emile de Antonio and Jerry Blumenthal are at opposite ends of the spectrum.

However, there is a strong thread of shared views running through the discussion of the network television battles engaged in by Douglas Leiterman, Tom Haydon, and Robert Vas. De Antonio, Cinda Firestone, and Raye Farr have very different approaches but they share the common problem of pursuing archive material, while Abe Osheroff reveals his own unique method in getting archive material out of the Pentagon.

Few prescribed films appear in the discussions, another sign of the changing times. Instead Mike Rubbo, Amalie Rothschild, and others describe how they had to revise preconceived film notions and structures in the light of insights gained during the filming itself. For Rubbo this meant a total change of direction in *Waiting for Fidel*. In *Nana, Mom and Me* Rothschild only discovered the point of her film when halfway through.

Finding films to illustrate different techniques and styles was easy. Choosing films to illustrate the movements and concerns of the seventies was far more difficult, because the documentary output of the period covered such a multitude of movements and areas of concern: Vietnam; the women's movement; urban decay; ecology. And for every subject there were often several good films. No list of films, whether for a festival or a book, is ever altogether satisfactory. I saw hundreds of films before finalizing my own list. I can only hope that my eventual choices were representative and fair, though they could not be truly comprehensive.*

One special consideration was to find a range of films that would illustrate the differences between working inside and outside "the system" comprised of such institutions as the BBC, the National Film Board, the CBC, and the American networks. I wanted to see what were the current possibilities of those systems, and what were their limitations. And I wanted discussions that would allow the free-ranging spirits outside the system to talk about their hopes, their strategies, and the more personal films they were doing.

I also wanted to contrast the views and experiences of those who'd done everything and seen everything with those who were just beginning. Al Wasserman, Roger Graef, Robert Vas, and Mort Silverstein must have made more than a hundred films among them. David Elstein and Michael Latham must produce a film or magazine item every other week or month. But *Harlan County* and *Attica* were the first major films for Barbara Kopple and Cinda Firestone, though they had worked on other films in minor roles. Will Roberts's *Men's Lives* represents his first serious work in film. Even more amazing is Abe Osheroff's *Dreams and*

*The categories into which I have placed the film makers are intended only to suggest resemblances and links among them, and should not be taken as an attempt at any kind of rigid classification.

4

*Nightmares*, a total plunge into the unknown by a fifty-nine-year-old California artisan.

I particularly wanted to explore an interest of my own which is seldom discussed in a documentary context: how film looks at history. "The World at War" was an obvious case for the study of this question and Jerome Kuehl both as producer and historian was the obvious man for commenting on film's historical overview. Film is today a major means through which the present reinterprets the past. No one who has seen "The World at War" can hold to the old two-dimensional view of the Battle of Britain or the old simplistic reasons for the dropping of atomic bombs on Japan. This demythologizing function of film is also central to Robert Vas's discussion of *Nine Days in '26* and forms the focus for Tom Haydon's remarks on his Australian film.*

And I am interested in another rather unfashionable question: the ethics of the documentarist, whose personal conscience is one of the things alluded to in this book's title. Calvin Pryluck has written about documentary ethics at length† but apart from his work and that of a few others the subject is shamefully neglected. How far can a film maker exploit a subject in the name of the general truth or the general good? Many perplexing questions lead from that one. How far does the subject realize what is going on? Does the subject realize the implications and possible consequences of his or her life being portrayed on the screen, or of being interviewed? When consent was given for filming, what was really meant by the film maker and what was understood by the subject? When does one have to shut off the camera, or destroy footage?

The interviews range over a number of these ethical issues. Sue McConachy talks about her conflict when confronting an old Nazi officer. Richard Cohen tells of his hesitation before filming the pain and humiliation of a mental patient in a hospital corridor. David Elstein goes on with a program even though it may mean prison for someone he's interviewed. Robin Spry shows his dilemma when a man wants to withdraw from a program months after the film is finished.

A fundamental complication of these ethical issues arises from the sometimes surprising complexities of how we see ourselves and how

*The Sorrow and the Pity* by Marcel Ophuls is extremely relevant to this topic but for reasons mentioned on p. 7 is not discussed in this book. I would also like to have tackled the implications of "Roots" and "Holocaust" but felt that these programs and their difficulties warrant a special essay to themselves.

†Calvin Pryluck, "Ultimately We Are All Outsiders," *Journal of the University Film Association*, Winter 1976, p. 21.

we wish to be seen. George Stoney has a great deal to say on this and it is one of the core questions in discussing *Grey Gardens*, which was widely attacked for having supposedly humiliated its two subjects, Edith Beale and her daughter. Ellen Hovde denies the accusations. She argues, and I believe correctly, that there was no question of humiliation and that the real discomfort arose from an audience which could not face itself.

This book has a wide range but it also has clear limits. I decided to limit my time coverage to a rough beginning point around 1972, though this limitation isn't too rigid. (Douglas Leiterman's *One More River*, Beryl Fox's *Mills of the Gods* and Al Wasserman's *The Battle of Newburgh* are all from the early sixties.) There were two main reasons for this time choice. First, after a dearth of material on documentary a whole group of books suddenly appeared together in the early seventies, ranging from interview studies such as my *New Documentary in Action* and G. Roy Levin's excellent *Documentary Explorations* to film histories such as Erik Barnouw's *Documentary* and Richard Barsaam's *Non-Fiction Film*. These books, together with Stephen Mamber's *Cinéma Vérité in America*, provide a fairly good history of recent documentary up to about 1971. I didn't want to go over too much old ground, so 1972 seemed a convenient starting point.

A more important reason for starting in the early seventies was that certain changes had taken place about that time in documentary—in style, purpose, ideology, and the very people involved in documentary. It looked as if a small revolution had taken place, though it was one almost entirely confined to independent film makers. The idea of documenting some of these changes interested me, and is one of the underlying purposes of this book.

Besides acknowledging the confines of time I also had to acknowledge the confines of space. Somewhat regretfully, I have only dealt in these pages with films made in England, the United States, and Canada, since I wanted to work from a cultural context that I have personally experienced. I was brought up in England, went to school and university there, played cricket in the evenings, and drank warm beer while in the RAF; it's still a place I know well. I also lived and worked in Canada for two years and the United States for four, and go back to both places fairly often. As a result I think I have a reliable grasp of these cultures, their histories, their social and political norms, and what they consider deviations from the norms. Documentaries, like fiction films, are often exceedingly hard to grasp if they come from an alien culture. By sticking to films from my own, whose nuances I could reasonably expect to fathom, I felt I would do a better job of interviewing than I could in cultures where I was less at home. But this geographical restriction was a difficult one to accept. It meant omitting Europe, Asia, Latin America. It meant leaving out Rouch, Marker, Ivens, and Alvarez, all of whom are vital names in the discussion of recent documentary evolution. It meant leaving out Antonioni's film on China and Louis Malle's epic *Phantom India*. And it meant leaving out two outstanding and controversial films by Marcel Ophuls, *The Sorrow and the Pity* and *The Memory of Justice*. This limitation also meant I had to exclude documentary in South America. This was especially hard because if documentary has anywhere a force and a passion, an urgency and a necessity, it is there. Most of this vast area is suffering under brutal military and fascist regimes. Open discussion and access to the media are extremely limited. Yet in spite of all the restrictions, the documentaries or documentary dramas that have emerged from South America in the last ten years have been simply amazing in their scope and force. *Blood of the Condor*, from Bolivia, needs to be mentioned in this context as does *The Brickmakers* from Colombia. The Cuban feature *Memories of Underdevelopment*, which has a strong documentary side, might also be mentioned in this context, along with many full documentaries from Cuba. However, the two most powerful political documentaries of the period are *The Hour of the Furnaces*, from Argentina, and *The Battle for Chile*, made by Chileans in exile. Both films have to be seen by anyone even moderately interested in documentary, and the whole area of Latin American documentary needs exploration.

I have chosen deliberately to omit films by, for, or about blacks. This omission implies nothing about the nature of the films themselves, but arises solely from my own inadequacy in dealing with the topic. I am not black, I know little of black society, and I felt there was no way I could get inside the black film maker to do proper justice to black films.

The reader will also find there are few films in this book by committed Marxists or from the extreme left. Such films have played a strong part in forming the new film consciousness of the seventies. Many of them come from left-wing film cooperatives or other tightly bound groups of political film makers. The groups are numerous, the best known being Newsreel, which was founded in 1968 to offer one alternative to the mass media. Among its key figures have been Robert Kramer and Norman Fruchter. Newsreel has been very prolific over a ten-year period. At the time of writing it has split into "New York Newsreel" and "San Francisco Newsreel," with the latter concentrating on films about women, blacks and the Third World. The most important films to have come out of the group are probably *The People's War*, about Vietnam, *Black Panther*, and *The Women's Film*. The group has had a certain influence but it is difficult to assess how much. Its main problem has been that its films speak almost entirely to the converted and have failed to touch or reach the urban middle or working class.

But I am wary of many of these political films. I respect their concern for a new, more just social order; I distrust them for their lack of compassion, and their tendency to condemn Western society's ills while tacitly condoning those of totalitarian collectivist regimes. My personal bias is toward skeptical humanism, and the reader should understand clearly that as the interviewer in the rest of this book I worked from the position of a middle-class liberal moralist—for better or for worse.

One final caveat: this is not a book about theory, but about how film makers work and how they perceive their efforts. Strangely little theoretical work has been done, either in the recent upsurge of film theory or in earlier decades, on the structures and techniques of documentary; and there is a grave need for theoretically minded writers to attack these questions in a serious way. Some lines of inquiry will concern formal matters: how documentaries are shot, cut, constructed. Others will concern interactions between documentaries and their viewers, and will bring to bear findings from perceptual psychology, information theory, and various social sciences. But this book, which is itself a sort of "print documentary," makes no attempt to formulate such issues.

In talking about the excitement and dynamism of the seventies I have in mind films like *Harlan County*, *I. F. Stone's Weekly*, *Union Maids*, *Attica*, *Hurry Tomorrow*, and Roger Graef's pioneering series "Decisions" and "The Space Between Words." In the sixties there was a similar blossoming. A comparison of these two decades is necessary to understand present-day trends.

The dramatic developments of the late fifties and sixties lay in the artistic challenge represented by the development of light-weight film equipment and in the influence exerted by *cinéma vérité* pioneers like Drew Associates in the U.S., Koenig, Kroitor and Macartney-Filgate in Canada, and Jean Rouch and Chris Marker in France. The combination of technical breakthrough and exploration of form by these film makers radically altered structure and approach in documentary.

The work of these film makers opened up possibilities for the direct capturing of real events, with synchronized sound, that had simply not been available to Grierson or Flaherty or the documentarists who came after them. Many remarkably revealing films were made. Looking back, however, we see that while Rouch and Marker addressed themselves to social issues of substance, the North Americans failed to do so; their films were chockfull of intriguing detail in the life of a race-car driver or a tobacco worker but somehow never brought the detail into focus. Perhaps this lack of ideational drive partly explains why the early *cinéma vérité* film makers, when they have continued working, have done so with less verve and passion. Ricky Leacock has turned away from film making toward technical experimentation with Super 8mm equipment. Drew Associates has vanished. Terry Macartney-Filgate works as a competent film maker for the CBC but rarely shows his full talents.

Only the Maysles brothers have kept on exploring new territory in a strong and passionate way. Even Fred Wiseman, who seemed in the sixties to be the film maker with the most developed social concerns and the most refined, poetically powerful style, seems to have lost something of his original brilliance. His aim is still to delineate the way American institutions work, and to show the dulling constraints of bureaucracy on human beings. Yet his recent films (*Primate*, *Essene*, *Meat*, *Canal Zone*, *Sinai Field Mission*) are somehow lacking, as if his basic technique breaks down when applied to complex political or economic subjects.

The Maysles, Ricky Leacock, Don Pennebaker, Bill Jersey, Fred Wiseman, and Allan King were pushing back the boundaries of documentary in the sixties. Their equivalents in the seventies are people like Barbara Kopple, Jill Godmilow, Jerry Brock, Cinda Firestone, Richard Cohen, Julia Reichert, and James Klein. What inspires most of them is an element we might loosely call radical fire. And yet we cannot really talk of a revolution or a "new dawn." Films like *Harlan County* and *Union Maids* are vital and stirring, but they are certainly not new. They are a renewal of an old tradition of American radical film making which has been neglected and laid aside for too long. *Harlan County* represents not so much revolution as rebirth.

Radical film making in the U.S. traces its origins to the Film and Photo League and other organizations of the thirties. Included in the League were most of the classic film pioneers, people like Thomas Brandon, Ralph Steiner, Paul Strand, Leo Hurwitz, and Willard Van Dyke. The aim of such film makers was clear—to document as forcibly as possible the social struggles of the thirties: foreclosures, evictions, strikes. While the feature film was confining itself to gangster melo-dramas or Busby Berkeley fantasies, Roy Stryker was making his first films and Pare Lorentz was documenting the destruction of the American landscape in *The River* and *The Plow That Broke the Plains*. In a pre-television age the social documentarist was beginning to use film to express anger and demand change.

Of all the groups of the thirties the most notable was undoubtedly Frontier Films, embracing Strand, Hurwitz, Irving Lerner, Sidney Meyers, Jay Leyda and others. Not only were their cameras turned towards America as in *People of Cumberland* and *Native Land* but the concern also went out to the rest of the world as in *China Strikes Back* and Herbert Kline's *Heart of Spain*. Again it is relevant to pause and consider the bonds that join *Heart of Spain* and Osheroff's *Dreams and Nightmares*.

This early radical movement of film makers was killed by three events—the Second World War, the rise of McCarthy, and the advent of television. The Second World War expanded the need for docu-mentary film making, and in effect pushed radical film making to the side both practically and politically. The media priority was devoted to films dealing with the war against Germany and Japan; the analysis of internal problems was almost forgotten.

The events of the McCarthy period are well known. What is often forgotten is that not only did hundreds of feature film makers like Dalton Trumbo, Herbert Biberman, and Ring Lardner suffer, but many documentary film makers were also hounded and driven to the wall.*

The final nail in the coffin of radical film making was, ironically enough, television. Superficially television might have been thought the documentarist's answer to finance, support and audience. In prac-tice this was far from the case. Few independent film makers got work in television, finding themselves either politically undesirable or un-willing or unable to conform to commercial network rules.

American television hit its documentary stride in the fifties. To be fair, many programs were brilliant, probing, and concerned. This was particularly true of the work of Ed Murrow and Fred Friendly, and of many of the CBS Reports and NBC White Papers. Often, however, there was an edge missing. Rarely did this have to do with a lack of moral fervor on the part of the film maker. The restrictions came from

---

*When I worked with director Leo Hurwitz on the filming of the Eichmann Trial in 1961 he told me it was one of his first major jobs since the blacklisting.

the very nature of commercial television, with its imperative of trying
to please everyone—or at least to offend as few customers as possible.
Thus a situation was created in which television *appeared* to have taken
over the task of the radical film makers and eliminated a need for them,
but in fact had done nothing of the sort.*

In spite of television the concerned independent film maker never
totally disappeared. Sidney Meyers's *The Quiet One* (1949), a fiction film
done in documentary style and co-directed by Janet Loeb, showed the
odyssey of a black boy in search of meaning in a strange alien world.
Herbert Biberman's feature *Salt of the Earth* (1954) battled on in spite
of immense problems. Lionel Rogosin's *On The Bowery* used hidden
cameras to penetrate the despair of the men and women on the New
York Bowery. Joseph Strick's *The Savage Eye* was more than the record
of a divorced woman's loneliness in the Los Angeles of the mid-fifties.
If it stood for anything it stood for a diary of the hell and alienation
in the twentieth century.

So films like *Dreams and Nightmares*, *Men's Lives*, *Attica* and the rest
are the continuance of a tradition. But why has this tradition suddenly
assumed a new force in the seventies? What accounts for such a vigorous rebirth? Certain tentative reasons seem obvious. One factor is
the whole upheaval of the sixties: Vietnam and Watergate, the student
revolutions, the growth of the women's movement, and changes in
perception of human socialization. In short the sixties gave us a whole
new social and political awareness which has to be followed up, analyzed, and fought for, and nowhere better than on film. A related factor, very much coupled to the first, is growing political sophistication
as to how the mass media work: what their power base is, how they
manipulate people, and their restrictions and inadequacies. People involved in political struggles have thus increasingly seen a need to turn
media to their own purposes.

This has become more feasible because the cost of making film has
gone down enormously. Light-weight 16mm film equipment has replaced 35mm in documentary filming with significant resultant savings. Sophisticated editing equipment is more widely and cheaply
available. The new 16mm equipment has much smaller crew requirements—only two or three people instead of nine or ten.

Another element is that we are dealing with a media rather than a
print generation: a generation which has studied film and television
techniques at school and university, and which grew up with TV om-

*I would agree, however, that public television—including the BBC and
PBS—does have a slightly better track record.

nipresent in their lives. Many in this generation find it at least as natural to express themselves through film as through print.

A last but important reason for the growth of independent film making is the changing financial situation. Films cannot be made without
money. Luckily this period has witnessed modestly increased funding
for films by arts councils and foundations. The sixties and seventies
have also seen a growth not only in the number of universities teaching
film but also in the number of institutions willing to allow their film
facilities and equipment to be used by students and others.

There are many positive ramifications of this film explosion. It has
opened up new subject areas. It has enlarged techniques and treatment.
And it has caused some reevaluation of the function of documentary.
Some of these ramifications are not new, just forgotten, and the new
documentary has rightly brought them into consideration once more.

The subject matter for the new independent film maker ranges from
the women's movement to aspirations of the young, people's socialization, and personal and family relationships. Some of the subject matter
is absolutely new and illustrative of the mood and feeling of the seventies. Other subject matter is more traditional but takes on a new
aspect and importance when treated at total variance to the usual om-
niscient television style.

The whole topic of Vietnam and American involvement was the
most serious issue to touch American society in the last two decades.
Its reverberations will be with us for a long time still. So far there has
been no widely published in-depth study on Vietnam and the media,*
but it is the supreme topic for investigating media policy, network attitudes and the role of the independent film maker.

The attitude of the U.S. government to its involvement in Vietnam
can be seen from two official films. *Why Vietnam?* was made in 1965
by the Department of Defense. Its avowed purpose was to make the
escalation of the war acceptable to Americans. A few years later the
United States Information Agency made *Vietnam Vietnam*. The film
was produced by John Ford for exclusive showings by the USIA outside North America. The film was so highly distorted and extreme in
its views that it became an object of ridicule and was eventually withdrawn from circulation.

The American networks for their part never stopped talking about
the war and examining the issues. The coverage was immense. Every

*An adequate introductory book, though, is M. Arlen's *The View from High-
way 1* (New York: Ballantine, 1977). See also Julian Smith's *Looking Away:
Hollywood and Vietnam* (New York: Scribner, 1975).

night pictures of bombing and fighting from Vietnam. Every night, Huntley, Brinkley and Cronkite with the latest reports. It was all being told, wasn't it? What more could one want! The answer was, everything. The problem, of course, is that "hard news" reporting does not really deal with history, context, or analysis, but with chronicling events—and encasing them in a reassuring consensus perspective. In retrospect it is clear that in spite of the immense coverage what was being told to the American viewer by the commercial networks was of almost total insignificance. The consensus perspective, subservient to government policy, turned out to have only a tenuous connection with political reality. Of the fighting itself there was coverage without end. There were the nightly network pieces of the correspondents. There was Pierre Schoendorffer's *Anderson Platoon*. There was Eugene Jones's *A Face of War*. But where was the report putting the war in a political context? Analysis was needed, but what was supplied was anecdote, and when Saigon fell, none of the network footage could explain why.

From the mid-sixties to the early days of the seventies the network hierarchies ran scared of the whole subject of Vietnam. In the beginning there had been some brave efforts but these quickly faded away. In 1965, for example, a CBS documentary took a slightly critical look at the war. Afterwards the CBS phones were jammed with calls accusing the network of being Communist. The networks obediently clammed up—though while they did, the massive antiwar movement was developing. In 1967 CBS tried again with *Morley Safer's Vietnam*. It was seen at the time as a courageous effort but in reality limited itself to interviews with soldiers and broad comments on the war.* Felix Greene's *Inside North Vietnam* originally had the backing of CBS but was eventually turned down by them. In the end 50 minutes of the film were shown on public television, but not before 33 congressmen, who had never seen the film, had protested the screening.

Besides Greene's film many others were available which discussed the war in terms other than simple victories and losses. The North Vietnamese themselves had made *The Way to the Front* and *Some Evidence*. East Germany had made *Pilots in Pyjamas*. From Canada there was Beryl Fox's *Last Reflections on a War*. There was the French *Far From Vietnam* and there was Joris Ivens's *The Seventeenth Parallel*. Many of these films were propaganda pieces for North Vietnam and as sus-

*For a general analysis of the difficulties of newspaper reporting as opposed to film reporting from Vietnam see Phillip Knightley's *The First Casualty* (New York: Harcourt, Brace and Jovanovich, 1975). For the best description and feeling of the war see Michael Herr's *Dispatches* (New York: Knopf, 1977).

pect in their own way as the Department of Defense's *Why Vietnam?* But they represented alternative ways of looking at and thinking about the war which would have been healthy for U.S. audiences to see.

Few of these pictures found such an audience. Many were seized by U.S. Customs as enemy propaganda. Those that got through were almost inevitably turned down by the networks. Various reasons were offered for the refusals. One was that the networks feared accusations of aiding and abetting the enemy if they showed them. The second reason, and an old network article of faith which has always restricted the free lance, was that the networks claimed they couldn't vouch for the authority and authenticity of work done by outsiders. Their responsibility to the FCC and to their audiences, they argued, precluded them from showing such films.

This excuse would have applied to North Vietnamese propaganda films but could in no way be applied to *The Demonstration*. *The Demonstration* described a 1968 antiwar rally in London outside the American embassy. It was made by the "World in Action" team, whose credentials were unimpeachable, for the English company Granada Television. This too was turned down by the American networks.

The cautious policy also infected public television. Beryl Fox relates how *Mills of the Gods*, a very early film about Vietnam, was shown on public television but only after being prefaced by a disclaimer indicating it did not reflect the views of NET.

Given the self-imposed blinkers worn by the networks one begins to appreciate the importance of the independent film makers in providing an alternative, if often a very left-slanted, view of the war. In spite of the customs restrictions, foreign films on Vietnam were clandestinely smuggled into America to be shown on university campuses. The Newsreel group was especially active in this matter as well as filming its own version of events in North Vietnam.

Slowly and imperceptibly the climate changed. The revelations of the Pentagon Papers and the My Lai massacre confirmed growing uneasiness about the war. The shocks of the latter event were further impressed on the public mind by Joseph Strick's independent film *Interviews with My Lai Veterans*. In 1971 Peter Davis made *The Selling of the Pentagon* for CBS, exposing the dubious ways in which the Defense Department manipulated public opinion to support the war. And from Canada came Mike Rubbo's *Sad Song of Yellow Skin* and *Saigon*, both of which avoided politics directly but provided moving and thoughtful impressions of everyday life in Vietnam.

Finally a film emerged which took up the challenge television had avoided for ten years: Emile de Antonio's *In the Year of the Pig*.

De Antonio's film analyzes Vietnamese history and French and American involvement, and does it brilliantly. It is made from a leftist position by an avowed Marxist, is extremely manipulative in its editing, yet for the most part is non-doctrinaire and coolly persuasive. Peter Davis's *Hearts and Minds*, made for theatrical release near the end of the war, also provides another broad analysis. On balance it tends to look more at the internal state of America than de Antonio's film, from which Davis borrows certain sections. *The Year of the Pig* was independently financed; *Hearts and Minds* drew its budget of $900,000 from Columbia Pictures. Davis's film was theatrically distributed but not by Columbia, which had got cold feet, despite general public revulsion for the war by that point. Like *Year of the Pig* it ended up making the campus rounds.

Besides Vietnam one of the main issues of the seventies has been feminism and women's liberation. The women's movement, though by no means new, was given extraordinary emphasis by the social climate of the sixties. The seventies saw the emergence of the feminist documentary as a new genre.

The new feminist films contrast markedly with usual television treatment of the women's movement, which has been limited and unimaginative when not a snide put-down. Feminism has been too often treated by TV as a media event or a joke, or relegated to quickie surveys or women's talk shows. Today, however, excitement about women's issues is growing outside television, not just around the new ways in which women are being treated in documentary, but also around the fact that more and more women are working as film makers.

Women are not newcomers to the American documentary scene. Perry Adato Miller, Shirley Clarke, Ellen Hovde, and Charlotte Zwerin are just a few names that come to mind. What one sees now though is a veritable outpouring of talent in Helen Whitney, Jill Godmilow, Barbara Kopple, Julia Reichert, Joyce Chopra, Susan Fanshel, Claudia Weill, Mirra Banks, and Amalie Rothschild—to name just a very few.* In England the list would probably be headed by Midge McKenzie and Joan Churchill.†

Some of the women are film makers with no particularly deep interest in the women's movement. Others are feminists who believe in a general liberalization of ideas within the existing social framework.

*For more see Sharon Smith's *Women Who Make Movies* (London: Hopkinson and Blake, 1975).

†Joan Churchill is relatively unknown in the U.S. but has done some brilliant *vérité* work with Nick Broomfield including *Juvenile Liaison*, *Marriage Guidance*, and *Tattooed Tears* shot in a California prison for juveniles.

And a few are radical Marxists who argue that there can be no female liberation without overturning the existing capitalist economic and political structure.

Most of the women work alone or in association with small commercial companies. What is new, however, is the growing number of women's cooperatives that have sprung up, such as the London Women's Film Group in England. (In the U.S. there are also a large number of collectives, a majority of them, like Newsreel and Kartemquin, including both men and women.) One of the main purposes of these collectives is to make a new kind of feminist film, but an additional purpose is to teach women basic film skills.

The new films about women range from politics to the description of ordinary details of women's lives. *The Double Day* studies the oppression of women in South America. Newsreel has *The Women's Film* on general liberation, while the British radical film *The Night Cleaners* considers a strike of cleaning women. Midge McKenzie's *Women Talking* and *A Woman's Place*, two important pioneer works, also helped pave the way for the new feminist film.

*Joyce at 34* by Joyce Chopra and Claudia Weill follows a less impassioned course than the above films as it examines the difficulties of a young mother who also wants to maintain a professional career. *Union Maids* profiles three women labor organizers, while *Woo Who? May Wilson* and *Antonia* document the spirits and verve of, respectively, a middle-aged painter and a world-class orchestral conductor.

Self-help is a key area in documentaries for women, and abortion, lesbianism, work and marriage feature fairly often as topics for discussion. *Janie's Janie* by New York Newsreel interviews a woman surviving on her own. Amalie Rothschild's *It Happens To Us* examines the feelings of twelve women who have had abortions. *In the Best Interests of the Child* makes a plea for the lesbian mother.

In *Growing Up Female* Julia Reichert and James Klein provide a broad picture of women's past and present expectations. These hopes feature in a satirical way in Sharon Hennessy's *What I Want* where she pleads for "total orgasm," "a man," and "to be ten pounds thinner."

What tends to be common to many of these new films is that they not only re-examine traditional roles and the inequalities of the sexes but also deal, more often than in the past, with the situation of the working-class woman, though middle-class concerns still dominate. Another innovation implied by the term self-help is that a large number of films are addressed to very practical matters such as contraception, maternity, and rape, as in Kartemquin's *The Chicago Maternity Center Story* and *Rape* by JoAnn Elam.

In an article on feminist documentary Julia Lesage makes two very important points about women and documentary which very well summarize intent and results.

> The women's very redefining of experience is intended to challenge all the previously accepted indices of "male superiority" and of women's supposedly "natural roles" . . . . Feminist films demand that a new space be opened up for women on women's terms.*

As regards technique, a central device used in many women's films is the personal monologue. Only rarely is a "neutral" commentator used and then with little sense of the shaping or inhibiting which we are used to from network commentaries. Another characteristic of these films is that they are often intended to be used in small group situations to encourage self-examination and self-help.

This objective of consciousness-raising and self-evaluation is also characteristic of another genre which might loosely be called the personal revelation film. These are films which often overlap with feminist documentary and deal with socialization, hopes, aspirations, personal relationships and family. Some of them look at the quality of present life and celebrate its small unexpected satisfactions as well as its frustrations. Another theme is sexual identity† and the place of role models. Will Roberts and Josh Hennig's *Men's Lives* is one of the first serious films to examine and criticize men's socialization into stereotyped "masculine" roles. Another aspect of the socialization process is seen in Liane Brandon's *Anything You Want to Be* and *Sometimes I Wonder Who I Am*.

The question of family and roots also provides the theme for a growing number of these revelation documentaries. Some of these films are shaped as investigations. Some are diaries. Some are portraits. Some are autobiographical confessions. What is common to this group is the need to understand the present through an examination of one's origins. Thus in *An Old-Fashioned Woman* Martha Coolidge looks at her grandmother while in *Joe and Maxi* Maxi Cohen looks at her father. One of the finest films in this loose grouping is Alfred Guzzetti's *Family Portrait Sitting* in which members of Guzzetti's family sit at home and

---

*Julia Lesage, "The Political Aesthetics of The Feminist Documentary Film," *The Quarterly Review of Film Studies*, Fall 1978, pp. 507–523. This is an excellent article and highly recommended for anyone interested in feminist documentary.

†Just as this book was going to press a number of interesting documentaries appeared on gay liberation, too late however for coverage in this work. See *Word Is Out* and *Gay U.S.A.* for two good examples in a growing genre.

reflect on their lives. Gradually all the shadows and memories emerge: Italy, emigration, marriage and children, work and politics. Eventually the family is seen very clearly, placed against the large socio-economic background of America, which gives one not just an individual story but a microcosm of a whole ethnic group's history. The subject of an Italian background is also featured in Martin Scorsese's picture of his parents, *Italian-American*.

Occasionally old and familiar names emerge in this genre. In *Reminiscences of a Journey to Lithuania* the experimental film maker Jonas Mekas takes us back to his early childhood. In *Milestones* Robert Kramer and John Douglas take a look, half documentary and half fiction, at their own lives and at the beliefs and passions of other radicals and students in the sixties.

Besides *Men's Lives* I have used two other films to illustrate this group for the book. *Nana, Mom and Me* looks at Amalie Rothschild's family and is a good example of the film of self-discovery and family revelation. *Grey Gardens* is slightly different in being made about the Beales of East Hampton by strangers to the family. Nevertheless it captures an intricacy and subtlety of family relationships seldom seen in documentary.

These small, intimate films rarely find a place on the networks. Occasionally, though, there is an effort. Following the inspiration of Allan King's *A Married Couple* PBS ran Susan and Allan Raymond's *An American Family*, about the Loud family of California. The efforts of filming were immense, the results questionable. By contrast "Six American Families" was a far more successful series in which individual film makers like the Maysles brothers, Bill Jersey, Susan Fanshel, Arthur Barron and Marc Obenhaus looked at six diverse American families and their life styles and relationships.

Some years back Arthur Barron, himself an outstanding film maker, noted the almost total absence of the film of human revelation and human dignity on American television. What the independent film maker has done is make the very films Barron asked for. That television declines to show them is a failure of the first order.

Besides questioning Vietnam, furthering the women's movement, and looking at personal and family history and socialization, the new documentary has also been regarding the face of America and its institutions in a more critical way. Since the early seventies we have seen many brilliant and devastating films that have inspected politics, class, poverty, war, bureaucratic behavior, and nuclear power in a way unheard of by the networks. These are the films that most closely follow the old radical tradition.

Many of these films involve the past. De Antonio's *Point of Order* investigates the McCarthy period and his *Rush to Judgment* examines the John Kennedy assassination. In *Dreams and Nightmares* Abe Osheroff reflects on the Spanish Civil War and American foreign policy. In *Hollywood on Trial* David Helpern reviews the era of the House Un-American Activities Committee, though it loses something by avoiding any issues of political complexity. In *Union Maids* Julia Reichert and James Klein not only portray the lives of three remarkable women but also provide a moving survey of trade union history after the depression.

Moving back into the present one is faced with *America: Everything You Ever Dreamed Of*. Little is left out of the seedy side of America in this scathing film by Rhody Streeter and Tony Ganz. Here is America the beautiful: plastic retirement villages, Jesus freaks, antiseptic kitsch motels for newlyweds. Also on the edge of the bizarre is *California Reich* by Walter Parkes and Keith Critchlow which takes an interesting look at Nazis in California, but ultimately fails to take a point of view on what is seen.

Nobody, however, could accuse Barbara Kopple of such a thing. *Harlan County* burns with outrage at the treatment of miners in a Kentucky mining strike. The same sense pervades Cinda Firestone's look at the prison slaughter in *Attica* and Richard Cohen's revelations about mental hospitals in *Hurry Tomorrow*. These three films are no simple statements, but torches lit with passion demanding that everybody see what is revealed by their flames.

This short survey suggests the power and dynamism of the new independent documentary. What has not yet been discussed is the sheer energy involved in making these films in the face of the difficult financial and distribution system currently prevailing in the U.S. Furthermore, it must be acknowledged that however difficult the system is in America, it is far worse in England.

Without money films do not get off the ground. Period. Even in an era of light-weight equipment and 16 mm stock it still normally costs anywhere between $15,000 and $40,000 to make a modest half-hour color film. Given this fact one appreciates even more the efforts of film makers such as the London Women's Film Group who for years have been putting out ten-minute and quarter-hour films on shoestring budgets of $300 and $400.

Where does the money come from for an independent film? Abe Osheroff got his $50,000 for *Dreams and Nightmares* through the backing of enthusiastic political supporters. Emile de Antonio told me how he picked up the $100,000 for *Point of Order* while having a drink with a wealthy liberal friend. Occasionally the money comes from the film maker's savings, or the proceeds of one film are plowed back into another. *Antonia* was backed by Judy Collins's concert earnings. *Men's Lives* was partially financed by a university scholarship. Tom Haydon's *The Last Tasmanian* was financed by company donations, state help, contributions in services, and preselling the film to a variety of television stations.

When Barbara Kopple started *Harlan County* all she had was the promise of a $9,000 loan. Even this fell through when the donor told her he didn't think a 26-year-old woman could make a major political statement. She then turned to friends and foundations. Amalie Rothschild's films have also been supported by foundations, as have a few of the films of Jill Godmilow, Julia Reichert, and James Klein.

Local arts councils and foundations have in fact been one of the chief sources of independent film financing in the last few years. The key principals here are the Rockefeller, Ford, and Guggenheim foundations, the American Film Institute, the New York Council for the Arts, the National Endowment for the Arts, and the National Endowment for the Humanities. Some money has also come from the Independent Documentary Fund for public television.

Funding from such sources is intensely competitive and dozens of applicants are turned down for every grant awarded. Barbara Kopple relates how she was refused again and again while trying to fund a film which is now widely reckoned one of the best of the decade. When money is granted, however, it may well be given in amounts up to $10,000 or $15,000 for an individual film.

The American foundation situation may not look bright but compared to England it is heaven. Hardly any money is available in England for independent filming. That fact, coupled with incredible union problems, is one of the main reasons for the abysmal plight of independent English film making.

In England there are only a few meager sources of money for the making of independent films.* The two biggest grantors are the Arts Council and the British Film Institute (the BFI). In 1976 the budget of the Arts Council for film making was £230,000. The BFI budget for independent film makers for the same period was £125,000 or about $230,000. By way of contrast it is interesting to note that the all-inclusive budget of the average film in BBC's "The British Empire" series was around £70,000,† more than half the yearly BFI grant.

*For further information on this sorry topic see *Production Board*, ed. Alan Lovell, (BFI pamphlet, 1976).

†This figure was quoted to me by one of the researchers on "The British Empire" and sounds about right.

Though far more money is available in the U.S., foundation funding has certain inherent difficulties. Many of these relate to the writing of the proposal. Most foundations require a proposal clearly stating the nature of the film, its limits and objectives, and a well-defined program relating to the filming itself. Though this is fine and acceptable for a simple scientific or art film it presents immense problems in the making of a film such as *Harlan County* where the film maker simply does not know at the outset what events may occur, which of them can be captured on film, or how the resulting footage will be structured.

Foundations also like to play it safe by requiring the participation of certifiable experts who will provide academic respectability to a project. Such requirements may make sense for films of popularization, but are obstructionist when a film maker is operating on the growing edge of a field where the scholarly mind has not yet penetrated.

Disappointments of grant applicants often arise through a failure to acknowledge the basically conservative nature of foundation activities. Many foundations are set up to fund programs related to the arts, health, ethnic or experimental matters. The art film, the classroom film, or sometimes the experimental film pose few challenges to a foundation's limitations. By contrast the critical, investigatory, or political film rarely finds a place in foundation funding without a great deal of trouble.

The establishment of the Film Fund has been a promising development in this area. The Fund is a tax-exempt foundation whose main purpose is to support the making of films and videotapes specifically dealing with social issues. The Fund is an outgrowth of the Haymarket Fund, a Boston organization of young heirs pledged to support projects linked with social matters.

Overall, the situation has improved slightly in regard to production funding but few similar words of hope can be said about distribution. Public exposure for the independent documentary outside universities is pathetic. In most American cities there are documentary showings at museums such as the Whitney or the Museum of Modern Art. Such screenings are prestigious, but they play to small audiences and bring little financial reward. The same is true of England where the National Film Theatre parallels the MOMA. But what of network possibilities and independent distribution?

In England and Canada it is still possible to sell an independent documentary to the BBC or the CBC. In the United States it is sometimes possible to sell a film to a local station but it is virtually impossible to interest the major networks, with the exception of PBS. For example, *Dreams and Nightmares* is a very human and personal look at the Spanish Civil War—hardly a topic of current hot controversy. It has been awarded major prizes throughout the U.S. and Europe. According to Abe Osheroff the networks refused even to look at the film. *Antonia*, though on a safe, topical, and noncontroversial subject, was turned down by the networks; only a part of it was eventually shown on "Sixty Minutes." *Hurry Tomorrow* with its startling picture of the drugging of mental patients in a California hospital made it to local television, but only through having a few minutes screened on a news show. *Attica* almost made it to PBS but was eventually rejected. (The history of these rejections is given in the interviews that follow.)

If we leave the commercial networks and turn to the independent distributors, the scene is still archaic and unfair. The lucky independent film will reach an audience, of sorts, but relatively few innovative films are taken by distributors. Reasons for rejection are often quixotic. Jill Godmilow was told that *Antonia* was too long for distribution because it did not fit conveniently into half-hour classroom use. She was told that the problem with her later film, *The Popovitch Brothers of Chicago*, was that it didn't fit into any simple film subject listing: instead of being about ethnic research, or music enjoyment, or social observation, it provided a blend of all three. Amalie Rothschild's films on women were dismissed in a similar way.

Even if a documentary is accepted by such a distributor the average returns tend to be farcical. In general an independent distributor takes from 75 to 80 percent of the gross rental proceeds. As Don Pennebaker once said, the independent film maker survives in spite of the system not because of it.

Given the depressing limitations of the system the independent film maker has continually sought alternatives. One solution adopted in the past by Allan King, the Maysles, and Leacock and Pennebaker has been for the directors to assume responsibility for the distribution of their films through independent cinemas and art houses. *A Married Couple*, *Chiefs*, and *Gimme Shelter* were all successfully exhibited in this way, as was *Antonia*. This sometimes works but only on the rare occasions when the documentary has some outstanding news or entertainment interest; and of course it keeps the film maker's energies away from making another film.

Another alternative has been for the film makers to set up their own nontheatrical distribution organizations.* These organizations use direct mail and other techniques to seek out specific audiences for their

*For further information see Julia Reichert, *Doing It Yourself: A Handbook on Independent Film Distribution* (Association of Independent Video and Filmmakers, Inc., 1977); and the *16 mm Distribution Handbook*, available through the Educational Film Library Association.

films in university departments, historical societies, prisons, unions, and women's groups. This form of distribution was successfully used by New Day Films in distributing *Union Maids, Men's Lives*, and *It Happens To Us* and is discussed in depth by Amalie Rothschild.

One of the more interesting developments in this kind of distribution is the growing number of film makers who go out to talk alongside their films. Kopple does this, so do Reichert and Klein, Will Roberts and Richard Cohen. These film makers no longer think of themselves merely as the originators of a "product" which others sell to an audience. Their personal presence, their urging of action and change, are as much a part of their activist role as the making of the film. They take their function of changing lives with total seriousness.

The work done by such dedicated independent film makers is like adrenalin to a lethargic political system. But no immediate assessment can really tell how important these films will prove to have been in promoting social change. Presumably even films in marginal distribution reach many "opinion leaders" and ultimately their effects trickle out through the society at large. On the other hand it is only the American networks, the BBC, the CBC, and a few powerful stations that can reach the mass audience. Changes in satellite technology and in government regulatory policies may one day produce greater competition and variety in television programming, but the prospects do not seem bright. For the foreseeable future, it will be through the network organizations that documentarists will make what contribution they can to general public perception of social issues. This is a major reason why I have interviewed film makers who work within the network bureaucracies.

I also believe that some of these network film makers have been unjustly neglected. One appreciates Barbara Kopple, Julia Reichert, James Klein and Richard Cohen but it was directors like Al Wasserman and Douglas Leiterman who have helped enlarge the boundaries of the broadcast documentary. And if Cinda Firestone now burns with outrage in *Attica*, her emotion is no greater than that felt and expressed by Mort Silverstein in *What Harvest for the Reaper* and *Banks and the Poor*.

In England, too, people like Michael Latham, David Elstein and Roger Graef have been enlarging the boundaries. Ireland would easily drop from the English consciousness were it not for programs like "The Man Alive Reports" and "This Week." And then there is the supreme keeper of the conscience, Robert Vas. In film after film Vas drew the attention of reluctant BBC audiences to the plight of the survivors of

23

Hiroshima, to the realities of the miners' strike of 1926, and to the fate of the Russian soldiers abandoned by the British army and murdered by Stalin. Robert Vas was a man without parallel and his early death in 1978 was a tragic loss not just to his family and friends, but to the cinema in general and documentary in particular.

Vas worked for years at the BBC. At the time that he joined it in the late fifties the BBC had already established a superb documentary tradition. During the early and middle sixties BBC documentaries scaled even greater heights. Ken Russell was working on music documentaries. John Schlesinger had done a brilliant film about Waterloo Station. Jack Gold had done *The Quorn*. Ken Loach and Jeremy Sandford were busy on *Cathy Come Home* while Peter Watkins had created a stir with *Culloden* and was quietly preparing a bigger bombshell called *The War Game*. Experiment was rife; the personal documentary blossomed. There was a sense of challenge, and anything was possible. But since the late sixties the BBC has changed beyond recognition. Superb films still trickle out but there is a sense of BBC documentary being in the doldrums. The personal documentary is out and the slick series is in. There has been a change of mood and loss of purpose which both Tom Haydon and Robert Vas comment on.

It is difficult to lay the blame on any one thing. All creative bodies have their ups and downs; occasional doldrums may even be a cyclic necessity. Or perhaps the BBC has become too conscious of its position. It has become hallowed and venerable, which is fine, but it has also become nervous about its status. Unlike the British independent television corporations the BBC is a public corporation which obtains its financial support through government-imposed licensing fees. Its charter is renewable but this is not automatic, and conscious of this the BBC has become extremely edgy in the face of various public and private attacks in the seventies. This has been especially true since the furor aroused by the broadcast of *Yesterday's Men*, a documentary by Angela Pope which drew a poor picture of the Labor Party in opposition.

In talking about *Nine Days in '26* Vas comments on the BBC's lack of courage in presenting his program at the appropriate time. This lack of courage is seen in other places, even in drama documentary. Drama documentary has always been the BBC's forte,* from the early days of Tony Parker's prison dramas up to the work of Jeremy Sandford. Today it is still going strong, but even in this area there are the occasional hesitations. A good example is the whole history of *The Naked Civil Servant*, a documentary drama based on the autobiography of

*While paying homage to the BBC one should not forget Yorkshire Television's *Jonny Go Home* or Maurice Kanareck's *Prisoners of Conscience*, a very good independently made film about the plight of Jews in Russia.

Quentin Crisp, a well-known homosexual. After the project was discussed for some while in the BBC it was eventually turned down for fear of giving offense to viewers. Luckily it was taken up by Thames Television, beautifully directed by Jack Gold, and finally acknowledged as one of the best television presentations of the year.

If one looks at BBC programming one almost suspects that the BBC hierarchy feels happier and safer in the past. "The Search for the Nile," "The Fight Against Slavery," "The Explorers," and "Edward VII" are fine and often very accurate reenactments of historic events and personalities. These programs together with "The Great War" represent some of the BBC's finest achievements. But even the past can be dangerous, as indicated by the events surrounding "The British Empire" series.

"The British Empire" started out as one of the most prestigious BBC series ever conceived for television. Its problem, as Tom Haydon recounts, is that it fell between two stools. It was neither romantic nostalgia nor was it historical critique and analysis. In the end no one was happy, as can be seen from the battles joined in the House of Lords and the storm of letters sent to the English newspapers.

Some of the blame for the depressed mood at the BBC may well depend on the aging of BBC documentarists who were in their experimental twenties when BBC2 started. Now in their forties, many are tired, and have simply been promoted to management. David Elstein, himself a former BBC producer, places a lot of blame for the low spirits on management structure. This view is seconded by Vas and other BBC producers I have spoken to. Part of the trouble started in the midsixties when the BBC called in a team of business consultants to rationalize the activities of the corporation. The result was the creation of a lengthy chain of command with decisions being shunted from functionary to functionary.

This state of bureaucratic nightmare was discussed in an unofficial letter to the Annan Committee* by ninety-two BBC film and television personnel. Their main complaint was put as follows: real control, *artistic* as well as financial, has moved further and further away from the program makers. This is a far cry from the heady days of the sixties when Peter Watkins merely had to get a nod from Huw Wheldon to make *Culloden*. Even where the possibility of direct personal responsibility still exists few people in management seem willing to take the flack that Wheldon and Kenneth Adam endured.

Again it is important to keep a correct perspective. Excellent films still emerge month after month from the BBC which would put other

*A governmental committee set up in the mid-seventies to investigate the future of broadcasting in England.

systems to shame. The series on slavery is one example, *The Family* another. And it was the BBC which allowed Roger Graef to go ahead with his remarkable *cinéma vérité* experiments in "The Space Between Words." But in all these there is a sense of "safeness," however fine the productions.

This playing for safety exhibits itself in the BBC coverage of the Irish situation, the most serious political dilemma to face England since Suez. A great many programs have been made on the subject, such as *Last Night Another Soldier* and *Christians at War*. Michael Latham also discusses the work of his own program, "The Man Alive Reports," in regard to the Irish question. Many of the productions are excellent but like a lot of the Vietnamese coverage have often been anecdotal rather than analytical.

The immense sensitivity of British television on the Irish issue can best be seen by glancing quickly at 1978. Early in the year the Controller of BBC Northern Ireland cancelled a major film on Northern Ireland by BBC director Colin Thomas, on the grounds that the film was too provocative. This was followed* by a decision of the Independent Broadcasting Authority (the governing body of British commercial television) to delay a Thames Television program about Amnesty International's report on the treatment of prisoners in Northern Ireland, *against the wishes of Thames*.

In spite of IBA intervention independent television has fared better than the BBC on the Irish question, perhaps because it is slightly less conscious of an establishment connection. All of the independent commercial stations have done Irish programs but the most outstanding is Thames Television's *Five Long Years*, which David Elstein comments on in his interview.

Over the years Thames has established itself as one of the best producers of documentary in England, and in spite of being commercial has kept a tone of sharp criticism in its work. It produced "The World at War," a series which must be rated as a landmark in British television. It produced *The Road to Wigan Pier*, still one of the finest documentaries on labor conditions in the thirties. And it continues to broadcast "This Week," one of the best documentary magazines of its kind.

Granada Television's contribution to British documentary goes back to its series "The World in Action." The series, which is still running,

---

*One of the points at issue here is whether senior policy-making staff had the right to over-rule directors and producers responsible for creative content. This decision of the IBA to ban a program, despite the wishes of the producers and of the company wishing to transmit, clearly raises very important issues in regard to broadcasting freedom.

is one of the oldest on British television, and became *the* finest documentary program of the sixties. This brilliant tradition has continued with programs like *The Man Who Went Too Far* about Soviet protesters, and *The Long Hand of DINA*, which describes the assassination work of the Chilean secret police. Another contribution of Granada at present is its sustained support for the pioneering work of Roger Graef.

In America the networks continue for the most part to follow the old patterns of the sixties. One sees almost nothing but stolid, noncontroversial films, and only occasional odd flashes of brilliance such as *The Selling of the Pentagon*, *The CIA's Secret Army*, and Helen Whitney's *Youth Terror*. Given the premise that networks are in business to sell audiences to advertisers, can we really expect anything different? The real wonder is not that so little is accomplished but how *much*.

The seventies has not been a great period for U.S. network documentary. The achievement of the Westinghouse Group W series "Six American Families" has already been mentioned, but in general television documentary has diminished in scope, challenge, and number of hours broadcast. In 1977 NBC produced eight long documentaries and four short ones. CBS planned twenty documentaries and then drastically cut back the number. ABC ran a few documentaries such as a spineless exploration of divorce, provided a certain spark with *Youth Terror* in 1978, but in general has preferred to put its efforts into highly profitable drama series such as "Roots."

On the public side NET has been replaced with the Corporation for Public Broadcasting and the Public Broadcasting System. The CPB structure, suggested by the 1967 Carnegie Commission on Educational Television, was originally viewed with great hopes by film makers and all those interested in public broadcasting. The events of a decade have not justified those hopes.

From 1970 (when PBS was set up) the CPB/PBS association has been rent by both internal and external difficulties. Internally it has been accused of being too bureaucratic; of being torn by internal squabbles; of failing to set up a strong central network core; of cowardice in relation to controversial subjects; and of failing to spend enough money on programming. Externally it has suffered from political attacks and problematic grant and federal support.

1972 is a good year for illustrating the external problems. In that year President Nixon vetoed the new increased budget of the CPB already approved by Congress. He then appointed or reappointed eleven of the fifteen members of the CPB board thus ensuring a fairly conservative overall CPB outlook. Details of the Nixon move and the crippled condition of CPB/PBS are given in the 1979 second Carnegie Commission Report on the future of public broadcasting. The report proposes an annual CPB/PBS budget of 300 million dollars by the mid-eighties, and obviously envisages an American system rivalling the BBC in international stature. Whether the recommendations will be implemented and whether they will bring the golden age remain to be seen. We know, however, that a decade of CPB/PBS has done little to foster or encourage innovative, provocative, and challenging documentaries.

Programs such as *The Police Tapes* by Susan and Allan Raymond are the exception rather than the rule. The dynamism and challenge of the "NET Journal" which backed *Banks and the Poor* and *Hard Times in the Country* is no more. Instead these programs have been replaced by BBC imports or by such safe series as that on American women artists entitled "The Originals: Women in Art."

This lack of strong central guidance might have been expected to encourage greater creativity by local public stations, which by 1976/77 were originating 60 percent of their programs. This hasn't happened. Instead the local stations have tended to concentrate simply on broadcasting the work of local cultural institutions such as the symphony orchestra or opera. Documentary, to say the least, has not been given high priority at the local level. Exceptions such as Michael Roemer's *Dying* (produced by WGBH, one of the few really creative local stations) are few and far between.

In such a sad situation "Eye On" and "Sixty Minutes" stand out like beacons on a foggy day. Of the two programs "Eye On," which is a local New York program, is more investigatory and assures one that the tradition of *Banks and the Poor* has not been entirely forgotten. "Sixty Minutes" deals with more general subjects. It covers a wide political spectrum but also runs entertainment profiles. Occasionally however "Sixty Minutes" runs precise investigatory pieces such as the study of *SAVAK*, the Iranian secret police, or Al Wasserman's look at oil company corruption in *The Daisy Chain*.

The network way or the path of the independent? The film maker does not always have such a choice. Where it exists, however, it is necessary to see what are the advantages and disadvantages of both and take the plunge with one's eyes open.

The chief advantages of working within the system are guaranteed financing and the ability to reach a mass audience. But there are unwritten rules regarding sacred subjects, limits of offense, and problems of style. And there is the knowledge of working within a body which is basically pledged to support the status quo. Luckily the rules are not static but are constantly being tested and probed and occasionally extended by the network film maker.

One tenet regarded dubiously by independents but accepted by even the most liberal of network film makers relates to common journalistic guidelines. All the network film makers I spoke to agreed on the validity of these rules. All argued that the substance of an investigation must be clearly shown so that the factual conclusions can grow from what has been demonstrated. It was also clear to all of them that this kind of journalistic objectivity and evaluation did not mean indifference or lack of concern. This is an important point and is often forgotten.

The disadvantages outside the system have been discussed. The advantages are lack of confinement in subject matter and technique, and freedom to express a sense of passion and urgency without outside interference. Within the networks limits are clearly defined. In the end Leiterman could not accept the confines of CBS and resigned. Such action seemed the obvious step to him, and he was right. Network rejection of *Dreams and Nightmares* and *Attica* should not have come as a shock to Abe Osheroff or Cinda Firestone. The rules were well known. They were outsiders trying to get in. With Robert Vas the situation worked the other way.

Vas was a network film maker yearning for the freedom of the outsider. What Vas fought for was the freedom of the network film maker to make a personal statement, in direct opposition to the rules enshrined in the BBC's handbook *Principles and Practice in Documentary Film*. The rules aimed at a formalized objectivity and neutrality, and made it clear that in BBC programs all opinions should be personal and attributable as in *Whicker's World* or *Philpott's File*. Vas, in spite of the freedom he was given, reacted bitterly to this approach. He rejected the idea of the film maker as a mere conduit pipe. He argued passionately for the acceptance of the artist film maker as legitimately expressing opinions in his or her own right.

Perhaps it is not a question of "either-or," and from society's point of view we are lucky to have both insiders and outsiders working in documentary. The solid responsible insider is needed to keep the official news coming, to provide balanced content for social debate, and to reach the mass audience on a broad range of subjects. The outsider is needed to wage an endless guerrilla war with the system, to criticize, to explore, to show new ranges and possibilities for film, and to break down taboos.

As we move into the eighties, technological changes pour down upon us in abundance. The video tape recorder is now an accepted toy. Computer films have become standard and the portapack revolution is old history. Satellites link up continents in milliseconds. Television

29

sets are available little larger than a pack of cigarettes. Miniscule microphones pick up sounds from a distance of miles. The wired city is seriously discussed by planners and "instant movies" are sold over the counter.

The production and transmission of imagery becomes cheaper and easier. Humankind, from children in California to inhabitants of African deserts, can now see themselves through their own videotapes, recapturing their images from outside "experts." Cable television spreads, open-access television links members of local communities. In England a fourth channel may be opened for independent film makers and video programmers.

Yet we may well wonder what, if anything, will really change through all this activity. Even the impact of a full network showing is small; the great wheel of society goes on turning with formidable inertia. *Cathy Come Home* was a tremendously moving film about homeless people which, when broadcast by the BBC, stirred up enormous public discussion and drew hundreds of volunteers into a political campaign. Yet, its writer Jeremy Sandford reports, after four showings of the film the situation of the homeless is worse now than when the film was made. Richard Cohen's *Hurry Tomorrow* stirred public opinion in California but in spite of the outcry little has changed in the state's mental hospitals. Occasionally there is a one-to-one relationship between film exposure and resultant action, but this is usually only in the very specific investigations carried out by "Eye On" or "Sixty Minutes."

This lack of effect can be seen not just in local matters but also on wider issues. It is often claimed, for instance, that television helped end the war in Vietnam. Edward Jay Epstein disagrees, and in *News From Nowhere* he claims that out of a large survey of television producers and editors, more than two thirds felt that television had little effect on changing public opinion about the war.

What has happened, then, is that we have reached a situation which could be termed a saturation of sympathy. Murders in Chile, atrocities in Cambodia, genocide in Beirut no longer appall us. The killings of Kent State students and the massacre of Attica prisoners shock us for a few minutes, but then the lethargy returns. One victim looks much like another on the small screen. Television turns carnage into entertainment. The child in the open heart surgery program gets a thousand weepy letters while Yuri Orlov and everything he stands for becomes a forgotten item in last week's news. For a film maker it is not the opposition that hurts—it's the apathy and indifference.

A few years ago, when discussing this question, I asked whether the crusading film maker accomplished anything besides salving his or her own conscience and influencing a small section of the open-minded who had seen the program at off-peak hours. I suspected at the time that such a conclusion was unduly pessimistic. I argued that though it is difficult to correlate specific films to specific responses, the overall pressure of television in the post war era has been enormous, even if the impact of any one single program has been small. I hold to this belief, but would add a few other shades to the picture.

I now see the concerned film maker not only as one who tries to bring about direct change, but as one who bears witness. This "bearing of witness" has two elements. On a modest level it means that the film maker is interested in telling us about a certain truth. It is not *"the* truth" or "the eternal message" but is rather a very personal statement that says: "This film arises out of my feelings, background, and integrity and on the basis of what I show and how I show it you can take it or leave it for what it's worth." It is this kind of modest personal truth that makes Mike Rubbo's quiet, seemingly rambling work so interesting, for example.

On a different level of bearing witness the film maker is one who says: "This is our world. See its joy and be happy. But see its sorrow and learn from it, and don't say no one ever told you what the world was like." This kind of bearing witness is not something one does logically. It is something one does compulsively. Kopple, Osheroff, Cohen and others like them are led not by reason, but by a conscience that says *this* story must be told, and *these* facts must not stay hidden. Robert Vas knew this better than anyone and expressed it as follows:

> I've brought with me from the other side a "baggage" . . . a great many things to talk about. This baggage, the message that nobody asked me to talk about, is absolutely central to me. I can't exist without it. And I must talk about it to audiences that never experienced these things directly.

This is what drives the concerned film maker: the baggage, the ineluctably personal message that nobody asks one to talk about. It is difficult, but the film maker knows that somewhere out there the witness will be heard and the message will find a response. And it is this knowledge, this sure knowledge, which makes everything worthwhile.

*Television History*

# 1

# *The World at War*

During the Fall and Winter of 1974–75, millions of TV viewers in both England and the U.S. followed, week after week, the events of the Second World War as depicted in the 26 consecutive episodes of the Thames Television production, "The World at War." That this documentary series continues to enjoy critical and popular success in its periodic rebroadcasts is all the more remarkable when one considers that it appeared after several other TV series had used wartime footage and interviews to recreate the events and personalities of the last world war.

"Victory at Sea" is perhaps the most famous, but "Crusade in Europe," "The Twentieth Century," and "Churchill: The Valiant Years" all depended largely on archival footage of the events that convulsed Europe and Asia between 1939–45. These programs also employed techniques that soon became familiar, however, establishing a standardized, routine approach for the compilation of historical documentary.

"Victory at Sea," made less than ten years after the war's close, set that pattern. Co-produced by NBC and the U.S. Navy, the series' narration frequently strained for dramatic effect, so that German military strategy was reduced to phrases like, "Hitler's legions attack with all the fury that has made them the terror of Europe," overlaying footage of advancing tanks and troops. And washing over all the visuals was the powerful musical score composed for the series by Richard Rodgers.

Reliance on standard footage sources also characterized "Victory at Sea" and the other programs—the official newsreels, the obviously re-enacted scenes, the footage of diving Stukas and the *Wehrmacht* on dress parade from German films such as *Baptism of Fire* and *Victory in the West*. The Second World War became an endless succession of predictable scenes, and many of the programs only made matters worse by their dependence on personalities, whether Walter Cronkite in "Twentieth Century" or Richard Burton reading Churchill's speeches in "The Valiant Years" in order to remind viewers of the importance of the events.

"The World at War" broke radically from these conventions. Instead of celebrity hosts or lectures by military historians on the real significance of events, "The World at War" featured interviews with the foot-soldiers, housewives, and others who could offer a personal perspective on the impact of the war on people's lives. From the series' opening episode, about an attack on a French village by an SS division on its way to the Normandy beachhead, it never forgot that it was ordinary men and women who were dying, whether they were combatants or "civilians who got in the way."

Avoiding the overdone and hackneyed war images, "The World at War" films are also incredibly well-researched, utilizing much new or rarely seen footage, with a conscientious effort made to verify the historical accuracy of the archival footage. This material has been superbly edited and blended with an effective understated narration spoken by Sir Laurence Olivier and poignant title music by Carl Davis.

The films range from depictions of life in England and Germany, such as *Home Fires* and *Inside the Third Reich*, to three essays on the bitter battles in Russia, *Barbarossa* (the German attack), *Stalingrad* and *Red Star* (the siege of Leningrad). The style and approach of the films was left very much to the individual producers and directors. Thus, John Pett's film on Burma is an impressionistic picture devoted to giving the feeling of the soldiers' war in the jungle. By way of contrast, David Elstein's *The Distant War* and *The Bomb* concentrate much more on political analysis.

The films also dared to admit the errors made by both sides, Allied and Axis. For Anglo-American audiences, it was a truly remarkable program that could give credit for a portion of the victory to Hitler's poor judgments, and show the price paid by the Red Army both for Stalin's miscalculations and the western allies' inability to invade Europe before mid-1944.

Such filmic and journalistic achievements did not go unnoticed by the industry. "The World at War" has won many awards including, in the U.S., an Emmy from the National Academy of Television Arts and Sciences and the George Polk memorial award for television documentaries.

## Jerome Kuehl, Associate Producer

*In 1974 the American Jerome Kuehl contributed a chapter to the book* The Historian and the Film, *and later reviewed the book itself for* Sight and Sound. *And why not—the qualifications for both tasks were there in abundance. Kuehl had done graduate work in history at the University of Wisconsin and at Oxford, had taught history at Stanford University and for a while was historical advisor to the BBC. In addition he'd made films galore as producer-director.*

*The relationship of history and film is one of Kuehl's main concerns. It was also one of the more debated issues regarding the "World at War" series. Were the films history or journalism? Is there a distinction? And what after all are the differences and limitations of the written word and the screen in covering the past? These were the areas where I knew I would get a good reaction from Kuehl.*

*We met for the interview at the Thames TV offices overlooking Euston Road. I was early and passed the time reading newspapers. Eventually Kuehl appeared. He came bouncing through the office, beaming all over, and distributing goodwill, gin and orange juice to myself and any secretaries, directors or personnel who happened to be within drinking distance.*

*Yet beneath the bonhomie and relaxed confident manner lies a certain scholastic pedantry. For example, witness his absolute insistence on time and place accuracy of all the footage in the films. This was all part of Kuehl's watching brief as associate producer of the series. As to the relationship between himself and general-series producer Jeremy Isaacs, he describes this as the difference between the chief-of-intelligence and the commander-in-chief.*

*Besides his general work on the series Kuehl also produced and directed* Reckoning, *which dealt with the end of the war and its aftermath, and was executive producer of ten "World at War" specials. From 1964 to 1968 Kuehl was chief writer-researcher for NBC's European Production Unit. Since 1968 he has been free-lancing for the BBC and Thames where he acted as associate producer on the nine-part series "Destination America."*

Q. Why, after so many television films on the Second World War, like the Churchill series and "Victory at Sea" to name just a few, did Thames Television feel it necessary to do another series?

A. There's an official history and there's an unofficial history of the origins of the Second World War series. The *official* history is that the series was made when it was made for technical and if you like psychological, moral, and political reasons. The technical reasons were that an enormous amount of film was shot during the Second World War, but once the war was over it was forgotten. It was put into archives and left there, uncatalogued and forgotten. And even when people knew of the material there was often no public access to it. Now this lack of access is important. Only when the archive footage was made publicly available was it possible for anyone to make a film using material which had not been seen before, and you can situate that point at about the late 1960's. Thus only from about 1965–1970 onwards was it technically feasible for an ambitious company, or an ambitious production unit, to set about using material which was novel—that is, which had not been widely seen by anybody other than the cameramen who filmed it, the lab technicians who processed it, and the people who had put it in the archives.

The second reason, and this is the moral political psychological explanation, is that there comes a point in everyone's life when they're prepared to speak candidly. I won't say to spill all the beans, but prepared to speak candidly about events in their own time. And that time comes at different times to different people. To some people it comes quite early on. For others it comes when they no longer hope for advancement in their careers or when they are disillusioned with the government which controls their destinies. Whatever the reason may be, they will talk about things that happened to them. For the generation which participated in the Second World War, that time, I think, came in the late 1960s or early 1970s. Men who'd held senior command, people like Brian Horrocks or General Montgomery or Lawton Collins, found that their active careers had come to a close.

Now some, like Montgomery or Bradley, whose active careers had come to a close long ago, were unwilling to be interviewed. They said, and I paraphrase their replies, "If you get us on a good day, we will give you a splendid interview. If you get us on a bad day we will not look at all good and we're proud enough and, if you like, vain enough not to wish to be remembered by our senile babbling in the twilight of our life." But for others, a bit younger, the time to speak out was the late sixties or early seventies or never. And as for the younger people, people who'd been lieutenants or captains or private soldiers in the 1940s, and were now in the fifties, they could look back with a certain amount of distance on the events of their young manhood or womanhood. So we had these two classes of participants who we thought would talk and say something fresh: those who had to say it before they died and the younger participants who were now mature enough to look back reflectively on what had happened to them.

The raw material for the interviews was there, and Thames had the wit and the foresight to see that this was the time to make this series and did so, beginning about 1971. And that's the official history.

The *unofficial* history is that everyone knew that there was going to be a series made about the Second World War for just these reasons. It was one of the great events of the twentieth century, if not of all time, and lavishly filmed. Now in England it was thought, by myself as well as by my colleagues at the BBC, that the BBC had a kind of monopoly on this prestigious pretentious kind of series. And BBC had a right to think so because they had made a series about the First World War, as their first historical, blockbusting documentary series in 1964 for the opening of their second channel, BBC2. So they thought that they had a moral monopoly on these kind of programs, and they assumed, along with everyone else, that when the series on the Second World War was made, it would be made by the BBC.

So there was the accepted gospel of the series going to the BBC, and then Thames TV stepped in and made it. Why did they do it, and how did they carry it off? Now I have a thesis on this, which I admit is just speculation on my part, but to understand it you must know something about the structure of British commercial television.

The Independent Television Authority, as it was at the time (now the Independent Broadcasting Authority) closely controlled not only the *nature* of the programs made by the contractors, but the profits made by the contracting companies. And when these profits got too large a kind of excess profits tax was imposed, and when profits were thought to be too small then the tax was lowered. This is a crude description of the "levy." What happened I believe is that in 1971 the levy was unexpectedly reduced. So literally from one day to the next Thames had quite a large sum at its disposal which no one had budgeted for. And the then controller of the features department, Jeremy Isaacs, in effect went to the senior executives of Thames Television and said, "I know what to do with that money. We will make the history of the Second World War."

The Board was delighted with this suggestion for several reasons. One is that as he explained it to them, it would have a large archive film component. That meant library film and a less expensive series than using live actors. The second reason was that because the series was about the war it would have a lot of gunfire. It would be a kind of heroic shoot-'em-up which could compete successfully for audiences against westerns and other forms of violent movies. And because it was about a great public event, the Second World War, it would also count as public service broadcasting. So they could kill three birds with one stone. So they approved the series.

It was Jeremy's great triumph that, having got the green light for what I think was expected to be a remake of something like "Victory at Sea," he turned that go-ahead into the series which it became: namely a series which never used known film when there was fresh unknown film never experienced before by the public. That was one characteristic of the series which made it so original. Another characteristic, which separated it from the former series, was that it was held as a guide line never to use mandarins—never to use experts— never to use pundits when the experience of ordinary people could be used to tell the story. So Jeremy's skill was in translating a mandate to make a shoot-'em-up into a populist, popular, and popularizing visual history of the Second World War.

Q. These things are seen very clearly in the programs. Was there much discussion at the start as to the style of the programs, their structure, where they would be different, where you were going? What happened at those first meetings?

A. I didn't come into the project until the first four programs had been made. So that all I can say about the tone of the early production meetings is what I gathered from talking to people who were there and I can work back to what must have been the case then, because of what was clearly the case when I arrived on the scene. I think that I've already implied that the overriding concern that Jeremy Isaacs had was to make the story of the Second World War intelligible to the Thames audience.

In socio-economic terms commercial television audiences in this country, like those of commercial television in America, are statistically very largely composed of men and women and boys and girls without a great deal of formal education, without high incomes, without a profound and abiding interest in the great literary tradition of the Western World.

Now the great difference between "The World at War" on the one hand and previous attempts to tell the story of the Second World War is that those other attempts (I'm thinking particularly of the BBC's "Great Commanders" series and indeed most of what the BBC does in this field) is that they make what I would call magisterial or mandarin history. Their approach is to get a revered figure, or perhaps even a controversial figure, but at any rate a *public personality* who tells the audience *what to think*. And since the only sort of people who are confident enough to do that in public are people educated within an inch of their life, what they tend to do is to speak not popular English, but Latinate professorial prose. And this doesn't make any sense at all to a Thames audience. I don't think it makes any sense to a BBC audience either.

40

For example you have commentators talking about "the constitution." Now if you want to get across to an audience whose formal education stopped when they were 14, I think it's better to talk about "the way things work" rather than "the constitution," because working-class people in this country don't talk Latin, they talk Anglo-Saxon.

What concerned Jeremy when he set up the unit and what concerned me when I was reading scripts and talking to people was our audience. Our audience was not the Staff College at Camberly. It was not the editorial staff of the *Revue d'Histoire de la deuxième Guerre Mondiale*. It was a lot of people who left school when they were 14. And the language suitable to the first groups was totally inappropriate to our audience.

Q. On the series Jeremy Isaacs acted as producer and you acted as associate producer. How were the functions separated?

A. Crudely speaking, the difference between Jeremy and myself, to pursue a military metaphor, was the difference between being a commander-in-chief and chief-of-intelligence. Jeremy set the tone. He set the pace. He made the fundamental editorial and possibly even more important financial decisions. "Yes, you can make another trip to the national archives to find the color film that you think is going to be there." "No, we cannot hold off the production of the program even though you know that the Wehrmacht film that you found six months ago in the German archives is being processed this very moment and so we will be able to show how most of the *Wehrmacht* walked to Moscow, and didn't ride on the backs of panzers, and didn't sing as they marched." All those kind of things.

My own job changed from week to week, from day to day, and even from hour to hour. The one thing I did more than anything else was continuously to try and make the production team aware of the consequences of what they were doing. I would never say you cannot say this and you must not show that. What I would say, and they certainly got very sick of it, was: If you say this then the following people are going to attack you on the following grounds. And if you show that then the following people who were there are going to say but that's *not* the 134th Brandenburg Light Infantry in the trenches at Anzio. That's the 736th Brandenburg Chasseurs Alpins before Vilna. And it's not 1944, it's 1941.

Whenever I did say that quite obviously there were two reactions. One was, "If we have to positively identify every foot of film in this program before we can use it, we'll never finish. Not only will we never finish, we'll never start." And the other reaction was, "You're absolutely right. I cannot see any way out of this terrible difficulty which you have made because I had a splendid sequence for the battle of Vilna and now you tell me it's all lies and I'm going to go home and put my head in the oven."

Obviously when you're making a series like this you don't want the second to happen, but you do want to get it right all of the time. You don't get it right as often as you can. And when confronted with an editor who has a sequence which contains dubious shots, all you can do and all that I felt that I could do was to not simply say, "That shot is wrong, take it out," but "If you've got to use that shot, I think there's another way around the difficulty. Don't say in your commentary '9:47 am, December the 13th, 1942, the Hungarians attack.' You shouldn't say that because it's perfectly obvious the film shows Romanian troops. But what you can do is say 'the kind of war fought in Transylvania was bloody and bitter' which avoids positively identifying, or I should say positively misidentifying the material which you know is something other than what you would like it to be."

That's really what I did, and sometimes I succeeded, and sometimes I failed because there was another element in all of this which was that I felt that in the unit itself we were fighting on two fronts. First to get things right. But you also fight for the independence of the producer associated with you which means defending his or her right to make editorial decisions which are then transmitted in the name of the company. So the fight that we fought was to let producers make, in the last analysis, the films they wanted.

I think it would be false to pretend that all of the films in the series are of equal merit. Some are conventional, because the producers wanted them that way. Equally, less conventional films were made because the producers wanted them that way. If you want an example of an unconventional film, look at the one David Elstein made about the decision to drop the atomic bomb. This film said, probably for the first time in a program destined for a very large audience, that the bomb was dropped in order to impress the Russians far more than it was in order to win the war against Japan.

The film about the Battle of Britain made it quite clear to anyone who had eyes to see that the Battle of Britain was lost by the Luftwaffe and not won by the RAF. And as I say the price that one paid for giving producers that sort of freedom (which fills up the postbag afterwards with opposition mail and brings Royal Air Force benevolent association secretaries down on our heads and is not something which any commercial company is eager to get)—the price that you paid for that was the rather more conventional programs and the only way you could get the two of them was to defend the independence of the producer. Not only against outside pressures, but against ourselves.

Q. In the end you made 26 films. How did you arrive at the particular topics? Were there other topics which you discussed which you eventually didn't cover?

A. Here again the question of what topics we included and what topics we left out can be answered with an official story and with an unofficial story. The official story is that we all thought very carefully about it and made our decision on our best knowledge of what film would be available and what subjects ought to be dealt with in any comprehensive history of the Second World War.

The unofficial story is the famous jotting on the back of the envelope. That the producer consulted the obvious person to consult—the director of the Imperial War Museum—and said, "If you were making the history of the Second World War for popular audiences what would be the 26 things you *could not leave out?*" And whether there is a real back of the envelope isn't very important. For my own part I'm convinced that it was very much like that . . . a rough, off-the-top-of-the-head set of suggestions about *what you could not leave out* modified by what film was available.

So one can see them jotting down: can't leave out the battle of the Atlantic. Can't leave out the bombing of Germany. Can't leave out Pearl Harbor, Can't leave out Stalingrad. Can't leave out the extermination of 6 to 12 million Jews, Gypsies, and Jehovah's Witnesses. Can't leave out the great battle for the Pacific. Can't leave out the invasion of France. And already you've got the first half-dozen programs right there.

The difficult decisions are when you're getting down to number 25 and 26. I bitterly regretted that we left out the neutrals. I thought that it was terribly important to show what was going on in Portugal, Spain, Switzerland, and Sweden. As it turned out it would have been very difficult to film in Dr. Caetano's Portugal or in General Franco's Spain. But now, for anyone who wants to, there is a splendid series to be made about what life was like in Sweden and in Switzerland from 1939 to 1945.

Q. Did you find when you went to the military consultants that their view of war revolved totally around the battles? Or did they in fact take into consideration the social aspects of the war? Were they interested in internal life in England or, say, the problem of genocide?

A. The question of the reaction of military figures as distinct from civilian figures to the subjects we proposed and to the questions we asked hasn't really got a simple answer. The most striking thing from an outsider's point of view about the series—and certainly it's something which must strike any military figure who comes to see the films—is that no one involved in the series was a professional military man. Indeed, none of the people who participated in it with two, perhaps three exceptions, had had anything to do with the Second World War except as child spectators. We were all, if not born after the war, at least born a short enough time before the war not to have participated as combatants.

We think, and this is where the official history and the unofficial history of the series coincide, that this was an advantage because we were not settling old scores. We were not paying off that son of a bitch from the 37th infantry division who stole my jeep, or whatever. There was none of that sort of thing as far as the production team was concerned. Which meant that there was a kind of innocence about some of our inquiries which perhaps predisposed tough old generals to treat us more—I won't say kindly, but to treat us more respectfully (that may be the wrong word) than they otherwise would have.

If you are asked by a personable lady exactly what went wrong at the third battle of El Halfiya, your reply cannot be "Come on, Jack, you were in Charlie's company. You jolly well know what went on there." It's got to be, "Well, let me explain what we were trying to do." To which you can reply, if you're the young lady or indeed if you're a 19- or 24-year-old young man who quite clearly has not done military service, "but I don't quite understand, sir. You mean you get men to stand up and run across a field where people are trying to kill them." Of course, the questions are not quite that naive. But there is certainly a kind of license which people who are not professionally involved in the job that you're doing have, when they ask *you* to explain the job that *you're* doing. That meant that professional soldiers had to persuade us. They couldn't take for granted that we would share either their preoccupations or their conclusions.

So the best films were not much influenced by any traditional military view of the war. And indeed I think that was one of their great strengths. For example, in John Pett's film about D-day, one of the participants, Joe Minogue, is recorded as saying, in regard to the evening after D-day, *not* "We fell down on our knees and thanked almighty God that we had had good hunting on the fields of Europe," which is Montgomery's language, but rather "We were absolutely astonished." He put this in rather more eloquent language than I can recall offhand. He says that at the end of the first day "we were astonished that this army of which we'd been a part for so long and we'd known how badly it fucked up everything it tried, actually managed to pull this thing off." What happens is that since no one ever says that in public histories, the first person who does say it enjoys an enormous complicity, or benefits from an enormous surge of good will on the part of people who hear their own experiences mirrored by the words of people like them.

So you can see, to come back to a point I made earlier, that kind of thing was the key to the popular success of the series. Joe Minogue saying "We got this message from Monty wishing us good hunting on the fields of Europe and being old soldiers we knew what a lot of cods wallop it was." That is not something that one hears very often in United States or British army recruiting films.

Q. How have professional military and other historians accepted the series? First, how have they accepted it as a series made by a group of people not connected with the war? Second, were there problems arising from their historic academic views of the war and how the series ought to have been, and your own realities of making it?

A. The reaction to the series has been favorable. It has been favorable not only on the part of the overwhelmingly civilian audience for which it was intended, but it has also been favorably received by military people.

Q. But how has it been received as history by serious historians?

A. It's a series which has had a varied career in the academic world. That's not a question of generation but a question of temperament. Historians, professional historians who take *visual evidence* seriously found it valuable. Their praise was consistent and of course very flattering. Historians who are word-obsessed cannot see what the point of making the series was and the reason for that is because they feel, I think, that the series has nothing to say to them. They know it all already. Not only do they know it all already but think it's a very superficial series.

The standard complaint (this is a hypothetical one) is "how can you possibly pretend to make a program about the rise of Hitler to power in Nazi Germany without talking about British rearmament." The answer is that even if the commentary of an hour program begins as soon as the main titles appear and doesn't stop until the end credits are finished, it can only contain about two thousand words, and two thousand words is rather less than what you can fit on a newspaper page. This is not something which is appreciated by very many professional historians. What *they* do is they look at a film like any of the ones we made in our series, see that it doesn't talk about things that they (quite rightly) think are of very great importance, and as a consequence dismiss our enterprise as being grotesquely misleading.

I think they have got hold of the wrong end of the stick because the stick they ought to be getting hold of is "who is the film made for and what is it supposed to be doing?" The film is made for an audience without much formal education and what it is supposed to be doing is to give them some idea of the significance of events which if they did not participate in, certainly had a profound effect on their lives.

Given this view it seems to be nitpicking to wonder what happened to the 134th Brandenburg Light Infantry or what happened to Chamberlain's memo to Lord Beaverbrook about Vickers's proposal to put eight guns and not six in a torpedo boat. That's not what the series was about and mandarin historians will never see that. But popular historians, or historians who do not disdain to try and reach audiences who are not themselves as highly educated as they are, who *do* have an interest in teaching those who are not professional historians themselves, most of these people rather liked the series. And young people who after all comprised more than a majority of the audience in the United States, find it's an entirely new world—one that they know nothing about.

Q. What were the key problems in trying to structure your films? And here one of the problems which interests me is historical memory. Were there times when you were conscious either of not getting an accurate view of the past or getting a distorted one? Did you allow for memory playing tricks or people bending history? How did you treat these and similar problems?

A. Certainly, the problems of trying to do visual history are quite as intractable as the problems of doing any other sort of history and in some respects they are similar. Memory is fallible. Even when people don't deliberately misrepresent events or their role in events, they get them wrong. And they don't get them wrong out of mischief-making or polemic. Often it's just that their memory is at fault. And it's a serious problem.

For instance, we interviewed a woman named Christobel Bielenberg, an Anglo-Irish woman married to a German. Her testimony was invaluable because she was British, but was part of German wartime society. She told a very moving story about the battle for Stalingrad and how the news of it affected the civilian population in Germany. And the story wasn't used because she misremembered certain crucial facts. For example she misremembered the point at which the German civilian population became aware that Stalingrad was not simply an important battle which was not going exactly the way the Germans had intended, but troops in Stalingrad had been *cut off*. She mentioned knowing this fact at a certain time when she couldn't possibly have had that information. She had *read back* into events things which she subsequently knew to be the case. And since I had no reason to wish to discredit her as a witness about other matters, I thought it best to advise the producers not to use that story.

In other cases it wasn't quite so simple. Lord Avon, Anthony Eden as he then was, gave a highly tendentious and self-serving account of his role in the diversion of British forces from Egypt and Libya to Greece in 1941. So what do you do? Short of having a kind of white triangle which pops up on the screen to alert audiences to the fact that this man is telling a very personal version of events—I think that's about as polite a way as I can find of putting it—there isn't much you can do. You might possibly suppress the story, but you can't really do that because it's important to know what *he* thought he was doing in office in 1941. So you let it go and hope people will take the trouble, if they are dubious about his account, to investigate further for themselves. There's a lot of that. Often there's not much you can do except assume that audiences are not stupid, and they can tell when people are being candid and they can tell when people are being self-serving.

In addition of course, producers and editors have ways of endorsing, or dissociating themselves from, what participants say by the context in which they place them, the music they accompany them with, and the length of time they let them speak and so on. There is nothing disreputable about that. It's the way film makers earn their living.

Q. You did mention somewhere, I think in one of your articles, about a need for passionate film makers who are concerned. And you said somewhere that this was one of the facets of your team. How in fact did this come about? How did it show itself? How were these people who worked with you on the team selected? Were you looking for just another writer or director, or a writer who had a particular interest in war or a director who felt very deeply about what happened in Germany or about what happened in the Pacific?

A. The way the team was selected, to continue to use a military metaphor, is very much the way the Chindits who fought with Wingate in Burma were selected. That is they were not people who were beating on doors saying I have a burning desire to tell you all about the battle of the Pacific, or in my heart I know that I cannot rest easily until I have given the world my version of the invasion of Anzio. Not a bit of it. They were mostly people already on the staff of Thames Television as staff producers and directors who were given an opportunity to work on a major series about the Second World War.

Now one very important thing to bear in mind is that television in this country, as in all the countries that I know, is a buyers' market.

Even at the best of times, about three-quarters of all members of the trade union are unemployed. So, in my own case, it wasn't that I was passionately concerned to do the history of the Second World War. It's that I was asked if I wished to be associated with a major series. I did, and the rent had to be paid and I sort of liked it, especially since it looked as if the job would last a year or perhaps even 18 months. As it turned out those of us that have stayed with the series worked on the Second World War longer than those who fought it. But that's not how it started out. It started out with serious professionals able to turn their hands to different kinds of programs. Being asked to participate and either finding that they loved it or hated it.

Q. Do you think such a series could have been made in the United States?

A. A series like this was made many years ago, "Victory at Sea." I don't think it was a very good series, but it was very popular. If such a series were to be made again or remade it would be done in much the same way. That is, a lavish musical score would be laid over very carefully selected but indifferently presented material. And by that I mean that America's film researchers are very good and America's editors are good. But I haven't got an enormous amount of respect for America's executive producers, who are the ones who make American television what it is, along with America's program directors.

What that means is that the present-day equivalent of "Victory at Sea" or "The World at War" would be "Doris Day's War." You'd have to have a host and you'd have to have a personality, like General Barry Goldwater or Colonel James Stewart to tell you the story of the 8th Air Force. James Stewart was a very good bomber pilot—he gave us a very good interview about formation flying—but he's not much of an authority on the strategic bombing campaign against Germany. So what the Americans would do is they would have a host. It would be a personal view by someone who has no particular reason for being entrusted with that task other than that he or she is a celebrity.

There is another reason why I think that this series would not have been made in the United States, and that is the economics of American television as distinct from the economics of British television. "The World at War" tied up an enormous amount of resources. It was originally budgeted for £500,000 in 1972. Today you could not make the series for anything under about seven or eight million dollars. I cannot see that any American network would bankroll such a series.

And once they began looking at the meaning and truths of the series and the implications of the events, the Americans would be even more reluctant to back the series. Because what do we say about the war?

America came into the war late. Didn't lose very heavily and got a hell of a lot out of it. We say the Russians could have beaten the Germans on their own. That the British didn't really win the Battle of Britain. All these things are really quite extraordinarily offensive, not to the professional historians who have known them for 30 years, but offensive to American executives and producers who simply would not wish to commit that kind of resources to that kind of series.

The paradox, of course, is that this series had an enormous success in America, and it's something which Americans in the business ought to ponder: why is it that in order to make serious programs which ordinary U.S. audiences find attractive, Americans have to come to Britain? It's very curious.

Q. What was your key "filmic" problem in making the series?

A. I think that the major problem in any visual history is this: that all that you can show is what has been filmed, and not surprisingly the cameramen will film that which is interesting to *them* when they're on their own. That which they think their editors would be interested in if they have explicit instructions, or that which their producers or directors tell them to film, if they're under direction. That means anecdotal material.

Television is hopeless at conveying abstract ideas, intentions, or any of the things that *go on in people's minds*. It can only show *actions,* so the problem you always have to face is that what you have before you on the screen is vivid, is riveting. It can be used to build and in some cases to tell a story. But it may not be what is *important*. What was important about the life of Hitler in prewar Germany was his *decision* to attack Poland. There never could be any film of that. What was and is important about the final solution is the multiplicity of *decisions* taken at all levels of the German regime to implement that barbarous policy. But they were never filmed. There is no way in which those decisions could be filmed.

And there's a kind of reverse story with trivial military engagements—trivial not to the people who participated in them but in the broad strategy of the war. Trivial events like the battle of the River Plate take on an importance because of the film that exists of them, but they are not important in the course of the war. This is the great problem that anyone who makes films has to deal with.

Q. All sorts of questions were asked by the critics when the series was first shown. What were the kind of questions that most annoyed you?

A. Well, a question which seems to me to be misplaced in a discussion of a series of this sort is what were your motives? What were you trying to do? What was the point of this or that episode? In a general way you know what you want to do with the series. You know the kind of stories you want to tell. You know the kind of episodes you are going to put in and leave out. But when it comes to individual programs and the significance of particular scenes which are either treated at length or cursorily, I think a great many critics could only ask the questions they do if they didn't know how films were made. When they ask what were you trying to do when you did that? the answer is "Good God, I was trying to finish the damn film. We were mixing in four days. And we still hadn't got the material from Washington."

Let me give a precise example of misplaced critical insensitivity. In the program which I made, the last narrative program in the series, there is a montage of victory parades. A group of dogs (the Canine Corps it was called in the Second World War) march down Michigan Avenue, in Chicago. That sequence is in that program for a very good reason. In the middle of the series we discovered in viewing that every program, up to that point, had a dog in it somewhere. Quite inadvertently. A dog climbing into an aircraft. A dog running along a street. A dog barking at a soldier. And from then on, as a kind of private joke within the unit we determined that every program would have a dog, and indeed every program did have a dog.

Now my program was the last program. So I said it's going to have a doggy sequence to end all doggy sequences. So there they are—150 Alsatians woof, woof, woof down Michigan Avenue. When I showed the film to a student audience in the United States, I was complimented on it in strange terms. They said, "What a courageous thing to do." "What do you mean courageous," said I. "Well," they said, "what is happening here, quite clearly, is that only a few Alsatian dogs guard the concentration camps and the extermination camps in the program about genocide, but American imperialism is far more powerful, far more dangerous than national socialism, so there are many more, and better organized, guard dogs." I said, "Thank you, I didn't know that."

Now there is a lesson there which is that programs are often typical only in their atypicality. Mine, for instance, was made during the three-day week. It was made in a month's less time than it ought to have had because suddenly the overseas sales department got an American sale for the series. That meant my program had to be transmitted a month before anyone thought it was going to have to be transmitted. That meant that instead of a very elaborate sequence of victory parades and whatever we had originally planned, it all had to be thrown together very quickly. So the answer to "why is that there?" is not "well

I thought we would have to make a balance in order to, etc." It's because the damn thing has to be ready next Thursday, and that was the only film there was.

Q. You have talked at length about the kind of audience you're aiming at. Youngsters who have never passed through the war. An audience who had probably not had too much schooling and so on. What have been the reactions firstly in England and then outside England to the films?

A. I think that the reactions of ordinary people have been as various as the audience is itself. Some people were delighted by the music and wanted to know where they could buy that wonderful record by Carl Davis. Others said "Dear Sir, I saw Uncle Freddy on a troop ship. I think it was him, in program number eight, and I wonder if you could give us a clip because he died and that's the only picture we've ever seen of him." That was very touching, and we tried to do that whenever we could.

A different reaction (and I can only judge this from the letters we received and conversations I had) was the sense of recognition, an acknowledgement that the programs had held their interest and had taught them things that they did not know. For example, very many people (not all of them under 15 by any means) were astonished to discover that the Soviet Union, the United States, and Great Britain were allies. They thought that the Soviet Union is our adversary today and has therefore always been our adversary.

Another fact about the Soviet Union which astonished even people in their forties and fifties was the enormous losses suffered by them in the Second World War. Twenty million dead. If I'm to go through my post bag and pick out the one single fact which appears spontaneously more than any other, it's the astonishment at the human price that the Soviets paid in the Second World War.

Two groups felt they had been very hard done by: the Polish community felt very strongly that we did not pay enough attention to them; and many Dutch felt that we had not appreciated enough the contribution of the Dutch resistance. There wasn't really any answer to the Poles: we didn't pay enough attention to them. The Dutch were a different matter. After all, the program was about the *Occupation* of Holland, not about the Dutch *resistance*. So of course we had to talk about collaborators and fence-sitters, as well as about resisters.

Q. What effect did working on the series have on you personally?

A. It changed me in one respect. It became impossible for me to view scenes of *simulated* violence. So a great deal of what has happened in the cinema in the past five years became and remains a closed book.

Apart from that I didn't learn a great deal working on the films. I knew what I thought about these events before I ever started to work on the series, and my mind wasn't really changed very much by what I learned. But what I did come to appreciate was the Soviet obsession with Western Germany, even now in the 1970s. It didn't seem to me that a superpower like Russia could be as frightened or apprehensive at the thought of a rearmed West Germany as its public utterances lead one to believe. I now see why. I didn't know that before I started working on the film.

Q. Do you think there's another level of reaction which may be important in America? I know from living in America on and off for four or five years that there's a very negative feeling with regard to the Vietnamese war. This then leads people to say that all wars anywhere are bad and that all American-supported or English-supported wars are capitalist-based wars. Do you think that a college audience in America looking at these films may now view war in a slightly different way other than the simplistic Vietnamese reaction I've given you?

A. I talked about the series to university audiences and I've tried to show them how we made the series. I think that it would be fair to say that the reaction to the series is one in which there's a sense of discrimination. That is the people I've talked to belong to a generation which entered college after the conclusion of America's military involvement in Southeast Asia. And they are able to make a distinction between America's military involvement in Asia and America's military involvement in Europe and Asia during the Second World War.

Now whether it's because of what they learned from the series or whether it's something apart from their exposure to the series is something I wouldn't be able to say. But certainly one of the extraordinary features of the Second World War, unlike any other in our lifetime that I know of, is that it's very clearly a case where there *are* good guys and bad guys. And the series (as does the war itself) begins with a string of victories on the part of the bad guys and ends with victory for the good guys. It's victory at a terrible price, and if the series has merit it's that it shows, more than other popular series have yet been able to, what that price involves. It's not a shoot-'em-up. There is not a single episode which is a glorification of armed combat. Horrible things happen in all of them, yet it's certainly not a pacifist series. When I finished working on the series, I thought, well the right side won, but Jesus Christ there must be a better way of ordering human affairs. And if that's the lesson which audiences get from it then it's four years well spent.

52

There's a further lesson in the series. It's that it's possible to be both true to one's material, and also make programs which large numbers of people enjoy watching. At its best "The World At War" demonstrated that you didn't need reconstructions, dramatizations, or on-camera celebrities to hold an audience. You could do it with archive film and the experiences of ordinary people. In other words, it was possible to make films which were both honest and popular. It still is. It ought to be done more often.

# John Pett, Director

*One of the misleading generalizations of the past has been that though documentaries can give the* strategy of war, *the* feel of war and the reactions of *men have to be left to the feature. This is sheer nonsense but has been repeated to me over and over again by fiction film makers. "The World at War" finally laid this myth to rest, and no director was more responsible for the burial than John Pett.*

*Pett's three films provide an incredible sense of how the war was perceived and suffered through by the ordinary combatant.* It's a Lovely Day Tomorrow *deals with the British defeat in Burma;* Pacific *covers the American invasions of Tarawa and Iwo Jima; and* Morning *deals with D-Day and the invasion of Normandy.*

*They are films made from the ground up, almost literally. Pett's method is to recreate an acute sense of place, feeling, horror and gut reaction. More than almost any other films in the series,* you are there . . . *whether ploughing through the mud of the Burmese jungles or shivering with fear waiting to land at Iwo Jima.*

*The films leave haunting impressionist pictures on the mind. Two scenes still reverberate in my memory as I write—the bitterness of the fighting at Tarawa and the battle of the Philippine Sea. In the latter American aircraft shot down 300 Japanese planes but had to return to their own carriers at sunset, with little fuel. This color sequence of carriers waiting—aircraft ditching in the sea—and the sun going down over the horizon in a blaze of red and gold—must rank as one of the most eerie-beautiful sequences of war ever filmed.*

*John Pett strikes you as very English, but in the best sense. An open air feeling. One thinks of rugby, tennis, and drinks in the pub. This is the casually efficient Englishman who will without doubt be the one to break out of the prisoner of war camp. And all of it coupled with sensitivity and talent.*

*Pett is one of those free-lance directors who's worked everywhere and done everything. He studied civil engineering but somehow ended up directing "B" feature films in Ireland. This was followed by a period in journalism and then writing, directing, and producing for Westward TV, a small regional television company. Since then he has worked for Granada, the BBC, ABC, and Thames. Apart from "The World at War" he is chiefly known for his series on the British Museum for Thames TV and a picture on artist Ronald Searle for the BBC's "Omnibus."*

Q. How did you come into the War series, and when you came in how were the areas defined that you would tackle? Did you have any choice of the films you would do?

A. I was working for Thames anyway, just completing a series, and I approached Jeremy Isaacs, because I very much wanted to work with him. Jeremy was setting up "World at War" at the time and said, yes, they would probably want film directors. So we talked, and he said, "Were you in the war?" I said, "No, because I did my national service about 1947, but my brother was in Burma." So he said, "How would you like to do the Burma one?" I said, "Fine." So that is how it started, and from Burma it became D-Day, and then it became the Pacific over a period of three years.

Q. Were there any ground rules which were laid down from the beginning? You must have had various meetings with the various producers or Jerry Kuehl as associate producer. How did you thrash things out, parameters, limitations?

A. The details of the series had not been thrashed out, but there were firm guidelines, and when I came in most of the programs had a treatment of some kind written by the writer. The programs weren't dealing with the chronological progression of the war, but rather with areas and campaigns.

Q. How did you cope with subject or area overlap with the other directors, and choice of film material which would obviously work for more than one film?

A. I'll give you an example. In *Pacific*, I wanted to use film of the kamikaze suicide pilots. Now there was another program dealing with Japan, *The Fall of Japan*, where they also wanted to use the kamikaze film because it is very dramatic. Eventually we went to Jeremy for arbitration. He, or someone else, then suggested that the other film should deal with the Japanese mainland and the kamikaze pilots taking off, while we did the American side, which shows the kamikaze pilots coming over and bombing the U.S. fleet.

Q. I am interested in your relationship with the writer. You come along and the treatment seems to be already set up. Was it difficult to work within the confines of that treatment? Did you broaden it out? When you started researching, were you prompted into different areas and breakaways from the original treatment?

A. John Williams wrote the script of *It's a Lovely Day Tomorrow*—the name of the Burma program—and he also wrote *Morning*, the real name for the D-Day film. He had written some very good books, but hadn't had much experience of film scripting—except for working on "The Great War" series for the BBC. But he was very cooperative and willing to help and even learn, as I was.

It was very difficult for me, in that I am used to writing my own scripts and one had to try and stop oneself altering points of style which didn't conform to the way one would have written it oneself. However, the easy thing was to trim all the wordy explanations of things which you actually saw in the film (it's a mistake many writers make with film) and thus avoid repeating visual statements. More difficult was the business of getting the tactics and strategy right. John was better at this than I was, but I wanted to get it down to a non-mystical level, to a human level . . . to get down to what it felt like to fight in Burma, or land in Normandy . . . and why.

There were three processes involved with the script as far as I was concerned. First, I got the shape of the film right with the editor and the sequences cut as we wanted them. I then wrote a rough guide for John Williams telling him the kind of things we would like for each particular piece of commentary, and he also saw the cut several times. After that he came back, and he and I went over the script without the film, making amendments and corrections, and then Jeff Harvey, the film editor, John Williams and I went through the scripts with the films, fitting where we could and altering again. Finally, Jeremy read a copy of the script and made his corrections (he would have seen the film several times by now) and then we had one or two more viewings where we thrashed out the final words. In the event, John's scripts turned out well.

I suppose many times I would have changed the script to suit my style, but that would have been wrong and lost any individuality for the writer. I think, in the end, we effected a fair meeting point.

Q. Where physically did you begin after you had your treatment?

A. I met Jeremy and I met John Williams and we agreed then on the whole outline. Then it was a question for me reading background material, and I read a lot. Burma was the first one I did, and I read masses of books including novels about it. I found the most difficult thing was sorting out how the actual campaign went, because no war progresses in a straight line. Then it's a matter of fitting everything in. How to make both strategical *and* emotional sense in just one hour of viewing. I think if you only show people a map and say the Japanese moved up there, and then the British moved down from here, without giving *the feeling* of what it was actually like, you are wasting your time.

On the film *Pacific* I was given a very competent and fairly complicated treatment by David Wheeler. Again I did masses of background reading. The problem was where did you start. Did you start in Australia and go out to the islands? Did you start in the Pacific itself? Did you end in Japan?

Finally we made certain decisions. One was we ought to concentrate on a landing and see what it was actually like. This would possibly last

56

10 or 15 minutes. Second we ought to concentrate on an area of battle, so we did Tarawa and Iwo Jima. Finally we thought we ought to concentrate on a naval engagement. And that was wrong, because there was very little material apart from stills. In the end we compromised. We concentrated on Tarawa and Iwo Jima, and on the Turkey Shoot, which was more aerial than naval engagement.

"The Marianas Turkey Shoot" or "The Battle of the Philippine Sea" was called a turkey shoot because the Americans said they found shooting down Japanese planes was as easy as shooting turkey. The battle took place over two days. First the Japs attacked the U.S. Task Force covering the Saipan landings and the Americans shot down over 300 aircraft, mainly because of the inexperience of the Japanese pilots. The Americans suffered damage to some of their ships. The next day, with each of the fleets looking for the other, the Americans sighted the Japs and sent up their planes despite the fact that the Japanese were out of range. Again, the Japanese were destroyed but the Americans had difficulty making it home as night was falling (a classic war melodrama situation) and the U.S. Admiral ordered the fleet to be lit up despite Japanese submarines.

One by one the planes come in in the dusk, some over-shooting, some crashing on the deck, and many ditching in the sea because they are running out of gas. I remember one of the interviews with one of the pilots. It was very emotionally dramatic, without trying for effect. He said something like, "On the radio you could hear the other pilots saying, 'I'm out of gas,' 'I'm ditching now,' 'I'm going down' and all the time it got darker and darker."

"Turkey Shoot" took place on June 19 to 20, 1944. The Japanese fleet lost 92 percent of its carrier planes, while the U.S. lost 130 planes and 76 pilots. Many, in fact most, were rescued after they had ditched. We tried to re-create the two-day battle, ending with the dusk return of the planes which managed to make it back. I suppose this was a little more romantic (if anything in war can be called romantic) than anything else in an horrific campaign. However, I had to remake the sequence after Jerry Kuehl saw it because much of the film material, although illustrating the action beautifully, was either not from the right period or the right place. Infuriating at the time and you think of all the arguments to retain the sequence or only alter it marginally, but Jerry was very good at this sort of thing, and you knew it was right to alter it in the end. I must point out that we had taken the material in good faith as being from that part of the battle.

Q. You mentioned having plotted the film in three sections: landing, area fight, and sea fight, but not finding sea material. Did this happen to you in any of your other films, that you conceptualized the film on paper as to what was important, and then material was just not available?

A. Burma is the obvious case in point, because the retreat of the British from the Japanese is the most dramatic thing in the whole story. There were so many good books written about these exhausted, weary British troops coming into India, and piling up on the frontier, and the Japanese minutes behind them.

So we set out, and we thought, God—it's going to be a very dramatic sequence. In the end it turned out there was not more than five minutes of film material. So we dug, and dug around, and eventually got a bit of the Japanese advancing, some propaganda film, and we built up a reasonable picture, but not possibly as good a one as we could have done, because it just wasn't there. I mean there were long trains of refugees. There was one very short piece of the Japanese marching through a deserted Rangoon. We built that up a bit, and it worked very well, but there was not enough material.

Q. One thing I personally liked, specifically in *Pacific*, was the use of the voice-over, the feelings of the soldiers at the time, their fear of death, their horror of war, of being killed. As a documentarist I very much like this personalized subjective view instead of the commentary voice-of-God. Is this very much a style of yours? How were you drawn to it?

A. It is very much a style of mine. This is very much the way I work, and sometimes circumstances made it a necessity. For example, I went to one Marine Corps reunion in the States, but could not film there, so I taped it instead. So in a sense it's like everything else in documentary, part of it is accident, but the desire is also to do as much voice-over as possible, as opposed to actually looking at people getting together and reminiscing. People relax and talk more when you have no camera, just a tape recorder.

I can remember one of the marines saying that in Iwo Jima the battle was hell. "If ever there is a hell it must be Iwo Jima." They remembered vividly what had happened to them and gave it to me very powerfully. And it was best non-synch. After all, how could you cut from a landing craft going into the beach to a synch piece of a man saying, "Yes, it was hell." It just wouldn't work, whereas it does with just voice-over.

Q. Were you working on *Pacific* by itself or were you working on one or two other films at the same time?

A. We were working on two at the same time. *Pacific* and D-Day. We had almost completed Burma, and D-Day was in its completion stages when we started on *Pacific*. And then I did two trips to America, one was for D-Day and Burma, the other one was for *Pacific*.

Q. Were the U.S. trips to get basic information, or primarily to get good interviews?

A. The latter. We were looking for good interviewees. The first trip was for the D-Day film, and I went to New York and Washington and Virginia. We would use a hotel room as a base and then bring the people to what was virtually a small studio. It was very exhausting dealing with the sort of total emotional recall that many American veterans seemed to have. Many of them were forthright and talked about their despair on Omaha Beach. They wanted it never to happen again. It tends to drain you if you get involved, as I do, in that kind of interview. We had so much good stuff from that trip that the difficulty was editing the material down. By good stuff, I mean memories which contributed to the feel of the film. I knew what I was going for, pre-invasion memories of Britain, the actual preparation for D-Day and then the ride over, the beaches and the aftermath as they fought their way out. I wasn't only looking for explicit incidents, but as much for how they felt emotionally, not just fear or excitement, but perhaps the despair, or how worthwhile it might have seemed then.

The second trip was again pretty specific, to find people who could cover the Iwo Jima and Tarawa landings, the Marianas Turkey Shoot and the kamikaze. The kamikaze pilots were in action from the Philippines onward, but we used them specifically for the invasion of Okinawa. Here the U.S. fleet battered the island with a tremendous bombardment, and then the Japanese sent wave after wave of suicide planes out against them. The impression from all the interviews was that this was worse than anything, because they knew the Japanese didn't care about their lives and the whole thing was so relentless. That's where this story was told by a man on the U.S. ship who said that one of the gunners suddenly had enough and after turning to his friend and saying "It's hot today" jumped overboard and they never saw him again.

I remember one session when some Marines in Washington had a reunion and again their memories of the battles were unnerving. While I wouldn't agree with their sentiments all the time, I must say I came to admire and learn something about what it was like then, whether you had liberal sentiments about war or not. One soldier told the story about how they were sitting around and suddenly a Jap ran out and blew himself to bits with a hand grenade. A chunk of the body of the Jap landed on one man's knee who then said, "Gee, am I hit that bad," and they all fell about laughing.

Now one saw his point. It was not callousness, or indifference, simply one way of releasing one's mind from the horrors all around, and the film proved those horrors in no uncertain way. Those unknown news cameramen deserve more than a mention. They got the most incredible shots and, at the same time, made it seem the bloody business it was. It's strange, though, sitting in a dimly lit hotel, listening to men telling you about some horror over and done with years ago, but still alive for them, and becoming alive for you. It blows your mind, as they say.

Q. There have been a large number of feature films made about both the Pacific war and D-Day . . . Zanuck's *The Longest Day*, to give just one example. Did the knowledge of these feature films affect you in any way, make you try for something different? Or was it a matter that you could put entirely out of your mind? And how did it affect you insofar as realizing that your potential audience had got a possibly very fictionalized version of these wars?

A. Two things. Taking D-Day first, I had seen library footage of the landings, not put into any order. I had also out of curiosity seen again the Zanuck film, *The Longest Day*, and with due respect to Twentieth Century-Fox, when you saw the real event, and then you saw the fiction, there was no comparison. I am sure that everything was done beautifully and precisely. It just did not work. It was *the feel* that was wrong. Once you saw those exhausted Marines on Omaha Beach after they landed with the sea lapping around, and the wounded and the dying, you knew you absolutely could not recreate that. I don't think anyone can or would want to.

Anyway, I said, right, we are not going to go for the big set piece, we shall go for this *feel*, and how the invasion affected people. What I wanted to do together with Jeff Harvey, the editor, was get as realistic a view of the landing as possible, without the heroics, and make people *feel* what it was like. Because it was pretty awful, not heroic. And they lost many cameramen getting that fantastic footage. And that too shouldn't be forgotten.

Q. In the D-Day film, *Morning*, you are using mainly black-and-white footage, and somehow that is how many of us unrealistically think of the war, in black and white. In *Pacific*, you used some absolutely incredible color footage, which I expect many others like me had never ever seen before, much of it very ghastly and dreadful in terms of the wounded and the bodies. How did you come across this particular footage? Was it new? Had there been censorship on it before?

A. The point about censorship . . . as far as I can recall, we were very short of marine footage on Tarawa Island landings and eventually

60

Raye Farr found some which had never been released because, apparently (and I hope I remember right here) the authorities didn't want the American public to see dead bodies of Marines floating about in the water—it was a point of morale. I don't know whether or not this was true, but Raye fought valiantly and got it for us, as she did many other effective pieces of film.

In *Pacific* Jeff Harvey and I were dealing with material which was sickening and harrowing, however you like to describe it. The problem was, and particularly if the film was in color, that it was very difficult sorting this film out so that it would give an accurate picture of what the war in the Pacific was like without using it to titillate or horrify simply for sensational and rather short-term reasons. It was a painful film to make and without those voices of the men who had actually landed on Iwo Jima and Tarawa and Okinawa it might have seemed just a catalogue of bodies, blood and death. Those men relived in those small interview rooms we used on the U.S. trip the experiences one saw on the screen. And, again, those cameramen—whose names would flash by on the slates at the top of the uncut rushes, or who were totally unnamed—deserve as much credit as Jeff or myself, and many of them didn't survive.

All this made it rather objectionable when one person called the material pornographic because of its violence. Neither Jeff nor I ever intended it as such, neither did the cameramen who shot it, and I don't think it was. I give it only as an example of the care which all of us from Jeremy downwards took to make the programs and to show that we were aware of the pitfalls.

Q. How did you work with Jeremy Isaacs and with Jerry Kuehl? As overall producer and associate producer, what were their influences on you? Were there any arguments? Was it totally agreed most of the time? How did they help you, specifically?

A. The differences with Jeremy Isaacs were few and far between. He had made the framework of the series clear and concise without making it inflexible, and so one knew in advance what one was aiming for. We might have had problems in the viewing sessions, because I tend to hug a film to myself until it is really ready to show, and also because I am not particularly good at *ex tempore* explanation—I find film making a very personal business until the film is finished. But this was fairly easily dealt with. The only really major point was on the construction of the first half of the film on D-Day.

I was worried that the first part of D-Day was about the build-up to the landings. Jeremy was adamant that it should be like this (rightly so—in retrospect), and it was very difficult getting the shape and pace right of this part of the film. However, he would never impose an idea on you, you could always retain your conception of the film and his was the overall shape of the series and in that was his supreme talent. I found it was a good relationship. You were left to work as you wanted to within the series framework. And I think we retained our own individuality as directors.

Working with Jerry Kuehl was a slightly different matter. Jerry is very useful, very annoying, because he was so pedantic about historical fact, but in the end I think he was extremely good. He did his job remarkably tactfully, but he was very dogged, very obstinate, and rightfully so. It sounds a bit pious, but I enjoyed working with both him and Jeremy very much. In fact it was a very good few years working on "World at War." You had a lot of talented, concerned people, not really knowing at the time that the series was going to be so great a success, and led by Jeremy, who had a flair for keeping the respect and affection of the people working with him, and perhaps that's why the series turned out as it did.

Q. You have major landing sequences in both *Pacific* and D-Day. Did you see yourself in danger of repeating certain film techniques and types of cutting?

A. I think we took the D-Day landing in a totally different way from *Pacific*. We concentrated on Omaha Beach and took the landing fairly quickly. In *Pacific* there was the danger of repetition, because we had landings at Tarawa and Iwo Jima. Because of this we decided to do each one a different way. In Tarawa for instance we dwelt on the build-up and the ships, and then in to land and a different kind of fighting. So it was quickly over. With Iwo Jima we did not have the build-up. We had the artillery barrages from the naval fleet, and then we went in with the landing craft fairly lengthily, and then it was a long, hard slug across the island. That was the idea. Whether it worked I don't know. You got the feeling of this awful business of going through jungles, very slowly, and eventually coming out. Someone says, "It was only about five days, but it seemed like five years," and I think that was the feeling we planned for.

Q. After you worked on these films, can you see any new perception in yourself about the Second World War, and do you think there are any particular things in your film, I won't say lessons, but maybe again perceptions is the word, which would have affected the viewer and your way of looking at the war?

A. "Teaching" sounds rather pompous but, in fact, through "World at War" I was made to understand what it was like to be pitchforked into the Burmese jungle from a quiet English landscape, or to land on

62

the hell of Iwo Jima when one's previous experience had been a small American town. The change must have been traumatic. It makes one re-examine all those "liberal" sentiments about war (because conscience-stricken liberals must have been rare on the beaches of Iwo Jima) and although it didn't change my horror of war, or make me want to glorify it, it did make me understand—say—the Marine who said quite dispassionately . . . "we didn't take prisoners."

Strangely, it made me understand my father's attitude to war (he had been badly gassed in the First World War) and see the reality behind what to me as a boy had been heroics. I think all the films one makes should have compassion (not sentimentality) and broaden the film maker's understanding, and, of course, you have to be committed, at least to the people in the film if nothing else. I don't think you can stand outside and feed off whatever is happening, neither can you use it as propaganda, but you have to use a part of yourself somewhere in your films.

# Susan McConachy, Researcher

The selection was difficult. How many interviewees had
carefully memorized wartime hearsay? Memory plays
tricks. Everybody, guilty or innocent, tells lies.

SUSAN McCONACHY, *SFTA Journal*

*A warm summer's morning. I'd done an interview at the BBC. Susan
McConachy lived nearby and had suggested we talk over lunch at her house.
Golden light streams through the window. Books everywhere. A make-yourself-
at-home atmosphere. And cold wine and a salad lunch served by a woman with
short honey-blonde hair to whom I'm unthinkingly telling my life history.
Tables turned! Interviewer interviewed! But what else to expect from a good
researcher?*

*McConachy makes you feel you've known her a long time. Without realizing
it trust is established. Suddenly, in the nicest possible way, I could see the charm
and quiet ability which had enabled her to research and interview some very
difficult personalities for "The World at War," including Traudl Junge, a secretary of Hitler, and Karl Wolff, Himmler's adjutant.*

*Because "The World at War" tended on balance to concentrate on people
rather than politics the realm of the human research was absolutely critical.
Three main people were involved in this field—Susan McConachy, Isobel Hin-
shelwood, and Alan Patient. Their task was to find people for the programs—
people who could personalize the general experience of war and provide witnesses
for both sides.*

*The research process was for the most part like other documentaries, but again
the differences lay in scope and sensitivity. The program on genocide, for example, called for talking to both concentration camp inmates and their perse-
cutors, and as the interview shows, created strong personal dilemmas for
McConachy.*

*The moral dilemmas for the researcher came in many kinds. How far do you
exploit trust you have built up with an interviewee? What rights do you have
to evoke shattering traumatic memories that have been dormant for so many
years? There are no general answers, merely answers that must be governed by
the sensitivity of the researcher to the feelings of the interviewee. Here I felt an
absolute trust in McConachy as a person who would never exploit, and who
would know where to draw the line to safeguard privacy and suffering.*

*McConachy's background includes a degree in modern languages from Bristol
University and early work in publishing. Her first BBC job was working on*

*"Choice," a consumer TV program. She stayed with the BBC from 1965 to 1969 and then went to work for Bavarian TV in Germany.*

*A little while later she returned to work for the BBC in Switzerland. While in the middle of the Swiss program she suddenly heard about the start of "The World at War." "So I wrote to Jeremy Isaacs saying I knew Germany backwards and would like to work on the series . . . and I only emerged three years later." Since the end of "The World at War" she too, like Raye Farr, has been working on Thames's Hollywood series with Kevin Brownlow.*

Q. When you started working on "The World at War" how was the series characterized as different from all the other tens of series and individual films about the Second World War?

A. There were two things. The first was, it seemed that we were far enough away from the war to be able to look at the whole of the war with a bit less of the really fierce feelings that were in each nation immediately after it. The way we wanted to do that was to look at the war from the level of ordinary people. We wanted to look at it from the level of housewives and ordinary soldiers. It was just far enough away then for the memory to be less bitter and yet not so far that the people who actually lived it were dead. The main idea was to look at the war from a personal rather than a historical level.

It was never meant to be a history of the war and what I found particularly attractive was that one was going to look at the war as to how it *affected* people. To me it was a very antiwar series. It was looking at the whole pointlessness of ordinary people getting dragged into what, in many ways, was somebody else's argument . . . and fighting for ideologies which people didn't really understand and hadn't been part of. We wanted to look at the war from an ordinary person's point of view, which is a very confusing way of looking at war because it no longer seems to be black and white. It no longer seems to make any sense.

Q. You look as if you were born in the early forties. Was your family involved in the war? Did you talk about the war? Was the Second World War in any way a reality to you before you started work on the series?

A. Not really. My father had fought in the First World War and was too old for the Second. Nobody close to my family had been killed or got lost and the nearest I ever got to talking about it was with my German friends. The father of the family I learned German with once took me out on his balcony and said, "From here, right across the town, was absolutely flat the day after the British bombers came over." That was the level I knew about the war. I had no particularly strong feelings, and I had spent relatively happy times with people of my generation in Germany who hadn't lived through the war. Therefore I had few prejudices.

Q. The first program you worked on in the series was *Keep the Home Fires Burning*, about the Home Front in Britain. Why did you concentrate the filming around Plymouth?

A. We had to look for a place *outside* London that had suffered fairly severe bombing as there was another program that dealt specifically with London. That film was a good place to start as I got my feeling as an English person talking to people who had gone through the war in England as to what the war had all been about as far as an English family was concerned. So I established my own English identity before I set off for Germany to do the mirror image program in Germany which was about their Home Front.

Q. I myself was brought up in England with the legend or myth "those were the greatest days . . . the greatest years," and I think we have a certain romantic concept of what England was like in the Second World War. But I use the words "myth" and "legend" cautiously. When you were doing *Keep the Home Fires Burning* what did you find out about myth and reality?

A. What I found out was that the reality had nothing to do with the myth. That again was something to do, perhaps, with the timing of the series. Enough time had gone by. People no longer needed to support that myth. They could talk about how awful it was in reality because they didn't have to pretend to be British and keep a stiff upper lip and to be winning the war. They'd won the war and a lot of time had gone by.

I talked to a lot of people on the practical level. There was an MP who was in charge of defenses for the whole of the Dover area. I talked to him about the preparations and, in hind sight, how badly prepared we were. When I went down to Plymouth I put an advert in the local paper for people who remembered the war and who had experience of the bombing raids. I asked people to write and to give me a brief idea in their letters of what they could remember. I recall being in the hotel in Plymouth and having people coming in almost like a production line, to tell me about their memories. We eventually talked to about a dozen people, though many more had written. For me, that was the first real experience of the war . . . meeting a man who worked in the home guard and had to go out and pull people out of the bomb damage. One woman had actually woken up under a pile of rubble with her child dead beside her.

Q. What were your general methods of finding people for the English programs?

A. One was putting adverts in the local papers. Then there were the obvious politicians. And there were the people who had roles during the war like publishing newspapers and organizing an area like say Dover. But I didn't spend a lot of time covering the political side because Phillip Whitehead who was producing and directing the Home Front film dealt with that area. But mainly we found people through advertisements.

I was also working very closely with Raye Farr who was doing the film archive research and she came up with two very interesting pieces of film. One was about the way they were kept going in Coventry in the face of the bombing. Taking that idea further we managed to track down the three boys who were featured in the wartime "Ra-ra" newsreel. Of course they were grown men now and I managed to find them around Coventry. They were very surprised. They hadn't seen each other for decades, but we found them through the newspapers. Unfortunately we didn't use that in the final film because there wasn't enough time or space.

The other bit of film was an interview with the first Bevan Boy— a public schoolboy called into the mines instead of the army. He told us how disappointed his mother had been that he wasn't going to be an officer. That interview we used.

Q. You mentioned before that people were now willing to talk because enough time had elapsed since the war. But wasn't there a danger of things also working the other way? That the memories didn't fit the reality? That people had built up a romantic conception of the war which didn't touch reality?

A. In England the passage of time hadn't made people romanticize the past. If anything, it had made them look back on it much more coldly than they might have done immediately afterwards. I think many of them probably said to themselves, "Look how well the Germans are doing now—so who really won the war? Perhaps it wasn't so great after all."

In England I talked about specifics. In Coventry I talked to the boys about *their* memories of working in that factory. I talked to a lady in Plymouth who'd lost her two children. I was going into the specifics of two bombing raids and the way I chose people for interviewing in the end was people who had specific memories and who weren't making any kind of heroic points. There was no room for comment, or for that story to be anything other than a series of facts of what war is

67

about and what war is like if you are a lady in Plymouth with a husband working on shore patrol. You're a family unit, and you come home one day and you find that that family has been smashed to pieces by a war which you don't understand anyway.

Q. There are certain things which you need for your program but which you realize involve people in extremely personal and painful memories. How did you cope with that? How did you decide where and how to draw the line?

A. I'll give you an example of a situation where that occurred and which we used in the film. There was a husband and wife in Plymouth who had lost their children in two separate bombing raids. They came to see me, and then they broke down when they told me the story of the children's deaths which they obviously had hardly talked about since the time. Since the war they had tried to pack it up and forget about it. But the fact was that they'd answered the article and offered to help. The fact of their pain was one of the areas I went over with them and I also heard that what happened to them was exactly the kind of experience that does bring war home to people.

I said to them, "I know and I can see that it is very difficult for you to talk about this. Are you prepared to do it all over again? We would like to do it and think it is important, but do you think it will be too painful for you? I think myself it's necessary for people to understand what war's about but I don't want you to do it if you feel it is something that is going to bring back the old memories." But they wanted to do it. They *wanted* people to understand. The husband felt it very strongly because he said "Here was Hitler doing all these awful things to us and all we were doing was dropping bits of paper." That was during the propaganda time of dropping leaflets. It was a war he didn't want to fight but somebody had killed his children and he wanted to go back and kill their children. He didn't actually want to kill their children but he wanted to *do* something. And one began to understand all the kinds of levels war is fought on.

Q. England won the war. Germany lost it. That would seem to me to put a very different dimension on memory, or on certain memories. What were the problems of finding people in Germany for your programs? I remember one of your programs on general life in Germany and one specifically on the death camps called *Genocide*. Was it harder to make people talk there, especially when you were looking not just into memory and experiences but also possible participation in guilt and atrocities?

A. You're right. It was more difficult because you had to get over the whole initial resistance of being English, of coming from British television and wanting to talk about the war. My German friends of the generation who lived through the war just heartily wished I wasn't doing this at all. Then I explained to them why and how we were trying to do it and they became more helpful.

Initially it was quite difficult to get people to open up. However, once they'd agreed to see you and talk, it was all much fresher than the English people's reminiscences and memories because it hadn't been told before. They'd never been asked or questioned about the war by the younger generation. They'd talked about it very little with their contemporaries because it was a nasty, closed chapter in Germany. People hadn't wanted to talk about it ever since the war was over. They may have muttered among themselves. There was a feeling, certainly with the old soldiers, and those who had been in the Russian campaign, that they had never talked about it—that whereas it was acceptable for Dad in England to talk to the kids about when he was in Africa, India, or wherever it *wasn't* acceptable in Germany.

Q. Were there certain areas of the war which were more acceptable to talk about?

A. Yes. The desert campaign was terribly acceptable, because that had been a good clean decent war and they all respected each other. So the desert campaign people talked very easily.

Q. And the Russian campaign?

A. Yes. They talked quite easily about the conditions in Russia, because that too was acceptable to talk about. But they became very reticent when you began to ask them what they had actually done as soldiers.

Q. Did you ever feel it was necessary to double-check your information?

A. The ordinary soldier's description of the cold and the frostbite and the food and the general physical conditions—all that we didn't have to worry about. It fitted in with what we knew. What one did have to double-check on, or often didn't use, were people who simply refused to admit or recognize there had been any kind of brutality on the part of the German forces in various places. This was particularly true once you got into the area of the Waffen SS. There were various people I talked to whom you couldn't use because you just didn't know what was true and what was false. Some of what they were saying might have been true but you knew an awful lot of it wasn't, or that

69

they weren't being honest about another whole area of their activities. Therefore, in the end, you thought it was better not to use them at all rather than have somebody who was making it all appear rather benign.

Q. I am very interested in the research you did on *Genocide*, the film about the German death camps. How did you get to people who were actually concerned with the running and operation of these camps? I can see many complex problems that must have arisen in trying to meet and get the truth from people who at best were under a cloud and at worst were probably war criminals.

A. The Auschwitz area was covered by two kinds of official people. One was Herman Langbein, an ex-prisoner of Auschwitz who organized the Committee of Ex-Prisoners of Auschwitz. He helped me a great deal on the side of the prisoners, tracing them and so on. There was also a German who had been made an Honorary Member of the Ex-Prisoner's Committee for all the help he had given the prisoners, although he had actually been an SS guard there. Herman Langbein had also written a two-volume book about the Frankfurt Auschwitz trials, which gave me information, and I managed to meet four of the people who had been involved in these trials, and had done their terms. Some of the accused were still in prison and the authorities approached them and asked them if they would be prepared to talk to me. They refused. Not surprising, really. But I did speak to two people who'd been in prison for several years and had been released.

Q. Did you find in regard to the death camps there were people who were willing to talk to you but would not be interviewed on camera?

A. Yes. Basically they didn't really want to talk to me but if a girl turns up on the doorstep and looks kind of harmless, they'll let you in. A lot of them were very polite and did talk. The people who'd been tried in the big Auschwitz trial in Frankfurt had a feeling that they'd done their time. They believed they'd paid the price, which they regarded as high, and they wanted to forget and get on. They'd had quite enough trouble and pain, so they didn't want to talk about it anymore.

Q. There were the publicly known figures and also the shadow figures. How did you get to the latter?

A. Often through a series of contacts. One was in a position of being given confidential information which one was not supposed to broadcast or pass on. You were only allowed to go and see these people on the understanding you gave nothing away.

Q. When you met these people, was there a willingness to assume responsibility for things like the death camps or was there still a desire to cover up responsibility, or to say it wasn't so bad? I'm thinking here of a book published recently in England and America which says that the death camps are just a work of imagination and didn't really exist.

A. The main thing, with nearly all the people I spoke to who'd been directly involved in the death camps and the extermination process, was of wanting to explain and still justify what had happened. They still didn't seem to realize what they'd actually done. They were often still so tied up in the ideology and old Nazi rationale that they still didn't seem to realize what they'd actually done or how the rest of the world saw it. And I found that the hardest thing of all to cope with.

There was one particular man whom we met who kept saying he'd answer all the questions and would be happy to talk about it. He'd worked in the Dutch area. I was able to check back there with people as to what had actually happened and for all his protests of being honest, he wasn't honest at all. There was another man who tried to tell us it was nonsense that six million Jews had died. That was Major Otto Remer who actually appeared. He was with the Berlin garrison and was supposed, in the 20th of July plot, to take over the propaganda ministry.

We spent an evening with Remer surrounded by vases with swastikas and him showing us his old arm band. No, he wasn't SS. He was straight army. He tried to tell us there hadn't really been six million Jews killed. "It is ridiculous. There was only something like 20,000 or so people who got killed. It is all a dreadful piece of propaganda and it really wasn't as bad as all that." We used him, but we used him in the context of the 20th of July plot because what he was able to give us on that was factual information.

Q. Did you get into situations where you were talking to war criminals and a problem arose between your relationship to that person, who had opened up a certain trust to you, and responsibilities to the police, your conscience, or however you want to put it? How did you resolve that conflict, if it ever came up?

A. Over the period of researching, particularly on the *Genocide* program, the director Michael Darlow and myself built up between us a fairly broad network of contacts who were handing us on. Now once you'd got on to a position of trust (and this was particularly true of myself), once you'd got onto the "circuit," you were handed on from one to the next. And it was an almost impossible situation because I was dealing with people who, in the period of their lives that we were talking about, had not operated with the same code of behavior, morals, whatever you call it, that I by nature and upbringing operate on. Yet I was being expected to operate along with their codes because they were handing me on in a trust situation from one person to the next.

There was one situation where the authorities wanted to know where one particular man was and the director and I decided that we should operate according to our own moral standards, which was not to betray a trust, and therefore we didn't say where he was. We also did this on the assumption that if anyone really wanted to find out about him they could have done it fairly easily.

Q. Did people vary or change their stories on different occasions?

A. We had some difficulties like that with Karl Wolff. I suppose Karl Wolff was the biggest person we talked to of the people most directly involved. It took a very long time and he kept us at arm's length, meeting in hotels. Over a period of time, and perhaps because he was a lonely old man, he loosened up and began to talk. Immediately after the war he'd suffered relatively little considering the position he'd held because just before the end of the war he'd had the sense to realize things were going the wrong way. He'd worked with Dulles and kind of bought his safety by making life easier for the Allies in Italy. So he suffered relatively little.

Wolff had been very involved with the philosophy and the building of the SS and the Marienberg which was where the SS were sent for refresher courses in the ideology of the SS. He went into that in great detail in the interview we did with him. The reasons that he talked to me were the same reasons that had got him into trouble immediately after the Eichmann trial—that he still believed in the basic ideologies of the SS which he'd helped to develop. He had a very stong desire to explain and thereby justify these things. He'd given an interview at the time of the Eichmann trial explaining the SS and as a result of that had stood trial and had been sentenced to some time in jail. He was now out on reasons of ill health.

One of the difficulties I always had was that when I went to see people like Karl Wolff I never argued with them. I knew that Wolff was probably responsible for the death of Langbehn, one of the Resistance members. Wolff had supposedly been protecting Langbehn, and yet Langbehn had died. When he told me about Langbehn it was very different. He was the supporter. So when I talked with Wolff it was very difficult because I knew if I argued with him, if I said, "That's a load of bullshit and you were responsible for that man's death along with others," then I would lose him as an interviewee.

You were operating in such a grey area that it became very difficult to hold onto what was right and what was wrong. And you knew it wouldn't make the situation any better if you treated that man as badly as he treated other people. You knew whatever you thought of what he'd done, you couldn't abandon your own set of standards that you'd built up over the years. Also, what he could tell us about the SS was very important to our understanding of its development for the completion of the series.

For example, he told me the story of the shooting at Minsk. He told it to me one evening during one of our research chats when I was standing in his kitchen cooking scrambled eggs. There was an instance of a shooting at Minsk where, according to Wolff, he and another SS chap were ordered to be present by Himmler, but they didn't realize exactly what they were going to be present at. It turned out, so he said, to be a shooting of Russian soldiers. Wolff described the incident in quite some detail because he said Himmler had never seen anything like this. Himmler went right up to the edge of the pit where people were being lined up, shot, and falling in, to be followed by the next batch. Himmler evidently got quite carried away by the whole thing whereas Wolff and his friend were standing some paces back, overcome by horror at being forced to see this shooting.

Wolff obviously had a very vivid memory of that and told us afterwards how Himmler had got up on his car afterwards and addressed the SS people who were there, saying how sorry he was they had to do these things but it was part of the fight, and they were the ones chosen to protect the ideology. The SS were the defenders of the faith.

So there was the situation. I was in the kitchen, standing by a stove, stirring a frying pan of scrambled eggs, and this grey-haired old gentleman—frightfully benign and charming—suddenly comes out with this story, prompted by the director, Mike, who was there as well. Now he was prompted into that in what one might call an unfair moment, because there was a certain amount of intimacy about pottering around in somebody's kitchen. Afterwards when we came to do the interview we were in a very difficult situation because we wanted to get the same story on film—a new piece of information that hadn't been made public before. He hadn't ever talked in public in such detail on that incident.

On the day of the filming we spent the whole morning letting him talk about things he wanted to talk about, such as explaining the SS ideology. After lunch he was more relaxed and Mike said, "Now pitch it to him," so I asked him the question about Minsk and the shooting. He did a double-take, and then the film magazine ran out and we thought "Christ, he's never going to talk now." And then I thought, maybe it's just as well that he does have time to think about it then I shan't feel so responsible. Though why I should have felt responsible about him I can't think. But we reloaded the camera and he told the story. It's in the series.

In all the times I had met him before that incident, I was not playing totally honest. For example, there he was telling me about how he had tried to protect Langbehn. Now in a normal situation I would have said, "Oh, come off it, that story is absolutely rubbish. How stupid do you think I am?" but because I eventually wanted to get that man up in front of the camera there was no point in contradicting him at the research stage. In almost every other program I've been involved in one could be pretty honest and straightforward about what we were aiming at. But in that situation it was difficult. I hope I didn't appear to totally agree with what they were saying but I never actually openly disagreed with them. I knew if I did that then this very very tentative agreement that one got from them to appear and be part of the program would be shattered.

When I talk of the problems of being straightforward and honest with the interviewees I suppose I really mean that it was a problem with the people who I felt weren't being totally straight and honest with me. With Traudl Junge I did have a different kind of basis, because she seemed to have come to terms with her own feelings about that period of her life and was able to be much more truthful about the things she would talk about. She made a particular point of only talking about areas where she had direct personal knowledge and experience. She would not go into areas where she did not know the details. This I respected. As you can see and hear in the series her testimony was invaluable and very interesting.

Q. When you interviewed people, particularly in Germany, did you make any agreement with them? Could they see transcripts? Did they have any control of the material or once they appeared was the material totally yours, to do with it exactly what you wanted?

A. In most cases it was done on the same kind of basis that we do all the interviews, which was that it was our copyright to do with it what we liked. There was also a verbal agreement that we wouldn't use the material out of context. We would only use it in the way it was intended and that we had discussed. But with Karl Wolff we agreed that he should have a transcript of his interview and if there were any facts which he found weren't right or which he wanted to change or delete, we would abide by that. We did that and I have never heard from him since. The director and I both thought that when he got the transcripts he would delete the incident at Minsk and other things. But we never heard from him. It's a total mystery. I don't know where he's gone.

Q. You were working with the programs a couple of years. How did you feel when you finished?

A. I felt I was only just getting into it and then it was all over. I felt I would like to have known at the beginning what I knew at the end. As far as I was personally concerned, it was, to use that dreadful expression, a learning experience. I learned about the war and I learned quite a lot about myself. Certainly for the first time in a fairly uncomplicated life I was forced to look at my own motives and to look at bigger moral questions with regard to the world.

## Raye Farr, Film Researcher

The more accurate the research, the sooner the compilation film will be rescued from half a century of bad habits.

PENELOPE HOUSTON, *Sight and Sound*

*When production started on "The World at War" the key film researcher was John Rowe, who handled the first four programs in the series. In September 1971 he was joined by Raye Farr. Later, when the going got even rougher, Michael Fox came over from editing to lend a hand.*

*The pressure on the film researchers was enormous. First, there was the problem of the sheer scale of the conflict—taking place over six years throughout the world. Second, it was a conflict that had been given absolutely immense filmic coverage. And last but not least there was the pressure of having to work to the demands of ten producers, five editors, and other program contributors.*

*The team spent eleven months abroad. John Rowe went to Holland, France, Japan and Australia, while Raye Farr concentrated on the archives in Germany. The work in the U.S. was split between the two of them. Talking about the American work Raye Farr says: "The National Archives in Washington suggested setting up a memorial Steenbeck in our honor. They claim that never in living memory has so much been viewed by so few."*

*How does one approach film research? Series producer Jeremy Isaacs says there are two possible ways. The first is to set an objective researcher to work for years to cover all evidence, and then plan the programs on the basis of the findings. The second is to work to timetables, budgets, and following clear guidelines. The first is an appealing way—but the scope of the series determined the use of the latter method, with beautiful results.*

*Looking at the series one realizes again and again how protected was one's usual view of war, or at least of the Second World War. In German newsreels no defeats or wounded soldiers were shown. When I grew up in England our own newsreels were cushioned and bloodless. No one dies in* Desert Victory, *and though Jennings's* Fires Were Started *is a fine film, it remains a soft reconstruction. What film research did on "The World at War" was reveal and show footage light years away from the usual compilation material.*

*Raye Farr seems an unlikely researcher for a war series. Too gentle and compassionate. Too feeling and too humane. I felt this especially when we talked about the screening of the footage of the dying soldiers and the families being split up. Even in recollecting these incidents she was moved to tears and was almost unable to go on talking. Yet it was obvious to me afterwards that it was this very quality of compassion, linked to a fine intelligence, which had made her such a good researcher.*

*Farr is American and grew up in Chicago. She majored in German at Oberlin College and traveled extensively in Germany as a high school exchange student, and then again while at college. The experience of these trips helped immensely in understanding the German background while researching Phillip Whitehead's* Inside the Third Reich—Germany 1940–44. *This was paralleled by research on the English social scene for Whitehead's other program* Home Fires.

*Besides her general work Farr also researched and produced two 90-minute spin-offs from the series. The first of these,* Hitler's Germany, *dealt with Germany in the thirties and was scripted by Jerome Kuehl. Writing about it in the* Daily Express *reviewer James Thomas called it "absolutely riveting." After the end of the "War" Farr moved back to America where she is still working for Thames on their current series about silent Hollywood.*

Q. How did you get into broadcasting?

A. I landed in television through translating some German wartime newsreels for Granada Television. It was for a documentary series "All Our Yesterdays" which Brian Inglis presented every week. Working on that series I looked at film of the war for three and a half years. Week by week, looking at the war in England, in Germany, in Russia. So I became very familiar with the film material of that period. And when the program reached the end of World War II I decided to leave and travel to India.

Q. How did you get involved with "The World at War"?

A. I had been away from television production for a year. Meanwhile Thames was considering doing "The World at War." They wrote to me and asked if I would be interested in joining them because they heard that I had looked at a lot of film of this period. In fact I was very reluctant. In my first discussion with Jeremy Isaacs I really asked him what they were going to do because I did not want ever again to see another tank in the desert. When he explained what it was he wanted to do with the subject I found it very much more interesting than I had expected.

Q. Why, after all, did you think this might be something new, interesting or different?

A. I think because there was a limited choice of subjects to be dealt with. It was not an attempt to do the entire war battle by battle. Jeremy was very interested in showing the Russian experience of the war, which had been one of the most striking features for me when I'd looked at film in the other series. As an American growing up during the Cold War I didn't know we fought alongside Russia in World War II. It was really that much of a revelation to me. So working with this Russian material was something I wanted to do more with. I was also

77

interested in the German side and German propaganda. And the language of Germany during that time was so compelling to me. Finally Jeremy agreed that I could do more of that kind of work rather than just viewing tanks in the desert.

Q. How was your job defined or laid out?

A. Well, it was simply stated as film research. To find films. Everything started at once. The cutting rooms opened up. The film research started. There were producers and directors working. But we all started pretty much at the same time. So there was a balance between going out and finding film which would then become a part of the concept of the program, and researching ideas and facts which we would later try to match on film.

Q. What were the specific areas or countries you were concerned with?

A. I concentrated primarily on Germany. This was because I had a good background in German and could often find films that were not easily accessible to somebody who was only English-speaking. I could pick up a lot of what was in the films.

Q. I want to get back to the guidelines and how you worked. Did the writer or writer-director define the areas he or she wanted you to research? Or did you research in a general way and then what you found helped the director to define the film line?

A. I would say it was different with each person we worked with. The balance between the producer, the director, the writer, the film editor and researcher shifted very much. It depended on the combination of personality and approach. For the most part we had fairly general guidelines, in the same way that the program subjects were briefly outlined at the beginning of the series by Jeremy Isaacs. On some of the other programs such as Phillip Whitehead's *Home Fires* and *Inside the Reich*—which dealt with the social background of England and Germany during the war—there was a ten- or twelve-point outline of subjects he wanted to touch on. I then went to Germany armed with Shirer's book *The Rise and Fall of the Third Reich* and my own curiosity, and dug up as much as I could through looking, watching, listening. Later I discussed with Phillip what emphasis he wanted and took it further. And that's something that happened throughout "The World at War."

What Jeremy Isaacs instilled in us was an attitude and approach rather than details. There was a clear purpose, in that we were attempting to get across *the experience* of the war. We weren't going to tell the whole story of the war. But we wanted people to feel what it was like. That way you could go into things deeply enough that people could identify sufficiently. So in the areas where there was a brief out-line there was a very free rein to look, bring back material, find things that caught your eye. Things that were sometimes very, very small. People walking together. Something like Albert Speer walking around with other Gauleiters at Hitler's headquarters allowed you to watch the human interaction between people that you've come to think of as mechanical. And that general kind of material was welcomed by some producers. There were others who had a very precise idea of what they wanted to say, who had a script, who had a narrative, and they wanted film to match it. And were sometimes impatient if the film did not match it. So it varied.

Q. I can see two key problems. First, where does one go to find the material—particularly new and fresh material? Secondly, I can see later problems such as authenticity of material. Can you tell me a bit about the first?

A. I must say we concentrated on sources that would not necessarily be a surprise but which held a lot of surprises. The Imperial War Museum in London has a vast collection of interesting material, but not all the cataloguing is up-to-date. Much of the material was cata-logued as it came in during the war, and was described in the simplest terms by someone who could not possibly realize the deeper signifi-cance of the material. So there were a lot of names missing. A lot of things weren't identified. And it meant looking and looking until you were so familiar with the people and the places that even locations in the woods became familiar to you. After a while you could figure out a time and a place just by looking at the stuff. But the subject indexes were very limited, and often not very helpful.

The War Museum had a lot of material on all countries, and all sub-jects. Some of it was captured enemy material. A lot, of course, came from the armed forces. It was the same situation with the National Archives in Washington. And we got film from the newsreels. But in many ways we tried to stay away from the newsreels.

The newsreels were the most familiar, the most often used, and all of the film that was shown had been censored and severely cut. We tried to bypass those familiar sources and to go to the actual army rushes, the censored newsreel material that had been kept separately. We went to those first to see what had been kept aside.

What we found was very interesting. There was film, for example, on the bombing of Coventry and other British cities which would cer-tainly have been a liability to morale in wartime if people had seen it. We viewed a lot of technical films, particularly on the German side where they were very thorough in film making. Technical films were a great source of interesting details of the war and much more realistic and interesting than what was shown publicly.

Q. Can you give me an example of that?

A. The first thing that comes to mind is in medical films, where there was much more evidence of injury, death, pain, and suffering. People left lying by the roadside. German soldiers dying. Did you ever see a German soldier dying in *Victory in the West*? We watched the Germans advancing along a country road in France while others of their comrades lay by the road reaching an arm up, moaning. You saw the pain of being shifted on a stretcher and moved around. But that was the only place you would see them, in the instructional films. It was something that the medics had to know about.

A more amusing example was an interminable film on orientation in Soviet Russia. Endless reels of film about snow and how to put newspaper in your boots. But one reel illustrated how to find your way when you are lost in the endless wasteland of snow in Russia where there is no tree, no building, absolutely white. And it showed discreetly from the knee down how a soldier could urinate in the snow in circles and and then follow those back to the base.

There were a lot of films on bombing which were really for air raid precaution films, but showed air raids in action, and would actually show damage. Show air raids and emergencies. Not staged nor heroic. But real situations.

We also found some very interesting things by asking people for personal films. Private films. Sometimes 8mm films. One that was very remarkable was the color film of Hamburg during the Allied bombing and fire storms in 1943. This film was in fact taken by the Hamburg fire chief. It was illegal for him to do it. Everything was supposed to go through the propaganda ministry. Yet there it is. One of the most vivid human documents of the war. And in color. Startling scenes of the refugees, of the aftermath, of the charred bodies—scenes which would unquestionably have been destroyed by the German authorities.

Q. When you searched the archives you were looking from an historic perspective of 1970 and the material would obviously be relevant to that 25-year hindsight on the war. And yet it might only be indexed, following up what you said before, according to what was relevant in 1945. How did you get over that problem?

A. I would say that it was only through the sheer volume of viewing that we did, that we got to know the people and got to know the personalities. And we looked over the material again and again. And it is certainly correct that there are, I would say, possibly, only one or two references to Martin Bormann on the subject cards of the personality index. And yet he appears so frequently in the films. Next to Hitler. Always nearby. Usually smiling. Glad-handing people. We now know what he looks like. We picked him out. We did not go to a catalog and find Martin Bormann that way.

The same with Albert Speer. There had been references added to his index cards since his books became known. But there were a lot of surprises where he appeared touring, and down in submarines, and rather happily organizing industry during the war. And he was clearly not someone who was known to a clerk in the Ministry of War Information in London who catalogued the films as they arrived during the war.

Q. Did you go to East Germany during your research?

A. We were very anxious to go. Sue McConachy made some initial inquiries and was in fact welcomed there. They have, of course, a treasure of material on this because of what was captured at the end of the war. But it was just at that point that the Russian trade commission was suddenly sent back by the London authorities. So Russia cut off all cultural relations with England at that point. Suddenly we discovered that not only were we not getting cooperation from Russia in terms of looking at their archives, but East Germany froze up for us as well. The visas were never approved. I was very disappointed since we did want to do a lot of work on Russia. As it was, it was done entirely from material available in the West.

Q. Were there any particular difficulties of researching in Germany? Human difficulties of people being involved in the war, with whom you're working, or anything else like that?

A. In terms of film there were no difficulties. However, in the everyday course of researching I was always met with a rather old question: "Why, why do you want to do this now? Why don't you think about the present?" But there was no attempt to hide material. They were cooperative. They were efficient. Anything that you recognized and you wanted to put your hands on they made available. It may have been rather different in terms of researching interviews. But for film research the Bundesarchiv, the government archive, was very helpful.

In the end they opened up to us with one of the most exciting discoveries of film on the whole project. It was film that had never been edited. Rushes of films, hundreds of thousands of feet which had been captured by the Americans at the end of the war. It had all been taken to the Library of Congress and apparently never viewed or catalogued, and then returned during the Kennedy administration. It still had Library of Congress numbers on it, and nobody at the Bundesarchiv had ever looked at it.

What happened was that after I had stayed there for several months, and they couldn't think of anything else that I should look at, someone mentioned that they had a room full of material which they thought had to do with the Second World War. We opened it up, and the first three cans chosen at random had the early stages of the invasion of France with German soldiers mingling with the refugees. Everyone confused. German officers with maps trying to figure out which way they were going. Unfortunately this material could not be made available to us until it had been copied, catalogued and rigorously and Germanically classified. It took a year and a half with heavy pressure on the German embassy in England from Jeremy Isaacs to make more money available so that they could process the material so that we could finally copy it. And by then we'd already finished many of the programs for which the material had relevance.

However, there were two striking scenes which we managed to use in the final program of the series. Both took place in Russia. One was of Russian prisoners in the early stages of the invasion of Russia. Herded together, below a bridge in the first days of the German invasion. Women are throwing them raw potatoes. And they are scrambling over each other. Just clawing each other. Fighting on the ground. And grabbing those raw potatoes and stuffing them in their mouths. And there are thousands of them. No fence. And in the background just some German guards with machine guns marching back and forth.

Another scene is in a Russian village where the Germans have just come in. And the men, bearded, possibly Jewish, but not necessarily, are being separated from the women and children. The men are being pushed to one side. The women in scarves and the crying children are being told to go to the other. A lot of it is in close up. Hands reach out, trying to have a last word. To stay with somebody. The officer is barking orders. And the camera stays on them as the women and children are told with a very abrupt gesture to move off towards the bridge. And you keep seeing them turning around toward the men who are left standing there. And you can imagine where they are going.

These films were full of scenes like that. A Russian hanging from a tree with a sign on him which we could not read. Just left in a beautiful idyllic landscape. An example? A collaborator? Impossible to know. But there were hundreds of cans of this film which seemed to touch the real experience of the war without anything intervening between then and now.

Q. You talked earlier of having had enough, three years of films of war in the desert. I worked for about five months with the Eichmann trial for television and I found that it was very difficult to take because one gets so personally involved and affected. What was happening to you and your co-researchers when you were going, day after day, through material like this? Just listening to it is so painful to hear about. Did you take time off? Did you try and get some kind of distance?

A. I didn't take time off. I don't think many of us took time off. I think there was relatively little distance from it. We were literally working twelve, sixteen hours a day, seven days a week, for over a year and a half. And I felt permeated by it. I dreamed at night about Himmler. Himmler oddly enough doesn't appear in very many films, but he appeared in a great many of my dreams. Goering appeared and had discussions with Himmler. They were real. They were not necessarily menacing. They were simply the people that I was living with. And the whole issue of death and loss and separation was magnified and permeated my life. And I still don't know what to do with it.

I remember the feeling of identification with a young, dying soldier, and feeling all the tenderness and loss of any loved person. It was a constant experience. In some way it drew all of us together in what we were trying to tell about the war. It was a greater incentive to make it true and not to allow the audience to have too much distance from what was happening. I think that affected the choice of shots. The choice of music. The choice of narrative. We tried to leave silence in places so that an audience could *feel*.

I had a feeling that there was no way in which the audience could have what I consider the privilege of sharing the discoveries I had by watching it happen day after day after day. I felt like I tramped through Italy with the British and American Armies. And saw little Italian kids and lovely women bringing wine, and the slow drudgery just occasionally relieved by human moments and warmth. I felt like I went through that campaign, and I wished somehow that there was a way you could put that into a one-hour documentary. But how could you do that? There was some attempt to do that with Stalingrad. That was the only program of the series that was so small a subject that we could stay in one place and one experience. We tried to do it through the diaries of individual people. What they felt. What was happening inside them.

Q. I'm very interested in your problems with the validity of the material. I think a number of issues arise on this subject and are important. For example, did you find that you were being fed what was feature material masquerading as documentary? Did this happen often or not at all?

A. It certainly happened. We became more suspicious of it I suppose concerning Russian material, because we knew historically that they had made such an elaborate effort, even during the war, to reconstruct events for their own propaganda. Perhaps that's putting too much emphasis on it. More gently we might say they reconstructed something that they missed at the time and they very much wished to have captured. So we looked very warily at some of the material. We didn't always get it right. We weren't fed material very often by anyone, so in that sense it was a question of looking at documentaries that had previously been made and trying to sort out what film footage within that documentary was accurate or fake, what was real and what was staged. And we felt very much the full responsibility of what we were putting together knowing other people would come to "The World at War" as an historical source.

Q. How did you recognize staged material?

A. Well, Jerry Kuehl looked very hard for that kind of thing. However, we all tried to familiarize ourselves initially with airplanes, with tanks, with uniforms, to pick out time. Did everything fit into the right time? Sometimes it was the camera angles that were improbable. Like the army charging toward the camera. If they were really on the front line you would not expect many cameramen to stand with their back to enemy fire to film the coming charge. We tried to put ourselves on the battlefield, imagining whether such a shot could have been taken under those conditions.

Q. When you looked at other documentary films and series, did you find that material had been misused? That material from one battle had been used to illustrate another?

A. Yes. Very often, and I think with the acceptance and connivance of the public and film makers because this had long been regarded as perfectly acceptable. If you wished to make a dramatic point, then if the planes were flying and the bombs were dropping or the soldiers were running, that was reasonable. I don't want to be grandiose about it but I think we helped to change that view by ourselves insisting, in ways that were very tedious to our film editors and directors, insisting that we would not do that where we know differently. And where we did do it we identified it so that other people knew what we were doing. And I think there has been a shift in attitude. Since then, I think more critical attention has been paid how material is used. It's a very difficult problem. The question is: does it undermine your own credibility? Why, in fact, should people believe anything you're telling them if the film that you're showing is not accurate?

Q. You mean once you go into any area of non-authenticity?

A. That's right. Your credibility is in doubt when you show something that is one thing and call it something else. I think that's an important issue. I think the public *should* doubt that kind of thing, because that's one area where distortion begins to take place in terms of what commentary goes over what pictures. How do you use something which indeed happened, because the camera has recorded it, but the audience sees your version, with your words, with your music, with your bias? This is a central problem for documentary. And we had a bias too. But one of our biases was to say to people, "Look at the bias. Look at ours. Look at the Russians'. Look at the Germans'. Look at it and then decide for yourself."

Q. When you were looking at material, or actually choosing it for the final film, were you looking at it in terms of "this *visually* is the actual record," or "this *emotionally* is the accurate record"? It may be that they are both one and the same. But I'm not sure.

A. I'll try to think of specific incidents. If you took a parade, a German parade with an audience, there are a lot of different emotions at work. They are different for the people marching. Different for the people who are watching. I can think of one example in particular, when we showed the victorious German soldiers returning from the invasion of France. And we showed people cheering. Now it's visually accurate, as I said before, on one level because the camera has recorded it, has been there. But we chose to raise the question: "Who were the people in that audience who were raising their hands because they were against Hitler and might be noticed as protesters against the regime if they did not raise their hands?" And when you look at that cheering, smiling crowd—how many truths are contained in that? Mostly what is conveyed is the truth that you feel with martial music. Victorious, cheering, which is, of course, how it was presented in the German films of the time.

There was certainly a choice of material and sometimes you had to choose between shots. There might be a very good shot which showed clearly and in color the airplanes on aircraft carriers that were in the Pacific taking off and attacking the Japanese fleet. The flags are waving. The sky is blue. And there are brilliant colors in the uniforms of some of the people. And that had a magnetism which was very, very seductive, that you wanted to show. But on the other hand, with so much material you had to lose something for everything you put in. And you might have another shot which was in black and white of a kamikaze plane which crashed onto the deck of one of those aircraft carriers. And the camera was moving and jolted and everything is out of focus and gives you the feeling of what it was like to be under that kind of an attack. Given these choices we would have tended to choose the latter.

Q. What would you say, taking into account all the stuff you've looked at, are the areas of life or history which were recorded but for one reason or another have *not* appeared in documentaries?

A. One area that is well represented and documented on film that does not get into documentaries or features is *time*: boredom, the length of the experience, the moment before, the moment after, the long, long, long periods of time between action. And action is what is usually in the feature, and action is what a documentary usually comes down to together with the personal testimony. You lose the sense of the experience as it fits into the rest of the time that it is experienced by someone in a war.

Q. How did the team work together? Although you were doing basic film research, were you involved in other activities in the film making?

A. Yes, I think it was an exceptionally close unit. Very much directed by Jeremy Isaacs's vision and clear perception of what he wanted to aim for. And I think that's very important in organizing something on that scale where we had ten director-producers, five film editors, assorted writers, yet were aiming for some kind of common purpose. And we were all allowed to share our discoveries and our doubts about things. We worked through material together. We shared viewings of films when they were, say, in a rough-cut stage. And the criticisms were allowed, taken and worked into the production, sometimes at considerable cost. That's another thing that was an important factor in "The World at War" that Jeremy as the person ultimately responsible was prepared to authorize and make the expenditure for correcting inaccuracies.

When we saw that something had gone astray or was going in the wrong direction, even if music had already been composed to an edited scene for which the commentary had already been written, we knew that program could still be revised. In a lot of productions I don't think that would have happened.

We talked a lot together. I often worked in the cutting room because of the German language problem. Translating and selecting the best words from interviews and speeches. And it's another thing I think that was especially good in "The World at War"—laying the English translation voices in such a way that the timing left enough of the original words which could be recognized by viewers. That was a very long and difficult job.

Q. Towards the end of "The World at War" you yourself made a couple of programs on life in Hitler's Germany. You'd been going over a great deal of visual material about that period. What were things you found, what were the points where you agreed or disagreed with the historian? What were the kind of new revelations you had for yourself?

A. There is a line of demarcation in that area between the prewar and the wartime experience. I don't think I discovered anything new.

I don't think there were actual revelations that could be pinpointed, except that you begin to integrate a feeling and in this case it was more from the interviews, more from the testimony of people interviewed twenty-five years later.

What was revealing was ordinary people, intelligent people, including Communists and Socialists, explaining how they were drawn into what was happening. Not necessarily in support of it. For instance, I remember a Socialist who joined the SS in 1933, when trade unions and political parties had been outlawed, because he and another friend said, "Well if they're going to get rid of all of those means for expressing political opinions, somehow or other we still have to influence what is going to go on in Germany. The SS is a new party organization. We'll join it and influence it from within." That's before anyone knew what the SS was. We tend to look back and say, "How could anyone join the SS except an evil, murderous, thug?" This man was a law student, someone who wanted to affect what was going to happen because there were dangers evident.

I heard a lot of contradictory evidence about opposition to Hitler. That in some cases people were very outspoken and defiant, and refused to go along with it. Particularly in Berlin. And that you got away with it. We tend to think that anybody like that got locked up. There was a housewife who was a teacher who said, "I'm not going to school on Hitler's birthday and helping my students to celebrate it. And if you don't like it, fire me." She did that several times in a row and was simply sent to a less desirable school.

You discover in small ways what it was like to simply lead an ordinary life in Germany. You see history becoming tangible on a human level and begin to understand the appeal of Hitler, particularly in the early years when there was such agony, political chaos, uncertainty, and economic despair. Hitler came into that kind of thing and provided a program. And I don't think that the things that he promised in the first two, three, four years in Germany sound so different from what Jimmy Carter or other politicians promised in their presidential campaigns. There was an appeal to *our* people. A manipulation of words to create the idea that he was one of them. That we should all have *one goal*. And that people deserve something basic, simple, decent and a claim on their own humanity. Hitler had a reasonable appeal at the beginning and I wanted to show that, even though we all know the tragedies and horrors that came after.

Q. How did people react to those programs?

A. I was very struck by the variety of responses from the viewers, some of which confirmed that we'd done what we'd tried to do, which

87

was to make sense of the period. But there was also more than one letter which said "Thank you for inadvertently helping the cause of national socialism. I'm sure you didn't intend to show what reasonable goals the Germans held but I hope this will help to influence the way things go in Britain now." There were Jewish viewers who felt outraged that the programs ended with a statement from Major Remer who had been in charge of the Berlin police at the time of the July, '44 uprising.

Remer states that there was never any intention to kill the Jews, that when he and others were shown the evidence of the concentration camps at the end of the war it was all a display put on to humiliate Germany and that the few deaths that occurred were natural, and that really people nowadays tend to forget the good things that Hitler brought to Germany. I wanted to use that to show the strength of *distortion*, believing myself that the facts are not disputable. But there were viewers who felt that by putting that there we were endorsing Remer's statement. Their assumption is: if a person's there on the screen, those people who make television programs must think what the person is saying is true.

Funnily enough, I thought we made a great effort to respect the critical ability of the audience to look and compare. I thought that Remer's statement was so outrageous that it seemed permissible to show it. We wondered a lot about it. It was the last thing in the film. It was also shown with pictures of the camp, briefly. But here were people saying "How can you deny that this happened?" So it certainly awakened in me an awareness of how gullible an audience is to what is shown. Or how they don't know what to judge as real and unreal because of so much that's shown on television.

*Television Investigation*

# 2
## Sixty Minutes
### Albert Wasserman

*My expectations were confounded. I'd expected a huge room, a polished mahogany desk, and a wall covered with journalistic tributes and photos of handshakes with the President. But Al Wasserman's room was a poky hole at the end of a crowded CBS corridor. A small desk. Books piled high. And no awards or presidential photos, only mementoes of wife and kids.*

*I'd first seen Wasserman's films as a student and studied them continuously. The one that particularly moved me was* Out of Darkness, *an hour and a half study of mental illness which he did in 1956. Then there was* Biography of a Cancer *in which Wasserman provided a detailed explanation of cancer treatment. These films were superbly crafted, touched you emotionally and were, so I thought, excellent models for a would-be film maker.*

*Wasserman is one of the unsung greats of American television documentary. As writer-producer-director he has won almost every award possible and his career covers the best years of "CBS Reports," the CBS "Twentieth Century" series, and NBC's "White Paper" series, which he helped originate. At present he works as producer on CBS's "Sixty Minutes," which is one of the best American television news magazines to date.*

*His film biography is immense. Among his most important works besides* Darkness *and* Cancer *are* Brainwashing, *an exploration of Communist persuasion techniques used on captured prisoners;* The Addicted, *about the effects and problems of drug addiction;* Sit In; Angola—Journey to a War; *and* Flight Deck, *which tells the story of the life and death precision of a flight deck crew.*

The U-2 Affair *was Wasserman's first "White Paper" and was followed soon after by the controversial* The Battle of Newburgh. *In* Newburgh *Wasserman analyzed the conflicts of a town whose city manager was totally opposed to welfare spending. A key part of the film was the moving interview with Tom Wiegand, a desperate and lost welfare recipient. Afterwards the city manager alleged that NBC had paid for the testimony, a charge that was totally disproved. Writing about* Newburgh *in the Boston* Evening Globe *critic Percy Shain called it "A searing study of Newburgh's handling of its welfare problem. It was compassionate in its treatment and damning in its point of view."*

*Wasserman is a relaxed, accessible man in his early fifties. His lithe figure hints at running, and his grin and handshake make you instantly welcome. He talks easily and listens intently. When we discussed film he rejected terms like "radical approach," "socially concerned," "pioneering." However, though Wasserman shrugs the terms off, a study of his films from* Out of Darkness *through to his work on "Sixty Minutes" shows a deep and pervading social concern. This concern can particularly be seen in* The Wilmington Ten *and also in* The Daisy Chain, *two of his many programs for the CBS magazine. Apart from work on "Sixty Minutes," Wasserman's recent films include* The Making of the President, 1972 *and* Prescription: Take With Caution, *a 1975 CBS special.*

Q. Can you tell me a little about your background?

A. I started as a free-lance writer of documentary films after World War II, and did that for a few years. I also did various educational films and some work for the United Nations in the early years after its formation. One of the films won an Academy Award, which was heady stuff for a 26-year-old.

Q. Was writing enough for you, or too confining?

A. Well, it became apparent very early in the game that it didn't make sense to compartmentalize functions. Many documentaries don't really lend themselves to a writer writing a script, then a director coming in and directing it, and somebody else editing it. So my interest ultimately was in doing my own films, and I spent a fair amount of time in the cutting room writing narrations, and I went out on location with crews whenever I could.

The television documentary began really around 1953–54 with a series that was done here at CBS called "The Search." Because there was a dearth of television writers at that time, I got a call from a friend of mine who was the script editor for this series, asking would I like to write a script. So that's how I got into television. And that's really what I have been doing since 1953.

Q. Did your early documentaries go in any particular direction? Was there a Wasserman style?

A. I think so. My background, unlike most of the people who have ended up doing what I am doing, was film, not journalism. I came in as a film maker rather than a journalist, and therefore had some concern for the medium itself as well as the content. I think the early concept, particularly in television, was that the function of the documentary was to present simple information and simple content. My whole approach, however, was that film is essentially an emotional medium, not an informational medium. I know it might sound platitudinous but I thoroughly believed one should not pack films too full of substance, but should try to make films that involved people, and that helped involve the audience in an experience. Then if they came away with one or two ideas, that is as much as can be expected from a film.

That's what I tried to do in my early films on this series of "The Search." And I would like to think it had some effect on the general orientation of the television medium, because fundamental and obvious as those notions were, they really had not been thought through in the infancy of the television documentary.

Q. You were involved for quite a while in the NBC "White Paper."

A. Yes, I was at CBS until 1960. Then I went to NBC along with Irving Gitlin, who was a very important figure in the evolution of the television documentary. Irv had been my boss at CBS and at NBC was put in charge of a unit called "Creative Projects." One of the things for which he was responsible was developing a documentary series to compete with "CBS Reports," and I helped produce those.

Q. One of your outstanding films of that time is *The Battle of Newburgh* on the problem of social welfare. Can you tell me how the film came about and whether it produced any changes in the town itself?

A. Well, I think the Newburgh film illustrates one effective approach to documentary, which is the *microcosm*.

The subject of welfare is an enormous subject, very complex and yet very important. We had been interested in doing something in that area, and the Newburgh experience gave us a very good focus for doing a specific story involving specific people, but yet with nationwide implications.

What made it desirable as a story for us was that the city manager of Newburgh, Mr. Mitchell, had been getting an enormous amount of attention nationally with his crusade *against* welfare "chiselers" and "loafers," and many people felt that this was a distortion and an oversimplification of a complex human and economic problem. So suddenly we had what seemed to be a good opportunity to go in and make a film by dissecting a community which had assumed a nationally symbolic importance. Its significance transcended the fact that it was a small town in New York State. So we went in and in effect anatomized that town and that situation, and I think that film reveals a lot of the meretriciousness and hypocrisy of the position the city manager was taking. Not too long after the film went on the air Mr. Mitchell left his position. In its time it was quite a controversial film. The powers that be in the city felt that their town had been maligned and they complained to the FCC. They filed suit against NBC, but the FCC upheld the network and ruled that our approach had not been unfair.

93

Q. Can you tell me what happened between "White Paper" and joining CBS's "Sixty Minutes"?

A. I left NBC around 1967 to set up my own film company. I had been doing documentaries for a good while and wanted to try something different. I was interested in a couple of feature film projects, and I wanted to be on my own. So I had my own company for about seven years and then decided that I had had that experience and wanted to go back to television. CBS was very receptive to my return. At first I worked on a freelance basis on one or two hour documentaries, and then I was asked to do a light-hearted film about "Sixty Minutes" for internal CBS use. And that's how I got to know the people at "Sixty Minutes." Not too long after that, in 1975, I was asked to join "Sixty Minutes" as part of the family. So I have been here for about three years.

Q. When you joined "Sixty Minutes," were you ever formally told where "Sixty Minutes" was going?

A. I don't think there was ever that kind of concrete discussion. It was known that I was a professional who had been around for a long time, and was presumably capable of doing good magazine work. The big change, of course, from hour documentaries to "Sixty Minutes" was the discipline of working in a short form. That does present certain difficulties, but in a way it is a lot easier, because one automatically looks for stories that are fairly small in focus, whereas the temptation in hour documentaries is to take such a large subject that one often ends up with a superficial survey, full of interviews and full of facts and without any impact. The fact that "Sixty Minutes" stories average around 14 minutes means that you have to exclude that kind of thinking. Sometimes you may get a subject that turns out to be fairly complex and the problems of distillation and compression can be very tricky, as are the difficulties of simplifying, but not distorting or oversimplifying.

Q. Can you give me the selection process of a story?

A. Story ideas originate anywhere. Producers on "Sixty Minutes" are expected to come up with their own ideas, but a good many suggestions also come from other sources. Correspondents often suggest ideas. We get a large amount of mail from the audience, and occasionally one of the audience ideas turns out to be a workable story. Again people working in the company may come across an idea and will feed it into "Sixty Minutes" and it will filter down to various producers. So the ideas can come from anywhere.

It is assumed that everyone is a professional and is responsible, so there are no rigid routines, no rigid rules of operation. As a generalization, most of the stories that producers do they dig up themselves, but certainly not all. Let's say I get an idea for a story I am interested in. I will talk to the correspondent with whom I work, Morley Safer, to see if he is interested in it. If he is not then we don't do it. Conversely if there is an idea Morley is interested in and he asks me if I would do it, and I am not interested, then I don't do it. Then he may well suggest the idea to another producer or whatever, but nobody stuffs anything down anybody else's throat. There has to be a concurrence, and that makes sense because there is no point in doing something that you don't like.

If Morley and I agree on a story that we are both interested in, then we will prepare a short presentation. It's a couple of paragraphs with a brief description of the essence of the story as we see it, and that will go in to our senior producer, Palmer Williams, who coordinates these things, and makes sure there is no duplication and that no other producer or CBS unit is working on the same story. Don Hewitt also takes a look at it at that time. And that is generally pro forma, assuming there is no duplication, assuming there is no serious objection to the story. Afterwards it goes on to the vice president in charge of documentaries, Bob Chandler, and he looks at it, again from a policy point of view to see if there is anything that might create any problems.

Q. Can you think specifically of any production ideas that have created problems that you have then dropped?

A. I can't think of any that were dropped because of policy problems. There have been some where the feeling has been, oh, this is too familiar a subject, it's not new enough, do you really want to do it? It's really that kind of thing rather than executive fiats saying, "Kill it." Sometimes we have been discouraged from doing a story on the grounds it's not a new subject, and then we have gone ahead and done it well, and the feeling has been, gee, it's great you did it.

Q. What is the production time on these?

A. It varies from story to story. As a generalization, we take about eight weeks for a story, that's including research, shooting, editing, and writing. But there can be an interview story that you can have on the air the same week. If we have a good personality and a timely subject we can get the whole story out of an interview. There may be others that have to be stretched out in time.

Q. How many producers are there?

A. About eighteen.

Q. Do you split anywhere between national and international stories? Do some producers tend to do the international stories, or in fact does everybody do everything?

A. Well, we have three producers who are based in London and they do most of our overseas stories, but there are exceptions. Occasionally some of us may be doing some filming overseas and will bring back a story, but generally we leave it to London.

Q. I am interested in your relationship with your correspondent, Morley Safer. Both of you are strong individualists. How do you find a balance in shaping up the story?

A. I fancy myself as being a competent writer as well as a film maker. Morley is a very competent writer with a style of his own. Certainly a good part of our early relationship was in getting to know each other, of my getting a sense of Morley's style and sensibility and vice versa. The balance of who does what varies from story to story. The correspondents do all the interviewing. There are exceptions, but in general the interviews, certainly the key interviews, are done by the correspondents. So they have to be familiar enough with the content to conduct an intelligent interview.

However, a correspondent may be working with five or six producers, so obviously he cannot familiarize himself with the details of the story or of what has been filmed on the same level as the producer can. So usually the producer will be the one who shapes the story in the editing. Different producers work in different ways, some may do a rough cut and then discuss it with the correspondent and shape it with him from that point on. Others, and I am among them, like to shape it and edit it as best I can and rough out the narration, so that when I go over it with the correspondent he can see it as an organic piece of work. In some instances there's a fair amount of re-writing. In others very negligible re-writing.

Q. Where does Don Hewitt, the executive producer, come into all this?

A. "Sixty Minutes" was Don Hewitt's brainchild and he was the one who sold the idea to CBS of doing a magazine series. In my own experience, Don's function is most crucial in the last stages of the story, at a time when it has been shaped to my satisfaction, or to another correspondent's satisfaction. At that stage we will screen it for Don and also for our senior producer, Palmer Williams. Don will be coming to the story fresh. He will not have been involved in the editing. He will not have steeped himself in the content of the film. What he does is function as a surrogate for the audience—a much more sophisticated viewer than the audience, but nonetheless as a surrogate—looking at the story anew, whether it's interesting, whether it's confusing, whether it's boring.

And Don is very much concerned on two levels. One concern is whether the story is solid in terms of content and in terms of information. The other is whether the story has interest. Does it drag? Is it paced so that it moves along so that people will want to watch? Does it start out in a way that engages an audience? Does it end in a way that is crisp?

I think that if anything is the hallmark of "Sixty Minutes" and has made for its mass appeal and success it's those two levels—doing solid stories, and doing them in a way that is succinct, well-paced, and interesting.

Q. I am interested in the stories that have been very analytical or investigative, and the problems that arise in doing them. For example, *The Daisy Chain* was an investigation into the oil industry. It was a program that named names, made accusations, and must have generated a lot of antagonism. Can you tell me something about that program, the difficulties and the reactions?

A. It was a story that was quite well documented, and obviously we would not name names and go into things in that kind of detail without a very solid documentation. We were in the fortunate position that a man who had been working for the Federal Energy Administration decided, as we say, to blow the whistle, and he had the documentation.

What made the story interesting to us, even before the beginning to work on it, was the fact that you had a specific story with larger implications. The story provided a microcosm of broader events. If we go back to the oil shortage and oil embargo of late 1973 and 1974 I think you'll recall there was a feeling on the part of the public that the increase in prices was not due simply to the raising of prices by Arab countries, but was also due to a certain amount of profiteering.

*The Daisy Chain* story laid out how a certain group of people, placed in companies dealing with oil, were indeed making unjustifiable and apparently illegal profits at the expense of the public. The events had happened a few years before but this was one of the first TV exposures.

The way in which the story evolved is also indicative of the serendipitous process of "Sixty Minutes," because I had not started out to do that particular story. I had been told by a colleague that there was a woman in Florida who might make an interesting profile for a "Sixty Minutes." Her name was Paula Hawkins. She was the chairwoman of the Florida Public Service Commission, and in spite of the fact that she was quite an active Republican, she had gotten a reputation as a kind of anti-establishment consumer advocate in Florida, bucking the utilities and so on. Altogether we sensed a good story possibility here.

I met with her, and while discussing some of the things with which she was concerned heard her make some references to overcharges to the customers of the Florida Power Company. She also mentioned that the *St. Petersburg Times* had done some articles about it. I went down to St. Petersburg, looked at the articles, spoke to the reporter, and said, this is a better story, because the paper had looked into it and had a fair amount of information. So that was the genesis of it. We started with one notion and it became displaced by a better one.

Q. In the program you show how oil company "A" sells to oil company "B" which sells to oil company "C," each time raising the price of the oil till it comes to the consumer at an astronomical price. You mentioned in the program that you tried to talk to the oil companies to get their side of the picture. What happened there?

A. We tried to talk to the key individuals involved at the various companies in the chain, and they, mostly through their attorneys, declined to be interviewed. This was possibly understandable because they were facing both civil and potential criminal action. The utility company, Florida Power, also chose not to be interviewed, maybe on the assumption that no good would come it from their point of view. It is not unusual for people in investigative stories to prefer not to be interviewed.

Q. Because it affects the whole of the oil industry, was there any reaction on CBS from advertisers afterwards?

A. No, I think we were very careful in the generalizations that we drew. Our facts were very well documented, and we had less backlash on that story than we had on a number of other investigative stories that we've done. Incidentally let me add one other thing about the *Daisy Chain* story, which is what interested me very much. The point is not just that the action involved the Daisy Chain rip-off, but also the fact that nobody was doing anything about it on other various levels. First the utility itself was not very effective in trying to keep prices down, in part because there was no motivation for them to do so because they could simply pass the prices along. Second, the State Public Service Commission had not acted very effectively to do anything about it. And third neither had the Federal Government and its watchdog agency, the Federal Energy Administration. So I think you had not only the fact that wrongdoing was committed, but the fact that none of the guardians of the public, who should be doing something about it, had come out of it very well either.

Q. Have any of these guardians of the public moved since your program?

A. On this one case, the matter was referred to the Justice Department for possible criminal action, and that action may be forthcoming next month. There are already civil suits against the companies and individuals involved, in addition to which I am told that the FBI has now been encouraged to look into this aspect of white-collar crime as an area for FBI investigation and that they are developing some other cases of a similar nature.

Q. In these investigative stories, a business, a corporation, an industry or a person will obviously realize the difficulty of their own position if such a story goes on the air. Has there been action in the past, on anything you have worked on, where people have tried to squash the story from the beginning?

A. No. I am trying to think of a situation I have been involved in where something of that kind happened, and I can't really recall any. In a story that I did which was called *Cold Comfort* about the man with the flue damper, there was an organization called the American Gas Association. They didn't try to put pressure on us, but they certainly tried to ingratiate themselves. This kind of action is much more common. An organization will try to be friendly, to deluge you with information with their side of the story, which is perfectly understandable and acceptable. Of course we are big boys, and presumably we can assimilate their information and we can also assimilate other information, and present a balance that we feel is objectively appropriate.

Q. What do you think of the capability of a network to do angry analytic social documentaries? And should a network take a partisan position?

A. The whole history of the documentary film, which of course precedes television, was to a great extent a history of social indignation, of allowing people who made films to express points of view about which the film maker felt strongly. With the evolution of the television documentary that is no longer appropriate. It is not appropriate for a television network to take a partisan position and to seem to be trying to force on an audience a predetermined editorial point of view. That does not mean that one can't do strong films, but the nuances are totally different.

An independent film maker who feels strongly about something can use all the art he can muster as a film maker to try to persuade the audience of the correctness of his or her point of view. But a television documentary is different.* A television documentary cannot seem to be saying to the audience, this is the way I feel and I want you to feel the same way. A television documentary must seem to be much more dispassionate. The film maker, the person who makes it, and the cor-

*AR: On review I find myself disagreeing strongly with this and Wasserman's following statements but they illustrate a very prevalent TV attitude. See also the discussion with Douglas Leiterman.

respondent who reports it should not seem to have come in with a preconceived attitude. Whatever the thrust of the story is, it should emerge from the substance of the film. There can be an emotional process, but it should be in the journalistic text of the story itself, rather than in what the audience would perceive as the orientation of the people who made the film.

I think that's in part what gives us the latitude to do stories that are strong and do have a thrust to them, because we are not perceived as having, and indeed do not have, one persistent point of view that we try to communicate. Each story stands on its own, and one story may have one kind of thrust, and another story may have no thrust, and a third story may have a different thrust. But in all of them whatever point of view emerges emerges from the characters in the story, the facts that are presented, and the objective research that has gone into the story, rather than from a predetermined "Sixty Minutes" point of view. Such a point of view would, of course, not be appropriate within the mandate of a news organization, and would also be self-defeating in the long run.

Q. What are the particular areas that interest you at the moment in documentary? What are the things you would like to do with your programs?

A. If there is one key word that I apply to documentaries, at least at this point in my 30 years of doing them, it's variety. My own very personal problem is to avoid boredom. Because I've done lots of films about lots of subjects I don't feel as passionate as I used to in terms of subjects per se. It's not that I am incapable of indignation, but I find that what keeps my juices flowing is to do different kinds of stories; and a story after all is in the doing of it. There is no subject so great but what you can't louse it up by doing it indifferently, and no subject so unrewarding that if you address yourself to it and really do it skillfully you can't make a good film out of it. But I try to do what interests me, and I try to do things that are somewhat distinctive and are differentiated from each other. "Sixty Minutes" does offer a rare opportunity for that—call it indulgence if you will: being paid to do what interests you.

Q. There are many film makers now, particularly young, new film makers, who think that the only thing to do is radical social documentaries on extreme points—riots, prisons, political action, and so on. Would you interpret your social documentary on a wider scale?

A. I am much less parochial in my view of stories that have social significance than I was during my younger and possibly more militant days. I think the most persuasive kind of film is one that does not editorialize per se. The subjective passion of the film maker may make for a very effective film for those people who already feel as you do, but I think the most effective kind of film is one which is not necessarily without emotion, but where the emotion is generated from the people you meet in the film, from the content of the film itself, rather than from the passion of the film maker. The film maker should be behind the scenes, rather than up front.

I like to do films that have ideas, that have significance, but that can occur in all kinds of contexts. *The Wilmington Ten* story that I did about a group of blacks who were in prison is an example. They claimed they were innocent and that they were victims of racial discrimination. So that was a story that got into racial discrimination head-on. But I have also just finished a film about a black composer and musician, a 95-year-old man named Eubie Blake. This is a man whose professional career spans almost eighty-five years. There is a lot of music in the film, there is warmth, there is humor, there is character, but you also get a sense of what it was like to be a black performer and entertainer during the early part of the century and the kind of discrimination and racial stereotypes and those kinds of difficulties; and that too, I think, provides a certain kind of social illumination, just as a more head-on film like *The Wilmington Ten* does.

Q. Is there any longer film project you are nursing, or do you just see the immediacy of "Sixty Minutes"?

A. Occasionally I do come across a subject where I wish I had an hour in which to do it, but that doesn't happen very often, and I can tolerate the frustration of not doing it because of the satisfaction of doing the kinds of stories I am doing now. In a way it's like having done novels for most of the years I've been in television. "Sixty Minutes" is the short story form.

# 3
## *Eye On*
### *Morton Silverstein*

*Is really investigative documentary possible on a flagship station subject to heavy commercial pressures? And if the answer is "yes" then what are realities within which the broadcaster nevertheless has to work? These were some of the questions that brought me once again to Mort Silverstein.*

*I'd known Mort for years and had interviewed him at length for* New Documentary in Action, *in 1969. Since then he'd written and directed* Banks and the Poor *(NET 1970), had worked for a while for ABC and had then moved over to WCBS New York in 1973.*

*Silverstein has a top reputation for probing documentaries. His films are far from simplistic and often deal with complex relationships of law, government, politics and social abuses. They are documentaries that require the most rigorous research as they often end up in naming names and pointing the accusatorial finger.*

*His two best known films in this genre are* What Harvest for the Reaper *(1967) and* Banks and the Poor. *Both were hour documentaries done for commercial free "NET Journal."* Harvest *is an exposé of conditions of black migrant workers on Long Island farms and rightfully rated comparison with Ed Murrow's earlier* Harvest of Shame. Banks and the Poor, *made three years later, is an intricate and moving indictment of the victimization of the urban poor by neighborhood banks and lending institutions.*

*One of the features of* Banks *is the use of the hidden camera, normally a very questionable practice but here well justified. Using this technique one gets right inside the ghetto lending office to watch the practices of loan sharks, and inside Caribbean casinos built with bank money "not available for housing." Fair as always, Silverstein interviews not only the black woman whose house has been repossessed but also includes the denials and rebuttals of bank officials and David Rockefeller.*

*"Eye On" is basically the continuation of the NET investigatory tradition but under the aegis of WCBS. I'd been skeptical whether a commercial station wished to or could allow much freedom on this type of program but was reassured by Silverstein. This is very much to the good. If indeed one does believe in the possibility of film affecting social change then the ability to reach a mass audience is a* must, *except for specialist or limited issues. Hence the importance of Silverstein's work.*

*Silverstein was born in 1929, went to a military academy and then entered Miami University "where I developed a good game of tennis but not much else." His first major job in television was working for "Night Beat," an interview program starring Mike Wallace and under the general guidance of Ted Yates. When "Night Beat" went off the air in 1958 Silverstein took up freelance writing for ABC radio and the* New York Times.

*This period was followed by documentary work for NBC, a short filming assignment with the United States Information Agency and then work for Westinghouse television. From Westinghouse Silverstein moved to NET which was the base for much of his finest work. Currently he produces "Eye On" and for a while maintained a general running brief over WCBS's current affairs programs.* *

Q. When I last talked to you, you'd just finished *Banks and the Poor*. That was November 1970. Can we trace your professional life since then?

A. One hopes, as another journeyman writer put it, that neither age nor custom would stale my infinite capacity to continue investigative reporting. When the NET documentary unit had its demise, which was in 1972, I left to do a freelance project with Don Dixon, formerly Director of Public Affairs at NET. We worked on a children's newscast project for King Features-Newsweek for several months. Subsequently, I went to the ABC Network for about four months where I did a half-hour documentary on breakthroughs in medicine, edited by Larry Solomon, with Jules Bergman as correspondent. It was called *New Hopes for Health*, and was a very visual magazine of various patients, ranging from infants in a life and death struggle in a pediatric ICU to new innovations for the blind at MIT. Though it won an award and was well received, it was quite unlike many of the previous documentaries I had been engaged in. There was very little investigative documentary going on at the networks and, as I say, there were none at NET after 1972.

Q. *Banks and the Poor* was a very strong attack on the attitude taken by the banks on lending for home construction, and so on. Have there been any practical results of that program?

A. Yes. There were certain House Banking Committee members who sold their stock. There was enormous public attention focused on congressmen and senators, who were involved either as lawyers for banks, or directors for banks. There were various conflicts of interest which they renounced or resigned. Other changes did take place. Chase Manhattan sold out its Resorts International Connection—a Nassau

*In 1979 Silverstein rejoined NBC as a writer-producer of hour documentaries for the network.

103

gambling operation. Principally, I think there was some consciousness-raising that went on, which showed how the Congress of the United States was indeed a bedfellow of the banking industry. Both were properly outraged because they were properly exposed. Unfortunately, it became the end of NET's investigative documentary tradition, because it was on a collision course then, with the advent of the Corporation for Public Broadcasting and the Public Broadcasting System which was just coming in as NET itself was being phased out. A long and complicated tale, and if we made it simplistic we would say that it was the good guys versus the bad guys, and the Nixon appointees won out for a few years—and are still winning out, as far as public television is concerned.

Q. How did you come to work for "Eye On" and WCBS?

A. Tony Hatch, who was then the Assistant News Director of WCBS-TV, called Larry Solomon (an outstanding film editor, with whom I had worked on many NET broadcasts in the past) and myself to come over to discuss the rebirth of a documentary series, which WCBS had generated in the early 1960's. It was then called "Eye on New York." In 1973 there was to be a revival of that documentary series, to be called "Eye On": *Eye on Banks, Eye on Hunger in the City, Eye on Slum Landlords*—whatever the subject was. Now, whether the rebirth was due to normal programming changes, license challenges, the sudden chicness of investigative reporting, or whatever (at any rate, not to be cynical about whatever the possible reasons were), Larry and I were both very excited about the potential of such a new series.

When I joined the organization I was concerned, immediately, with what would be the distinctions between a commercial broadcasting organization and NET, where I just spent eight very happy, advertiserless years—years of making films that were completely funded by the Ford Foundation, who never let you know one way or the other whether your show was terrific, banal, or whatever—and that's the way it should be. Here I was, for the first time in probably ten years, back at a commercial operation.

I also had reservations about reaching a local audience as opposed to a national audience, which NET had been reaching, with over 200 stations throughout the country. Even though New York is hardly local, nonetheless it was a tri-state audience as opposed to a national one. Then I read in *The New York Times* that first week, in the Business section, that a number of ad agencies for banks and their clients had taken a tour of WCBS. Having come through *Banks and the Poor* not too long ago, I wondered if the editorial freedom to choose the topics, to investigate again without fear of favor, which we had been able to do at NET, would still hold true at WCBS-TV. Almost five years later, I can report accurately, authentically, and enthusiastically that the same editorial freedom and the same measures of support from management still prevail. Not once have I been enjoined from doing a particular subject.

Indeed, one of the strongest shows that we were able to do here was called *Conflicts of Interest: Banks and the New York State Legislature*, which continued the tradition of *Banks and the Poor*, and in which we made links between the legislators of the New York State Legislature (as we did with the United States Congress and Senate in *Banks and the Poor*) and the banking industry. That broadcast went on the air and was given full support by the news director, general manager, and the CBS broadcast organization, and, indeed, "Eye On" has continued its editorial freedom and self-determination to this day.

Q. Regarding the program *Banks and the Legislature* and *Industrial Cancer*, you just stated that you had this editorial freedom, and that nobody put pressures on you. But were there, in fact, any pressures put on WCBS-TV by advertisers trying to say that such and such a program would affect their advertising—would not be good for the sponsors? In other words, although the pressure may not have hit you, can you say anything about pressures that were put on management or on the sales organization of WCBS when they heard about these programs?

A. In the instance of *Eye on Industrial Cancer*, the scenario was as follows. The documentary was broadcast. About two weeks later there were two sources of protest: one was from Owens-Corning, troubled about our citing the National Cancer Institute study that fiberglass was a potential carcinogenic—a cancer-producing substance—and the second was from GAF.

If you recall, the broadcast showed that GAF had buried a mound of asbestos—a proven carcinogenic substance—right near the river in Bound Brook, New Jersey. GAF protested that they had never disguised it and so forth, but I think that they were essentially troubled that we did discover their pile of asbestos, which they failed to seal entirely. They attempted to bring pressure upon the station. They sought to discredit our investigation. They set out to discredit our film. They sought a retraction. They claimed that they had met all the Environmental Protection Agency's standards, and so forth and so on.

The fact of the matter was that we had not only discovered their bungled job of burying a carcinogenic substance near the drinking supply of some communities in New Jersey, but the EPA also confirmed, once again, what we had stated in the broadcast, which was that GAF had failed to properly dispose of the material, and that they, the EPA, were continuing to investigate.

Owens-Corning was quite another matter which showed pressure at its most refined. Here, the president of Owens-Corning wrote to the president of the CBS Broadcast Group. Letters came down through division, and down to the station level, and, finally, to me, where I was requested to make a response. Owens-Corning was very upset that we had directed our audience's attention to certain government studies showing that fibrous glass had produced cancer in laboratory animals, and that there was increasing attention being paid to mortality rates of workers who had installed fiberglass.

Owens-Corning, as the principal manufacturer of this form of insulation, which has succeeded asbestos, believes naturally enough that fiberglass is wonderful and good for your health, and should be sprinkled on your cornflakes every morning. Many of the points raised in the Owens-Corning letter had nothing to do with the broadcast itself, which is very typical of these affairs. So, what you do then is that you find yourself re-researching not only what you accurately researched in the first place, but also researching a series of *non sequiturs* which had nothing to do with the original research, nor with the original broadcast, just to make your reply as comprehensive as possible. This takes endless amounts of time, and ties everyone up, and you're damned angry about it. But you try to be constrained and civil, rational, and as accurate in your reply as you were in your original investigative piece.

Q. You said, Mort, that the management of WCBS-TV has been basically very supportive of you, and has not limited your investigation. Would you say that it is generally true of network television today, that investigative reporting is being produced in an atmosphere of greater freedom and of more support from the management? Or is management still looking over its shoulders at sales?

A. To demonstrate the supportiveness of WCBS-TV and Ed Joyce— then News Editor—and Tom Leahy—then General Manager—and to answer once and for all, my original reservations about doing investigative documentary for a commercial broadcast organization, not only was the show repeated once, but four times. Not only did they stand up to Owens-Corning, they invited them to express their beefs up front, if they had any. My reply was given to them. It was supported by management.

Now, to respond to your question about networks. I think there is an enormous, aching void—a vacuum in network investigative documentary, except for an occasional foray on the part of "Sixty Minutes" and one hour films at "CBS Reports." More is always promised. Our local documentary on industrial cancer was followed by a network version—and, perhaps one day Lincoln Steffens will look down and smile benignly upon all of us, whether we toil in the network or station vineyards.

Q. Can you tell me how you go about selecting your topics? What you use for input on the topics, how you narrow down your topics, what interests you at a particular stage?

A. Well, social injustice continues to interest me and impel me. I hope my capacity to continue investigative reporting and whatever motivated me to begin with, that's to say my inherent convictions and sense of outrage at people being exploited and people without voices, which mandated most of the documentaries I did at NET, still prevail here.

*Banks and the Legislature*, as you say, began with *Banks and the Poor*. *Industrial Cancer* dealt with people at the workplace who were innocent victims of corporate greed or indifference, such as the submarine workers at New London—at Groton, at General Dynamics. This sense of repression continued in the "Eye on Bookbanning" show, which, incidentally, was a collaborative effort with Barbara Gordon, with whom I had worked at NET. The same sense of values, of my own ethics of being true to myself, still prevail and mandate the selection process, as well as the film making process.

Q. Do you think these shows really effect change, or do they merely set up a certain climate of inquiry? Can you coordinate show *A* with result *B*, or are you lost in the wilderness?

A. One always tries to affect the conscience and effect social change. *Banks and the Legislature* resulted in (1) tighter disclosure laws in Albany, (2) certain of the legislators who were up for re-election were not re-elected. I would like to think that possibly our broadcast helped result in those returns. Our broadcast was in June, and the election was in November. I do know for a fact, because they told me, that members of the banking committee who had gone on various junkets subsidized by the banking industry were troubled by the exposure and were not going on any further junkets and were going to mind their P's and Q's. Other journalists in Albany told me they were watching their steps. Now, whether they have reverted to their original ways or not is another matter, but I would hope that we had some impact.

Q. How fully do you research before you go into a show? Would there be issues that you have read about in the paper, and then you said, "Ah, yes, this is an issue that seems worthwhile investigating; this seems to be a clear good and bad," and then you go into the show and find, in fact, that the issue is far less clear cut and therefore you have to abandon it?

107

A. I think that each of the broadcasts that you've seen, such as *Industrial Cancer* and *Banks and the Legislature*, were topics that were originally researched by ourselves. They were not extensions. My working mandate, as you know, is not to find a clipping or an article and translate it into television, but, rather, through my own contacts and conversations with activists or victims, to somehow get a sense of repression, of wrongdoing, of injustice, and then to launch an original investigation rather than to translate a *New York Times* or an *Atlantic Monthly* article into a half-hour film.

Your question was, if we don't get into a simplistic good guy-bad guy situation, do we abandon it? Rarely do we get into that kind of a situation, because we are usually sniffing at something that we sense to be some original sin—one that has not been dealt with before. If it ever turns out that everything is hunky dory, that there was simply nothing to investigate, we'd call off the infantry. But I can't think of an instance where that's occurred. Not to be sanctimonious about it all, but I just can't think of one offhand.

Q. In many of your shows, as with other documentarists, there appears to be, on the surface, a balance. A problem or bleak situation is pictured and presented and then, superficially, you give the other side a chance to reply. But, in all of the shows that I've seen of yours and of many other documentarists, the reply always comes out slightly worse, whether we are talking about *Banks and the Poor* or *Industrial Cancer*. Are you really being fair to the other side? Do you think there are situations where there *is* really only *one* side? Are we using documentaries to say that we are talking about balancing and being fair to both sides, when in reality we know that we are not?

A. I think there is often only one side to a story, despite the aphorisms to the contrary. There is only one side to the truth. There is only one truth. As the late Bill Greeley, the *Variety* critic, used to say: There were no two sides to Hitler. Thus, there are no two sides to economic repression, or to social injustice. I don't think we bring in the villain in a way you characterize. I believe *people* are ultimately accountable. There are people within institutions who are accountable for given acts of social repression. And these are the people, whether they are crew chiefs at migrant labor camps, or farmers, or members of major corporations manufacturing potential carcinogens, who should be put on camera and asked, "how come?" and "why?" and made to respond to accurate statistics about repression or exploitation or shortened mortality. We don't deal with it superficially. If any spokespersons look poorly, it's possibly because they haven't persuaded you or the audience of their verity, but only me of their voracity.

Q. Some years ago, in talking about *What Harvest for the Reaper* we discussed the problem of the person who is left behind. You mentioned talking to migrant workers who were very open, very exposed to you, and very truthful to you, and you mentioned to me that you then went back to your hotel. You'd completed your film and were free, but these people were left with their problems. These days, do you show people the results of your interviews, do you let them evaluate how they look on your film?

A. No one sees the results of the film, except while watching the broadcast on the air. You take me back to something I still feel guilty about, which is moving into people's lives and then being able to split to a decent hotel or a decent restaurant—and being out of their lives whenever our own filming needs are concluded. I've tried to help in whatever way I can.

In the case of our broadcast *Hunger in the City*, for "Eye On," obviously we tried to make sure that people were getting fed by contacting pertinent agencies—or brought food ourselves. In the case of the earlier migrant workers film, I sought to explore and update the conditions there and, along with Reverend Arthur Bryant, who was in the film, subsequently testified before the Senate.

There are certain ways that you can follow up, and, yet, there are not enough ways. I think your question is as good and valid today, and as guilty-making today as it was back then. There are only a limited number of things that a film maker can do about the lives of people he has put on film. There is damn little that really can be done subsequently, except giving the victims another life, I guess. It still grieves me, and I wish I could be more responsive to the question. I wish I could say, very glibly, "Well, here's what we've done, which changed the system after the migrant or bank show, and here's what we've done to change the world." In the Valhalla, we'd do five documentary follow-up days a week. Each night we'd show that there's still a camp that practices slavery, and continue to expose it until finally it comes clattering down.

Q. Do you think there is a diminishing-returns effect on these investigative shows—that the mere fact of having them on one per week or one per month might, in itself, turn off the audience? They know that *Investigaton of the Week* is going to come up, and again they are going to be asked to be concerned about cancer among workers or abuses of legislative responsibility. Do you think that the mere fact of repetition is going to stop people from looking at your show? Again, are you going to be out to catch a general audience? Or are you merely capturing a committed audience from the beginning?

109

A. A good question. You always wonder if you are addressing the same people all the time, who'll cluck their tongues and nod reflexively—what some cynics have called "knee-jerk liberals," who say, "Yes, isn't it a bloody shame about migrant laborers," or about workers who contract industrial cancer, or about any other oppressed group. I like to feel that the investigative documentary form is constantly seeking out new members of the audience to persuade them to take some action, perhaps within the simple democratic process of hounding their legislative representative to reform the condition.

In regard to holding an audience I feel that in exchange for the viewers' time, you must strive to present information in an arresting, filmic, involving way. The documentary, too, is entertainment, albeit in its most difficult and demanding sense. So our mandate continues. We try to focus on injustice, but not by treating the documentary as a dull, unread social tract, but rather as a film which is responsive to and respectful of the viewer.

Q. Do you see much difference, or any key differences, between newspaper investigative reporting and what television can do?

A. I think TV, through the power of its imagery, can persuade more quickly; can arrest the attention more instantly. But there have been some tremendous newspaper investigations and I don't have to provide a testimonial to Woodward and Bernstein for their work on Watergate. One of the differences is obviously space and time requirements. The metropolitan staff of *The Washington Post* is encouraged to seek out wrongdoing. They have as much space, as much sanctioning of their enterprise as possible. Television, on the other hand, only has random time periods for investigative reporting, or any other kind of documentary, and probably tougher space strictures.

Q. You're working for a local New York station. Do you find any constraints in dealing with what are basically local documentaries, instead of being able to deal with major issues facing the nation? Would you like to do the latter? I felt, when I looked at your film about bookbanning on Long Island, that although this was a local issue, throughout the substrata of the film I could feel that you were asking many questions about where American society is at, at this particular moment in 1977. Would you like to go into these broader range documentaries—the hour documentaries on national issues—and, if so, what are the kind of subjects which would interest you?

A. This is a question that troubled me at the beginning, but no longer troubles me. I think every issue, every broadcast that you referred to, embraces a national issue, but we show the local symptoms.

The bookbanning documentary on the removal of books from high-school libraries is a national issue. There have been instances of this in Ohio, Pennsylvania, in the Far West, as well as Long Island. We had a Long Island expression of it and we did that because that's our audience—the tri-state New York, New Jersey, Connecticut audience. Industrial cancer is a national issue, and we had instances of it in New Jersey. CBS indeed followed by a few days with their own strong documentary on industrial cancer. Banks and the legislature is a national issue—it could be done in any state legislature in the country.

What frustrates me, admittedly, is not being able to reach larger numbers of people, but perhaps that is only an ego thing. New York probably has the world's most important and influential audience, but I suppose I miss reaching greater numbers of people, and I miss being able to influence or get input from people all throughout the country. It is not a question of diminishing an issue, or taking a smaller piece of the issue—you just take on the challenge to do in 23 minutes what you once were able to do in 58 minutes.

The real problem I found I faced when I came here was how, after a wonderful period of really having a blank check, if you will, at NET of doing a 58-minute documentary, without commercials—how to then not compromise your convictions, nor your principles, nor your own artistic and journalistic standards. How to get to a story and tell it powerfully and persuasively in 23 minutes and 18 seconds, because that's what the actual time is, when all is said and done, in a commercial half hour, as opposed to educational television's 58-minute span. What that requires is going very quickly to the heart of the story, rather than having the luxury of a long development. This means focusing on one salient example of the issue, as opposed to many examples in many locations.

But that's something which relates more to the disciplines of the writing and film making process, rather than to the issue of short-changing the audience by compromising on the thrust of the documentary. To put it simply: Just because there's less time to tell the story doesn't necessarily mean one should tell less of the story, or do it less investigatively.

Q. If anyone said to you, "Here, Mort—here's X thousand dollars to make any documentary you want," is there any particular documentary that fascinates you?

A. I'm still fascinated by the prospects for making a documentary truly an instrument for social change. The subjects themselves are never a problem, unfortunately. I say "never" and "unfortunately" because there are all those injustices still with us which keep perpet-uating themselves in the same systemic problems. I'd rather talk about the opportunities.

Today we have a thing called ENG: electronic news gathering. Doc-umentaries are going to be increasingly made via portable videotape equipment. The topics are still there, the freedom to choose and do the topics is still there, so therefore, what do we do with the medium itself? If we now have this thing called ENG, if we now have these minicam units on location, we have to ask what advantage does this new hardware give the documentarian? What does it give me today? Journalistic opportunities are there—to take a studio-based talk show and bring it out to the community. What other possibilities exist to break down the claustrophobia of the studio and go out into the turf of the people? What advantages are there, in terms of mobility or ar-tistic texture—indeed in terms of using the *present tense* which is, I find, the province of *videotape* as opposed to the *retrospective*—the past tense of *film*. Is that an advantage or a disadvantage? Is that an opportunity or an obstacle? I think the next few years will tell, and it's something that is swiftly coming into our industry, and something I'm addressing myself to right now.

So, it's not a question of topic as much as it is, this moment, of seizing the opportunity to create new techniques and development for-mats, as newer technology comes into television and into journalism. It's having an electric typewriter, as opposed to a manual. Only the technology changes and makes new demands, but the integrity and commitment of the documentarian must always, must enduringly re-main the same.

# 4
## *This Week*
### David Elstein

*"This Week" started off in the mid-fifties as a light-weight current affairs magazine produced by Rediffusion.\* It was hailed as commercial television's response to "Panorama," the BBC's main documentary report. In 1963 "This Week" was taken over by Jeremy Isaacs,† a former Granada producer, who transformed it into a single-subject half-hour program with both a national and an international brief. It was from that moment, almost, that its reputation started rising.*

*In 1965 Isaacs moved over to the BBC to run "Panorama." At the time both "Panorama" and "This Week" were dealing with the crises of the mid-sixties such as the internal problems of Africa and poverty in India, with Vietnam somewhere on the side. Both programs responded quickly to urgent issues and also occasionally took reformist paths. While "Man Alive," another current affairs program, tended to be domestically oriented both "Panorama" and "This Week" were slightly tipped in favor of the international story.*

*After a brief period at the BBC Isaacs moved back to "This Week." Isaacs is silent on the matter but Elstein, who knew Isaacs at the BBC, maintains that Isaacs's move was made because of the BBC's resistance to innovation and to genuine investigative and political reporting.*

*On his return to "This Week" Isaacs proceeded to raid the BBC of its finest current affairs reporters and directors, including Phillip Whitehead and John Morgan, who probably sensed greater freedom and openness at "This Week." A little while later they were joined by David Elstein, then regarded as one of the brightest of the junior directors at the BBC.*

*Elstein had had a brilliant career at university and then joined the BBC as a trainee. After a few years at the BBC he too was lured by the freedom of "This Week" where he began to work as a writer-director. When this interview was taped in 1977 Isaacs had moved on to the upper echelons of Thames Television and Elstein had become the current executive producer of "This Week."*

*Under Elstein's leadership "This Week" has continued the sharp political aim that characterized Isaacs's tenure. Among many outstanding reports one would*

\*Rediffusion is the former name of one of London's independent commercial television stations. Later it changed its name to Thames Television.

†I interviewed Isaacs at length for *New Documentary in Action* where he provides more details on the early years of "This Week."

*include the programs on Chile, terrorism in Germany, the Biko inquest and David Dimbleby's exposure of famine in Ethiopia.*

*When I met with Elstein we talked mainly about Ireland and its problems, the coverage of which has generally been very poor on English television. "This Week"'s record on Ireland is, however, good, with Elstein's joint program with* Peter Taylor, Five Long Years, *being one of the best analyses of the situation.*

*Besides running "This Week" Elstein also occasionally directs other films for Thames. Notable among these isolated efforts is* The Bomb, *about the planning and use of the first atomic bomb, which Elstein directed for "The World at War" series.*

Q. How old were you when you left the BBC for Thames Television?

A. I came to "This Week" when I was still fairly junior. I was twenty-three, but I'd had quite a few years of experience in television and had served a basic apprenticeship of making film after film in the half-hour format on all kinds of subjects: long-sentence prisoners in British prisons, racial discrimination in Rhodesia, Norman Mailer running for Mayor of New York, decaying villages in the North of England, and pollution. Then, three years ago they asked me to become overall producer of "This Week," and I've been concentrating on that end ever since.

Q. When I talked to you earlier you surprised me by saying that the drive and analysis of Thames films was better and deeper than the BBC. I'm interested as to why. In America, for example, the tendency is that once you have commercial backing for your programs and have to think about a sponsor or an advertiser, your programs generally become slightly softer, slightly gentler with a great deal of attention being paid to avoid giving offense. What accounted in the past and what accounts in the present for this difference between the BBC and Thames?

A. Well, it's a paradox of structure. The BBC is overwhelmingly unitary. It tries to have a BBC line on all administrative questions. BBC Northern Ireland is very much part of BBC, not of Northern Ireland. In ITV things are much better ordered and it's partly accident and it's partly deliberate. In ITV the structure that was settled on was very much a regional structure under a public service authority. The authority, which is now known as the Independent Broadcasting Authority, is instructed by an act of Parliament to insure that programs will be of a standard and will inform and educate as well as entertain. Very similar wording to the BBC's own charter. But the authority then licenses contractors to operate the commercial franchise in geographical areas and they have a monopoly of advertising space in those geographical areas. That gives them financial security.

For the most part ITV companies are rich. They are not at the behest of any advertiser. No programs are sponsored. Programs are decided on by the ITV company, approved of by the IBA. And advertisers have no access to program makers at all. Because of this there's no possible pressure that advertisers could put on them. So the problems of sponsorship never arise. Indeed, I would say that political pressure is much severer on the BBC than on ITV, and I'll explain why.

In ITV there are five major companies which contribute to network programs. The vast majority of programs are networked and five major companies, each totally independent from the other, contribute to the network. They tend to have very short managerial structures. I sit next door to my head of department and he sits next door to the director of programs. And that's the management chain for current affairs programs in Thames. In the BBC you might have a chain eight long before a program goes on the air. You might have the program editor, the assistant head of current affairs group, the head of current affairs group with several chief assistants and special assistants, the deputy head of news and current affairs, the head of news and current affairs, the director of news and current affairs and the deputy director and the director general. All of whom can and do kill programs from time to time. So a program can get through much quicker at Thames than at the BBC.

Equally, where a program has trodden on dangerous ground, or upset some politician, that particular politician may have it "in" for that particular program company, but he can scarcely blame Granada Television for Thames's mistakes. In brief, you can't attack the ITV system, if you're a politician, in the way you can the BBC. If one BBC program makes a mistake, the whole of the BBC is under pressure. And the whole of the BBC is therefore infinitely more sensitive than any individual company within ITV. I've always seen the BBC as much more repressed by the political pressures that are put on it than the ITV system as a whole.

Even advertisers, funnily enough, find it easier to get at the BBC than they do with ITV companies. ITV is so supersensitive to any accusation that advertisers might have an influence that they take particular pleasure in proving that they're not under influence. For instance, "This Week" did four programs on the perils of smoking. The final one, about Phillip Morris, was as devastating a program about cigarette manufacturers as has ever been made. The BBC has never attempted anything like that, and never would, because it would come under terrific attack from the tobacco industry and the advertising industry. For knocking Britain in some peculiar way. For putting jobs in danger, national responsibilities, and so on.

Q. Do you remember any specific examples of differences in political treatment between the BBC and Thames?

A. There's an interesting example from Northern Ireland. Before Phillip Whitehead came to Thames he was working on BBC's "Panorama" as a producer and wanted to make a film about the political structure in Northern Ireland. This was in 1966, before the troubles. It was basically going to be about how housing was manipulated by the Protestant majority. How the boundaries were gerrymandered. He put up his proposal. It was approved by his program editor and then vetoed by the BBC's controller in Northern Ireland and the director general, who said the program was too sensitive and could not be made. When Phillip Whitehead was hired by Jeremy Isaacs to produce "This Week," more or less the first program he produced was this exposé of gerrymandering in Northern Ireland.

Q. When you came in to head "This Week," you already had a fine reputation for investigative journalism. Can you recall now where you hoped "This Week" would go? What were the particular projects or ideas you had in mind at the time? How many of them have you been able to put into effect?

A. Well, the areas of concern have been the things that interest me and interest the production team. We are very interested in Northern Ireland. We do a lot of programs there. We have done four programs about Ethiopia, including one program about the famine in Ethiopia which helped bring down the Ethiopian Emperor. We have felt duty bound to go back there and report since on the problems of the revolution, on the Eritrean war. We have made a large number of sophisticated programs on the Middle East. We have done four programs on Cyprus because once you do one program on an area you are sensitive to developments thereafter in the same area.

We do what I regard as less soft stories than we used to. We don't do much general duty political coverage. I'd much rather do analytical programs. We've done a lot of investigations on corruption in local government, on wrongful convictions, on the reasons why the DC-10 crashed in Paris, which was one of the biggest air crashes that ever happened. On the poisoning of Michigan recently. We have tried to be harder headed and more political than we have been in the year just before. We're very interested in social issues, such as smoking, alcoholism, bad housing, rape. I'm interested in the treatment of sex offenders. And very occasionally we do programs which are completely out of the normal path, but which just strike a chord somewhere.

Q. What have been the biggest problems for you as a production team in this kind of investigative journalism?

A. The biggest problem is the television act which laid down that ITV could not broadcast libels even if they were justified, which is a problem. It goes way beyond what happens to newspapers and we have had instances in the past where we have assembled the information on a particular subject and then we were told we couldn't publish it because it was in breach of the television act under which ITV was created. And we're then rather galled when the following morning national newspapers would run all the details of our story in a way we couldn't.

So one of the things I've done is to become very expert on what we can say and what we can't say and how you can say something without it being libel. It means that in order to get an investigative program on the air you've got to have absolute factual support for everything you say. You cannot rely on "these people dare not sue—we think this is right, and we're pretty sure that we're right and we reckon that we'll win in court." You've got to be dead certain about every single thing that you do and have the physical evidence for everything that you say which means that you have to invest large sums of money in investigations and a lot of effort.

When I first came to "This Week" I discovered that an investigation which had gone on for six months had just been abandoned because our lawyers had advised that to broadcast the program would be strictly speaking a contempt of court because there was a prosecution pending of the people that we had investigated. And in those days it was thought that that made the subject impossible to broadcast. What was then needed was someone with enough energy and enthusiasm to lift up and re-enthuse the production team that had done it and had been shattered by the legal decision, and then reconstruct our case so as to clear it legally and just drive it through till it was on the air.

Q. How do you get the co-operation of people and industry? I would have thought that a program like yours begins to spell danger to anyone with a bad conscience. And if I were a cigarette manufacturer I'd run a mile before I ever spoke to you.

A. That does happen. A lot of people won't talk to us. Why Phillip Morris wanted us to make a program about them after the programs we had made about the British manufacturers, I can't for the life of me understand. And you do in any case have particular problems on television that you don't have elsewhere. For instance if you're doing a radio investigation, a voice can be disguised and not named. However, as long as the *bona fides* of the person giving you the information are acceptable you can do the story. In newspapers you don't have a face. In television you do, and it normally has to be identified.

117

Q. I'm interested in questions of ethics involved. Very often you're trying to get somebody to cough up his guts or say something interesting on the air. Do you ever give these people a chance to see themselves, to vet the interview afterwards?

A. No. It's a delicate area. I am more sensitive to this than most producers in television. With the majority of interviewees in any program I will always make sure that they realize when they take part that they can withdraw at any stage. If we're doing films in very sensitive areas where we're asking for people's co-operation, I will agree to making our investment, which could be 10 or 15 thousand pounds, entirely conditional on their final approval of the finished, edited film.

Where people are giving you information as part of a general investigation you've got to be rather more hardheaded. First of all, you've got to make clear to them that they might be required to confirm their evidence in court and if they're not willing to do that then you really don't want to interview them. That in turn puts them on guard and makes them doubly certain that what they say is what they want to say. Thirdly, you've got to be sure not to pay them too much money. That's so you can't be accused of having induced somebody either to break a trust or to give information simply in exchange for money. Fourthly, at all times you've got to respect the IBA rules for the editing of interviews. These state that interviews must be edited fairly to reflect accurately what a person said in his interview.

Now over and above all that you've got another problem where someone tells you something and then for one reason or another wants to withdraw later. Then you have to make judgment as to whether the reasons for withdrawing are valid or not and whether the public interest outweighs the individual's reasons for wanting to withdraw. Here's one example.

Someone gives you the inside story of how a multimillion-pound company has bribed its way into a particular contract, and gives it to you in good faith. And you film it in good faith and you complete your program. At the last minute the informant suddenly has cold feet. The cold feet are to do with "someone's going to assassinate me if you put out this program." Obviously, you abandon the program. Or they might say, "My life is going to be shattered. My wife has not realized that I've been involved in a bribery. She'll leave me. My children will be devastated." Again, I would guess that we would abandon the program. If it's "I've been fired," I think I would take the view that the informant knew that was a likely consequence of spilling the story in the first place.

Q. Can you think of any programs in the last year or so where these kinds of things actually happened?

A. Yes. In an investigation of corruption we had an interviewee who told how a series of county councillors had been bribed with expense accounts, fur coats, and so on. He had been an actual witness to the bribery. Just a week before transmission he got very anxious. Would we indemnify him against any possible libel suit? We said no, we wouldn't. Would we pay him an increased fee to cover his legal expenses? No, we wouldn't do that either. "Well, I want to withdraw." "Well, you committed us this far, you can't withdraw." "What if I'm prosecuted for bribery?" "That's a risk you'll have to take." He finally decided to go ahead. In due course he was prosecuted and got a two-year jail sentence on the basis of what he had told us. This was the kind of decision where you just have to work your way through to the point where he knows *exactly what is involved*. And without putting any immoral pressure on him, you have made clear what the balance of the decision is for you.

We have been in situations, for instance making a film about an abortion clinic, where the finished program was shown to the participants and one or two of them wanted to withdraw. And we agreed to withdraw. Abandoned that version of the program. Reshot it with new people until we got everyone's agreement to doing it. But I think that's standard practice, or should be standard practice for all kinds of programming like this.

Q. When you do these programs do you go in for anything theoretically called balance? You're making an accusation. Do you give the other side a chance to reply?

A. It depends how good their case is. We wouldn't give them a chance to reply if what they were saying was waffle, was rubbish. We would put accusations to them and if they're interested in replying they could reply. When we did an exposé of ballot rigging in the engineering union, we desperately wanted the union to take part. And we invited each member of the executive, individually and collectively, to participate—and they all declined. So we put out the program, and the chaps who did the ballot rigging are still serving their jail sentences.

When we did our programs about smoking we very much wanted the advertisers and manufacturers to come on. They didn't want to, for obvious reasons. The one thing that we occasionally do which is of dubious morality is secret filming and secret reporting, which does put the person involved at a disadvantage because they're not four square with you when you are exposing their activities. And to do that we always have to get special permission from the IBA before filming.

We did a program exposing franchise frauds, the fast-food companies which offer you supplies if you buy the ovens to put them in. After we had done all the investigative work proving the people were frauds

119

and were breaking the law and deluding people out of funds, we then got permission to film one of the salesmen at work. We prepared an elaborate trap and used a hidden camera and a "would-be sucker" who happened to be one of our researchers. The guy did his spiel and we were able to expose every single lie in his spiel. That kind of thing you would only do if it was pretty important. You wouldn't use that kind of sledge hammer to crack a nut. And we're currently in the business of doing tape recordings of bribery inside a very major British company which we'll get on the air in a few months' time. And here again we had to get permission for that.

Q. When you're doing your films in England, you and your team are working as people living in England, familiar with the social and political scene. And the viewers are also familiar with the same scene. I can see that your films covering foreign situations might offer many more delicate problems, both in the state of knowledge of the viewer and your own knowledge of the foreign situation when you go in for a week or two weeks and suddenly have to become experts. I'm particularly interested here in the films that you've done in Ethiopia, and on Israel and the Middle East and the problems that these kinds of films have created for you.

A. Well, this is the area where we become journalists more than film makers. "This Week" has a structure whereby I'm the overall producer. Under me there are four film directors, four journalist reporters, and a half dozen researchers. And they tend to team up into teams of one of each to make films. When we go to foreign locations I always expect the journalist to be pretty expert on the area before he goes. And one of the things that I have to do is to keep up-to-date myself with situations all over the world.

We try to anticipate a subject rather than just run with the daily news. We keep our eyes on a situation for a period of months. We think about a film on Quebec separatism and work out which is the best week to be in Quebec and maybe that time is the week of Jean Baptiste Day: the celebrations of French nationalism, and so on. And we will gear our whole film to that particular week and make sure that the journalist and the director and the researcher are going to be expert by the time they get there. If we go to the Middle East we will make our film about Egyptian politics and the nature of Sadat's domestic policies at a time when he himself is of interest to the general public because he is pressing for peace in the Middle East.

You have to pick the moment when people will be prepared to listen to you. We made a film about Guatemala which was essentially about the nature of the class society in Guatemala. We made it in the period immediately after the earthquake, because we reckoned that the audience would be interested in the earthquake and this was a good chance to tell them something about a typical Latin American country, which they would never have bothered to watch but for the fact that Guatemala for the first time was familiar to them. But we would have been following events in Guatemala, and indeed in South America generally, for the last year waiting for the moment in which to make the film.

If we go to the Middle East, as we will be doing next month to do a program about the Israeli position on Geneva, it will be on the basis of very detailed knowledge of Israeli politics as we have managed to cull it from the State Department, from Israel itself, and from political and journalistic contacts that we have. It won't be "Gosh, this is Tel Aviv. Isn't it hot. Which side of the road do we drive on? Let's make a travelogue." The level of sophistication amongst the journalists has to be very high in order to get across the essence of a situation, the essence of a society as far as we can see it, and then present it to a British audience.

Q. There's a certain body of opinion in England, for example part of the group characterized by Mary Whitehouse, who tend to see all television today in England as run by trendy lefties. What is your view of left-wing or right-wing bias in television in England, and what do you think should be the base rock of the investigative TV journalist?

A. This is a very big issue and an important one. I think the BBC is essentially right-wing as an organization. And I think a program like "The Money Program" which is a weekly current affairs program about business is monstrously biased in the way it presents financial issues and yet the BBC lays claim to some kind of objectivity. I have never subscribed to the myth of objectivity in journalism or in television current affairs. I'm a great believer in committed programs. That doesn't mean that people have to be overtly socialist or fascist or whatever it might be. It's just that the reporter, the interviewer ought to have commitment. It can be the scandal of a coverup or a mass poisoning of a state. It can be anger over unnecessary starvation in Ethiopia. It can be the passion of caring about a subject, say in Northern Ireland where the reporter who files regular reports from there really does care. He's not a republican and he's not a loyalist in his own political opinions, but he cares about the issue.

I find that BBC programs are exceptionally wishy-washy, cautious, conservative, and if committed in any direction, it's usually on the side of authority. I think it's probably true to say that the most effective current affairs programs are largely inhabited by left-leaning journalists, producers, and directors for a very simple and obvious reason. Those are the kind of people who are interested in investigating society, in challenging subjects, in asking is the status quo acceptable. And those people won't be receptive to a Labor government as opposed to a Conservative government. Indeed they'll be just as critical of any government, left or right, as they are of foreign governments, because they don't accept necessarily the rightness of the party.

Occasionally "This Week" does get directly accused of bias. Sometimes, if it is a program about Northern Ireland, it will be accusations of bias from both sides which usually means that you have probably been more outspoken than either side likes but you have an overall balance one way or the other. Some of our programs, particularly on overseas issues, are attacked as being left-wing. Programs we've done about South Africa, Rhodesia, the Palestinians. My own view is that the reason that this accusation is made is because the reality of the situation in those areas is one where the left has a lot of right on its side, so to speak. Fairly right-wing people will complain about our interviewing black movements in South Africa. Saying how dare you put these law breakers on television.

We have been bitterly attacked recently by a Conservative MP about the campaign he has been running attacking what he calls "scroungers"—people who collect welfare payments without apparently being entitled to them. And he was afraid I might expose the malevolence of his campaign. So we were heavily attacked by him and his supporters for being politically permissive. Myself, I must say I was delighted we did the program and it brought a lot of comfort to people who are very downtrodden—people he described as scroungers—to see television prepared to commit itself on issues like that.

Q. In the U.S., where the networks occasionally do the investigative or analytical program, the program makers sometimes give the right of reply to the person attacked. The classic case is the Ed Murrow broadcast on McCarthy followed by a reply a few weeks later. On "This Week" do you ever give people the right of reply?

A. Never. The right of whose reply to what? It begs so many questions. It may be in our attacking the cigarette industry that we had been idiotically mild in our attacks. Maybe the right of reply should lie with critics even further to our left rather than with the tobacco industry. We made a program about South Africa where we interviewed four black men saying how the police treat them. Who had the right of reply? The South African government, the police who beat them, the thousands of blacks who have been killed so far by the South African government? I mean that just begs too many questions.

If someone *asks* for a right of reply, we'll consider the request. We'll try and assess whether they have a legitimate complaint. When the South Africans complained about the film we made, we also tried to do a program in which we interviewed the chief of police. That we would have regarded as a right of reply, but they turned down the invitation. Yet they still complained that they hadn't got the right of reply. If we had patently only done one side of an issue such as the Arab conditions for peace in the Middle East, we would go out of our way to search out the Israeli side of things because we owe it to our audience to be balanced in our approach to the world. If we exposed a crook I'd give him a chance to defend himself in that particular program.

The whole point is to retain our editorial control over what we transmit. Otherwise we're basically an access channel. I approve of access but it has no part in communicating current affairs programs to the audience. The audience relies on us to exercise our editorial judgment otherwise they wouldn't know what to make out of what's coming out of the set. Even when our journalists wear their colors fairly openly, where they're very hard hitting, in a particular interview, at least the audience knows where that journalist stands, especially if it's a journalist who's on regularly. If someone is thought to be right-wing then someone socialist in the audience watching will use a filter and interpret what that chap says and vice versa. But if you abandon your editorial standpoint then the audience has no means of assessing whether it's being got at, brainwashed, or whatever.

Q. In America since about 1966–67 there have been various programs on the Vietnam war. The biggest kind of war-political issue in England the last few years since 1968–69 has been Ireland. "This Week" has made a number of films looking at the Irish situation. What have been your problems and targets within this area?

A. Well, the first thing to say about coverage of Northern Ireland on British television is that it's generally pretty bad. And it's pretty bad because it's caught in the classic colonial trap. And I'm sure it was exactly the same in our coverage of Aden, of Cyprus, of Palestine, ten, twenty, or thirty years ago. It is extremely difficult for a British journalist to expect a British audience not to identify with British troops whether British troops are carrying out correct or incorrect policy. Now that means that British television coverage in Northern Ireland is wildly at odds with television coverage practically everywhere else around the world. It is very difficult for British television to raise the question of what the hell are we doing in Northern Ireland after all these hundreds of years. Why are we still laying claim to this piece of territory which we conquered centuries ago and happen to be clinging to for obscure reasons? The assumption that Northern Ireland is British is very deeply ingrained, particularly in the BBC, and I think the BBC in Northern Ireland is an exemplar of British colonialism. I'm interested to know what'll happen to the BBC Northern Ireland office if Ulster becomes independent.

"This Week"'s coverage has been better I think than anybody else's because we are consistently interested, and we do this at our own peril because the British audience is not interested in Northern Ireland. To the British audience Northern Ireland is a place a long way away about which they know little, want to know less and where beastly things happen to British soldiers in the streets of Belfast. To the British audience the Irishmen are blackguards and come over here and fiddle and make bombs with which they blow up the law courts. There is absolutely no sympathy in Britain for Irish republicans. And not much more for loyalists. There's total incomprehension about why it's such a bitter issue and why it's one which should cause so many deaths. Therefore, when I say "at our peril" I mean our ratings dip alarmingly every time we make a program about Northern Ireland.

I feel, however, we have a duty to report because it is undoubtedly the biggest single issue in Britain. The most important, the most intractable, the one where successive governments have been successively wronger and wronger. I don't think we are totally honest in our coverage. I think that we allow ourselves to deal with Northern Ireland issue by issue, week by week, 27 minutes by 27 minutes. This week we're doing a film about last week in Northern Ireland. We will be asking: was the Queen's visit a triumph for the army and the Queen, or did it simply re-emphasize in sharper form than ever before the essential conflict in Northern Ireland? It will upset an awful lot of people among those who watch it because it will challenge certain assumptions. It's rare that we ask that question. In a few weeks we'll be doing a film about the status of political prisoners in Northern Ireland, which is a narrow issue. We did a film about five years after Bloody Sunday. How did Derry feel? A narrow issue. We take issue by issue and very rarely impose a perspective and I'm not too happy about that.

The only perspective we imposed was in the special program we did called *Five Long Years* where we took ninety minutes of air time to try and give some depth to the British involvement in Northern Ireland. And people, those who watched it, were absolutely amazed to discover for the first time that the Protestants had been abusing the Catholics in Northern Ireland all these years. That the British troops were only meant to go in for a short period. That internment was a terrible mistake. That we've tried to impose solutions. That there are politicians who have never been to Northern Ireland and don't know what it's about. When you actually see it in some kind of context it is astonishing and revelatory. And you get the idea that this is something that ought to be covered. Why isn't television covering it? Because you are faced with the classic problem: people aren't interested.

Q. On that program *Five Long Years* Peter Taylor acted as the journalist-reporter. And I think you were the producer-director. How did you split responsibilities and directions between you?

A. Well, the program was made three years ago, when I was a director on "This Week" and not the producer. At the time I'd already made one film with Peter Taylor in Northern Ireland when we made a film about Strabane, a little town which had had a very heavy toll of casualties in bombings in the four years since the troubles had begun. And we discovered that we worked together very well and that what we were able to apply was a common political judgment.

The beginning of *Five Long Years* was very curious. Peter and I had just been talking off hand about Northern Ireland and why couldn't we do something a bit deeper than "this is a town where people have died—where people have suffered." Maybe we could try and explain some of its causes. Then Peter, just out of the blue, composed a memo saying we should produce a program called *Five Long Years* which would be a special "This Week", which would analyze what has happened. We sent it off to the Director of Programs and eventually the reply came back "yes." We gave ourselves a very short time to do it— thirteen weeks from start to finish, and we're talking about a 90-minute program.

We plunged in on the basis of trying to make sense of the period from 1969 to 1974. We knew the twelve to twenty people that we would have to interview—key figures in the army and the various political parties. We just had to make sure that we covered the ground with all of them. We hoped that we could draw it all together after we'd got all the interviews. While Peter went off to see them all in Northern Ireland, I dived into the film archives. Later we joined forces to do the interviews which took us about a fortnight. Any interview would be Peter asking the questions and me being there with him so that nothing was covered inadequately on my side as far as I could tell. Then we went back to London to assemble the material.

Q. The program is really the build-up of the British involvement in Ireland and the growth of the IRA. Most of the figures you talk to are

British generals, politicians, Irish MP's, and a few members of the IRA. I can't recall you talking to many Protestants in the program and asking them their viewpoints.

A. There were quite a few. In fact, we had a problem with the Protestants. The trouble was that when some of the leading Protestant politicians discovered we were interviewing IRA men they refused to take part in the program. Paisley, for instance, didn't want anything to do with it. William Craig, who was the leading Protestant politician at that time, was convinced the Protestants were under-represented in the program but it was curious because in a sense the problems of those five years '69–'74 weren't Protestant problems, they were Catholic problems—Catholics trying to come to terms with the army being there ostensibly to protect them, but quickly becoming the enemy. But I think the balance of the program, particularly the last third of it, was very much the Protestant resurgence. One of the Protestant para militaries was explaining how they had organized the strike which brought down the power-sharing government and one got a sense at the end of *Five Long Years* that the Protestants were very much in control of what they wanted to be in control of. I think we did a fairly careful balancing job as far as we could within the limitations that the Protestant politicians themselves imposed.

Q. What have been the actual physical difficulties in filming in Ireland—trying to shoot and trying to report in the midst of civil war? I'm thinking of the difficulties in regard to the crew, difficulties of access to people whose own lives are on the line, difficulties of getting and cross-checking information, and so on.

A. The crew difficulties were overcome by always having volunteers and by having a much smaller than normal crew so that you aren't particularly exposed when you're on the streets. You're four people, not eight or ten as might otherwise be the case. The problem of access isn't great and because "This Week" has been on the ground for a long time we are on good terms with all the parties involved. We have close contacts with the Protestants, the Catholics, the Provisionals, with the UDA, with the Northern Ireland office in Westminster, with the army. In fact, the only peole we're a little cool with in the last four months are the army people because they have changed their view of the conflict and now have refused to take part in programs where paramilitaries are shown. That's their decision and it means that we no longer cover the army's point of view on "This Week" because we would have to accept the ultimatum they give us.

There are two basic difficulties. The first is the sensitivity of Ulster

Television which is the small ITV company which is based in Belfast, which broadcasts in the Ulster area and which has to live every day with the Ulster problem. We go and come back, but they're on the spot and reporting constantly. They're identified with what we produce because it's on the same network. They have to live with the consequences of a bad program by bullets, riots, bricks in the window. No cooperation. Therefore we're careful to stay well in touch with them when we're making a program. We let them see a program before broadcast and very occasionally they opt out of the network for our transmission. It hasn't happened for at least four years, but it has happened. They have said "This is too much. This is too sensitive."

The other problem is, of course, the Independent Broadcasting Authority, which is very tough on things like interviewing the IRA. We have to get special permission before we're allowed to approach the IRA for interviews because they're considered "enemies of the British people." And the IBA are very anxious that we don't overstep the bounds.

I've had many conflicts in the past with the IBA and on one occasion they banned one of our Ulster programs. It was a film about fund raising and gun running by the IRA in America called *Hands Across the Sea* and was the first exposé of the IRA front which was organizing Irish politics in America at that time. We wanted to transmit the program on the night after a day of voting in a particular election. The IBA decided this was the wrong time to put it out and banned it sight unseen. This was very upsetting and bad for us because it made people think we were somehow suspect. But for the most part they have now accepted the tone of what we do in Northern Ireland, that we are more prepared to be vigorous, to understand loyalist and republican extremism, the conflicts, and people caught in between them.

Q. Over the years you've tackled an extremely large number of very sensitive issues. You told me before that the executive chain of command above you was very short as compared to the BBC. Have there been any issues where you have run into conflict with your head of department or something like that?

A. It's happened to me in the BBC, but curiously enough not at Thames or at least not in terms of where it's actually affected me. My head of department has never censored an idea as being politically unacceptable. Just came to me and said, "That's not a very good story. Why are you doing that?" And my director of program has never censored any idea as such. Occasionally the director of programs or the managing director of the company or the chairman of the company who didn't have direct contact with me will, after the program has been transmitted, have a word of reproof. "If you hadn't included that particular statement to camera it would have been better" or "Aren't your films about South Africa getting a bit similar to each other?" "The way you describe Afrikaans as a dialect as opposed to a language is bound to cause unnecessary offense." Generally there has been amazingly little internal conflict or hassle.

The only conflict I've had has been with the IBA, the outside authority. They banned a program on Northern Ireland, but it was reprieved the following week. They banned for some time a program we did about abortion on the grounds that some of the scenes in it might upset the viewers. Nobody here at Thames TV agreed with them. The whole company bitterly fought that decision, and eventually the program got on the air with the most minor of modifications. They have prevented us doing a couple of programs at what they regard as inopportune times. They thought a film about Tony Benn, who's a left-wing cabinet member, should be delayed during the run up to the referendum on the Common Market when he was a key participant. So we delayed it. They tried to stop us from doing a film about the National Front, which is a very right-wing Fascist organization, but eventually allowed it through. They've taken odd little things out of films once they've been finished, saying that's a bit much—that's over the top. In general though, I think that it's a remarkably free atmosphere—even with the IBA.

Q. Over the years you must have formed a pretty realistic appraisal of the ability or otherwise of your programs or films in general to affect social and political change. You told me before that one or two people had finished up being charged or in jail, but what have you seen of the wide effects of these kind of programs? What do you think about their influence?

A. I'd say that we don't have much influence. The simple direct cause-and-effect programs happen. We say these boys should *not* be in jail for a murder they didn't commit. Eventually they're released. We say these men ought to be in jail for an offense that they *did* commit. Eventually they go to jail. We say those policemen over there beat up demonstrators outside a factory. We name them. We expose them. They are still being promoted within their own police force. Nothing happens at all. They're still being promoted as far as I know. These two chaps rigged the union ballot. We named them. We showed their photographs. They should be prosecuted. They get prosecuted. That's too easy.

At a more advanced but still not very sophisticated level we do a program saying smoking can kill you. Two hundred thousand people stop smoking. Six months later two thousand have gone back to smoking. You can have a short term dramatic impact when you're making a short term dramatic program. We did a program saying all our attitudes about drinking and driving are totally confused. Which wasn't intended to have any particular direct impact on people. And it didn't as far as we know. It just made people aware, those who watched.

Of all the programs we've done the one with the most impact was probably the film we made about the famine in Ethiopia. We were simply exposing the horrendous scale of a famine which had been completely concealed by the Ethiopians. In itself that one film destroyed the Ethiopian empire. And the reporter who made it became a national hero in Ethiopia and had streets named after him. The film was shown on Ethiopian television twice a night after the revolution took place. That is bizarre. An absurd direct cause-and-effect relationship between television and society which was neither intended nor possible to anticipate. But the vast majority of what we do is simple information and the stream of information.

You can tell people things of great sophistication or not even very great sophistication on television and ten seconds later it's totally forgotten. The amount of stuff that's pumped out is truly terrifying and it really does make you wonder what the bloody hell are you doing. Why are you bothering. If people can absorb and eject so immediately what you have produced is it because you're a very poor communicator; is it because the limitations of the medium are too great; is it because the nature of the learning process simply hasn't been understood? Whatever it is, by any normal standards of judgment we are undoubtedly failures. On a monumental scale. We spend vast amounts of money, and we put in a terrific amount of effort, yet the net increase of information relative to the amount of information we put out is, I suppose, only five percent.

Q. How have your films and programs been affected by practices of the film unions?

A. The ACTT, the Association of Cinematograph and Allied Technicians, has got a closed shop in every ITV company. All film crews and studio crews are manned by ACTT agreement. This applies to directors and researchers as well as cameramen, soundmen, production assistants, and so on. And the result is that the ACTT has an immense hold on everything that we do. To film with safety in a war zone means reducing the crew to an absolute minimum. A standard crew is seven, or eight, or nine strong. But the maximum that you want on the street in a civil war is about five—better still only three or four. To get agreement to that you've got to ask for union permission. Occasionally it's not given. If they're in any kind of a dispute with the management over whatever it might be they may use this as a lever to gain bargaining power elsewhere.

We lost a whole year's coverage of Northern Ireland because the union withdrew agreement to short crewing worldwide. We couldn't cover Beirut. We couldn't cover Belfast. We couldn't cover any dangerous zone for a whole year. And this was a major ITV current affairs international reporting program stymied because of a dispute between the union and a company over insurance rates.

The union also has very strict regulations about special filming requests we might have, such as black technicians working in films about black people, or women technicians working on films about abortions say. More importantly the unions can attack you at any time through blacking films in the pursuit of any particular industrial dispute that they might have. You are constantly at risk as a result of disputes that may arise between union and management. Now I happen to be a member of the ACTT for the reason that I couldn't work at ITV if I wasn't a member of it. And I've been a national negotiator and spent a lot of time on a lot of subjects for the union. But I think it's a very incompetent and unorganized and ill-run union which makes serious mistakes,and which makes life for a current affairs outfit very difficult.

A lot of that has to do with the historic bad relations between management and unions in ITV. And I have no doubt that "This Week" as a program would be infinitely better off as an independent organization simply contracted by the IBA to produce a half-hour current affairs program every week, which is what we're doing. That way it would be isolated from all the union-management disputes that go on about crewing, studios, hours, whatever it may be.

For instance, another union called NATTKE, the National Association of something or other—mainly scene men, props men, projectionists and so on—demanded that all Thames film locations be accompanied by one of their members as a driver irrespective of whether he was needed. Irrespective of whether he would be an embarrassment on certain locations where we already had such a large crew that you couldn't actually get enough hotel accommodations for all the people that had to go with you. And "This Week" was threatened with blacking by that union because the company wouldn't negotiate a system whereby "This Week" would automatically have to take NATTKE drivers. We were vulnerable at that level.

130

The union also puts immense pressure on the program simply through bad practices which have become institutionalized. I always have the problem with being caught between company and management, on money. I keep trying to persuade the management to give "This Week" more money to make better and more interesting programs. The company's rolling in money. It's embarrassed by the amount of money it takes in on advertising. But it won't give more money to "This Week" than say inflation allows. This is partly because so much money is wasted by restrictive practices of the union. For instance, all air travel beyond a thousand miles has to be first class— a union restriction which simply soaks up the budget. There are immense penalty payments for working before seven AM, working after midnight, working without a proper lunch break, working without a ten-hour break between the end of one session and the start of the next.

The journalists who are breaking their backs trying to piece together what might be a very complicated political story are constantly hassled by technicians who are claiming union rates, union hours, etc. Now this of course is a worldwide phenomenon in the industrialized countries. But it makes life misery for what otherwise would be very effective and very good journalism. And I see no way out of it. It's very exhausting, very debilitating, and the one thing that I'll be glad to be shut of when I get off producing "This Week" in a few months' time will be all that idiotic, unnecessary, pointless aggravation which comes from bad labor relations.

# 5

# *The Man Alive Reports*
## Michael Latham

*Michael Latham was born in Winnipeg and before entering television was a journalist, film critic and broadcaster. An urbane man in his mid-forties, he looks like a comfortable and pleasant family lawyer. Appearances deceive, as Latham is one of the most experienced BBC documentarists around. He learned "the trade," as he calls it, in outside broadcasting. "It was football on Saturday—Church services on Sunday—and riots on Monday. Whatever they wanted, you did."*

*Later he moved on to feature documentaries, producing the first programs in the classic BBC-2 science series "Horizon". He was also Editor\* of "Tomorrow's World" on BBC-1 for three years, producing during that time* Barnard Faces His Critics *and* British Heart Transplant Special.

*Between 1973 and 1975 Latham produced "The Explorers" (screened in the U.S. under the title "Ten Who Dared"). "Explorers" was a drama documentary series which investigated not just geographical explorers like Pizarro and Columbus but also people who probed ideas like Von Humboldt. It was an excellent series and remains, along with another British series "The Search for the Nile," in a class of its own.*

*Currently Latham is Editor of the weekly "The Man Alive Reports." This is a series of documentary reports covering the general British social and political scene with occasional forays abroad. Along with "This Week" and "Panorama" it is part of the standard viewing of anyone in England who is even mildly interested in the current scene.*

*In the talk with Latham I tended to press television coverage of the Irish question and the prison scene as these were two topics that interested me very much. Afterwards I looked up the six-month program coverage from January to June 1977 to see what else the program had done. Topics included marriage and divorce in the U.S., problems of North Sea oil, colored immigrants, professional boxing, the Gary Gilmore case and a strike of British automobile workers.*

\*In England the term "Program Editor" is equivalent to the American use of "Executive Producer" and occasionally "Producer."

*"Man Alive" is a well-made, hard-driving program but, as Latham points out, this kind of program lacks both the money and time to do really investigative journalism. Money problems have in fact been acute (as all over the BBC) and in recent years more and more programming has had to be done in the studios rather than on film. However, in spite of these difficulties "Man Alive" still remains one of the best programs on the BBC today.*

Q. What kind of subjects were you covering in the early "Man Alive" series?

A. Do you remember the Great Train Robbery? Some of the robbers were caught and went to jail and then they started jumping over walls and escaping. For one of the "Man Alive" programs we decided to find out where one of them had gone, and also try to locate some of the missing money. Since half of the police in the world were doing the same thing our chances of actually finding anything were minimal. Except that one used the ground rules of the kind of journalism that we were fairly good at—you got yourself some good underworld contacts. We did just that, and in circumstances that I won't go into here we found one of the escaped robbers hiding away in England. In order to get the story we had to use hidden cameras and planted radio mikes. In those days it was all entirely acceptable. Now, of course, it isn't. Like a newspaper journalist you followed the story to the bitter end, but instead of coming back with a notebook full of stuff, you came back with film rushes and then made your films.

Q. What were your areas of concern in those days? How was "Man Alive" differentiated from "This Week" or "World in Action"?

A. Both of them were doing things quite differently. "World in Action" has always followed its own investigative path. We were trying to make documentary *stories*, rather than taking issues and trying to find out who was right and who was wrong. We wanted the viewer to observe and then make up his own mind. Occasionally we did do the investigative story but by today's standard they weren't really investigations.

It was a relaxed and freewheeling time. In that first year of "Man Alive" I made fifteen films all over the world. One day we said, "Let's go to America and do something. We'll buy around-the-world tickets. We'll get a story set up in America so that we've got a guaranteed start and then we'll continue around the world and pick up other stories as we go, sending them back with cutting orders and linking commentary on tape." And that's what happened. We made a film about the Duke

133

of Edinburgh's first visit to America. Then we moved on to Hong Kong, Australia, Fiji, and so on. It was an exciting time to work in British television.

Then Aubrey Singer, who was then running what was to become BBC-TV's Features Group, said one day "Why don't you use these techniques to do something really worthwhile?" So along with Gordon Thomas I researched and set up a film about a woman who had just discovered she had an awful brain tumor. She was going to have an operation and she thought she would die. We lived with her and her family over a ten-day period before she went to hospital. Would she live? Would she die? What did the situation do to the family? Mum-in-law came to look after the kids. That's all it was about. It worked well, because by that time we'd learned how to shoot *vérité* well. We'd learned how to handle the long take and the walking track. We'd learned how to work in very, very low light conditions. We'd learned a lot of things. Most of all we'd learned how to keep the technical side of the film making from swamping the subject. The film won prizes all over the world and then one day I got a telephone call from Huw Wheldon who was at the Monaco festival and said, "They've voted the woman the best actress." I said, "Well, you better stop them fast. It's all for real."

Q. One of the questions that concerns me is responsibility to the person you're interviewing, or who's involved in your program. If you're doing a story for a newspaper the person's name is mentioned, but they're not seen, they're not heard, they're not felt. It's always seemed to me that in film there's a much greater responsibility because that person is very fully in front of the screen, is totally recognized and has to live with the story afterwards. Did you have any problems with that going from print journalism into film journalism? Were there specific occasions when you were confronted exactly with that kind of problem? I would have thought, for example, the film of the woman with the tumor would have brought up all kinds of questions like that.

A. Fortunately, she didn't die, because it would have been an appalling film had she done so. One even might not have been able to show it. But for me it's not a theoretical ethical problem, it's a straight human problem. By the time you've met somebody and decided to make a film with them you have built a relationship based on mutual trust. That's the only way you can do it. Otherwise they're going to be embarrassed every time you turn over the camera. That trust is based on the earliest conversations with them. They want to know everything. And if they're normal, average human beings they are flattered by your attention but they actually don't want to take part. Why should anyone want to take their underpants off in public? You have first of all to try to convince them that you're trustworthy, that if at the end of the day you have film which will be damaging to them if it is seen in public, you will be very careful not to cause that damage to them. You might even let them see it and decide along with them. Let me make it clear that I'm talking about people who, but for the film, would remain private individuals for the rest of their lives. I'm not talking about politicians or other public figures.

Q. Do you in fact normally do this? Let participants see what you've filmed?

A. When you're dealing with the sort of social and intensely personal problem like the woman with the brain tumor, of course. We followed her into the operating theater and filmed the operation, intercutting with what was going on in the home where her family waited. Later we showed it to her and her husband. They sat and wept because they were reliving something whose emotional intensity they had forgotten. You always forget pain. We made one small cut, that's all. And it was a cut requested by the husband because in a moment of stress his mother, the woman's mother-in-law, had said something rather unkind about the wife who was in hospital. It didn't make any real difference to the film, so we cut it out.

Q. There have been vast social changes in England, in the sixties and in the seventies. How have they affected the programs you are trying to do?

A. Let me put it this way, as far as social documentaries are concerned. In the sixties, when people were being shot to the moon we seemed to be on the verge of a new kind of age and the programs one tended to do questioned everything very hard. Very hard indeed. The reason you did a program was because you wanted to observe something closely that otherwise might be glossed over. That's why people did programs questioning the validity of sending people up into space. Shouldn't we be spending the money elsewhere? Politically naive, but that's why people were doing that sort of program. Nowadays things are harder and though nobody's got a lot of money the gulf between the haves and the have-nots is more marked. Because of this the tendency now is to make programs about social injustices and social issues that would be an absolute downright disgrace to ignore.

For instance, look at the programs we've done in the last two or three series of "Man Alive Reports." When Dr. Sheila Cassidy came out of Chile we were the first people to pick her up and get her onto television

135

in this country. She faced people our researchers had found who said she was a liar. That led to an explosive 50-minute live program. We did a program about people who suddenly, after years of protesting about motorway building policies, got fed up and began taking things into their own hands. Now that's a small parochial issue in one sense, but the program seemed to tap a vein of common feeling and it was followed by a wave of protest about road building policies throughout the country.

We did a program about people who believe they see things going wrong where they work—and they try and get things changed, and they get fired as a result. We were sued for that. We did a program which resulted in an enormous argument in the studio about whether or not new legislation in Britain which demands that in certain circumstances you must join a union is right and proper. Another program was about people who steal from their places of work.

Q. Can you tell me about the way these programs would be prepared, researched, and your timing and financing of them?

A. The "Man Alive Report" is structured around an editor, which is me, four or five producers and four or five assistant producers. Any one of these individuals can make a program. When somebody walks through that door and says I'd like to do a program about this or that— we talk about it for five minutes, no more because it's only a gleam in the eye at this stage. If I want to go ahead he's got five days, one working week, to go out and see whether it stands up. If it doesn't stand up it will probably take him only a day and a half to find that out. After five days he may return to tell me that research for the program idea about shrimps, say, has revealed a much better story about herrings. Now I'm faced with a totally new situation. I thought I was buying shrimps and now it's herrings. So we talk about herrings for a while and he's got another five days to see whether herrings is really going to make a worthwhile program. Except in the most extraordinary circumstances, two weeks is all we can afford to spend on the research state.

Around here the cheapest commodity, thank God, is "the idea." So after a fortnight if I agree that the idea is worth putting into production I assign a reporter on the story (later on there may be another one added). I also assign a producer who's going to make sure things run properly, and who is also going to have a hell of a lot to say editorially during the making of it. There will also be a production assistant, a secretary, and the original researcher on the team. The average program takes about another three weeks to make and then you're on the air. So the average is a five to six week turnaround.

There are exceptions. A member of the team reported one day that there was a suggestion going round that some long-term inmates in some British prisons were being fed drugs to keep them controlled and placid. The tip-off wasn't very reliable but it was worth looking into. After a week's work the producer-researcher came back and said "I'm not totally certain but I think one of the prisoners, who claims to have been drugged up to his eye balls, is about to be released. If we hang on a while we can pick him up when he comes out of jail and see if the story is worth anything."

That's what we did about a month later. The prisoner turned out to be unreliable, possibly psychotic, certainly very ill. At that stage I hired a guy who had spent half his life in jail to tell me whether one informer was speaking the truth. The advice was: "Well, he *thinks* he's speaking the truth." So we took it from there.

By that time we were way over both the research and the production period. We were also into terrific budget problems and that, incidentally, is why investigative journalism doesn't actually exist in television. Investigative journalism presupposes that you are going to throw away years of work if you're not getting anywhere. When people generally talk to you about investigative journalism they're usually talking about material and stories that present themselves by luck.

Anyway the producer began digging and eventually made contact with the Home Office which controls the prisons. We had long meetings with them and they said they would help in any way they could. By this time we had amassed a lot of so-called evidence from ex-prisoners—a lot of it hearsay. But there were other straightforward cases that turned up in research where people claimed very clearly to have been given drugs in prison. When the Home Office learned that we were likely to use these cases they withdrew all support overnight. We lost prison governers. We lost medical officers. We lost everybody who said they would take part. It took another two months to persuade them to come back in, with the Home Office apparently resisting the whole idea of the program every inch of the way. In the end we got on the air with a former Home Secretary, a former Chief Prison Medical Officer, and a former Prison Governor. In other words, with participants who were no longer answerable to the Home Office. It caused a hell of a row, as you can imagine. So we'd taken four months to make the program. Expensive—but worth it.

Q. There has been some discussion recently of a former permissive era in the BBC being supplanted by a more restrictive era. Is that true? If so, has it caused any changes in the style and nature of your programs?

A. I think that when you actually get down to it, the freedoms that you're talking about as a producer are very much of your own making—as are the shackles. If you're making a film and you believe that it's important and valid, but you're afraid that someone may rap your knuckles, and because of that you start your own private self-censoring campaign, then that's your bloody problem, nobody else's. If you look around the place at those people who make programs carefully and honestly you will find they are more concerned about their programs and their audiences than they are about so-called censorship. In my experience it's usually the second-rate or inexperienced producer who frets over the idea of censorship.

Q. There's one BBC instruction book—I think it's sometimes referred to as "the green book"—that seems to lay down certain ground rules for making documentaries. One of the key things in it is the necessity for objectivity and balance. Those are marvellous words, but what do they mean and how possible has it been to obtain those objectives in your programs?

A. I actually got rid of somebody working around here because he demanded to make a program from such a politically committed point of view that he had ceased to be a usable journalist. He was being totally unprofessional. The basic rules of journalism *must* be applied to television documentary. If you get one side of the story you must check it and then get the other side. That doesn't mean to say you don't have a personal point of view. It just means that your point of view is irrelevant when you're collecting the material. Now when you cut film and you put one shot up against another that's when you start facing problems of subjectivity and objectivity. Because, as you very well know, very often you can put two sequences together because they work dramatically, but whether they are an accurate account of what happened is another matter. And that's when the individual producer has to come to terms with being a professional documentary man. All the green book did was to present the ground rules for newcomers as seen by people who'd been working at the BBC for some time. Whether one took notice of the book or not was up to the individual.

Q. When you're doing a film abroad for "Man Alive" in a situation that you know comparatively little about, how do you go about the process of checking your story, seeing that you're only on the spot for a few days or for a week, and that you yourselves as reporters haven't got in-depth experience of that situation?

A. Well, we've just been making a film about a prison on the east coast of the United States where the lifers, pretty tough men who are in for ninety-nine years for murder or rape, are used to scare the be-

138

jesus out of young offenders who keep getting into trouble with the police. Whether it's good psychology or not I don't know, but it's a damn good story. And so we said, great we'll do it. But we'll check it first with our New York office. We've got people who live there and know the scene. They came back to say the story existed but it wasn't new. It just happened not to have been done before. We were told that the lifers had their own office, and their own telephone.

So I rang the number I was given and a voice said "Lifer's office," and I was speaking to a guy who was in jail for ninety-nine years. I said we'd like to make a film about what they were doing. And he said, "I can fit you in but I've got a very busy diary. I've got to see a judge who's coming and I've got to see some social workers." It was like talking to the president of the United States. Finally he said that he would see us about three and a half weeks from then and only then. So we went and we're now cutting the film. But by the time we got there we knew that in a sense these weren't ordinary prisoners. So the original story idea, which was about ordinary prisoners setting young kids right, was not accurate. These were men, perhaps unusual men, with privileges outside the experience of ordinary prisoners.

Q. The obvious political problem recently has been the Catholic-Protestant troubles in Northern Ireland. At the beginning of this year you did a major program on Northern Ireland. Can you tell me about the circumstances surrounding that?

A. We did a program about the peace people and it was transmitted about six months after the peace movement had been formed. What it was going to try to do was to assess the importance of the movement, as distinct from its headline-getting significance. The peace women were nonpolitical, and had no political axe to grind. It would have been suicide to appear to be anything else at that time. Research showed up some remarkable personalities and some very brave people, and we talked at length about the kind of film we were going to make.

It seemed to me the best thing to do was to have two crews, two directors, two reporters. One crew would cover the Catholic side of the story, the other the Protestant side. That would avoid the problem of crossing both the physical and political boundaries. After all, if you were talking to a Catholic yesterday am I going to trust you today if I'm a Protestant, or vice versa. Can I trust you? Each night each crew briefed the other on what had happened and the shape the story was taking.

What we discovered was that the peace movement was also running an escape organization. At that time nobody knew that. We discovered this by pure chance at a secret meeting we were invited to attend with people arriving under cover of darkness. Somebody started talking and it began to sound like a sequence out of a rather bad film about the French resistance in 1944. People getting out of the country through an underground escape network. They were getting out IRA provisionals who didn't actually want to fight any more, but if they stopped fighting they'd become targets for their own organization. So their families and they were being spirited away.

Now that was a marvelous journalistic scoop. The question was what were we going to do with it. We had marvelous sequences on film but to show it could blow the entire escape network. On the other hand if we didn't use it what were we in the business for anyway? I decided that we either did it properly or were not going to do it at all. Doing it properly meant that we had to get the peace people's cooperation. We stopped filming for a day and the producer spent hours talking with the peace people. They agreed that eventually the story was bound to get out because people simply don't keep their mouths shut forever. They said if we would hang on for six to eight weeks they would help us. If not, we'd better get out. There was no question of us getting out. In fact, they told us everything they were going to do, and they announced news of the escape network within days of transmission of our film, which was just fine for us.

Q. Why on earth would people in such a delicate situation put their trust in you, an unknown person from the BBC? And were there any pressures from the police to pass on to them any information which you'd obtained in making the film?

A. No. No pressures at all. We had cooperation from everyone. We even did interviews with people in a pub whom we subsequently learned were UDA assassins.

Q. Why do you think so many people talked?

A. I suspect a lot of people in Belfast knew about the escape route, but newspapers hadn't found out yet. When we stumbled upon it we were being tested. Could we be trusted? When all is said, earning that trust was more important to us than a news story. And when we in fact kept our mouths shut that was the moment when everybody started trusting us quite a bit more than they had.

Q. I gather there's now utter rejection by journalists and photographers about going to film in Northern Ireland. Was this a recent instance or was this already in existence when you were filming?

A. Well, not utter rejection, but I'll tell you that film was a pig to make. I think we used four different crews. We couldn't get people to go to Northern Ireland. Mention Northern Ireland at that time and it was a switch off. Many crews would not go. We found that we had to use free-lance crews—that is, non-BBC crews—for more than half the time, but in the end used the local BBC crew in Belfast.

Q. One of the comments made on news documentaries is that the very presence of the film crew tends to provoke a certain amount of action. Did this happen to you?

A. I know exactly what you mean. And it can and does. We have all had experience of this, but it didn't happen on that film. The big fracas we were filming was a punchup that was preordained. We knew it was bound to happen and it did. It didn't happen only where our crew was—it happened all the way around that area. Yes, of course, when one looks at rushes of that sort of material, one turns to the director to ask, "How much of that was caused by our presence?" But here I don't think it was true.

Q. "Man Alive" has changed its format slightly the last year or so. Much more is being done in the studio. Why did you make those changes?

A. The reason was that we simply couldn't afford to go on making the kind of films we had been making. So we were forced to rethink our approach or risk disappearing into an overdraft. We were all film makers, as you know. There were only two people here, apart from myself, who had experience in studio documentary. We sat down and we talked about what we could do and after half a day of going around in circles somebody said "Let's face it. We're all scared, we're terrified of the damned studio." And we all pretty well agreed, with embarrassed shuffles, that this was probably what the real problem was about. It wasn't making programs in a studio, it was dealing with our own fears of a studio. And we realized this was also a fear of participants, and we should have to reckon with it in our studio presentation.

I then talked to many people, including psychologists, about why people are scared of television. If you stick a microphone in somebody's face they're likely to dry up and go cold. Why? Because of momentary insecurity. Because of a sudden feeling that you won't live up to your image of yourself. For some people a television studio is a bit like an operating theater with a brain operation in full swing.

So we had to create a studio that wasn't like that—not just for our benefit, but also for the sake of our participants. After a lot of advice we came up with two simple concepts: the first was to get people into the show rather early; the second was to give them protection. And the protection had to be physical. We were told that it was no coincidence that people become garrulous when they're drinking in a bar. It's because they feel physically protected by the bar itself. And they talk.

We couldn't supply the alcohol because unfortunately it's not allowed in the studio but we built a set which was based on the principle of a bar. That way people could lean on their elbows even when they were sitting. We had to make a lot of adjustments, and then it worked.

We bring people in anything up to an hour and a half before we go on the air for a live transmission. We serve coffee and sandwiches and have a serving bar built into the set which you can't see on the screen. When they arrive they all whisper because the place is so big it's a little like walking into a cathedral.

For an hour they drink coffee, eat sandwiches, begin to talk and eventually the voice levels begin to rise. When it gets to about cocktail party level that is the moment for the studio lights to come up—very, very slowly. And then the lights are on and nobody's really noticed it. Then we start cleaning up the coffee cups and people are led gently to their opening positions. And when it's all working you slide onto the air. There's none of this: "Stand by! We're going on the air."

It works astonishingly well. We've discovered how to interview ordinary people and make them feel as easy and relaxed as if they were in their own homes, or almost as relaxed. We are getting the sort of material you associate with *filmed* documentary, not the rather stiff interview of the live television studio. And that is the fundamental basis of our new success.

*Television Documentary*

# 6
## The British Empire
### Tom Haydon

*In 1976 I spent four very happy months teaching documentary at the Australian National Film School. Professor Jerzy Toeplitz headed the school and had assembled under him a group of teachers which included some of the best film makers in Australia such as Storry Walton and Bill Fitzwater. Also much in evidence was a lanky long-haired fellow with a perpetual quizzical grin, whom I used to see propping up the odd corner. This was Tom Haydon who gradually became friend, mentor, instructor in Australiana, and drinking companion.*

*Haydon, Walton, and Fitzwater had been the leading stars of the Australian Broadcasting Commission in the mid-sixties. All had succumbed to the Colonial itch and come to London and Earl's Court, and all three had worked for the BBC with remarkable success. And all three had returned to Sydney to try and inject something into an Australian television scene increasingly overwhelmed (at least in the ABC) with petty bureaucracy and political restrictions.*

*While at the school I saw a lot of Haydon's films. They were for the most part models of film making, involving every style and technique from vérité to drama documentary. They were also full of a wit and humor very characteristic of Tom himself. But beyond the technical brilliance, which could sometimes be too good and slightly off-putting, there was often a saving compassion and involvement.*

*Haydon started in television as a trainee producer with the ABC in 1961. Most of his early films were made for the schools' programs, the University of the Air, or the ABC Science Unit on areas like soil erosion and wild life. These were seemingly not the most dynamic of subjects but Haydon infused them with a freshness that brought national acclaim.*

*One of his main interests has been anthropology. In his hour documentary* The Talgai Skull *(ABC 1968) he traced the story and historic implications of a skull found in Queensland in 1886. In* The Long Walkabout *(ABC and BBC 1973) he returned to anthropology to trace the origins and prehistory of the Aborigines, creating a marvellous detective story out of the events.*

*The film that brought Haydon to the attention of the BBC was* Dig a Million, Make a Million *(ABC 1969). This was an exploration of iron mining in Australia and the wheeling and dealing of multinational corporations like*

*Rio Tinto Zinc and Kaiser Steel. On the strength of that film Haydon was offered a short term BBC contract that led eventually to his involvement in "The British Empire."*

*"Empire" was a high-budget prestige series of thirteen films on the history of the British Empire. The series covered three centuries, ranged over most of the world, and used a variety of techniques including straight documentary, dramatic reconstruction, and animation. Though it appeared a "safe" series it excited considerable controversy and was heavily criticized by both the extreme left and the extreme right—no simple achievement!*

*The quality of the individual films, made by four different directors, varies from the outstanding to the banal. Some of the more farcical historical reconstructions such as that of the Indian Mutiny were particularly scored by the British press. To add to the controversy and difficulties an underground BBC pamphlet alleged special Time-Life influences on the programs.*

*My interest this time was in trying to understand the complexity of the creation of such a series. I wanted to know about guiding lines, interconnections, the power of the individual producer in relation to the series producer, and so on. All these questions were answered by Haydon during a couple of evenings in his London apartment.*

*Haydon himself did three films for the series:* Oh! the Jubilee, Beyond the Black Stump, *and* The Gift of Endless Dreams. Jubilee *(screened January 1972) was the opening film of the series and centered on the Diamond Jubilee of Queen Victoria in 1897. Writing about it in the* Guardian *Nancy Banks-Smith said: "I don't suppose there is any point in walking around the word. The episode was superb."*

Beyond the Black Stump *was an exploration of the Australian character. It dramatized the story of the Jolly Swagman and Eureka Stockade and went on to explore contemporary life in the outback.*

*Writer Elkan Allan called it "the best British Empire program yet." Other comments were less favorable. The Australian expatriate community was divided, with many feeling very insulted. An emotional correspondence raged for some weeks in the* Times, *and Haydon himself was badly criticized in the House of Lords. Meanwhile an Australian newspaper ran the headline: "With friends like Haydon who needs enemies."*

The Gift of Endless Dreams *was Haydon's last film in the series and possibly his best. It relates the rise of the British in the Far East and continues with the story of Singapore and its fall to the Japanese in 1942. It is the most moving and human of the three films and full of a compassion and human understanding too often missing from the series.*

*At the moment Haydon commutes between Sydney and London. His major films since 1972 include* Skipper Pitts Goes to War *about the British-Icelandic cod war,* Epitaph to a Friendship *(1974) about Russell Braddon, and* The Last Tasmanian *(1978).*

146

Q. How free was it within the ABC at the time you started?

A. The ABC then was making a fairly brave effort at being a kind of colonial child of the BBC. I remember at the time, however, feeling very cramped in the ABC and feeling the strictures of bureaucracy and so on. But when I compare the ABC that I knew then with the ABC that I have come to see and experience ten years or more on, I recognize that it had certain qualities then that have quite disappeared since. At least at that stage there was a certain *caring* about things. There was a certain concern for at least getting techniques right. The first few years of my working life were spent just trying to learn the nuts and bolts. I was working on educational programs for schools and adult educational programs. This gave me an excellent chance to learn. And people seemed to care.

However, the overwhelming feeling was of belonging to a blinkered, limited organization. I was actually accused by one head of a department at the ABC of being "a film maker." This was actually a criticism, and a very strong one, because I suppose I should have been a "broadcaster," or shall we say "a professional officer of the organization," not a film maker. All the pressure of the organization was bending you towards something very bureaucratic, very much like being in a government department. There was a faded BBC sort of sense of holding responsibility toward the community, and so on—protocol and procedures. You had to fight to be creative and the whole current was against you. All this tended to make you very careful. It trained you to think and prove each position you took, especially if you were in any way going to be outlandish.

I remember an amazing case of this when I did a film dealing with mining, *Dig a Million, Make a Million*. This was a kind of exposé of the power of overseas finance, which was at that time turning Australia into a great big open cut mine and taking the profits away for the overseas companies. When I made that film, which was done fairly conservatively and relied on a lot of innuendo, the print had to be "lost" in the laboratory in the week before we went into the air, lest certain members of the Commission (the governing body of the ABC), who were on the Melbourne stock exchange, might demand to see it. There was also concern that the government might actually cut the ABC's budget, because it was a film highly critical in some ways of government, and so on. That was the kind of situation you operated in.

Q. You told me some while ago that a documentary director has a responsibility to the person appearing in his film. In *Dig a Million, Make a Million* there are many members of big English mining companies, Lord this and Lord that, who come out as rather caricature figures. Do you think you were being fair to them?

A. I think actually I was being scrupulously fair. When I arrived in London to film Sir Val Duncan, who was then head of the Rio Tinto Zinc Corporation, England's largest and richest mining corporation, we were rushed into his rather plush room. Sir Val Duncan then told me what we would do. He told me what he would say and what I should ask him, and he walked up and down his carpet, rehearsing all his lines and told me the kind of questions I could put to him. So I did just exactly what he said, more or less. And what we captured on film, in terms of himself, and also many of the other people, they themselves were very happy with.

It was an extraordinary situation. On the one hand, here was a film where some of the audience, people like you, felt the people on the film were portrayed as caricatures and you laughed at them. At the same time, Sir Val Duncan bought a dozen prints of the film for the company to show to the trainee executives who joined RTZ. The point I am making is that there is a way in which people are happy with themselves if they are shown just the way they are. They do not see themselves as funny or as caricatures. I think this is the aspect of documentary which in its ultimate sense I find the most beguiling.

Now when I talk about the documentary maker having to be fair to his people, to the people in his films, I mean he should be fair to present them as they themselves are prepared to be presented. If he takes advantage of something that occurs when they are off guard, or takes advantage of getting them on a very bad day, perhaps, or exploits people who are not too aware of the fact that he is filming them—things of that kind—then I think you are entering into very serious questions of misrepresentation. But there is a whole world of people, in fact a whole set of attitudes and behavior which is absolutely normal and absolutely acceptable to the people themselves, but seems strange and funny to you and me.

Q. How did you get involved in "The British Empire"?

A. I had come to England in 1968 to do some scenes for *Dig a Million* and was well received by the BBC, who'd bought my film *The Talgai Skull*. I met Noble Wilson who was then chief assistant to Aubrey Singer in features, and Noble said, "Do you have any particular ideas?" I said, "It sounds silly, but ever since I was a student I have thought it would be splendid to do some great television series on the decline and fall of the British Empire." Noble then got me to meet Max Morgan-Witts who took me to his office and showed me a wall map of the world, on which he'd divided the empire into four parts. Evidently he was looking for someone who would be producer for that part which included Australasia. He said he had liked my film *The*

*Talgai Skull*. So that began what was virtually an offer at that stage. But nothing was definite. Nothing was signed and I went back to Australia to finish *Dig a Million*.

Q. Were you given three programs from the start?

A. Yes. Max used to write me letters and gradually the project was starting to come together. Max said that it looked like I might be able to do two or three programs, and they firmed up once I got over here. I was very fortunate, because two other departments were also offering me work, and I suppose a bit of bargaining went on. I did not realize till long after that in fact the producer positions for *The British Empire* had been much coveted within the BBC and that there had been a great deal of juggling among all sorts of people trying to get into them, and here was I, come from the antipodes, and had secured one of the posts. But all of that kind of background was a total blank to me.

Q. When you came in was John Terraine still the script writer and what happened between John Terraine and the producers?

A. Yes, John Terraine was the script editor, that was his function, always had been. He had been signed up some months before. There was a rather strange structure. There was the editor, Max Morgan-Witts, the script editor John Terraine, and then there were four producers.

Now the four producers, of which I was one, had been told by Max that we would have control over our own programs. We were not being employed simply as directors. However, during the period of two months or so before the producers joined, there had been a series of intense script conferences, wherein John Terraine, Max, and others had developed a whole set of detailed outlines, which all landed on our desks the day after we joined. We were then to be given just enough time to read these things, to assimilate them, and then go on to the next step and go off to do reconnaissance for the films and so on.

The producers responded adversely to this. They felt they had been misled in terms of what their role was to be. When this was put to Max, he said the producers of course were right and of course they were in charge of their programs, and John Terraine would be subordinated. But according to John Terraine, when we each had discussions with him, he had been told the opposite by Max. There was a certain kind of, shall we say, confusion.

It also became clear that we were going to work according to a production system which gave us, as producers, very little room for initiative. According to this original set of treatments, the programs were carefully linked together to follow one after the other, and each program would include film shot in different parts of what had been the

Empire. This meant that each producer would be contributing film to a number of programs besides his own. Max coined the term "father-figure producer." Each of us would be a father figure of a program where we would be in charge of editing, but we would each of us also be doing bits and pieces that would go into everyone else's program as well. You would not have any one program, where one producer-director was shooting, shaping and editing the whole thing. This bothered us very much, because it seemed impractical.

Q. What was then conceived of as the guiding line of the series?

A. The notion was that we would go around the Empire to locations where things had happened and we would try to bring to life the events of the past without any full scale dramatization. This places a great premium on personal imagination in directing the shooting so as to interweave it with old photographs and paintings.

The business of trying to achieve what I've described by a scissors and paste method, undertaken by an assortment of individuals, working on their own in different parts of the world—well, we really doubted it. Maybe this kind of film could have worked if archival film existed, but for the most part it didn't. So, as producers we began very much to doubt that the series would work as originally conceived.

Q. Some of the films in the series are good, some are very indifferent. What often seems to be lacking is a point of view. What was the unifying theme, if any, in Terraine's original script outline?

A. A somewhat *Boys' Own Annual* view of the Empire that Baden Powell would possibly have liked: that the Empire had been a great thing, that the Empire had always been progressing towards a great British Commonwealth of white nations. The story of the blacks and coloreds did not matter nearly as much, that side of the Empire was just an accident of history, and Australia, New Zealand, Canada, and hopefully South Africa and Rhodesia were the great achievement. This was a story full of heroes and the achievements of heroes. This seemed to most of us to be a dated and distorted view of the Empire, but perhaps it was also a view of the Empire shared by a certain proportion of the public. It rather represented the old-fashioned liberal view of the Empire as white man's burden and doing good to the natives, and progressive material achievement.

Q. When you finally got together with Max Morgan-Witts what were the guidelines that he finally gave you when he allowed you, for the most part, to write and direct your own programs? What were the guiding lines as far as you saw them?

A. They were very loose. By that stage, after the wholesale revision initiated by the producers, the programs had become essentially geographically based. For example, I was doing one on the Far East. The principal guideline concern was that we should try to start and finish each program at certain points in time so that we would have some kind of connection both to the previous and the next episode. There was very little in the guidelines that dealt with basic thematic approach or point of view. Max actually presented us with a document, "We shall neither praise nor blame, we shall neither say it was good or bad," and so on. There was very little that was *positive* in terms of a guideline or an approach.

On the question of method and style, there had been a lot of talk about playing it straight without dramatization. Then, just a few weeks prior to the main shooting commencing, we were all told that in fact we should consider utilizing dramatization. This idea was strongly supported by Max's superiors who were concerned lest the series might not have the desired "color" and impact and so on which they were so anxious about, since this was the BBC's first major co-production with American Time-Life.

I don't want to be unfair to anyone but most of us went off to shooting with a confused sense of what the guidelines were. The Indian programs had fallen upon especially difficult times because the original producer and the BBC had parted company and India had also said the BBC could not go there, and the new producer was necessarily having to get the thing together at the last minute and by incredible ingenuity in view of the ban. So none of us had much idea of what was going to be in the India programs and India of course was *the* central core of the Empire story. I remember standing one day on a beach in Malacca and looking across the Bay of Bengal, wishing I had some vague idea of what my colleague might be thinking of doing in India. Whatever he was doing had to be kept secret because of this ban in India. We were like a number of people being shot off in different directions to keep up to a schedule which was perhaps unrealistic, given the uncertainties we were facing. I think one of the things that "The British Empire" series revealed more than anything else was a lack of adequate communication within the BBC between hierarchy and producer.

Q. What in fact was your schedule and what were the budgets of these films?

A. Schedule? The total period originally was something under two years and in fact it extended almost to two and a half for the whole series. It was worked out very carefully in advance, the idea being that we would go through a succession of meetings, and then each producer would go off on a three months' reconnaissance trip to his part of the Empire to be followed by a carefully planned shooting period.

The trouble with this scheme was that it assumed that the scripts, or at least the notions of what the series was to be about, were all well worked out before the schedule began. Because of the disagreement between the producers and John Terraine, this was not to be the case. So when everyone went off, there were still no notions or script ideas sorted out, and yet the schedule had to go on relentlessly.

One reason for the schedule being fairly inflexible was because of the co-production arrangement with Time-Life. There was no content influence by the Americans on the series (though many English people thought otherwise) but there was influence in terms of schedule. The first of our programs had to go to air at the same time as the first issue was published of the two-year weekly magazine series which Time-Life was to produce in conjunction with our films. The first published issue had to come out in February, so come hell or high water, that is when we had to go to air.

Q. So you were researching without a script and without a guideline?

A. Yes, about the most anybody could do before the reconnaissance, was to arrange the reconnaissance logistics such as plane trips, hotels, local contacts, and government permissions.

Q. When did you work out the lines and thrust of the three programs you eventually did, and how far did you have to coordinate your line with Max Morgan-Witts?

A. Initially, I tried my damnedest, in conjunction with some of the other producers, to work out some kind of overall coordinated approach. Most of all we argued for time. Give us some time so that we can all just sit here, see each other and work it out. We managed actually to hold a conference after a great deal of argument that was not necessary, in between the reconnaissance trips and the shoots. We met at the Hurlingham Club on the banks of the Thames and there, around the table, again with precious little time, we pushed through the outlines for the scenes. I remember feeling it was totally pointless trying to work internally within each of my programs without having some sense of the overall theme and shape.

For example, there was such an immense mass of material in say, the story of the British in the Far East. There was no way you could tell the whole story of the British in the Far East, in China, in Hong Kong, Malaya, from the seventeenth century through to the fall of Singapore, in one fifty-five-minute program. And what I found there were naturally *all* the elements of the Empire. Just as in Africa or India you found there district commissioners, governors, planters, all these things. What was I to choose? It seemed to me it would have been marvellous if I could have known, for example, whether the India man was going to concentrate on district commissioners? If so, then maybe in Malaya I could neglect them and concentrate instead on the planters. There was no sound basis for selection because you had no idea of what anyone else was going to do. So in the end you came back thinking, I have somehow within each of my programs to tell the whole story which is in that place.

I remember a meeting with the other producers somewhere near the end of the first twelve months. We were discussing whether we should all pull out and let the series go into limbo and take whatever uncomfortable consequences might occur, or whether each producer should just try and make his own program as well as he could. And that's how it turned out for me, in effect three "one-off" programs.

It was the same with the others. We wanted to change the title from "The British Empire" with its implications of a comprehensive unified series to "Echoes of Britannia's Rule." "Echoes" would have suggested a series of individual essays. I believe that would have been more honest and would have settled the objections of some of the critics.

Q. Your program, *Oh! the Jubilee*, started off the series. What were some of the ideas you played around with originally, and how many of these ideas got into the finished film?

A. The brief for this program was to utilize Queen Victoria's Diamond Jubilee in 1897 as a way of encapsulating the British sense of empire, at its high noon point in the nineteenth century. The moment I got into researching it, I realized that the Jubilee had been a facade—a way for people to convince themselves that everything was still great, marvellous, at the very moment when the rising power of Germany and the United States meant it was going the other way.

The canvas, of course, was enormous. We researched the Jubilee events, not only in Britain but throughout the Empire, and everything else that was relevant including pictorial magazines, photographs and so on. The general problems of the series bore especially on this program. This program was to be the opener and was the legacy of the first plan, that the series would cover "50 years of change" in the Empire story, from the Diamond Jubilee in 1897 to 1947. But as the whole structure of the series then changed, it emerged that the *second* program would then go back and start with the West Indies and the slave trade in the seventeenth century, and the series would then gradually go forward and reach 1897 again round about program six.

Now for the life of me, how could I set off in the opening program to make people slightly apprehensive of the future and the doings of the Kaiser and the French, and so on, if the next program went back 200 years? What I was called upon was to give a taste of the froth and bubble. I had to contrive to tell the story, without in fact indicating the reality, and in a way just exploit the Diamond Jubilee to show the kind of euphoria then present in Britain and the way people felt about the Empire. So the program had to be impressionistic and could not really come down to brass tacks. Now with that in mind I sat down and wrote a detailed script, shot by shot, because the film had to be a contrived one, just creating an amalgam of emotion.

Q. Several of the comments on that program were quite interesting. *The Sunday Times* review said "the program was beautifully made, but impeccably bland." Another review said that your program lacked a point of view and lacked a commitment. Do you feel that was a fair comment on your program and a fair comment on the series?

A. That is a difficult question. I agree with the comment on the series, because it had many points of view, not one, for the reasons that I have explained. I do not agree with the comment on the Jubilee program of mine. I think the program had a point of view, but was not presented very blatantly for fairly obvious "Realpolitik" reasons. My point of view was that the Diamond Jubilee was a defensive act by someone, Britain, who is about to be clobbered and knows he is. So he shows off in national, imperial self-deception. That to me gives the program interest.

Q. It seems to me, looking at the many newspaper letters particularly in *The London Times* that your program on Australia, *Beyond the Black Stump*, was totally misunderstood by a number of viewers.

A. It was an idiosyncratic film. I am not surprised it was misunderstood by some people who took it too literally. I had been asked to make a film in that slot of the Empire series about the development of "the Australian character," as seen as one particular response to the fact of the British Empire! Again the subject struck as a facade and unreal. We've all heard about the idea of "the Australian character," especially the one built up while Australia was still part of the British Empire. Australians are seen as stoic, courageous, tough in adversity, resisting authority. It's all part of a nation's defense against reality. A defense image built up over time.

Against that I was trying to come up with something much deeper. In one sense the film was a portrayal of how the generally accepted idea of the Australian character came to be. In another sense it was the story of how the fact of the British Empire shaped and determined Australian attitudes and values in the nineteenth century.

I see what happened in Australia as a straightforward case of imperialism. The British Empire exploited the country and exploited a great many of the people they sent out there. This reality has been coated with illusions and dreams and fantasy history. There is the notion that the Australians were free and independent and equal. Much of that is fantasy bullshit and what I sought to do in the film is say so.

I couched the film within a historical narrative, from Captain Cook until World War I, but I used a great many present-day people and situations that I felt were symbolic of the fantasy-like images of what happened in the past. I feel the response of these letters to *The Times* as totally authentic. I could quibble and say, look, they were misrepresenting the program in their letters. This program was a historical presentation of Australia in the nineteenth century, which happened to use some modern scenes and those people totally missed the point. Their response was in fact authentic, because I suspect that what I was also commenting on in the program was their own views of Australia. And the fact that they responded with such alacrity and so vociferously does indicate to me that the film worked.

Q. When the series started to be broadcast, there was a fair amount of criticism. One comment was totally to question the validity of the series; I think the comment went "such a series will encapsulate revolution in a cliché and will trivialize history." A second comment was that the series was not very good history, with many important episodes of the British Empire left out, such as Ireland and Palestine. A third major comment was that it totally failed to look at the impact of the working man in the building of the British Empire and totally failed to see the British Empire as a process of degrading subject colonies. You worked on three of the programs and worked very closely with the whole of the series. What do you think of the series as history?

A. Well, I think it is very hard to think of that series as history at all. I would view it as a series of various films made by a group of BBC producers in the early seventies who went out into various bits and pieces of the world which had once been part of the British Empire. They then communicated some of their responses, told various anecdotes and stories, and commented on certain historical events that had occurred. Actually I think some of the programs were at their strongest when they were more specific than when they attempted the usually impossible kind of overall historical sweep. There is no way the series as such could be history, because the series had no central over-riding editorial voice—no central theme. When the presentation people came along at the last stages to ask what they should put on the trailers as the theme of the series, all that they could be told by the Editor was "The British Empire"—full stop. That is not history. History calls for a point of view.

Q. Which of the three films you did moved you most emotionally?

A. What probably most moved me as a person was what I did in Singapore. I found myself among a group of left-over British colonial officers and rubber planters from the 1930's and through their memories I retold the story of the fall of Singapore. Initially I had seen them almost in a caricature sense, sitting there in the Cricket Club still and yelling out "Boy" and what have you. But as I grew closer to them, I couldn't help realizing how much they themselves had truly believed in this thing called "Empire." I saw how they had been somehow betrayed by their own illusions, and how tragic the whole outcome for them was. That was a minor kind of turning point in my own view of the Empire.

That film, which was the last one I did, was rather different from any of the others. I almost became imperialist in terms of the effect those people in Singapore had on me. They were real people, you see. This was one of the problems, I think, that the series often labored under. You were looking at these funny photographs and the old speeded-up film and those pompous ways of writing letters from the past, and it was very hard to see the people concerned as human beings. Now when you come to know a small clutch of them as people who were genuinely very pleasant, very sincere, it moved you even though they would sit there and say things to you which would seem very pompous, like "we had a way with these people," and "the people loved us because we had integrity" and all those kind of sentiments which we now regard as terribly passé. When you saw that these people *meant* it then you recognized that they were deluded, but no more than you or I are about other things. Within their context they were sincere. For them the collapse of the Empire was a mortal blow.

Q. The film you are working on now, *The Last Tasmanian*, is extremely committed. What prompted you to make it?

A. Yes, this film is very much a response to a sense of outrage. The genocide of the Tasmanian aborigines is one of the great untold and yet terrible stories from Australia. No race of man was ever so completely and so rapidly eliminated as were the Tasmanians, at least within historical times. Initially I felt, I suppose, simply a desire to tackle this subject because it has always been pushed under the carpet and I wanted to bring it all out. I have certainly become more and more knowledgeable about it, it has taken on many varying shapes.

I found as I got into the film that there are some pretty unhappy truths about the aborigines as well. They were not terribly bright and were not without some responsibility for their own demise. In a kind of way I find myself now committed to asserting my own right as a thinking human being and film maker to investigate a subject, and to present it as I discover it, even if it does not fit into any particular obvious niche.

156

Q. This is a film made outside the standard BBC or ABC unit. How did you set up the financing of the film?

A. At first I tried to set it up as a coproduction, between the BBC, the ABC and a few others, and at the last moment this fell through as the ABC had its budget cut. Well, the first thing I came to realize was that whatever I was going to do, I could not just go in and chat someone up and give them a half page, like you could in a good old BBC sort of situation. I had to give them something fairly solid, if they were going to let me have their money.

I then managed to get a little bit of money from the Australian Film Commission and with that I did research. At that stage, with no backing promised anywhere, nothing definite at all, I sat down with Rhys Jones, a brilliant archaeologist and historian, and we started to work it out. I did most of the writing and we spent almost three months preparing a very full treatment. I also did a very detailed budget. I sought to make the thing impeccable, so that we could not be challenged. It was going to be an expensive film with a budget of 104,000 Australian dollars, which is quite a lot of money for a documentary. That brochure, hard-cover and with lots of illustrations, was what I then used for the next six months in raising the money.

The usefulness of the brochure has been extraordinary, because as and when people did become interested in backing the film, there was never a case of having to convince them about the idea or the storyline, and so on. That was all there. Never once did anyone question the budget and say is this too much or too little. Everything was answered in advance.

Q. What was the precise arrangement you finally came to?

A. I took the plunge with my own money and went to Tasmania to shoot the funeral of Truganini, the last Tasmanian. While I was in Tasmania filming the cremation, I established contact with the Tasmanian Government, and that started the ball rolling. The final arrangement is this: the Tasmanian Government, through the Tasmanian Film Corporation, supplied facilities and cash, and some of the crew and equipment. We provided the key personnel in the crew.

The Australian Film Commission had already assisted with a small development advance and also became an investor in the production of the film, giving vital backing all the way. My company Artis Productions is also a major investor with Rhys-Jones, myself, and a few others taking deferred fees.

Société Française de Production, SFP, the French government and television production organization, also came in as there is a French aspect to the story. They provided all the shooting and crew in France, all the lab work, and in return they get the rights to French-speaking Europe, Oceania and Africa. We then wrote to twenty major firms operating in Tasmania proposing that each invest $1,000. We needed $5,000 then and Cadbury-Schweppes came in and said they would prefer to give the lot. With the BBC I had managed to do a prepurchase sale, which means they pay half in advance and half at the end, and we also managed to include an additional arrangement with BBC Wales.

Q. You seem to have developed over the years a very strong sense of the realities of film making. You have also produced a number of films which one could call concerned films, yet there is very little "artiness" in your films or in your approach. How generally do you see committed or concerned film making today?

A. I think there are in some ways all kinds of dangers about the term "committed film making." It is very easy to acquire a certain kind of status as a "committed film maker" among a certain clique of people— and you can become quite trendy as a committed film maker. All sorts of bad things about your film can be overlooked if people can just say, look at this man, how committed he is, how concerned he is. The film might be too long. It might be pretentious. It might be manneristic but that "commitment" shines through it all.

Now I am all for commitment, but I think you have to take it under the cold shower sometimes. What you can do is place yourself in situations where your ideas and convictions are tested in this. If there is something I really want to get across or make people aware of, or have them share my feelings about, then what concerns me most of all is how I get my message across. It might upset people. It might anger them, maybe they won't like it, but I want to get it across, and I am not essentially concerned about film and its methods, except insofar as they help me to do that. That may mean, if you like, that I am manipulating film to communicate. Well, okay, I do not think film per se with all its methods and devices and possibilities merits particular veneration.

# 7
## *Cathy Come Home (Aftermath)*
### *and*
## *Edna, the Inebriate Woman*
### ⁄ *Jeremy Sandford*

*Most film makers would admit that in spite of its versatility the straight documentary may not be the best form for the propagation of certain social ideas. When that limit is reached it often becomes time for the drama documentary to take over.*

*The drama documentary is a television form which though not that much practiced in the U.S. has been brought to perfection in England. Writer Jeremy Sandford is one of the best practitioners in this area and his two plays,* Cathy Come Home\* *and* Edna, the Inebriate Woman, *are fine examples of the form.*

Cathy *described the situation of the homeless in England in the early sixties. It was a devastating attack on slum conditions and bureaucratic apathy and caught the public's attention in an unprecedented way. It was screened four times by the BBC and may well be the most effective drama on contemporary social and living conditions ever shown on British television.*

*After its transmission* Cathy *also came out in novel form. At the same time three people wrote to Sandford and claimed they were the authors of the play. In short the film, backed by the novel, achieved publicity, notoriety, and calls for action. Did it change anything? Sandford claims that in spite of the immense hullabaloo the situation of Britain's homeless in 1978 is probably worse than when the film appeared in 1966.*

Cathy *dealt with a likable working-class girl from a recognizable family and social environment.* Edna *goes a dimension further. It deals with the derelicts and the tramps—the true down-and-outs of society. It deals with the forgotten classless people totally without home, family, and friends.*

*Although not acclaimed as highly as* Cathy, Edna *won awards from both*

---

\*For an in-depth interview on *Cathy* see Alan Rosenthal, *The New Documentary in Action* (Berkeley and Los Angeles: University of California Press, 1977), pp. 165–175.

*the Writers' Guild and the Critics' Circle as best television play of the year. Actually it's rather a formless play that drifts through a very large number of scenes and incidents. The character of Edna the tramp is written and played with humor and brightness, but this merely serves to offset the sadness and pathos of her life.*

*What we are shown are many people like Edna to whom violence has been done by society. Though adult in appearance they are often only at a child's stage of development. What Sandford demands is that we stop persecuting them and ask instead what we can learn about them and how we can help them.*

*Jeremy Sandford himself could well pass for a rather tall, shy, unkempt undergraduate. Born in 1930, Sandford read English at Oxford where he produced among other things a musical poetry show called* Flagrant Flowers. *After serving as a clarinetist in the Royal Air Force band, Sandford worked fairly extensively for BBC radio, directing about forty documentaries on various aspects of British life and writing three radio plays for the BBC's Third Programme. Sandford also wrote a play called* Dreaming Bandsmen *which was produced at Coventry Theatre, and which was described by one critic as giving the feeling "of being dragged through a sewer backwards."*

*Though Sandford is best known as the author of* Cathy *and* Edna *his television work predates* Cathy *and includes his controversial film on the Savoy Hotel. In the last few years Sandford has written several linked social plays for BBC television, a book on social conditions called* Down and Out in Britain, *and a travel book on Mexico. He has also produced an interview book called* Gypsies, *and for a while edited the Gypsy journal* Romano Drom.

Q. What difference did *Cathy* make to your career, and how did it alter, if any, the situation of the homeless?

A. *Cathy* made me famous overnight. Life was all television and newspaper interviews. The response was terrific to it. And various things happened as a result of it. I think I mentioned to you last time round how, subsequent to articles I wrote in Birmingham newspapers and to a public meeting which Ken Loach and I called in Birmingham in the wake of the excitement caused by the film, the city of Birmingham announced that they were going to discontinue their policy of separating between three and four hundred husbands a year from their families. This was perhaps the most important of all the results of *Cathy*. A month or so later "Shelter," a campaign which aimed to draw public attention to the position of homeless people in Britain today and provide accommodation for them, was launched. The effect of *Cathy*, according to Shelter's director Des Wilson, was that it immensely strengthened their hand in that they were able to point to *Cathy* and specifically refer to the social problems that they were talking about. I remember Des saying, "Cathy was worth half a million to us."

It was only later that I learned that quite strong pressure had been put on the BBC to not stand firm by the film but instead admit that it was a fabrication and this sort of thing was not going on in Britain. It's greatly to the credit of three men in particular that they stood by the film: Sydney Newman, head of drama group, Kenneth Adam, director of television, and Hugh Greene, director general.

Q. Do you think the establishment of the BBC today would stand so whole-heartedly behind facts which were so controversial and unpalatable?

A. Certainly what happened to Roy Minton's film *Scum*, about conditions in borstals,* suggests that the BBC establishment today might be less courageous about putting on a film that bears the same sort of relationship to reality that *Cathy* did. *Scum* was made but not transmitted.

Q. How much did *Cathy* help change the situation of the homeless?

A. When I first realized that despite all the hullabaloo surrounding altogether four television transmissions of *Cathy*, there were still more homeless families, I lost some of my faith in the power of the media to change anything. There is one thing that can be said, though. Certainly *Cathy* alerted social workers and the public to a grave injustice in this country—one of which most of them had so far, largely, been ignorant. Perhaps without *Cathy*, the situation might even be worse than it is. This at any rate is what people in the caring professions tell me, and I'd like to believe it.

Q. When *Edna* was broadcast it caused almost as much commotion as *Cathy*. Was this a project you brought to the BBC or did they approach you?

A. Irene Shubik, a BBC producer, had every now and again been writing to me asking me if I would write another play for the BBC and my agent asked her out to lunch. We discussed various projects and she commissioned what was to be *Edna, the Inebriate Woman* (at that time designed to be one of three linked plays about injustice).

At the time when the contract was signed little more of it existed than the working title *The Common Lodging House* and my feeling that, having written about the problems of homeless families, I'd now like to turn to the problems of the single homeless. There was one other ingredient in this. Ted Kotcheff, whom I'd continued to be in touch

---

*Correction centers for juvenile offenders in England.

with, had for some years been saying that he'd like to combine with me on a sort of British version of *The Lower Depths*, which I actually have never seen.

These three strands came together in about October, 1969, when I received a letter from the Rev. Kenneth Stoneley, of the Christian Action Hostel in Lambeth High Street, in which he said that he wondered whether it might be possible for me to write something which would bring to the public as forcefully as *Cathy* did the problems of the single homeless.*

I had already written articles in *The Observer* and other newspapers about the world of the dosshouse† and the common lodging house, and in the course of the research had stayed in dosshouses and spikes,** descending into "the lower depths."

Christian Action helped a lot with research. They were pioneering hostels for women at that time and I was drawn to the idea of having my protagonist be a woman. One of their hostels was about to be closed, and I went to a special inquiry about this, and a lot of the special inquiry in *Edna* is drawn, some of it verbatim, from that event.

Q. Can you remember your first reaction when experiencing these "lower depths"?

A. I found descending into that world an incredibly depressing experience. Once some years before I'd started *Down and Out in Britain*, and the unhappiness and hopelessness of that world had caused me to despair. I shall never forget the first time I went down to the Thames Embankment and saw, within sight of Big Ben and the Savoy Hotel, the vast numbers of dossers sleeping in the open air on a cold night beneath the stars, wrapped just in cardboard boxes and polythene. Some of the huge dosshouses were quite horrific, with dormitories housing up to 100 of the derelict and lost—dumping grounds for people whom society seems to have abandoned.

Q. Again your chief character is a woman. This time a cheerful-spirited sixty year tramp-wanderer. What were the generating seeds for Edna?

A. I was casting around in my mind all the time as to whom I would like to cast as the protagonist for my play, but hadn't come to any conclusion. Then sitting in the foyer of the Christian Action Hostel

---

*At the time when Sandford started writing his play there were over 100,000 single homeless in England.

†Cheap or sometimes free overnight lodgings of the very lowest standard for "dossers" or tramps.

**Reception center; so called because, in the old days, in exchange for a night's shelter you had to break a certain number of rocks on a spike.

one afternoon I glanced through a little glass window giving on to the corridor outside, and framed momentarily at the window looking in at us I saw the wizened face staring in at us of a little old lady in a great coat with a huge collar and a little porkpie cap. She was only there for a moment. She tapped and one of the staff went out to see her. I was entranced by the little sad interesting face that peered through the window at us. I immediately asked whether I might meet her and one of the staff got up and went out to ask her. But she said that she didn't want to. Next moment the front door slammed and that was the last I saw of her.

Q. Was there any special reason why you chose a woman protagonist rather than a man?

A. What I felt was this. I wanted to do a film about Britain's thousands of single homeless, and they're often uncouth in appearance. They do not have the immediate charm of Cathy, the young mother with children. Many of them would be thought of by the general population as filthy old tramps, or worthless. It was going to be a lot harder to get an audience to sympathize with our protagonist than it was with Cathy.

The male stereotype, the ancient tramp in his ill-fitting overcoat, was so familiar that I thought it would be difficult to break through the built-in attitudes of the typical audience to such a person. It therefore seemed to me that a clever way round this would be to follow a lady tramp. Although they've become fairly common now, at that time they were really quite uncommon, and it seemed to me that there would not be such built-in prejudices against such a person.

Q. What were the key things you wanted to show in *Edna* as opposed to *Cathy*?

A. In *Cathy* I showed only the tragedy and some of the forces that produced it. In *Edna* I decided to show more than this. I wanted to show, as well as the tragedy of the treatment of our single homeless people, what I felt should be the solution. This was that instead of shoving them round on an endless treadmill between common lodging house, psychiatric hospital or spike or prison at vast expense to the taxpayer, one could provide small permissive hostels presided over by a kindly father figure which could provide a haven for such people until they were ready to return to society. And all this would cost only a fraction of the other places.

So the basic structure of my screenplay early on became fairly plain. I would show Edna in the typical lost spirals of the world of the down-and-out—this decrepit dirty old lady staggering from the door of psychiatric hospital to dosshouse, to prison, to spike, and back on the road.

I would show her momentarily rescued from this in a hostel based on the hostel run by Christian Action. And because such hostels are rare, are always being closed down, or having to eject people, and also, no doubt, because of some strange disturbed longing in Edna herself, I thought that at the end of the film she must be back on the road again.

I follow her, this drunken quarrelsome old lady who wears an ill-fitting overcoat and porkpie hat, on her continuous journey through town and country, showing the shortcomings and absurdities of a society whose response to her predicament is insensitive, inappropriate, and expensive.

Q. Beneath the text of the play one senses terrific passion on your part!

A. Yes. The play was written from my anger and impatience with our reluctance to help those who wander through the twilight world at the bottom of society. For those who didn't see *Edna*, the best way I can describe it is with a couple of quotations from the book version. It begins:

> Out of the darkness, out of the night, a frayed decrepit fragile old figure was emerging. At first she was a speck lit up fitfully by the headlamps of passing cars. Then as she got closer, it was possible to see in the moonlight, her solitary trudge and the painful and uneven motion with which she moved forward.
>
> One of the old lady's feet was encased in a polythene bag, lined round inside with tiny drops of moisture, and tied tightly around her ankle with string. Under one arm she carried a polythene parcel apparently containing old bits of newspaper and old clothes.
>
> Now she was leaving the countryside and entering town. She reached, at last, in a terraced street, a battered door. It wasn't locked. She entered.

And so it goes on till the end of the book, but not of Edna's journey. And she finishes up still wandering.

In an essay in the book version I wrote more about what I was trying to achieve:

> Concern about the homeless family has been mobilized by "Shelter" and the Squatters, but this equally grave problem has so far received little attention—the problem of homeless single persons. Such people are often dubbed by society "socially inadequate," and information about them is fairly hard to come by.
>
> Kenneth Stoneley, representing the National Association of Voluntary Hostels, an organization that tries to find homes for such people, told me, "We alone now try to find homes for four thousand such people each year."

164

In the essay I went into much more detail on what makes people into Edna—and who is the homeless single person. Often it's a person who has suffered a series of rejections, or suffered a series of acts of violence. In the research I asked a doctor what makes these people like they are. Some have never had a loving relationship with parents and now can't make contact with society. Others again were institutionalized in psychiatric hospitals or prison. Some are alcoholics. Some drug addicts.

The events of *Edna* are based on real events, and she passes through many of the traditional lodging places of persons of her type. Sometimes she sleeps out in derelict buildings. Occasionally she uses the "spike"—or reception center. Then a rung above these come the kiphouses. I wanted to show the brutality with which many of these people are treated, and the way they are often moved on by the police without any feeling. Newspapers still sometimes carry stories about "tramps," still treating them as figures of derision rather than as human beings in need of as much compassion and help as anyone else.

Q. How long did the story take you?

A. I worked on the screenplay through November and December 1969, and January, February, March 1970, and went to Irene Shubik the producer with a draft in April, which differed little from the final draft.

Meanwhile I'd been keeping Ted Kotcheff posted on what was going on, and I sent him a draft too, hoping very much he might be able to direct it. I also, as a way of getting to know the story better, was writing it alternately in the form of a novel and a screenplay.

Q. What were the difficulties and benefits in working with Kotcheff and Shubik?

A. I'd worked with Ted Kotcheff some years before all this on a play of mine called *Dreaming Bandsmen* based on my experiences in an RAF band. This was directed by Ted for the Belgrade Theatre in Coventry, the first time I think that he'd directed outside television. It was a wonderful occasion, and Ted, freed for the first time from the shackles of television, let his imagination run riot. The play worked well and we got on very well.

Ted and I worked for a number of days on the script up at his house in Highgate, beginning in August. Once in a while there came "script notes" from Irene which, so I felt, failed to grasp the essential importance of the irrationality of the script. Most of her comments in these script notes seemed to be an attempt to impose some sort of rational flow onto it whereas the essence of the thing I'm sure is that it should be disjointed, with its own sort of wild poetry. So I ignored her notes and kept it that way.

Q. You obviously saw *Edna* as being technically very similar to *Cathy*?

A. Yes. I was most anxious to have disembodied statistics on the sound track chipping in where relevant, as in *Cathy*, and also to have the voices of real dossers and down-and-outs on wildtrack, in order to give a strong sense of reality. Ted, however, is a different sort of director from Ken Loach, and *Edna* is in fact far more theatrical than *Cathy*. Fairly late on, Ted felt that the film would be better without these statistics, and I acquiesced.

Q. You knew the background inside out. Did you show this all to Ted Kotcheff?

A. Of course I took Ted round the common lodging houses, doss-houses, and to a psychiatric hospital I knew. I also took him down to the Embankment to see the hundreds of people sleeping out, or huddled against the railings outside hotel kitchens to pick up a bit of that warmth.

After that I left it largely to him and I gave him a list of what I thought might be likely addresses and the production team got on with it. I scripted parts for some of the inmates of the Christian Action Hostel, and some of these, in the production, played themselves. We used a real psychiatric hospital in South London, and a real ladies' Common Lodging House which had just closed with the inmates from another Common Lodging House.

For the "legion of despair" sequence, where Edna's predicament is shown in relation to the predicament of hundreds of others—sleeping rough and scrambling after the mobile soup kitchen run by nuns, we used in part those who were actually there sleeping on the Embankment, and partly the inhabitants of one of the Rowton Houses, one in Hammersmith which itself was to be closed not so long after.

Q. Why did you add the words "the Inebriate Woman" to Edna?

A. I gave the work the name *Edna, the Inebriate Woman* ironically. Society may dub her "inebriate" but of course her problems are far greater than just this. Thus I have one of the characters say:

> . . . if there is no hostel provided for these people they have nowhere to go, poor dears, except to the mental hospital or the streets. Or to prison . . . Going there, not because they are really criminals or mad, but because there's nowhere more suitable for them. These people are referred to in official reports as inebriates, alcoholics, schizophrenics, drug addicts, the disabled, layabouts, failures. These words are alibis to help us to ignore why they're really like they are. Stack the cards against us, these people are the same as us—you and me in a mess. The answer, so I believe most sincerely, is in the sort of hostel that we

have set up. Let us help them. They can exist and be happy in a hostel like ours. They *can* live fulfilled lives. There should be hostels like this everywhere. One every four or five streets.

The places where they're put at present are no answer. The huge institution, so vast, so impersonal. What they need is a small place, a place to be a typical home, the home that most of them never had. They escape the help that is their right because they can't dress up their needs in the correct form. And so they get kicked from pillar to post. And there are thousands of them. I reckon something like one hundred thousand of people littering lunatic asylums, prison, Common Lodging Houses, spikes, sleeping out in the open, mostly men, but a few thousand women.

And the need is desperate. Every day I have to turn women and girls, even men, families away from my door. I don't want to have to turn these away as well.

Edna is not a typical homeless person in the way that Cathy is a typical mother of a homeless family. The reason is that there is really no typical single homeless person. This makes it that much harder to write a book or screenplay about them.

Q. I saw the film a year later than its first screening. What was the reaction at the time?

A. Public reaction to *Edna* was good. A critic in *The Telegraph* said, "Mr. Sandford forces attention and involvement. The strength of his portrait lies in its depth and dimensions, comedy and sadness together springing naturally from the character." And Colin Hodgetts in *Church Times* wrote, "When *Edna* was first shown, many people commented that it seemed exaggerated . . . Those who work in the field know that [it is] depressingly accurate."

In arrangement with the BBC Press Office, a press showing was arranged for the morning of the transmission at the Christian Action Hostel in Greek Street. There I spoke about the reasons I had for writing the play, and invited some of those who had appeared in it or who were in Christian Action Hostels to speak. Later, on television, I insisted that people actually from the down-and-out world should be present and there was a dramatic moment when one of them became over-excited and chased the camera crew into an alcove and started unzipping their flies.

I was most anxious that those actually working to fight these conditions should be represented, in the same way as Shelter was directly involved in *Cathy*. In addition to Christian Action I involved the Cyrenians in the enterprise, especially their director Tom Gifford. In the months, indeed years that followed *Edna*, I worked mainly with Tom,

showing the film and lecturing, encouraging people to enter the field
of caring for the single homeless, fund raising, and generally spreading
information. The relationship continues, and I am indeed now a director of the Cyrenians.

Q. Obviously people must have compared *Cathy* and *Edna*. What are
your own feelings about their relative successes, their styles and their
differences?

A. *Edna* was successful, and was transmitted three times, but it
wasn't the tear-away success that *Cathy* was, partly because the production veered perhaps more towards drama and less towards documentary than *Cathy* did. *Edna* looks more like a traditional drama and
some people have said to me that they felt that it was a betrayal of the
idea to choose an actress in the grand histrionic style like Patricia Hayes
for the role. I don't know. I think that with a subject which is lacking
in attraction for a lot of the population, one might have got a lot of
people switching off with a more realistic production. At any rate with
this, people got involved in Edna's situation and above all in her courage. More people watched than would have watched a more Loach-like
production and perhaps the message thus may have got through to
many more people. Certainly the performance by Patricia as Edna was
magnificent.

Q. Can you see any broad way in which *Cathy* and *Edna* have influenced drama documentary in England?

A. I don't want to make extravagant claims for *Cathy* and *Edna* but
at any rate *Cathy*, I hope, helped shift the field of drama on television
just that bit closer to reality. I would say that for a number of years
British television drama just wasn't that concerned with reality. Today
I think that's generally changed, and that drama documentary in particular has become much more common.

In the famous *Jonny Go Home* real people were used to reconstruct
events in which they had participated. In *Dummy* a script was drawn
up from the real life of a deaf and dumb prostitute. This was then
played by actors, and the only criticism that I have heard is that the
tragedy of this girl who ends by stabbing her tormentor is not particularly related to the society in which she lives. One is not clear, watching it, whether the anger one feels is anger about the society which has
driven this girl to this condition, or anger about the human state as a
whole.

The dramatized documentary form has become increasingly popular. The justification for it must be, as I have said, that the events
portrayed are inaccessible to true documentary treatment, either because
they are in the past, or because they lie in some area of secrecy or

168

inarticulacy, such that to shoot them as straight documentary will destroy the very thing that one is trying to show. I do think, boring though it may be, that the viewers should be told the relationship of what they're seeing to reality—as we did tell the audience in the final captions in *Cathy*.

In the historical category, the immensely moving "Roots" used the method to look at the events that led to the descendant of an African finding himself in the social position that he does in America today. "Washington: Behind Closed Doors" needs a different justification. Real people would not have been prepared to confess to the apparently typical events that this drama showed. And the lyricism of its treatment made it attractive to watch.

In the other area of inaccessibility, namely that the camera may destroy the very thing it aims to portray, there have been *Leeds United*, and quite a number of films from Loach and Garnett, including *The Divided Mind*.

Q. Can you remember any cases when the straight drama and the documentary have covered the same subject recently?

A. Yes. An opportunity to compare a dramatic treatment with a documentary treatment of the same subject came with the play *Destiny* and the documentary *The National Front*,* both transmitted on the BBC within a few weeks of each other. My experience of these two was that I was made angry at the National Front film, and frightened by it. In the case of the play *Destiny*, I felt horrified and alarmed but also that sense of "the pity of it all" which seems to be often present in literature and seldom in documentary.

A *cause célèbre* has recently been Roy Minton's *Scum*, built up from interviews with about 100 former inmates of borstals. The arguments used against it being shown by the BBC establishment were that though all these things do happen in borstals, not all of them could happen to the same person in so short a time.

This sort of point of view raises questions as to the relationship of dramatic time to real time. Nobody is saying that Cathy passed from marriage, had three children, lived in a slum, and got evicted seven times, all in the space of three hours. My view is that there is so much of television mildly or highly supportive of the establishment that in the interest of balance it would be a good thing to have programs which showed a less rosy side of such things occasionally.

Q. Do you still believe that certain documentaries can only be done as drama?

*The National Front is an extreme right-wing semi-fascist and racist political party which grew up in England in the mid-seventies.

A. Yes, tremendously. There are so many areas into which, because of their remoteness in time or their sensitivity, cameras cannot go. That is the area of dramatized documentary. Writers must come forward and be given space on the telly to give their message of the world as they see it. Drama is a persuasive medium. Television drama is our national theater. Space must be given for writers old and young to contribute to public debate about the sort of society we want, the sort of world we live in.

One of the strongest feelings abroad at the moment in Britain must be contempt for the old order, immense impatience with the mystique and small-mindedness and dishonesty of the old ruling class. Television I believe has contributed vastly to this, especially in its documentaries about the bungling of the First World War, and also in programs like the Garnett-Loach *Days of Hope*. This in its turn has caused people to question much more the blind authoritarianism of our society. And that is very much to the good.

# 8
## *Decisions*
### *Roger Graef*

The original goal of the work I've been doing was to
make people aware of their own ability to be critical of
the world around them.

ROGER GRAEF

*I'd seen some of Roger Graef's films in America, had wanted to meet him but
was slightly put off by the biography. The man was obviously such a doer,
achiever, and go-getter. Graef was born in New York in 1936, did pre-law
at Harvard and was working in the professional theater by the age of twenty-
one. Between 1957 and 1962 he directed eighteen plays on the East Coast and
also found time to supervise two dramas for CBS.*

*In the early sixties he moved to England and shot* The Man from Sotheby's
*for the CBC and* Günter Grass's Germany *for the BBC. Since then he has
produced and directed thirty major documentaries including one on the British
Communist Party, has written for a number of newspapers in England, published* Is This The Way to Save Our Cities, *lectured at universities throughout Europe and the U.S., and become a Governor of the British Film Institute
and chairman of a public planning group.*

*All of which conjured up a forbidding prodigy figure which turned out to
be at total odds with reality. When we met, Graef was open and friendly and
showed a great capacity to listen as well as talk. Later, when we started discussing his films he took great pains to bring in the comments of his cameraperson, Charles Stewart, who was also present.*

*I consider Roger Graef and his crew the most important and significant film
team currently working in* cinéma vérité. *They have shaken observational
cinema out of many old worn grooves and have shown how the* vérité *style can
be of true social and political significance. One might say the same of Fred
Wiseman, but in the end I think Graef's films are fairer and deeper and also
stick to chronological order in a more honest way.*

*Although Graef has a considerable reputation as a film maker dating back
to* The Life and Times of John Huston *(NET 1960) his importance regarding* cinéma vérité *dates from the three series he produced and directed
between 1972 and 1976. The first of these, "The Space Between Words," was
made as a coproduction between the BBC and KCET (Los Angeles). "State of
The Nation" (direction only—1973–75) and "Decisions" (1975–76) were both
made for the Granada ITV network.*

*"The Space Between Words" consists of five films dealing with communica-
tions. Using pure* cinéma vérité *techniques (no interviews, no interference,*

*and even no lights) Graef took his cameras into such diverse situations as a dispute at an electronics factory, an emotionally charged family situation, and an economic and social council session of the UN. The series was extremely innovative for England in terms of access to private situations\* and in the presentation of personal, industrial and diplomatic relations on television.*

*All five films dealt with situations that would normally have been considered too undramatic for conventional film treatment. Where they succeeded beautifully was in showing the function of role playing and public ritual in daily life and in illustrating the complex fusion of verbal and non-verbal behavior.*

*Following "Space" Graef used the same techniques to film inside the Brussels Headquarters of the Common Market and inside the Department of Trade and Industry. The two films appeared on "State of the Nation," and again highlighted Graef's ability to capture and condense a series of events as close as possible to the original flow.*

*The "Decision" series of 1975 and 1976 consists of three films, Steel, Oil, and Rates. The films were shot during discussions over vital decisions made by three groups, each operating with huge sums of money on behalf of immense numbers of people. The British Steel Corporation had to consider whether to invest fifty million dollars in a new steel plant. Occidental Petroleum had to "guesstimate" the yield of a North Sea oil field and future tax before committing themselves to an investment of 400 million dollars, and Hammersmith Council (a local London council) had to choose between a growth in social services or a cut in rates.*

*The problems Graef faced in gaining entry to the corporations, winning their confidence and doing the actual filming are fully covered in the interview. But the importance of Graef's films goes beyond the solution to technical and human problems. Their value lies in the fact that they enable one to understand processes vital to the running of our society yet normally hidden from film coverage, or at best obscured by indiscriminate news reporting.*

*Summing up his own work Graef talks about the necessity of "demystification," and breaking up the aristocracy of information whereby key society decisions are privately and secretly exchanged between elite political or managerial groups. This demystification seems to me vital and essential in a healthy society, and Graef's work in promoting it strikes me as one of the most important contributions of documentary film to date.*

Q. When you went into film were there any models for you in terms of style, content, or the politics of film?

A. There was a Canadian film shot by Richard Leiterman and directed by Douglas Leiterman called *One More River*. That was the film that most persuaded me to go into documentaries. I saw it on television

\*But see the work of Allan King in Canada, and Susan and Allan Raymond in the U.S.

and was so stunned by the power of those images without any commentary that I said, "What the hell am I doing in the theater. This is really something else far more powerful." And I've never forgotten it. That was the film that meant most to me.

Q. You are most noted now for a very political use of *cinéma vérité*—observational cinema. You study institutions, like Fred Wiseman, but your work is poles apart. How do you see the differences between the two of you?

A. Our work differs very dramatically because we have a completely different relationship with the institution that we're filming. It seems to me that Fred Wiseman has an adversary relationship with his institution. He comes along to try and rip the place open. He's very personal with his use of *vérité* and edits it in any sequence that suits him. And it's very much a personal statement about the institution in the film. What we've been trying to do is to use *vérité* over a number of years to develop a highly specialized observational technique where we're actually interested in these institutions. We're interested in capturing them alive, reducing the material to an effective hour and a half, and having the people in the institutions say: "Yes, that's exactly what happened."

Before we start shooting all the political implications and reverberations start. People in our films have usually never trusted media people before. They're businessmen, diplomats, trade unionists, and civil servants. We come along and say: "Look, we're not out to get you. We might afterwards disagree with what we saw transpire but we really want to see just what goes on and get it right. Get it straight." And so that's a very different use of film.

Wiseman is political, but in a very personal, artistic way. He's against big institutions and doesn't like small people getting abused by them at the bottom, and I think one gets that. We are really fascinated by what goes on at the top. Our first concern is how these places tick. Criticizing these places, if that's appropriate, comes afterwards. What we're really saying in the film is: "Are these officials mysterious and remote, or are they indeed a series of human beings struggling, perhaps caught in webs, but nevertheless struggling with things you can recognize and needn't be left alone?" And they represent a large share of human life these days—bureaucracies, institutions, and so on. And because they're not considered good subjects for television, they tend to be left alone.

Q. By these subjects not being considered "good television" I assume you mean the *reality* of the business world as bureaucratic institutions, because there have of course been a lot of TV series based around big business like "The Brothers" or "Mogul."

A. Yes. The general television attitude as shown in "Mogul" or "The Planemakers" and so on is that what really happens in business isn't by *itself* interesting. It's only interesting if people are cheating, cheating on their wives, doing something wrong instead of doing something well or just struggling with the problem. There's got to be some extra spice in there.

What we set out to do was to leave all of those kind of crutches behind. We were interested in the formal decision-making problems themselves, and how human beings grapple with them. That's interesting enough for us. I wouldn't go so far as to say that all those theatrical images of business are pure fiction, but they actually obscure the understanding of business. They totally mislead you.

They simply bypass all the real drama of risk. I mean there's tremendous drama in whether you invest 500 million dollars. One of our films is about North Sea oil—about a marginal field. If you read the papers you think the North Sea is just a piece of cake. You just send your boats out, sink the wells in, collect the money, and retire to the South of France. The truth is even if you know or think there's oil down there, you *don't* know exactly where it is or how fast it might come up. And you've got tiny, tiny, tiny holes two miles under water to give you this information. And then you must decide irrevocably whether or not to spend 500 million dollars on it that may never pay off. Now that's dramatic enough for me.

Q. You keep referring to *we* and in a preliminary discussion you were talking about *the team*. How do you work as a team?

A. The *we* is very much an *operational* we. The decision about *what* we're going to do and how we'll do it is mine. But the way we do it, the actual process of film making is very much a collaboration. I really look for help and I'm delighted when people show the same kind of willingness to involve themselves as I do. And I've been very lucky to find myself working with Charles Stewart the cameraman, Ian Bruce and Mike McDuffy, the sound men and the three editors, Terry Twigg, Dai Vaughan and now Tom Schwalm. These are guys who've stayed with us over the years, developing this, and learning from our mistakes.

Q. Your *vérité* filming is very different from the classic reconstructed documentary, and investigative reporting with straight question and answer. You've done both these types of film but have now adopted a different way of communicating information. What impelled you to move to this form of *vérité*?

A. I've done the investigative documentary and also lots of classic documentaries. One on Islam for example was called *In the Name of Allah. Why Save Florence?* was another one that was shown in America.

They're both good films, but they rely on a form of communicating information that I don't think film is very good at. It's a literary form translated with pictures onto television or onto screen. It's basically visual/verbal.

What we're doing with our *vérité* films is saying that in real life the way you learn is by *experiencing things*, by *sharing* them. Just simply being in a situation and decoding it. Your brain has to work to figure out what's going on. You throw yourself into a new room. Suddenly we open the door and you're in the boardroom of British Steel and you don't know who anybody is. You don't know what the rules are. You don't quite know what they're talking about. And your brain races along to figure it out. I like that. However, if I simply stood there in front of that boardroom and told you everything that was going on, you'd relax and you'd think: "Oh, my, he knows a lot." We're trying to make the viewer work hard. And they do work hard when they stay with our films and are surprised and delighted in the end that they have stayed through an hour's struggle about an investment of ten million pounds in a steel mill or whatever.

Q. Can you tell me about the research?

A. Well, the pre-filming research really just involves going and sitting and winning the confidence of the people in the companies. Showing them that we are straight and keep our promises. We allow them to see our other films and ring up everybody we've dealt with before so they can find out if we are what we say we are. And in a sense that's what the first period is about—establishing mutual trust. We develop trust for them. We're filming in the British attorney general's office right now. That kind of thing was totally unheard of in this government. We discussed it for ages. Finally they decided we were straight, but it took us a year.

Q. What ground rules do you use when you are filming a company or a corporation or diplomats?

A. We developed the ground rules seven years ago when we did the BBC series "The Space Between Words," and I've never changed them. They were based on asking, if I were a businessman or a diplomat or a politician, and didn't trust journalists, what conditions would *I* require in order to trust *them*? Rule one was that there'd be no scoops, that we would not release our information in advance, or tell anyone about anything else that we'd happened across while we were there. Rule two was we would film only what we agreed to cover. Three, we wouldn't show the film until we both agreed it was time and safe to release it—in other words, we weren't setting out to embarrass them. Four, in exchange for the above we demanded access to everything to do with the one or two subjects that we agreed to film.

175

That's what we ask of them and it's a kind of a test of their trust in us. It helps us verify whether we're getting access or not. Can we walk through closed doors? Can we listen in on conversations? It's a way of our reading them as well.

We also said we would never use lights, would not do interviews, nor would we ever stage anything. It's that kind of interference which is the usual excuse for not letting film makers in: too much trouble, too much time involved, too many lights, too many cables. None of that applies to us. We keep our equipment under the table. Everybody in the crew dresses according to whatever the manner is in the situation. We do everything possible to avoid drawing attention to ourselves and have a minimum number of people in the room. It's really a very austere experience, our film making. So if you like, the general line of what we do is to say we do absolutely nothing avoidable to disturb the situation that we're in.

Q. You've done a number of films on British big business. Can you tell me about the number of companies you approached and the reactions of these companies to being filmed?

A. For the first "Decision" series we approached nearly a hundred and very few would talk to us seriously. What we found was that the PR men, if they were good, saw the virtue in what we were doing. But often they knew they were working for people who wouldn't take that kind of risk. What got us into British Steel was that both the boss *and* the head of public relations saw the virtue of it. We needed both of them, because in a sense the kind of leap in the dark that letting us in really involves meant that they both had to hold each other's hands for a bit. You see, in a sense we were coming along and saying we will tell the truth about you. If you're good that will show and if you're bad it will also show.

Q. Do they have any veto over the material?

A. They do have certain vetoes which journalists of a conventional kind might be frightened by, but that kind of thing has never bothered us. When we show the finished film to them they can veto confidential material, a trade secret or a diplomatic secret, or personal secrets as well. And that's never proven a problem. We always offer that because it's the *process* we're interested in, not embarassing details. We're not out to do a story about a particular thing even though that's the usual shape of the film. It's the *process of the institution at work*.

We did a series called "The Space Between Words," that was on communication. One of the films was on politics. The film followed the deliberations of the Senate equal educational opportunity committee under Walter Mondale, then a senator. He was one of the very few senators who would even consider this project, and wasn't apparently out to use us just for his own end. He actually liked the idea. But in practice again, even Mondale who was very good—I'm delighted he's vice-president—had his political antennae out all the time. His aides, who were not running for anything, would still remember months later the tiniest gaffe or criticism that was made of them in front of the camera. They were all so unrelaxed about it. We have found again and again over the years that politicians, because they're the most experienced with the media, are the least relaxed with us. They're the worst subjects for this kind of film making.

Q. Can we pursue this subject of wariness? One of the comments I've heard about your programs is that although you may be in there filming fifty or sixty hours over a period of weeks or months you miss the real decisions—that people clam up when you're there and the real decisions are made when you're absent.

A. I've heard that argument as well. I think it depends on what you call a decision. We think that we have been present at the *turning points* in the decisions. We never claim to be showing the whole decision. We're very careful to say what we've missed, and to say what happened earlier or whatever. And again, a lot of film makers just cheat that. It's very easy to leave that sort of thing out and make people believe they've been there for the whole event. But that wouldn't accomplish my purpose politically, which is to show people the real dimensions of such decisions and not give them a false sense of completion.

Another criticism I have of other peoples' films on these subjects, particularly fictional ones, is the implication that from the beginning, the middle, and end of the film, you have the beginning, middle, and end of the event. You don't. But they don't want to tell you that. They don't want to say, "We only had a week's shooting. So we turned up in Ireland and this is all we got of a particular Protestant-Catholic event." Instead they say "It began on July 15th and it ended on July the 20th and these are the five days." We don't do that. We say these are fragments of a much longer process.

Q. You said before that one of the exciting things is you appear and just start going with the process of the meeting and stay with it. Can we take that a bit further?

A. What we do is we sit in at a number of meetings, maybe over weeks. Then Charles with his camera and Ian or whoever's on sound will come and sit in there with the equipment for the odd day, just to get used to it. And then we start filming. Wherever possible that's what we like to do, acclimatize ourselves and the other people first.

Q. In the more conventional documentary, or the older kind of documentary, the film maker made a great effort to place the situation against a certain background, a certain history, a certain experience.

Your films tend to be rather like the tip of the iceberg. You don't know what's underneath or behind it all.

A. True. Mind you, if you had the whole iceberg in front of you you'd never see any detail. What we say here is that seeing the details and feeling the experience may tell you more than all the careful story setting.

In the *Work* film in "The Space Between Words" series an impending dispute that never happened tells you more about the kind of communication in class relations between management and labor than a big epic which shows marches and strikes. Because most experience, 95 percent of it, is much less dramatic than what goes on the box. That's 95 percent of the bulk of people's lives. If they wait for a strike before they think they're alive, they'll miss the point of what real industrial relations are about.

Q. In the *vérité* of the sixties one of the key film approaches was to follow a particular crisis which you knew was going to be resolved. That crisis and resolution gave the form. In some of the films of the Maysles and Allan King you sensed the film maker searching desperately for some kind of conflict, some kind of old-style dramatic structure. In your films you seem to take ongoing processes with hardly any dramatic structure. Are you ever frightened there's just going to be no story there?

A. Certainly. We're always at risk in this. The stories we are following can fall apart. We've been very lucky, and it would be misleading if I said we weren't deeply conscious of the need for dramatic structure. But we try to temper that kind of temptation with our understanding that things don't end so neatly. We are after the ordinary but also after a bit of development. Fortunately, it almost always comes. We're working on a film at the moment which has yet to get it. But in another film we're doing, on the British Communist Party, they split apart, for the first time in the history of the party, right in the middle of the film. And with British Steel, something that should have been a rubber-stamp decision turned out to be very difficult with a deadline and lots of dramatic phone calls across Europe. What I'm saying is that by being open to modest surprises, if your scale is modest, they become dramatic.

Q. What would you say is the average amount you shoot? Is there an average?

A. Yes. It's quite interesting. I think my intuition was good. When we did this first *vérité* series that I mentioned to you, I put in a budget without any idea of how we were going to do it, with 33 to 1 as our film ratio—65,000 feet. We were shooting about 17 to 1 on conventional films, and always pushing that up because we liked to let things surprise us and so kept filming more and more. I guessed at 33 to 1 for "The Space Between Words" and we really haven't varied that much.

Q. In the editing process in other documentaries or fiction one often goes for the visually very dramatic, visually very interesting things. These visual points often give one a guide to the film structure. How do you work out your structures? How do you work out what to eliminate?

A. In one film we shot 100,000 16 mm feet. That's fifty hours. It takes two weeks to see that in the rushes. We usually see it when we've shot it and we see it again at the start of the editing. And the editor will see it a third time. These *vérité* films are usually best in the rushes. All fifty hours tend to be interesting. It's like a long-running serial. Strangers wandering through our viewing rooms tend to sit there and come back, and back, and back because they want to know what's going to happen next. It's got that kind of excitement to it.

There *is* a problem in structuring them. The films tend to be next best at something like six or eight hours. They're very good between four and eight hours. And then there's a terrible problem because all of the subplots, all the nuances, all the things that aren't going to survive, but do feed the sense of reality, all have to be cut. And although I'm pleased with the results from the films that you've seen and that we've made, the best versions of those films were probably two or three times as long.

Q. What are you trying to bring out in that final version?

A. In the end what we do is to try and focus on the core moments, the moments in which the decisions really are taken. The moments in which the communication did or didn't take place. The kind of most revealing (in the best sense of the word) details of the whole picture. Because of that we usually start with good basic scenes which we know have to be in the film and embellish them with the other scenes that we'd like to keep in. And compress them and prune and prune. It's not like a granite block. It's more like big hunks of clay which we add on to the basic body of the thing and then pare away at.

Q. I remember a film of yours about a family being interviewed by a psychotherapist. It was interesting, but painful. There are obvious difficult ethical questions concerned here for the film maker about intimate exposure, and privacy, and pain. What are your guiding rules here? What guided you in the family film?

A. For that film we asked for volunteers through the newspapers. A hundred families including the one we chose volunteered to take part. After they volunteered we went out to see the families, ate a meal with them, and talked to them about what was likely to be going on. We talked to the social worker who had been working with them. We talked to the therapist who was going to interview them. We went back and back to the family so that they were aware of what they were getting into. I felt that they were adults and we had to give them the responsibility provided we hadn't withheld anything from them about the possible consequences.

Before we showed the film to the public we showed it to the family, to the psychiatrist, and to the social workers. We showed it over and over to ourselves and we felt that we'd been honest to them and that on balance the verdict was similar for everybody. "Look, we don't know what good it will do but we don't think it will do any harm." And on television we were confronted afterward by an interviewer saying, "What do you think you did for the family? People will criticize them for exposing themselves." The father then said "Anybody who doesn't like us from this film, doesn't like us—period." In the end we were satisfied with that.

Q. The films you've been doing have been about decision-making in government circles, in international circles, in big business. While making these films have you been aware of any of your own biases or attitudes to the problems creeping in? Is it possible to be objective?

A. I don't suppose it is possible to be objective. What we try to do is be *fair*. That's why we allow people in the film to see the edited version beforehand, and also let the key participants tell us if they think it's accurate or not. And the words *accurate* and *fair* are the kind of words we play with. We don't use the word *objective* because that's nonsense. But if the people in it say: "Yes, bearing in mind it's an hour, what you have represented of my activities and words is fair," then we reckon that's as good as is required.

*Charles Stewart*: One example of objectivity is what happens in the camera work. One has to be aware of the implications of the angles you pick. You don't emphasize. I have consciously to ensure that the film angles are neutral and that the close size of the shots is controlled.

*Roger Graef*: Also in cutting. It'd be very easy to lay very dramatic cross cuttings and make points, which of course most film makers do. Fred Wiseman does that to a certain degree. We leave the pauses in. One of the things that we're most known for as well is having these enormous pauses and silences in the films, because they're there. And that allows people not to be embarrassed or souped up or forced into falsification of their experience.

Q. Where do you see yourself going in the next couple of years?

**180**

A. Well, I think we've bitten off more than we can chew in the last two films, to tell you the truth. The two films we're working on now are 18 months long. And they are based around meetings and appointments, occasions which we have to turn up for. But the most successful films we've done have been when we've had total immersion in the situation. Where we had an office next door to the directors of British Steel. Or where we were really floating around the Palais des Nations in Geneva. And we really developed such a high intelligence network at that point that we knew things that were happening that nobody else did. We knew more about the situation than everybody else in it. And that's when we're at our best, when we're enjoying the situation and it's going on. It doesn't need to be a crisis, but I think it needs to be reasonably contained within a period of time and place. Eighteen months long, too many interruptions, too much detail that needs to be provided from the outside—I think our technique isn't equal to that.

I'm also very interested in returning to the work of two other films that we did that a lot of people have stayed involved in. They show these films over and over again. They are booked up all the time in this country anyway. One is *The Family* and the other is *School*, a film where we followed a teacher for a month with her class in a comprehensive school. Bright woman, very attractive, nice, intelligent. But having a hell of a time with a bunch of active fifteen-year-olds. But those are films where there are ethical problems, difficulties, and they're not polished in the usual television way. The reality of this family and this teacher in trouble is priceless. They're used all the time for study. I think we ought to get back into more intimate predicaments than we've been doing.

# 9

## *One More River*
### *Douglas Leiterman*

*Douglas Leiterman was unknown to me till I started working in Canada
in 1969. Yet soon after I arrived people kept dropping his name all over the
place as a director to be seen, studied, and listened to. Finally we met at one
of those conferences on the future of Canadian broadcasting or the like, and had
time to get to know each other and swap ideas on film and documentary. At
that point Leiterman was just getting out of network broadcasting and establishing his own company, being as he put it "a bit fed up with the constant
management fights."*

*The management fights, or "interminable discussions," were basically in the
context of Leiterman's work for the CBC and CBS. Leiterman worked extensively for both organizations in the sixties, establishing during this time a reputation as one of Canada's top documentary journalists.*

*The son of a gold-mine accountant in Ontario, Leiterman graduated from
the University of British Columbia in economics and political science. After
working for a number of years as a political and financial journalist he finally
joined the CBC in 1957. His first major documentary was a study of the Dou-
khobors, a Canadian religious sect.*

*During the sixties Leiterman produced and directed over twenty-five docu-
mentaries including* Forty Million Shoes *(an Intertel report on Brazil),* Fas-
ten Your Seat Belts, *and* The Image Makers. *The last was a merciless
examination of how public relations people help shape images for such diverse
bodies as the Bell Telephone Company and Jane Fonda. During this time Leiterman also produced "This Hour Has Seven Days" a current affairs series which
is often referred to as the most successful program series in the history of the
CBC.*

*Leiterman's trademark is a very honest journalistic approach plus a genuine
compassion for the underprivileged. There are a few critics, however, who argue
that Leiterman is often too biased and subjective. In discussing* One More
River *critic William Bluehm\* takes Leiterman to task "for exercising a style
governed more by emotional effects than by journalistic resolve," and adds that*

---

\*William Bluehm, *Documentary in American Television* (New York: Hastings
House) p. 238. Bluehm's book is a classic statement of the old-guard view.

*Leiterman's filmic omissions "hopelessly distorted the situation (of the American blacks)." I think Bluehm is wrong. What he really objects to is the element of individual passion in Leiterman's voice, such a change in the early sixties from the usual neutralized plastic observations. In contrast, Maurice Wiggin of the* London Sunday Times *described Leiterman's films as "terrific torrential television with the impact of a high pressure hose."*

*To my mind the two most interesting examples of Leiterman's work are* One More River *(Intertel 1964) and* From Harlem to Sugar Hill *(CBS Reports 1968). The first dealt with the situation of blacks in the U.S. South while the second dealt with the black middle class. Both were subject to severe management interference and* Sugar Hill *finished up being shelved by CBS as being too controversial.*

*This relationship between network management and documentary producers is one I really wanted to explore with Leiterman and we finally talked about it while sprawled on the grass at his farm near Toronto. There was no bitterness with Leiterman, just a full recognition of the difficulty all networks have in making films that even fractionally rock the boat.*

*Since 1970 Leiterman has had his own company, independently producing television network programs. Major series produced have included "The Fabulous Sixties" and "Here Come the Seventies." Another interesting series took the form of over a hundred mini-documentaries dealing with the shape of the future. As Leiterman said, "If I place my controversies in the future, who can argue . . . ?"*

Q. What were some of the key issues you started dealing with in the sixties? Where did you want to go? Were there any issues where you found you were running up against internal or external censorship as to what you could deal with?

A. Initially the field was wide open because we were breaking new ground. The CBC management generally had very little knowledge of what we were doing and very little concept of what was taking place. Initially it was carte blanche. We could deal with virtually any issue. There was in the first year or so virtually no supervision and certainly no censorship. However, as we began to get the range of national matters, we began with our video artillery to begin to hit the target now and again. Then the cries of alarm began and we became more and more closely watched, and it was always, of course, on matters of national sensitivity.

I'll be specific. I think the very first thing was a program made by Allan King for the series "Close Up," on unemployment at a time of high unemployment. Now, Allan's approach differed somewhat from everything we had done up till then, and everything anybody had done

183

in television on unemployment. Generally we had been going out and interviewing unemployed people. Allan said, "Let's find a way to have people understand what it's like to be unemployed," and he and I talked about it at length. He knew what he wanted to do, which was to find a family and live with them and film them for a while, and he did that.

He found a family in Hamilton after we'd placed a blind ad in the papers asking for unemployed people. Allan had checked all the replies and one of them turned out to be suitable. He then did a very moving program about this unemployed family. Of course, when it was telecast in prime time on a Sunday night, the roof fell in because the government had been proclaiming that there wasn't very much unemployment, and there wasn't much to worry about. This program for the first time touched the central nerve of the general question of unemployment.

Now unemployment sounds like a very dull thing to get anybody upset about, but like most key national issues which tend to be dull, if you *can* get to the sensitive nerve, the body politic and the nation will react. And that's what was done in that program, and there was hell to pay. And from then on, sensitive nerves were constantly being touched by my colleagues or myself as we developed these programs and developed our techniques.

Q. How did that work out in practice in the CBC? If you had a topic, who had to pass on the topic? What were the questions asked as to whether it affected national consciousness? Were the questions asked before the program, were they asked after the program? Did you find that there were certain areas which were almost too dangerous to touch and if so, did you still go ahead?

A. You'd have to divide my experiences with the CBC into two periods. In the initial period, which was prior to "Seven Days," there were no areas that we feared to touch, and no places we feared to tread, and no one who would have stopped us from exploring a subject. In fact, the supervision, though constant, was very sympathetic and understanding. This was mainly because there were three current affairs supervisors who had a very deep and compelling understanding of what the nation deserved from its television current affairs.

These men, Frank Peers, Bernard Trotter, and Reeves Hagan, were men who had come the long hard route through CBC radio and television, understood what was necessary to survive in a corporation like the CBC, but were never cowed by the political pressures that were on them and were a tremendous backup and support. As a result of their skill and guidance, we young turks felt quite comfortable in launching into any areas that interested us. When we had finished a program, the supervisor would look at it, and generally he would take a deep breath and gulp and say, "Okay, we're going to go with it. It's fair and it's honest." Again he might say, "You neglected this angle or what about this?" or question us thoroughly on conclusions that the program had drawn us towards. But if he was satisfied, and we were satisfied, then the thing would go, and he would fight afterwards to prevent the boom being lowered because of the trouble that these programs caused.

Well, over the years this process became less and less flexible as management began to understand the immense powers of television. As it became aware of those powers, management gradually began to look for and to find means of controlling the output, *not* with any specific aim in mind but generally just to make it possible for the president of the CBC to sleep at night without being disturbed by telephone calls from members of Parliament or other important pressure points.

At no point did I encounter a management who sought to pursue a specific point of view or to withhold or to keep a specific kind of thing from getting on the air. But what management was afraid of and backing away from and eventually found means of hindering was *controversy*. And although I never met a senior manager of the CBC who didn't give lip-service to the importance of controversy, the problem was that the definition of controversy that these men universally used was what you or I would call *safe* controversy.

Q. What program either for the CBC or done outside the CBC gave you the most problems in the sixties or in the early seventies? I'm thinking of a program which was very definitely political or social, and not just a descriptive documentary.

A. The program called *One More River* raised the most specific and difficult problems. *One More River* was commissioned by the CBC for its Intertel series. That was a loose cooperative documentary organization which had been formed between the CBC, a British television production organization, NET in the U.S. and the Australian Broadcasting Corporation and a couple of others. The group decided that the CBC would do a program on race relations in the southern United States. This was 1961 or 1962. The program was based on the notion that an outsider might be able to do something a little different from what an American would do on that problem. I was selected to produce the program, and I had with me Beryl Fox as co-director and my brother Richard as the cameraman.

Through the great concern of the CBC over nepotism, my brother was never identified as a cameraman and the credits of the film say it was filmed by Allan King Associates, which was the organization that he worked for. But Richard Leiterman was the cameraman. And the crew set off on the assumption that it should report what it found in the state of race relations nine years after the Supreme Court decision granting equal rights and facilities to all Americans including blacks.

Before I left to even survey the subject I produced an outline of the film which suggested that there had been great progress made in that nine years. This was based on most of the print reports which I had read. Then we went into the South, and we found that although there had been some progress, the crucial central story of race relations in the early '60s in the U.S. and the most significant fact was that there had been *very little* progress and that, in fact, the southern U.S. was sitting on a keg of dynamite. And we reported that. We simply interviewed a lot of people and put together a program which we called *One More River*. And we were very excited about what we got.

We managed to film a Ku Klux Klan's grand dragon and his partner in the dead of night on a farm many miles from any major population center in Georgia. Beryl Fox had been successful in doing an on-camera piece with a black escort where they both attempted to go into a movie house and were turned down; and my brother was kicked in the belly I believe and his camera damaged while filming an attempt by some blacks to sit in at a lunch counter. All this stuff was successfully filmed, and we put the film together.

Then it was ready to be aired and had been approved at every level of the CBC. However, when it got to management, management felt that it wasn't a fair picture of the southern U.S. and they decided the program would not be shown. No member of the committee of management, including the president, Mr. Alphonse Oimet, had ever been in the southern U.S. This created an impasse because I refused to make substantive changes in the program. I couldn't permit myself to soften what the actual facts were. So the program was held up and was not shown to the other Intertel members.

Eventually, I was able to persuade the management that the program should run with a footnote which was to say in effect that what the viewer had just seen didn't really represent the facts of the situation! In the end I wrote what I thought was a very clever footnote which simply turned around the wording which management had suggested. It wasn't quite what the management had in mind, but it got us by. It kept my view of the situation and the program was aired and was a considerable success.

The British loved it and ran it without the footnote. The Americans at first held it up and eventually, after it had been acclaimed by the British and the Australians and had had a good reception in Canada,

NET decided to run it, and to follow it with a one-hour panel whose purpose was to smother and soften the force of the program itself. But of course footnotes and discussion groups and panel groups never really soften the thrust of a genuine piece of film.

Q. What do you think, specifically in regard to *One More River* and generally in regard to documentary film making, of the so-to-speak foreigner coming into a situation, trying to understand it very quickly and then transmitting it to viewers a couple of thousand miles away. When the truth comes down, you had read a great deal about the South, you were *not* from the South, you had *not* lived that experience, yet you're willing to come in for the stretch of a month or so, and then give what is to a certain extent a god-like overview?

Another question related to that is how do you specifically know that the interviews you're taking are typical, that they *do* stand for a generalized situation and are not a very enclosed point of view?

A. Well, of course the outsider will always tend to have a less sharp and certainly less detailed view than the insider. And my own feeling is that there is room and need for both. Generally the insiders are constantly dealing with their subject and sometimes can't see the forest for the trees. An outsider may bring a fresh point of view, and I think through the entire history of television documentary, this has been a very important factor.

I happen to think that there has never been a film about Chicago or any American city which even approached Dennis Mitchell's *Chicago* which was done under precisely the circumstances that you describe, a few months of filming in the city by someone from the other side of the ocean. But his perceptions were very fresh and in fact so startling that the city of Chicago for years was able to prevent that film from being shown anywhere in the United States, and it wasn't shown in Chicago for ten or fifteen years after it was made except to very small private groups.

As to how balanced and fair a job a film maker can do, it obviously depends on his experiences and his skills, and it also depends on having a pretty adequate budget. My own technique has always been to cast a very wide net, to interview an awful lot of people, interview a few of them on film at considerable length and talk to a great many more who never make the film and may never even make a tape recorder, but who begin to enrich my own perceptions of the situation. I then put it all together in the editing room and try to come up with something that seems to me to reflect the important aspects of the situation.

Of course, you're subject to all the limitations and the shortcomings and the prejudices that you bring to it and so on. If you've had experience as a journalist, you have some protection because the journalist is always going into situations that he knows nothing of. The better journalist will generally do a competent story and the man who sets out to prove a point of view along the lines of let's say *Time* magazine, at least in the years that I worked for them, will come out with a very prejudiced piece.

Q. You said you had difficulties with the CBC in getting *One More River* shown. Did you have difficulties with any other films in the sixties?

A. I can't remember a major half-hour or one-hour documentary that *didn't* have difficulties. But the important thing about the sixties was that we generally prevailed, and that management was less scared. When I say "we" I'm talking about the current affairs infrastructure from supervisors and executive producers down to producers and directors. We managed to get the material on the air. But there were casualties like Ross McLean who left because of a program on a divorce co-respondent which was challenged in the press. CBC chained Ross, and he was never able to regain the confidence of management.

Q. What were the problems around the film *From Harlem to Sugarhill*?

A. This is a film I did at CBS after I'd left the CBC. In 1967 CBS asked me to do a program on the black middle class. At that time, no such extensive program had been done. I was given a year to do it, a magnificent budget, well over $150,000, an hour of air time and an adequate staff, researchers, black assistants and so on. Unfortunately after completion the film ran into trouble at the senior management level.

Now at CBS management is considerably more layered than at CBC and there were five layers between myself and the president. The film successfully navigated four of those layers. The day it was shown to the president of the CBS news, Dick Salant, all of the four supervisors who had previously approved it and myself were at the screening. Salant watched for about half an hour and then walked out. This was well before the program was over. Half an hour later he called me into his office and said, "That program will never be aired on CBS."

His chief problem with it was that he saw the black middle class as generally accepting the racial situation in the U.S. in the year 1968. When I started that program, like the previous one, I had no preconceived view. I didn't know much about the black middle class, but we recorded with the black middle class in many parts of the U.S. over many months. We simply put the interviews together. And the picture that emerged was one of a smoldering revolt among the middle class. But this was contrary to management's view. Indeed, management at

CBS had the intention of running a program on the black middle class in order to demonstrate how well the middle class was fitting into the American way of life and how they were coming up very rapidly and were accepting the American way of life. And we found that the facts were somewhat different. Management was not content with the film that resulted, and in the end the film was never run by CBS. The money was simply dumped down the drain, and the film put in the morgue.

I had a long final discussion with the president, and it was agreed between us that if I wished to say and do another kind of film (I was at that time on a seven-year producer's contract at CBS) he would be happy to have me stay. However, I would have to accept and understand that if the films that I produced were not in accord with management's view of the kind of film they wanted and expected, then I would have to accept changes or have the film not run. In the end I decided that I would be happier outside of CBS and shortly thereafter I left.

Q. But you knew those were the basic preconditions when you came to the job.

A. No, I went to CBS with very high hopes. CBS was not only the best of the American networks, it was the inheritor of the Ed Murrow tradition. Fred Friendly had in fact left shortly before I came (which should have warned me, I suppose) but CBS had shown tremendous courage in standing up to government. You'll remember that my problems in Canada related to the difficulty of the CBC as a quasi-government Crown corporation standing up to the government of which it was a creature and which paid the bills. CBS, being a private enterprise, has had and has today in my view a magnificent record of standing up to government. But there are other areas in which CBS is vulnerable to pressure, and I very quickly learned what they were. I very quickly learned that there were certain programs we would never be able to do at CBS.

Q. What were these programs?

A. At CBS, one would tend to submit anything from fifteen to twenty-five subjects in order to get one cleared and be able to make a film out of it. The ones which were a little bit taboo were generally examinations of aspects of the American way of life which CBS as a corporation felt did not merit scrutiny. Anyway, these fifteen to twenty-five subjects included examinations of defense policy, examinations of the corporation generally, of monopoly, of trade union practices, of the plight of the poor people and the not so poor people, almost anything which you might imagine a corporate board room considering

189

and deciding, well, let's leave that one for another year because, if we're only going to do six or eight one-hour documentaries this year, why should we do one in an area where we are uncomfortable? That was the basic philosophy.

Q. What were the kind of programs you knew would go over, which would be attractive?

A. Well, after a while you found yourself designing them very carefully. Designing programs which would satisfy one's own need to deal with some controversial or significant element of American life, and at the same time not violate what you knew to be the unwritten rules, the unwritten law of material that would never get on the air.

I always managed this process by envisioning myself in the president's Cadillac as he was driven from Connecticut to his office watching the CBS morning news on his television set in the back seat, sheltered generally from any view of how the rest of New York and particularly the citizens of New York had to live, well protected from any problems. Here was a man who never rode the subways, who was not in danger of beging mugged or robbed, who was protected at all times, who had no driving problems because his chauffeur took care of them, who had no problems relating to paying his medical bills, who knew no one who was unemployed, who had little direct experience with any of the criminal elements of the country, who generally was willing and able to support the status quo. You know, when you really come down to it, you could even examine elements of the society which were controversial so long as the basic approach was "don't rock the boat."

Q. Were there any actual rules for film makers that you had to follow? I remember talking to a friend some years ago who said that everything had to be 100 percent authentic. You couldn't use fantasy in a CBS documentary. If you heard music on the program that had to be identified. Were those kind of rules still around at CBS?

A. Yes, and by and large I would say that I supported them, and I thought they were valid. Some of them were abused and distorted. The prohibition of music for example came about because Ed Murrow had never used music. So when Salant took over CBS news he was told Murrow never used music, and a rule was passed that we could never use music. So we didn't use music. And in some respects I thought that was not a bad policy, music often being used in a way that made me uncomfortable, to overdramatize a point. I'm not saying I'm against it all the time, but I think there is a point. If there was music, we always showed a picture of a loudspeaker.

I would just add that in general the practices and the rules at CBS news were directed towards maintaining the integrity of the broadcasts, were very important and I was wholeheartedly in favor of them. Such things as proper identification of the person speaking, and very stringent practices regarding editing. We had a practice, for example, that any subject who was interviewed had the right to come and examine the outtakes or examine a transcript of the entire interview and we made bloody sure that in the editing process any condensation of anyone's remarks represented fairly what he had to say because we knew that he had access to those outtakes, and that this is a very crucial thing. By and large the practices were good, the supervision was intelligent and proper, and I'm very much in favor of those kinds of practices in any organization which attempts to practice television journalism.

Q. Well, that strikes me as a very fair news comment but the general practice would seem to make for a rather dull documentary, as if you're neglecting half the possible forms within your field of film.

A. Well, sure, I grant that there is a place for drama and a mixture of drama and documentary and programs which do both. I tend to be a little old-fashioned, and feel that the audience is entitled to know which is which. I don't think that necessarily kills the thrust of the documentary or of a dramatic documentary, but I think the audience should know, is this a real person speaking, has he been coached, is he speaking lines that someone has given him, is he an actor who is reading lines, and are those the actual words that he is reenacting and which is when? And there are means of doing that.

However, I think that if you open all the doors and you say, "We won't make any rules. We'll let the film maker as an artist practice his craft and do what he wishes," then you're totally dependent on the sense of integrity of that film maker, and I don't believe that every film maker has that integrity or is entitled to my vote to do what he wishes.

Q. It seems to me that in the middle years of the sixties CBS and the other networks were making fairly good, fairly interesting news documentaries, but totally neglected the film of human sensibility, the film about the ordinary human being. Had you or any of your other colleagues tried to make that kind of film while at CBS?

A. I think the criticism is a valid one. My own approach has always been to try to see the story through the human equation, and I did have difficulty doing that at CBS because of the basic preconceptions. I suppose that the problems I had at CBS related more to that than anything else. Because as you and I are both aware, when you begin

191

to deal with an abstract problem in human terms, then you begin to get at people where it hurts. And it's at that point that management or, let's say upper-level concerns, management concerns, censorship restrictions, begin to be imposed. However I also feel that within the general rules of permissible techniques at CBS, that you could really do just about anything that needed to be done and that I don't feel that those rules were an impossibly hobbling thing. I feel that they resulted in many dull documentaries which reached nobody, but it was possible, notwithstanding those rules, to do human documents.

I seem to be coming down on both sides of this, and I suppose I am. In other words, I'm very much afraid of giving the film maker, in a television journalistic sense, complete license. I want him controlled. I want to know what I'm watching. If there aren't rules then I want some process to be established whereby people of great experience and integrity and background and judgment are making those judgments. I'm not afraid of a Marcel Ophuls taking a couple of years and looking back at the process of the Nazi occupation of France. And I don't care what method he uses because I trust the man. But the run of the mill documentarian who gets his hands on the levers of a public network should not, I feel, be given those kinds of freedoms.

Some process is needed to protect the public and indeed to protect the man against himself. And if they are rules that CBS had or simply practices that grew up as have grown up at CBC, I think that many of those are essential and I would rather see networks err in the direction of being overly cautious, because it's an immensely powerful medium. There's nothing which approaches the power of television in dealing with subjects.

If CBS does *The Selling of the Pentagon*, a vitally important program, I want to know that all the proper regulations have been carried out because the program is explosive. In these kind of programs I want to know that the interviews that I see are fairly edited, that they can stand the test of the publication of the entire transcript, that music is not brought in when a tank is sold to the Arabs in order to dramatize the point, that some process of experienced, journalistic judgment has been imposed on the generally young film maker who is at work so that he isn't given complete license. How you do that and still allow venturesome controversial work to be done is the problem, and it's always the problem in every network.

# 10
## *Youth Terror:*
### *The View From Behind the Gun*
### *Helen Whitney*

Youth Terror, *directed and produced by Helen Whitney, was broadcast by
the ABC network in June 1978. Filmed mainly in New York, it provides a
powerful insight into juvenile deliquency from the perspective of the delinquents
themselves.* Time *magazine called the film "possibly the most disturbing and
dramatic news program ever seen on American commercial networks." Tom
Shales of the* Washington Post *said that the film makers had turned "a sociological cliché into riveting and profoundly disturbing television reality."*

*The teenagers in the film are street kids and use street talk. Some of this
language was found to be outrageously offensive by a dozen ABC affiliates who
elected not to carry the program. But the shocks are not in the vocabulary but
in the content. Here are accounts of acts of aggression that would make the most
hardened criminal pause. A young pale boy is asked why he preferred an ice pick
as a weapon in a previous assault. "Internal bleeding," he answers. When
Whitney asks some young men about limitations of violence, one replies "Ain't
no limit. If I gotta kill you to get what I want, I'll kill you."*

*The interviews provide the heart of this documentary, from the teenager who
declares at the start of the film, "This gun is what talks around this neighborhood," to the Brooklyn youth who says, "We're raised like animals, so we act
like animals." And when the film ends searing portraits remain like the rec-
onciliation of a Puerto Rican boy with his mother, a former drug addict.*

*Youth Terror shows the deep despair, hopelessness and cynicism of the
American urban slum jungles, with the teenagers seen as much as victims as
aggressors. Solutions are discussed—better jobs, schools, neighborhoods and housing—but in the end this is, as critic John O'Connor calls it, "a tale of pow-
erlessness coupled with the fantasy of being powerful."*

*The grip of* Youth Terror *lies in its sense of reality and unvarnished truth.
Thus there were shockwaves all round when, subsequent to its broadcast, the
Black Producers' Association charged that sections of* Youth Terror *had been
specially contrived and staged.*

*In its request for an FCC investigation the BPA claimed that ABC News
misrepresented many of the profiled youths as still involved in delinquent behavior when that was not the case. The BPA also claimed that the producer*

*had staged scenes of gang violence especially for the cameras. The FCC subsequently investigated the complaint and in its report of February 15, 1979, totally cleared Miss Whitney and the ABC and stated that no further action was warranted on its part.*

*I'd done my interview with Helen Whitney just after the broadcast and at that point none of the complaints had been raised, and so of course they are not discussed in our talk. Originally I'd met Whitney at a film seminar in Boston in 1977. One of her films had been shown and the audience had been extremely critical. I myself had very much liked the film when I saw it in New York and thought the seminar audience was wrong in its judgment. Helen and I talked about this and afterwards became good friends. So when* Youth Terror *came out I was eager to see what had happened to Helen's filming over the years.*

*For Whitney* Youth Terror *marked a return to ABC after a few years' absence. She had begun in film at the age of 26 by working for Fred Freed on the NBC "White Paper" series, first as a researcher and then as associate producer.*

*After six years at NBC she went to ABC news to become associate producer on a documentary called* Fire, *which was produced by Pam Hill.* Fire *went on to win two Emmies and a Peabody award.*

*Whitney then decided to take a year out from television and worked for a while as an editor on the* New York Times. *Her filming then resumed when she teamed up with independent producer Dewitt Sage. Together they did two films. The first was a 90-minute special on modern immigrants called* To America. *The other film was* First Edition, *which shows a day in the life of a newspaper, and was the film I'd seen which aroused so much criticism at the seminar.*

*Whitney is a graduate of Sarah Lawrence and also has an M.A. in English Literature from the University of Chicago. Her specialty is Victorian literature, and she taught university for a year before taking up filming.*

Q. When you came to ABC what was your specific job?

A. I was to co-direct a film with Pam Hill about juvenile delinquency. It was to be without narration. Within a few weeks after my arrival, Pam was promoted to executive producer of all ABC's documentaries so I took over the film. I spent nine months working on it, and my credits were producer, director, and writer.

Q. At that stage did you feel any particular tradition at ABC of documentaries, or could you sense anything that distinguished an ABC documentary from those of NBC or CBS?

A. When Av Westin was an executive producer about four years ago he started the "Close Up" series, and it quickly got an excellent reputation. The *Fire* documentary that Pam and I had done together came out of his shop. His documentaries were primarily investigative news studies with less focus on innovative film making. The "Close Up" series had a deservedly fine reputation.

Q. You came in as director, producer, and writer. Had the films you'd done before had this kind of analytic quality to them? Or was this style something new for you?

A. The films on which I was researcher and associate producer for Fred Freed's "White Paper" series were, in effect, essays. The emphasis was less visual than journalistic. The emphasis was more on the information to be disseminated than on the picture you'd be seeing. But *First Edition* was without narration and that was a very valuable experience.

Q. Now this film, which Pam left to you alone, eventually became *Youth Terror?*

A. Right.

Q. What were the guidelines laid down when you came in, and what was your reaction to the subject?

A. Well, we wanted to go without any narration at all, which was unprecedented for a commercial network. Pam wanted to do it. I thought it was a terrific idea and the network acceded. Of course Fred Wiseman had been doing it for years, but it was a style the commercial networks had never used.

Q. What was the brief that Pam gave you?

A. The subject was to be the origins of juvenile delinquency.

Q. What research did you or Pam do on this?

A. We read all the important studies. We talked to people from Harvard, from Stanford, from the University of Chicago. Talked to psychologists, to streetworkers. All this is before we got to the kids. Pam began it and I finished talking to so-called experts. I also read an enormous amount.

Q. What happened to the sociological and educational theories when you actually met your subjects? And was there much conflict among the experts?

A. We decided to have a strong theoretical base before we went out into the field. But the theory was certainly altered for me by the kids that I met. The experts didn't agree; there was very little consensus. Of course, everyone roughly agrees that the family, institutions, and jobs are the important areas. But everyone has their own priorities.

Q. You steeped yourself in the literature and the experts. Where did you go from there?

A. To the kids. And that was the most difficult for personal reasons and for practical reasons as well. One's fears had to be overcome. I spoke to at least 500 kids, and found them in a variety of ways. I found them through jails and I found them through diversion projects (these are projects that divert kids from jails). Then I found them through various kinds of institutions. Through reformatories. And most important, most of them I found through word of mouth out on the street.

Most of the kids I ended up using were referred to me. I would talk to kids in a jail or I would talk to a kid in an outreach program and he would say I should talk to his friend who lives in Bushwick. Then I would go out to Bushwick with him and I'd meet twenty other kids that day. The best kids I met were out on the street. But as a necessary stage for myself in overcoming my fear I began with the institutions. There was some protection there. For a few weeks I was meeting them there. And then I started going out by myself or with them or simply going out on the streets alone.

Q. Can you say more about your fear and also the reaction to you as a white middle-class woman?

A. I met Roger, the most articulate kid in the film, through a diversion project. He told me if I would come out alone to Bushwick, he would introduce me to his friends in the area. I went out alone and I knocked on the door. Roger and I had had a long conversation before, so I felt I had made some contact with him. I also thought it was necessary that I go out alone as evidence of some reaching out on my part and saying well, I trust what I see. So I walked into a room in which there were eight strangers. I assumed all of them had long jail records, and were savvy in the ways of crime. "Heavy hitters," as they described themselves. Some of the feelings I had that day—I remember it well—were fear mingled with embarrassment. It's difficult asking questions like, why are you robbing? Why are you stealing? Why are you angry? Why have you raped that woman? Why have you killed somebody? These are not easy questions to ask. Fear and embarrassment really sort of slipped into each other.

That was a difficult afternoon. I had to assume they wanted to meet me, and they wanted to talk. And I didn't want to appear afraid or naive. But I was nervous, very nervous. I also have a relatively tough-minded approach about personal responsibility. I agree that these kids have been assaulted in a variety of ways, yet I finally do feel that it's simplistic to say that is *the* reason why kids are doing these things.

Q. Did it ever get to the point where they were really angry with you?

A. Yes. That afternoon in Bushwick I asked questions like, "The immigrants made it. And if *they* could do it, why not you?" "Do you really want a job if you don't show up?" "What kind of salary do you think you're entitled to if you haven't finished high school?" A lot of heat was generated that afternoon. I was told they respected me more for asking those questions that afternoon.

Q. How long did you spend on this kind of research?

A. Four months.

Q. Having done the research, did you know pretty well what you wanted to draw out of the interviews or was there still a surprise?

A. There were surprises, but I knew what I was going for. I had spent so much time with the youths that I knew, both visually and intellectually, what to expect. I had an editing outline on paper and in my head before I went out to shoot, so I had a pretty clear sense of what the finished film was going to look like.

Q. How did you select the actual kids for the film?

A. The more I talked to kids the more I became certain that our original research idea areas were important ones. The family, the institutions, the jobs, the street. But I also felt there was a very important theme of identity and power running through all of them. Identity and power are central to the origins of delinquency. Again, after two or three months into my conversations I began to listen for and to look for kids who could illustrate certain kinds of problems. Certain kinds of problems within the family where anger and disorientation begin. Certain kinds of problems within institutions. Certain kinds of problems in the job area. And I began to look for the kids who could best articulate and illustrate those problems.

Q. Were you also changing your mind about some of the theoretical research and expert advice at that stage?

A. None of the experts with whom I was familiar were placing what I thought was the appropriate importance on power or identity except one caseworker by the name of Bob Siegel. He was extraordinary, truly extraordinary. More knowledgeable, more articulate, more tough-minded and compassionate than anyone else I met. He was the most important "expert" that I met and greatly influenced my thinking.

Q. When you selected the kids or young people, were there any ground rules which you laid down for them or which they laid down for you?

A. One of our ground rules was that there would be, as in all network films, no quid pro quo. There were no assurances or promises from us of money, favors, or anything like that. Another ground rule was to try to protect them where possible when talking about specifics of a crime that had been committed and that could subject them to prosecution. Also no names would be used. Only first names occasionally if they came up naturally. Otherwise they would be identified only as a subtitle shown in the film as "Brooklyn Youth," "Bronx Youth," "Newark Family." So identities were protected.

Q. And yet they knew that the mere fact of appearing on television might put them under greater surveillance. Some of them said some pretty outrageous things like the fellow who talked about using the ice pick as a weapon.

A. The police have so much crime happening in front of them that stories of the past don't seem to interest them particularly. Obviously I spoke of this at length with criminal lawyers. Also my husband is a criminal lawyer and was concerned over their safety. I was assured by him as well as countless other criminal lawyers I consulted that nothing was going to happen as long as no specifics were mentioned.

Q. Did the parents try and put any controls on the filming?

A. No.

Q. Now when you talked to them did you get a sense of what they said being mostly true or a sense of the stories being exaggerated for the film?

A. Anything that I felt was exaggerated or untrue was simply edited out. Also one of the advantages of spending so much time with these youths, hanging out with them, going to see their families and their friends was that I got to know them pretty well. And I got to know them to the extent that when the bullshit started, as it always does, I'd simply say, "Cut it." I also had a pretty good idea of their criminal records and their particular specialty of crime. So I'd know if someone was being evasive, dishonest, or simply hamming for me or for the camera. So that gave me enormous leverage with them. I didn't want to embarrass anyone but I wanted to ask questions about violence and personal responsibility and self-awareness.

Q. Were there any scenes or particular elements which you developed which you cut out of the final film?

A. We had an important character who was finally dropped. This was a woman whose brother had been a gang leader who had been killed. She was articulate and expressed ideologically the basic themes of the film. She explained what drove the brother out onto the street was the need for identity—wanting to feel like somebody, because he couldn't feel that way in school, or in the family, or in the neighborhood in which he lived. There were many scenes filmed with her at home, or on the Staten Island ferry where she would go to relax and escape from her environment. We filmed a scene at the graveyard where she and her mother had gone to visit the grave of Husky, her brother. We dropped all these scenes because they lacked the immediacy that a live subject could give us.

Q. There is one scene in the film where it's clear that while you are interviewing one of the family, somebody else in the family has used that opportunity to steal your bag. How did you handle that situation?

A. I'd left my pocketbook in the kitchen, and while I was interviewing in the other room it was stolen. When I realized what had happened I turned off the cameras and asked who had stolen my pocketbook. It was the kind of family in which, on any given day, thirty extra people were in that very tiny chaotic apartment. There were eleven kids and their thirty friends. Everyone, as you could see in the film, said they were innocent. And it could well have been one of the strangers that had come in. I tried to find out who did it. Then I asked the mother, who returned from work, how she felt about the situation. This is what you hear in the film.

Q. In the film you have some terrific interviews and discussions where the kids really open up to you. But you also include here and there some really violent scenes which illustrate youth terror pretty horribly. How did you get these scenes?

A. They happened spontaneously.

Q. Can you give me examples of two or three of them?

A. There are three violent scenes that you are talking about. We filmed them in Williamsburg, Brooklyn. Williamsburg is six blocks square. On any given day everything seems to be happening. One of the youths who lives there describes it as the Wild West. Do you remember in the first minute of the film you see a woman being thrown on the hood of a car? That woman is me.

We'd arrived one afternoon to do some filming and there were some prostitutes rolling around on the dirt. Crowds had formed. We started filming them. One prostitute raced towards the camera. Obviously the camera aggravated the situation which was already serious by the time we arrived. I jumped in front of the camera, and they threw me on the car and my cameraman went on shooting.

The second scene was with the gang kids. That violence was more the theater of self than actual violence, in a way. They put their colors on. They were strolling up and down the street where they knew we were filming. They enjoyed it. That's what being visible is all about. They started horsing around and it got out of hand. We were there. We filmed it.

Q. And the third scene?

A. We rode with the police one night in an area that some of the kids had come from. And there was a stabbing and we simply filmed it. I felt the scenes of violence were necessary because this is the world that these kids live in. They see violence at home, they see violence out in the street, and they participate in both. I felt it was an essential part of the film. In fact, there's probably a good deal more violence in their lives than the film suggests.

Q. The films looks beautifully shot. It's one of those documentaries which is much more than just filmed interviews strung together. It really exists as film in its own right. You must have worked very hard for that. There is a real feeling for composition, movement, and texture.

A. I have a fantastic cameraman named Don Guy whom I worked with on my previous film. He has a rare combination of qualities. He has a feature eye—a sense of form and style. He also has documentary fluidity and is incredibly smooth. He can move like a human tripod. But I made an enormous attempt in the research period not only to find the kids but to find those parts of their lives that were real and visual.

Q. When you brought the film back for editing what were the problems or complexities you were faced with at that juncture?

A. I had to structure the whole thing. It was a monumental task.

Q. There always are problems of structure in these kind of things. I was thinking more of problems with the network, problems of violent language.

A. Language was not mentioned at that point. I was left alone up to my rough-cut. During that period I worried about transitions. How and why am I going to move from scene X to scene Y? How could I make it clear? How could I make the transition from Harry and his pigeons to the streetworker and his kids smooth and organic?

Q. What was the reaction at the rough-cut stage?

A. It was good. Pam liked it but she felt that it needed more pacing. It was too cerebral. Now I had deliberately saved eight shooting days, so I was able to go out to find visually supporting material to make better transitions, and to make the whole piece hold together.

Q. The reviews were quite ecstatic, which must have made you very happy, and I personally like the film very much. Do you think, however, that some of the reaction might have had to do with the fact that finally a network was offering a non-God-narrated film?

A. I got a lot of letters and most of them were very positive. Many of the people who wrote said how refreshing it was not to be told how to feel about something. There wasn't a single letter I received that said "Oh, I missed not having X anchormen there summing it up or telling me what to think." Not one. I was pleased about that because I wasn't trying to say anything I thought particularly original—I was trying to dramatically render important journalistic truths about the

200

problem of juvenile delinquency. I was trying to get to the viscera of the audience and they seemed to respond in that way.

Q. Did any of the young people get back to you after seeing the film?

A. Yes. Many of the kids called me. They loved the film. But it was Roger's and Harry's reaction that I most worried about. They were the main characters. It really meant a lot to me. Roger was the most articulate youth on the show who had responded so passionately and so eloquently to my questions.

Q. How is the film being used apart from the network showing?

A. Well, McGraw-Hill have bought it for distribution in schools and colleges. Conferences on delinquency are sending in requests to buy it from them or rent it.

Q. Are you now being asked to talk as an expert on delinquency?

A. I'm beginning to, but I do not describe myself as an expert on delinquency.

Q. Have you got to the point where you can think about your next film or are you just taking a breather?

A. Exactly. I just want to recover my life. Read, think, just put back those dimensions into my life that are gone when you're so narrowly focused on one subject.

"The World at War": Episode 3, *France Falls*. Pilots at a Royal Air Force aerodrome in France race to their Hurricane aircraft to attack invading German planes.

"The World at War": Episode 4, *Alone*. Londoners sleep in Underground stations during the Blitz. November 1940—the Elephant and Castle station.

"The World at War": Episode 9, *Stalingrad*. The symbol of Russia's stubborn resistance, Stalingrad holds out against Hitler's besieging armies until they are encircled and destroyed. Women take supplies into the almost destroyed city.

"The World at War": Episode 17, *Morning*. The D-Day landings pushed the Germans away from the Channel for the first time since 1940. Paratroopers synchronize watches for their drops behind German fortifications.

"The World at War": Episode 23, *Pacific*. Marines landing on Japanese-held islands faced impenetrable jungle and heavy enemy fire.

"The World at War": Episode 17, *Morning*. British tanks
and infantry go ashore on the beaches of Normandy.

"The British Empire": *O the Jubilee!* The landau used
by Queen Victoria in 1897 is filmed for the program.

*Edna the Inebriate Woman.*
Patricia Hayes in the title role.

Emile de Antonio's *Point of Order:*
Roy Cohn and Senator Joseph McCarthy.

Emile de Antonio's *Underground:*
De Antonio (left) and Haskell Wexler (with camera)
confront the group of Weatherpeople.

*Action: The October Crisis of 1970.*
Police cavalcade as Canada is put under martial law.

*In the Year
of the Pig:*
"Found footage"
of American
involvement
in Vietnam.

*Sad Song of Yellow Skin*, by Michael Rubbo.
Monks on the Island of Peace pray almost all day.

*Vietnam and Politics*

# 11

## *In the Year of the Pig*
### and
## *Underground*
### Emile de Antonio

*During the late sixties a number of films were shown in the U.S. which discussed the Vietnam imbroglio from a leftist view. While parts of Felix Greene's* Inside North Vietnam *were shown on PBS most of the other films were totally shunned by the networks as political dynamite. Besides Greene's work, other films which claimed attention were Joris Ivens's* The Seventeenth Parallel, *and* Far From Vietnam. *However the most stimulating and politically sophisticated of all these films was Emile de Antonio's* In the Year of the Pig *(1969).*

*In* Year of the Pig *de Antonio provided an encapsulation of forty years of Vietnamese history. In so doing he also presented a background and perspective of the war totally missing from the then current U.S. television programming.*

*The film's method is superficially simple. Historic newsreel material culled from both Western and Communist sources is edited alongside or together with in-depth interviews with Vietnamese experts who range from journalists and politicians to Buddhist historians and philosophers. There is no commentary. Instead statement builds on statement till a picture of immense French and American folly is revealed.*

*It is not, of course, a fair film. De Antonio speaks from a particular viewpoint and uses almost any filmic trick to emphasize his point. Thus the material is wickedly manipulated with statements of presidents and army officers being taken out of context and then intercut with scenes that make the officials appear total fools if not villains.*

*We know all this but still accept a lot of de Antonio's reasoning because it makes coherent historical sense. There are tricks galore. There is subjectivity galore. But there is also an essential truth and reason that goes beyond all that and which gives the film its weight and importance.*

*When I met de Antonio all the things were present that I'd ever heard about him. There was the robustness and the sheer energy. There was the talk about giving up drinking. There was talk of the five wives and love of women, and the recounting of the history of the various careers (barge captain, longshoreman, peddler and so on.) And there was the humor and warmth of a man who de-scribed himself to me as "a middle-aged vampire."*

*But these were minor things—almost parodies of the expected de Antonio image. What came across of a more serious nature was a generosity and openness of mind, a certain directness and human understanding, and a surprising lack of polemic from someone so left-leaning. Above all the sense of a man who really cares, which was something I'd already heard from other friends whom "De" had helped at early stages of their careers.*

*Gradually we eased into the interview and the core of things, and often I found myself disagreeing with de Antonio's viewpoint. For example my own tendency is to distrust not only American policy but also the idealization of North Vietnam, and justification phrases like "customary post-revolutionary excesses" don't fall easily on my ear. But it was de Antonio and* his *opinions that mattered, and the need to bring out the political concern behind most of his films.*

*De Antonio's importance lies in the intelligence he has applied to an exami-nation of the politics of the sixties, and his ability to get a critically left view seriously considered by a complacent middle-class liberal audience. In* Point of Order *(1963), for example, de Antonio required his audience to review and rethink the Army McCarthy hearings; in* Rush to Judgment *(1966) he reex-amined the Kennedy assassination and the Oswald case with Jay Epstein;* Year of the Pig *looks at the Vietnamese war while* Millhouse *(1971) presents a devastating satirical portrait of Nixon.*

*Stylistically de Antonio has done three things. First he has avoided straight* vérité, *which tended to be the main path of the sixties. Second he has revivified the collage documentary dependent on historic material; and third he has es-chewed commentary and elevated the importance of the lengthy interview in serious analytic documentary.*

*The interview as documentary can be seen in its fullest form in* Under-ground, *in which de Antonio and his colleagues talk to five Weatherpeople who have eluded the FBI for years. While the film was being made de Antonio and his colleagues, Haskell Wexler and Mary Lampson, were in fact severely har-assed by the FBI which issued a subpoena against them and their work. Even-tually the subpoena was dropped and the film finished.*

*The interest of the film lies in the insights it provides into the background, thinking and hopes of the five self-styled revolutionaries. On that score it is fine, if a little long. However when the film tries to illustrate the Weatherpeople's contentions about U.S. decadence and corruption it begins to fall flat.* Un-derground *is not a particularly good film (in fact that kind of qualitative term just isn't relevant to it) but it is a unique film. It is social comment, tract, manifesto, and confession. In a decade when so little alternative argument or*

206

*serious radical discussion gets shown on the media a film like* Underground *is absolutely necessary even if one disagrees with most of the arguments it puts out.*

Q. How did you get into documentary? What was the starting point for you?

A. I began in 1961 with a film called *Point of Order.* My life up until that point had been very much living by my wits. Unlike most film makers I was an intellectual. I went to Harvard and did graduate work at Columbia. At college I joined the Young Communist League, and the John Reed Society. In fact, for someone who is not much of a joiner, I joined everything political I could. Later I taught philosophy but thought that was a mug's game. So I became a one-day-a-year business person. I made a lot of money one day a year. I was a Marxist among capitalists but became depoliticized by my army experiences in World War II. Afterwards I got into alcohol and women. I was married five times and lived with countless other ones. I read a lot and led a generally chaotic bohemian life.

In 1959 I became a communist again—unaffiliated—and also got interested in film, which I had always disliked. I had admired the Marx brothers, W.C. Fields and the early Soviets, but I did not go to the movies as Americans did. I mean a year would go by without seeing a picture.

Q. Why did you suddenly become political again in 1959?

A. I think I sniffed in the air that politics might work again. I knew Kennedy and I was more uncomfortable with his election than I was with Eisenhower's or Truman's. I started meeting young radicals who were political for the first time. During the fifties I had as friends what you might call the homosexual avant garde. My best friends were John Cage, Rauchenberg and Jasper Johns who used to come to my house in the country, and get drunk, and talk.

Q. When you started off in film, why did you choose the McCarthy question?

A. Well, he was surely the most powerful and important political figure of the fifties. He defined that decade that was coming to an end. And there was absolutely nothing about him on film except that rather empty-barrel TV show which was made four years after he had been running over the country.

The choice of the figure was clear, and then what further appealed to me was the idea of working with dead footage—a kind of collage junk idea I got from my painter friends.

When I first approached CBS about acquiring the McCarthy foot-age, CBS claimed they did not have it. They were not lying. They had masses of material stored in a bonded film warehouse in New Jersey all jumbled up, confused and forgotten. However friends of mine at CBS conducted a search within the organization for me and found 188 hours of raw material in this warehouse.

Now, to the film itself. I wanted to make a political documentary and, in a certain way, the initial idea came from Dan Talbot. Incidentally it was Dan, who owned a theater called The New Yorker, who actually reshaped the taste of the American cinema audience by running very unconventional material at his movie house. One day Dan said, "What is the most interesting thing on television that happened in the fifties?" and we both said "the Army-McCarthy hearings." Dan didn't want to make a film—he just wanted to gather a big chunk of the hearings or even their summaries and make a program about McCarthy.

I knew nothing about film but I wanted to make a film out of the material. Dan, who is somewhat more timid than I am, said, "You don't know anything about film, let's ask Orson Welles to do it." He cabled Welles but Welles wasn't interested. We then hired a professional to do it. He started but then we fired him and I took it over. The fundamental idea of the film was that there would be no narration, and I think one of the important things about it is that it's the first full-length political documentary without one line of narration. It is totally organic.

Q. There was obviously a possibility that Dan would make the film. How did the final decision come to you?

A. I said to Dan, "I'll match you. Either you'll make a film or I will. We'll toss and whoever wins will make a film without any interference from anyone else. When it's finished we'll look at it together." Dan then said, "That's unfair. I can't do that. I own this theater. I have a wife and children." So I said, "I'll do it." And he said, "OK," and that is what happened.

Q. How did you raise the money?

A. I have always been good at raising money. I have raised over one million dollars to make left-wing films. I don't come from a poor background and I have always known people with money. Anyway, there was this nice liberal millionaire called Eliot Pratt, who gave his occupation as sharecropper. He was a liberal, very rich, and he hated McCarthy, and I went to see him. We met at his house and then went over to 73rd and 3rd where there is a place called Allen's. We had a hamburger and a couple of drinks, and I told him what I wanted to do. Eliot thought and then said, "Well how much money do you think that would cost?" I said, "I don't know. I have never made a film." So he said, "Well, what if I put up $100,000 to start?" I said, "Wait, first I have to get a corporation established." Later the meal check was brought and he tipped 20 cents, and then did indeed give me the $100,000. In the end, the film cost a lot more.

CBS having a monopoly on the material demanded $50,000 for the copyright (it didn't matter the material was dead and useless) and fifty percent of every dollar made after that. CBS has made more money out of *Point of Order* than anybody.

Q. What was your goal or guiding objective when you started cutting?

A. There are two concepts that seemed in part what I wanted, which were form and content. The formal aspects were a lot more intriguing. What I frankly wanted to make was a commercially successful film and *Point of Order* was the first political non-TV documentary after World War II that was successful financially and played theaters. I wanted the feature line to be organically contained, unified, without any external noise, without any narration explaining anything. I wanted the thing to be self-explanatory political statement. There is something in narration that to me is inherently fascist and condescending in the sense that you are telling other people what it is they are looking at while they are looking at it. If the film works you do not have to narrate it, it narrates itself.

Q. When CBS agreed to make the archive film available was it worried about your political background, or the use to which you might put the material?

A. CBS was so nervous about who we were, and was I a communist, that clause 14 of our contract with CBS stated that if the CBS name was ever mentioned, the contract would be null and void, and the $50,000 forfeited. When the film was finished, however, and all the reviewers loved it and *Time* magazine said, "A psychedelic experience," CBS took all those reviews and published them in a very handsome brochure. And that outraged me, because the critics and CBS missed the point. And all the liberals who had their ejaculations looking at the film, thinking about what it was they should have been doing during that time, also missed the point.

The film is not an attack on McCarthy. The film is an attack on the American government. My feeling is that if you look at the film carefully, Welch comes off as badly as McCarthy. He comes off as a rather brilliant, sinister, clever lawyer who used McCarthy's techniques to destroy McCarthy. There has certainly never been a more craven Secretary of the Army than Stevens who was humbled and crumbled by

209

McCarthy, and there has never been more patent window dressing than those idiotic generals sitting bemedalled behind the Secretary of the Army. I am thinking now of making a play out of this—a kind of Dada piece of theater, in which the generals will be painted fifteen feet high and Welch will be played by Oscar Lee Brown, as a kind of sibilant wild homosexual. But all insinuating, because Welch wasn't a homosexual. He was clever and McCarthy knew he was being gored to death. Don't misunderstand me. I wanted McCarthy gored to death but I also wanted the whole system to be exposed, and the only people who saw that were a few Marxists. The good bourgeois critics loved the film and made it successful.

Q. What were your problems of "innocence" in terms of making a first film? What were the mistakes you made?

A. Well, on the whole it was a generally satisfying experience. There is nothing that I would do differently in that first film. In other films after that, yes. But I have never worked so hard in my life. It was my introduction to real work. I mean I had done all kinds of physical work, and I enjoyed it, but that was different from spending two years, seven days a week for probably ten to twelve hours a day, fiddling with all that stuff.

Q. What were you looking for? How did you select your hour and a half out of the 180 hours?

A. For me the most important thing in film is structure. Now I knew the material very well before I saw any of it because I had watched the hearings and I have a good memory for that kind of thing. There were certain key moments, but the basic idea was to tell the story of what happened and to reveal the softness of the system, and to reveal how a demagogue was undone by a machine, because he was not undone by any principled stand or by morality or by anyone being against him.

Q. Can you tell me something about your restructuring of the material of the Army hearings in *Point of Order* and why you did it?

A. The most obvious restructuring of what happened is at the very end of the film. Now in real life, no point was made. The actual hearings ended quietly; the Senate wanted them over—the President wanted them over—too much of the American system had been revealed. So the hearings actually ended with Senator Mundt banging the gavel, and everyone cleaning up his papers and walking out.

I wanted to reveal what really happened, and I did not want to *say* it—I wanted to have it done *cinematically*. What really happened is that McCarthy lost the American people. When those hearings were over, so was McCarthy. When those hearings were over he never had any strength left. When those hearings were over the Senate finally had the guts to produce a censure hearing. And that's the reason that that last sequence is made out of many days and in addition has that immediate cut to the silent, absolutely empty room. That emptiness is indeed the emptiness that fell on McCarthy. He had nothing left to say to anybody, and he died of drink almost exactly three years later.

Q. It seems to me that besides the end, you manipulate words and pictures quite extensively in the film.

A. Frequently. The material is totally manipulated. *Cinéma vérité* is first of all a lie, and secondly a childish assumption about the nature of film. *Cinéma vérité* is a joke. Only people without feelings or convictions could even think of making *cinéma vérité*. I happen to have strong feelings and some dreams and my prejudice is under and in everything I do.

Q. Let us just come back to *vérité* in a minute. What I would like to understand is how you can say narration is fascist, because it tells you exactly what to think and yet you can use a very deliberate, manipulative editing to do the same thing.

A. Well, it is not just fascist, it is boring, and this is what's wrong with television documentaries. It's boring as hell, and maybe more than fascist there is a kind of contempt built into it, and it is too easy. When you come to a filmic problem you solve it by just having a voice telling you what it is.

Q. But if I am manipulated by your editing, by your structuring the film's A against B against C, why is that any more creditable?

A. Well, if it is more creditable it is because it works better.

Q. Why are you so down on and angry at the *cinéma vérité*?

A. Well, first of all the phrase. What I am in favor of in *cinéma vérité* is the technical stuff that was developed—the light cameras, the effective sync sound systems. But it is the empty-headed pretentiousness that gets me. The belief of lack of prejudice. There is no film made without pointing a camera and the pointing of that camera is already, in a sense, a definitive gesture of prejudice, of feeling. You cannot cut a piece of film, you cannot edit film without indicating prejudice. The *cinéma vérité* people are essentially apolitical, so that they go for high moments. Does anyone still call himself *cinéma vérité*? No! I think it is fairly dead.* Leacock does not make films anymore; Pennebaker is a foundation entrepreneur, and the Maysles say their films are better than fiction or documentary. So I don't know who in this country makes *cinéma vérité*. But there is not one of those *vérité* films that

*AR: This is obviously de Antonio at his wildest as *cinéma vérité* continues to thrive and grow. See for example the work of Joan Churchill, Richard Cohen, and David and Judith MacDougall.

couldn't be challenged on the basis of whose truth was it. It is much better, I think, to make a film from the position that you really occupy, rather than pretend you occupy no position, since that is almost a physical impossibility.

Q. Do you make films for specific audiences or just films for yourself, or a combination of both? Who is the audience?

A. I am a Marxist and I am a bad Marxist, because I do not make films for audiences, I make them for myself. I have thought this out very hard, and it seems to me to be as contemptible as television to assume that I am going to make a film for this kind of an audience. I have no measuring devices, nor am I interested in measuring devices that would measure what kind of an audience.

I usually make films because of anger or opportunity. I made *Millhouse* for example because I had been angry with Nixon since the Hiss case, since 1946 when he began his political life, but I didn't do anything till the opportunity presented itself.

Q. What was that opportunity?

A. I was over in Movielab working, when the phone rang and someone said, "Look, I have just stolen all the footage of one of the networks on Nixon and I'll give it to you for nothing, if you will make a film about him." I said, "I cannot give you an answer on that, let me have ten minutes." He called back and I said, "Ok, I'll do the film on Nixon, I will put aside what I am doing (which was *Painters Painting*) but I never want to see you, and I won't pay you for it." He said, "I don't want money."

Then I said, "Come to the Movielab building at midnight tonight. I'll have the superintendent let you in, and you leave everything in the middle of the room." When I came in at seven in the morning, there were 200 cans of film there. I can say that freely now, because the statute of limitations has expired. That was in 1970.

I was the only film maker on Nixon's "enemies" list for making a film. There are ten White House memoranda that begin, "The White House, Washington, D.C. Subject: Emile de Antonio." Those memoranda are actually more interesting to me than some of the prizes I have won. Those ten pages are the ultimate prize.

Q. As the sixties progressed did you get any feeling of being watched by higher-ups or by officialdom because of the nature of your films?

A. Not until my second film, which invited interference.

Q. That was *Rush to Judgment*?

A. Yes.

Q. What happened?

212

A. When we went to film in Dallas the Sheriff's department simply followed us around with a pick-up truck with a lot of shotguns.

Q. Do you think this was political, or does it generally happen to film makers? I have a friend who was filming in the South and had exactly the same experience, and it was not a particularly political film.

A. Well, I think this was for political reasons because of a good many other things that happened. I now have two suits against the government. One is before Judge Sirica against the FBI, the other is before Judge Bryant against the CIA. This one has to do with the FBI because Mark Lane and I uncovered a great many people the Warren Commission could not seem to find.

I'll give you an example of the atmosphere. Jean Hill was probably as close as anybody when Kennedy was shot and she was one of the many people we called. When we first phoned her she said, "Sure, why not." We didn't lie. We didn't say we were CBS or NBC, we just said we were an independent group of people making a film who doubted the assumptions of the Warren Commission.

When we went to film her she was really scared. There was obviously a short circuit between our call to her and our appearing. This happened in many cases. She said, "Look. I am divorced. I have two kids, I teach in public schools, and I was told I would be fired if I talked to you. Now please go away." This happened in one form or another of more or less severe intensity right along the line. People knew where we were going to be, and they knew the people we were going to see, and it could only be done by wiretapping or a combination of wiretapping and following.

Well, it was the very first night I was in Dallas. My crew had come in from San Francisco and I was there alone and was briefing them. Suddenly there was a knock on the door, introducing two very pleasant-looking young men, wearing suits and ties with Stetsons. They produced some grey visiting cards—they were both members of the Dallas homicide squad. They were very polite. And right then you have to make a decision; you claim your constitutional rights and you get run out of town or you play with them, truthfully. I said, "I work for the Judgment Film Corporation," (which is a corporation I created to make that film) and told them what we were interested in. They were very sweet until the name of Benavides came up. Benavides was the person who was probably closest to Officer Tippet when he was killed. At that point the police said, "You are not going to interview that 'boy,' Benavides." And we never did. He was frightened right out of town, and it happened with plenty of people.

213

Q. Can you go into the origins of *In the Year of the Pig*, the decision to make the film and what you thought the media had or had not done until that time?

A. Well, the media never did anything substantive or critical. That was part of the greatest hype that the American people have ever suffered from the media. Every day we saw the war. Every day we saw dead Americans, dead Vietnamese, bombings, all kinds of rather interesting things, but never one program on why; never one program on the history of it; never one program attempting to place it in context. I wanted to do an intellectual and historical overview of the whole thing going back to World War II and just before, then through the French experience down to the Tet offensive which was when I finished the film.

I was angry about Vietnam and wanted to do something. Then two academics came and said, "We have seen your other films, we think you should make a film about Vietnam," and it all suddenly went 'click' for me. I had good connections with both the NLF and the DRV and connections in Eastern Europe, and was able immediately to raise a lot of money and go all over Europe and collect Soviet footage, East German footage, Czech footage, and so on. I then did a lot of shooting of all kinds of people like Jean Lacouture, Philippe de Villers, and various Americans, and some really crazy stuff like Senator Morton calling Ho Chi Minh the George Washington of Vietnam.

Q. You really have to pay attention to the film all the time. Did you have any fears of losing your audience with such long stretches of interviews?

A. None. I always had the feeling that people will accept what is well done. It is meant to be historical and argumentative. I am not worried about boring people in films. In some of my films, like *Painters Painting*, I have sequences that are meant to make people sweat and strain to hear what is being said. Going to movies is too passive. I want the audience to strain. I don't want it to be easy for them.

Q. When you did *In the Year of the Pig* did you work outwards from the transcripts?

A. I do everything at once. I used to have a very big office space and also had a friend who makes cardboard boxes. So I used to get enormous pieces of cardboard, almost as big as that wall, and I would start pasting up transcripts of the track, along with ideas of images. I'd then try the track material on a Steenbeck with different images, so the process was always one of collage. You are always cutting away

214

and always trying to make two or three things happen at the same time, and those who get it, get it, and those who do not get it, do not get it, and it doesn't really make any difference anyway.

Q. Were there sequences that you had in the rough cut which you took out?

A. Of course. In the finished film there is one sequence which I dislike, that I would cut out today, which are the six minutes on the negotiations. I didn't like it at the time and I don't know why I left it in. That was a weakness, but I would never change anything once the picture is there. Then these are the sequences which you put in at the last minute like that great sequence with Colonel Patton, who later became General Patton.

Q. Is that where he says, his men are the greatest killers?

A. Yeah. I had already finished the film when somebody from one of the networks called and said, "Listen, I got this whole goddamn thing on Patton. He sounds goofy." So I went to have a look at it and said, "I want it." I then recut a whole segment of the film to include it although we were just prior to mix. Later that sequence was lifted from the film and included in *Hearts and Minds*.

Q. Somebody discussing your film said something like, "These films have the authenticity of history. This is history in the documents speaking for themselves." Now in most historical research one eventually lays out all the documents. A few people have said, however, that in *Year of the Pig* they were very carefully selected. Those were some of the comments brought up when the film was shown at American universities. Do you think that's a fair comment?

A. I think that is correct, but not necessarily fair. No one produces all the documents filmically. I think they confused the different pace between film and books. No one lays out all the documents in film—it's impossible. But what I have been willing to do (and my films have been seen by a lot of people who disagree with them) is to answer any questions as to where the stuff comes from and what the context is. I have a full text of where everything has occurred.

Roy Cohn appears in *Point of Order*, and we have become friends out of that animosity. He still attacks *Point of Order* and me personally. He still says the film is prejudiced (which it is) but he has never been able to find one distortion and he knows that text—all thirty-six volumes of it.

Q. In your films, do you try to match an intellectual experience with your own human experience? For example, in *Year of the Pig*, Ho Chi

Minh and North Vietnam always come out like God and Kingdom Come. But you had not been to North Vietnam nor did you know that society through actual contact. Do you find yourself on the one hand challenging things about American society or a capitalist-European society, and on the other hand, because of your politics, accepting stuff from and about North Vietnam far less critically? Does it happen to you? Are you aware of it?

A. Well, it's war which I regarded from the beginning as being unjust on the part of the French and then ourselves. In Pauline Kael's review she said that Ho Chi Minh is the hero of the film and she is totally correct. Ho Chi Minh was meant to be the hero of the film. It was not an objective statement, but it was not a lie either. I mean there is a difference between being passionately involved in what you work with and believe in, and lying. There are no lies in the film—there are prejudices in the film. I wanted the Vietnamese to defeat the United States, and the Vietnamese did defeat the United States. The Vietnamese government, the DRV, is not the perfect government. There is no doubt that it is committing customary post-revolutionary excesses. There is no doubt that the retraining of various reactionary elements is harsh and there is no doubt that it does not conform to the luxury of democratic procedures which I prefer.

I believe, as a Marxist, with Marx who said, "Thank God I am not a Marxist." No one, not even Marx, not even Lenin has written holy writ. The way of change changes with time, place, circumstance. Marx found the way. It is up to us to apply it and in doing so to change it. I think you could have a genuine Marxist revolution in the United States without scrapping the Bill of Rights. I do not mean communism under the party of Gus Hall and run by the Soviet Union. Each country is a different situation. It adjusts in the arts. I think the Cubans have produced more interesting films than any other Marxist country since the Cuban revolution in 1959. There are no films in the East that can match *Memories of Underdevelopment* and some of the other Cuban films. And it is not an accident. I have been in those eastern countries, and they are very heavy, oppressive, stifling.

Q. I think it's Pauline Kael who says that selections in your film are made to show the basic rottenness of America.

A. Absolutely.

Q. She then goes on to say that you present a thesis that the whole West is collapsing.

A. I think that the West is fairly rotten. Collapsing is her word. I think that with our German and Japanese allies we are rather formidable.

216

Q. The two key documentaries on Vietnam, besides the work of Ivens and Newsreel, are *In the Year of the Pig* and Peter Davis's *Hearts and Minds*. What do you see as the principal differences between your film and that of Davis?

A. I would say there are substantial differences. The first difference is *when* they were made. It is a little luxurious to make a Vietnam film after the war, when it is safe enough. It is a different position, and it makes it even a different political position. But that's not the greatest weakness of Davis's film, because you can write a book about a war a hundred years after it's over and it will be totally valid. Its greatest weakness is its snideness. As somebody who has fought in a war, I cannot be very sympathetic to the treatment of that pilot from Linden, New Jersey. We see a sort of mocking Beverly Hills view of his mother, his family, that little schoolroom sequence, and the stupidity of the guy who said that he would go back and bomb Vietnam again.

That sequence to me betrays the political emptiness and the human emptiness of the whole enterprise. There is not one ounce of understanding of that person which means that you have no political understanding of this country. That person was a prisoner of the Vietnamese for seven years, which ain't exactly apple pie, and the fact that he was a full lieutenant in the navy, equivalent of captain, was a big class rise for him. We need to understand the nature of what we are involved in—and to laugh him off, to tick him off the way he was, is to avoid the real politics of what was in the film.

The rigged scenes in *Hearts and Minds* like the whorehouse scenes are just cheap. It's the old network mentality to manipulate people rather than film. In the football sequence, for instance, the coach and the players had no idea they were going to be used in a film about the war. They thought they were going to be used in a film about high-school football. Well, they are not the methods I would use, nor do I think they are particularly effective.

Q. You criticize Peter Davis for making a film after the event, when the Vietnam war was almost over. Isn't your McCarthy film a little like that, or do you see McCarthyism and other excesses still rampant?

A. *Point of Order* was made seven years after the Army-McCarthy hearings took place. It was made because its lesson was forgotten; because it was something new; it was the first time a *film* had been made out of television's old and wavy images. The footage was manipulated, certainly. The point of *Point of Order* is that there was an ending to the hearings which the American people never saw. It meant the end of McCarthy because the establishment pulled the rug out from

217

under him and because those cameras ground on relentlessly for thirty-six days. It's not when a film is made but the passion and filmic energy that are brought to the film.

I objected to *Hearts and Minds* because even though it was made late in the war, almost as the war was coming to an end, it had no more perspective than US television and the latter didn't have much.

When I reviewed *Hearts and Minds* I said, "Network television and Hollywood have always been uncomfortable with the documentary. The networks used to spew them out and give awards, like National 4-H Clubs, to one another; long White Papers, etc. They take place in Trotsky's dust-bin—so objective, life is bleached out. Objective enough to be mindless, so that no sponsor or his grandchild should be offended. Hollywood's discomfort is more practical; it avoids them, finding Godfathers, Airports, Poseidons, and a kind of ritual cinematic cloning of the works of Fitzgerald, Hemingway, and Zane Grey more profitable. *Hearts and Minds* is the *Godfather* of documentaries. My guess is there is one big difference: it will never find an audience. I found it both heartless and mindless. Heartless because of an inability to understand either the United States or Vietnam. Heartless because it sneers with a japing, middle-class, liberal superiority when it should be doing something quite different. The distance between the more hip parts of Beverly Hills and Linden, N.J., is vast and those who made *Hearts and Minds* don't understand it."

Q. Your most recent film is *Underground*. What was the background to it?

A. Well, there is nothing left from the sixties; little left of that youthful movement to whose cause I rallied, SDS, which at one point some people would say numbered 400,000, others 200,000. It was surely the largest radical movement young people ever put together in this country. Nixon destroyed the peace movement through two simple strokes; one was getting the middle class out of it by destroying the draft; and the other was to use violence which scared people. So in a very short period of time there were few people left who were willing to play for all the chips, and I liked that game myself.

I thought at first that the Weatherpeople were ridiculous. I thought the bombing was silly. It had a certain kind of courage and panache that I liked, though I would not have done such a thing myself. But it was silly. But then they published *Prairie Fire* and to me it was such a reversal of the European experience and my own experience. Being characteristically pragmatic and American we developed techniques of street fighting and college destruction, and all of that. We did it all rather well *without any theory*. *Prairie Fire* was kind of an innocent ex-

218

ploration into *theory*. I interpreted it, whether rightly or wrongly, as a move out, away from bombing.

So when I read *Prairie Fire* I got in touch with them, and I suppose part of it was based on the challenge of middle-aged kicks. I went underground. It was hairy. It was dangerous. You have read the papers and know that the Weather Underground was the subject of the most intensive FBI scrutiny ever, as well as the most intensive FBI illegality. I met with them many times before recruiting Haskell Wexler and Mary Lampson.

What appealed to me was the whole idea of filming in impossible conditions; a film about people whose faces would never be on screen. All that appealed to me, and yet it is already dead. It was shot May 1, 1975, when the movement itself was splitting up. But that doesn't affect the film because a film always captures a moment of history at twenty-four frames per second and that is it. I am not interested in keeping up with it or doing an addendum on the Weather Underground.

I found them exciting, interesting people, curiously uneducated at one level and fantastically educated at another level. Anybody who can keep a group of 200 people underground without ever being caught—who can walk in the Capitol and stick bombs into it and get away with it—these are people who have more than average sensibility about what the country is all about. But you cannot exist just on the run, you need help, and they had help and have help. They have aboveground support, and they obviously function in the system somewhere.

When I first met them, we just went to restaurants and ate. It was very interesting, because I like my adrenalin charged. When the police came by the restaurant they were very cool. I was the one who got a kick out of it. But I didn't make the film for middle-aged kicks. I wanted one last report from the left, one last documentary, before I went on to what I am doing now.

Q. How long were you out shooting?

A. Three days. We could have made that film even quicker, which was my original conception, only we listened to them about including certain things. We filmed aboveground, which was OK—that made sense. But then they wanted to go to the Martin Luther King hospital. Now rule one is you never go to racially mixed areas if you have people who are fugitives, because there are just too many police cameras, and we realized within five minutes of being there that we had to get the hell out. Luckily we were much faster than the police.

Q. How did you manage to process material you wanted kept secret?

A. Haskell has a commercials company through which he put the film and it was processed over the weekend. I took the quarter-inch tape sound track to a soundhouse and said, "Look. This is a new kind of 'transactional psychoanalysis,' and I will pay you your regular rate if you will get out of here and let me transfer it myself. You see I have signed a contract with this shrink, and this stuff is confessions of men and women about their inner sex lives, and the contract states that if anybody else hears it the contract is null and void." So the guy was perfectly happy to take my money and let me transfer. We were all done by Monday and everything was sequestered. Then the FBI started bullying us.

Q. How did the FBI appear in this?

A. Well everything is slower for the FBI. They obviously took our pictures when we were at the Martin Luther King hospital, but they didn't process them until a few days later. Then the intelligence members of the police looked at them, and they saw Jeff Jones and Cathy Boudin and Haskell and Mary all together, and then this was turned over to the FBI. Within forty-eight hours the FBI was standing around pretending to change flat tires. They also began harassing a woman I was living with at the time who happened to be a totally apolitical person. She had no idea what I was doing. I didn't want to get her into trouble so I said, "I am going to be gone for three days, like a traveling salesman or something. But don't worry—I'll be back." Then they started investigating her mother and that kind of thing. So I got very angry and just called up the FBI and said, "Get your fucking gumshoes off my back!" That was a very good thing to do because it made them angry and the FBI does not easily lose its cool. So they served us at once, and that was their mistake.

Q. They served you with warrants?

A. They served us with subpoenas to appear before the Grand Jury. And I suppose the most important and notable political event in Haskell's or my life was the fact that we were the first people, along with Mary, who had the support of the whole Hollywood community. We were the only people to beat the system. I mean this goes back to the Hollywood Ten when the Hollywood community withdrew support at all the blacklisting, grey-listing—everything. We had the support of every star in Hollywood, every producer, every director. The president of the Screen Directors Guild came and read a statement which went into the Congressional Record and the government simply withdrew the subpoenas. We had in the meantime hired three of the best lawyers in the country.

Q. They subpoenaed you, just to talk to you and go through your material?

A. That is right, but there are certain things which we are guaranteed under the First Amendment of the Constitution. Under the concept of prior restraint they still had no right to go through our notes or unfinished material. If I committed a criminal act in making that film they could have attacked it when it was finished and projected on a screen, and then I would have had a right to defend it. Then their attack would have been legitimate—but to choke it off just after filming was a clear violation of free speech.

The free speech idea had been brought up to date to include film by a series of decisions from the Supreme Court, and the foolhardy FBI and the assistant district attorney for the southern district of California issued that subpoena too quickly. The subpoena said, you will bring with you all films, tapes, negatives, which is really odd, and this outraged the Hollywood film community. There was a lesson to be learned, that if you can home in on a narrow specific cause like a film, you can get the whole Hollywood community or X or Y community to support you. Many of the people who supported us were totally nonpolitical but just did not want to see film interfered with.

The one person among the supporters whom I admired and I wrote to was Elia Kazan who himself was not only an informer, but took a full-page ad in the *New York Times* in the fifties to list the names of all his friends who were communists. He knew what would be involved in coming forward to support us, and that his name would be splashed around the papers as a former pigeon who squealed, and who now supported our stand in making a film on revolutionaries. I thought his position took more courage than all the obvious Hollywood liberals who would have supported us anyway.

Q. Was there a problem of gaining the trust of the people in the film? Did they limit or restrict your questions?

A. Well, much of the best part of the film, Mary and I cut out, which was the process of how we got to these answers. We eliminated all the give and take that is ordinarily the most dynamic and interesting part, because we wanted their voices to be heard didactically. They were, in my estimation, a little lunatic—or maybe overly puritanical rather than lunatic—about refusing ever to say "I." Finally I said to them (and we kept this in the film), "We are film people and this doesn't work. We have to be interested in who you are and how you got there. How does a middle-class American (and in some cases they were really super-upper-class American) get to call himself a communist revolutionary and go around blowing up buildings? It is precisely *that process* that is interesting."

They finally agreed but this took a whole night of arguing, and they would not talk about the town house explosion, nor would they talk about the Capitol explosion. We had to stay up after the filming and go over tapes very carefully to see that they did not compromise themselves, and nowhere did they say ever that they bombed anything. They always say "the group" or "the organization" because one slip could become an indictment and could mean a number of years in prison. But that was not what motivated them as much as that they did not want to be regarded as egomaniacs or people developing the cult of personality. They wanted everything to be "it, the organization" and not individuals.

The first two reels we shot were so boring that they were never used, because we were totally unaware of the fact that in their collectives they had a rule that no one could ever interrupt. They started speaking and went on and on. We were shooting color film, it was sort of crazy, and after two rolls I said, "What's going on? Why is this so damn dead? I ask a question and then you all sit and talk at great length and this is costing $120 a roll, and we have so far wasted $240 out of Haskell's and my pocket." So they said, "You don't understand. We never interrupt one another." And I said, "Well, I am going to interrupt you all the time when we cut this. You don't think we are going to let you make an eight-minute speech? Maybe I'll just take one sentence from all that." They got very wise but they still wanted to preserve what they had developed.

Q. What sort of working agreement did you make?

A. The one agreement that we made was that we would never see each other again. We knew on both sides that that would be very dangerous because once the police knew that this film was done there was no doubt that Mary, Haskell and I would become the object of very intense FBI surveillance and wire tapping.

Q. They obviously had enough trust that you were not going to rip them off?

A. They knew me and my work, and they knew Haskell, and both Haskell and I were respectable middle-aged leftists. Mary had worked with me on three films and earned a few badges also. I took them to Haskell and Mary and they had long conversations with them and they passed on them both.

Q. What was the import of Mary in the film?

A. She and I made it and Haskell was the cameraman. It was very hard for Mary and me, because Mary had worked for me in the past and now we were working as equals. And this turned out to be a very good thing.

Q. Were you both asking questions?

A. All three of us were questioning. But what was more important was that Mary and I determined the input of the film itself. We had hours and hours of stuff which we cut into an eighty-eight-minute film, and Mary and I did that equally. We had a lot of fights and a lot of arguments, and a lot of yelling at one another, because I had once been a boss figure, and she had been a worker figure, and there was the man-woman thing, and the middle-aged man and the younger person and all the rest of it, and it came out equal.

Q. Was there any stuff you cut out, not because it did not work in the film but which you thought, given the circumstances, too dangerous for various reasons to put into the film?

A. Well we had a hairy life for a long time, because Haskell had trained himself for a long time to get the maximum clarity of image and the maximum subtlety and nuance. Suddenly he was being asked to obscure and defocus that image and he made a lot of mistakes. When we put the materials through the Steenbeck viewer, you could see faces so clearly that they could be put up on FBI posters. You have to remember that the FBI had not seen any of these people since 1969. So Mary and I would paint a little blue and have it go through the frame and shoot a new negative, and destroy the original negative.

This was the most time-consuming. You see, it was a film without any staff. Just two people. I have ordinarily eight or ten people working. We were the messengers, the editors, the directors, everything. Those Sundays we worked fourteen or sixteen hours, because we knew we would not be interrupted, and finally we destroyed everything revealing—every single frame. I used to drive out to my house in the country and get a big fire going and burn all that stuff, staying up half the night, with a drink in my hand, poking around to make sure that not one frame was left.

Q. After all these seventeen years of film making, do you see these films or films like yours causing change or are they just making a statement? Are you hopeful or cynical about it all?

A. I am not at all cynical. I am skeptical about individual films changing the world. But there has never been anything, including organized religion, to compare with the media in this country. TV is on the air twenty-one hours a day and you can see what garbage is destroying the minds of our people.

Q. When I came here you were looking at a piece on the evolution of young film makers. You seem to be very supportive of young film makers. What is the help you give them?

A. Political. Cinda Firestone who made *Attica* had a first job with me, and there are a lot of film people who started with me who are now doing their own work. That was because I learned as I was going along myself which made a good experience for them. I have been a curious employer in the past because I could never stand the sight of people around me who were not working. So I would just say, why don't you go to the movies, or go home, or something, but then I would expect them to work Saturday and Sunday and all night, if things were going well.

Q. How do you advise young film makers who are looking for money? You said you helped one guy get a grant of at least $84,000.

A. He got that from the Public Broadcasting System. It is very very hard and it is going to be harder. Let's face it, the source of money for radical film makers in this country has been with the liberal movement which is no longer interested, and money is very hard if you are interested in radical or political films. And every disaster at the box office of pseudo-political films like *Memory of Justice* and *Hearts and Minds* makes it harder for others.

Q. But most of your documentaries made back their cost.

A. They made back their cost and they played in limited cities. We never had grandiose ambitions of playing them in a thousand theaters, which is what happened to *Hearts and Minds*. *Hearts and Minds* will make its money back in 16mm but it's going to take a long time to recoup. In the case of the Ophuls film, *Memories of Justice*, they will never make their money back.

Q. Do you see yourself staying with documentaries?

A. I have always found documentary very interesting but there's a fictional film I want to do about my own life. It began as an obsession and I started thinking about it before we did the Weather film. It began with my suing the government under the Freedom of Information Act. I was into the Weather film but hadn't started shooting and suddenly got from the FBI almost 300 pages of documents collected by the FBI on my life up to my twenty-fourth year. But no documents were available after that except with a struggle and using two lawyers. Fortunately they are friends of mine.

The early pages were interesting and I cannot describe my feelings when I sat alone and read all the material collected before tape recorders and before computers. Material collected by some FBI guy who wrote it down on his little green pad, went back to his hotel and typed it all out. All this was initiated by my applying for flying school and a commission. And these hundreds of pages about me went back to the age of twelve, the year I went to prep school. They went to my mother who said Emile is an atheist therefore he has no moral scruples. And to have that same sentence appear in a colonel's mouth . . . it gave me an eerie feeling and an angry feeling and then the anger went away.

So I am doing this story *cum* film very dispassionately, and I am

224

doing it as a fiction, because of the libel laws. I have been advised by my counsel to do it that way because there are a lot of people in it who talked about me who I thought were my friends. But now it has become much bigger than that. I originally titled it "A Middle-Aged Radical as Seen Through the Eyes of His Government," but it is now something which is really my life—the whole damn thing!

Q. Your films have a consistent left-wing view. You talk about yourself as being an early Marxist. Where do you think you are now? Do you belong to any recognizable group?

A. No, I haven't belonged to recognizable groups since I was a teenager, and I suppose I am now sufficiently cynical to think that I will not see revolutionary changes in my lifetime. I care most about change in this country, and if anything, I have probably become some kind of anarchist. I believe in strong violent responses. I find it curious that the Spanish communist party should be the most interesting communist party in Europe, and that the Soviet party should be the most deadening and oppressive. There is not much room, and it is very lonely here. There are very few people here who have left-wing politics. People share left-negativism and there is a big difference between negativism and real left politics.

There are a lot of people I know in $300 jackets with their Mercedes waiting outside, who will make snotty remarks about the peanut and about this country, but that's too easy. It is very hard, I think, to make those same remarks for the right reasons and to have something to say beyond. And that is where one gets stuck in this small no-man's, no-woman's land in which there are very few women or men who really see there is anything happening.

Q. What do you see now, at this moment, as the vital and necessary documentary subjects for a film maker?

A. To me the most interesting documentary would be about television itself. That's the ultimate pollution that we have, but there is no market for that. You know, couldn't get any money for it. It would play theaters, maybe, but TV would never play it becuase it would have to be hard about the manipulation, the planning, the lies. *Network* was nothing compared to what it is all about. *Network* is an avoidance of the whole thing: the fighting for ratings, the amount of money moved, Barbara Walters, and children, and the concept for women.

If the women's movement would look at television for five minutes as a woman, they would burn the fucking stations down. The idea is that women are nitwits, so therefore you give them gameshows all day and soap operas, and that sort of thing. The news comes on at six, the

225

big news at seven, because that is when the man is home; that is when the purchasing power and the king of the family is home, he has come off the train at Greenwich to hear Cronkite.

The news has become an industry. The news has grown from a half hour to an hour and a half and in some cases two hours, because the news now produces more income than anything else, and this is why the news cannot say anything. The news cannot offend anybody, that is why the news cannot analyze anything, and has to be sort of blanched out until it is a nothing that deals only in personalities. And this is why there is no investigative journalism.

You make a tube to place in the ground for the year 2077 and all you need is the TV page of the *New York Times* for one week with the TV material to go with it. Do that and you will see why this culture will drop like a ripe fruit, if there will be anybody to push it off the tree. The thing is we are so empty we don't even have the strength to knock this ripe fruit off the tree. It is going to hang on the bloody tree.

# 12

# The Mills of the Gods: *Vietnam*
## Beryl Fox

*Beryl Fox is not only one of the most prolific film makers working in Canada today but must be rated as one of the best documentary directors in North America.*

*Beginning with* One More River, *an hour-long documentary on race relations in the U.S. (1963) her films include* Balance of Terror *about NATO (1963);* The Single Woman and the Double Standard *(1965);* Memorial to Martin Luther King *(1969);* The Visible Woman *(1975) and* Take My Hand *(1975) which was made for the Children's Aid Society of Toronto.*

*Most of her work has been done for the CBC, but she has also done a number of films for NET such as* A View from the 21st Century *(1968) and "The Fabulous Sixties" (1969). Since 1970 while working for Hobel Leiterman Productions and others her work has ranged from the political and social spectrum to nature studies, travel, and an examination of the seventies.*

*Fox began her career as a script assistant at the CBC. In the book* Women Who Make Movies *she's quoted as saying, "The only reason I advanced was because of an overriding inferiority complex which drove me to do everybody's donkey work, night work, work for free . . . never refusing any kind of work."*

*The two best known aspects of Beryl Fox's work are her films on the U.S. South,* One More River *and* Summer in Mississippi, *and her three films on the war in Vietnam,* The Mills of the Gods *(1965),* Saigon *(CBS 1967), and* Last Reflections on a War *(1968).*

*I'd originally seen* The Mills of the Gods *on the BBC and had been struck by the power of the photography, the sharp feeling of the agonies of war, and a cool but committed viewpoint of its senselessness. One felt from the film the horrors of a war being inflicted on noncombatant villagers and the lack of trust the Vietnamese had for both the Saigon government and the U.S.*

*It was almost unthinkable at the CBC that a woman film maker should go to Vietnam though many women newspaper journalists had worked there or were to work there. Not only did Fox go in but went back again to shoot* Saigon *and* Last Reflections on a War. *The latter is about Bernard Fall, a noted war correspondent who died in Vietnam and who was a good friend and guide to Fox in her first days in Vietnam.* Last Reflections *won the Atlanta Film Festival Peace Medal.*

*Getting Beryl Fox to talk was possibly the hardest interview of all. I'd known Beryl some years and admired her and her films immensely. She is vocal and can be very impassioned. Yet when I met her in Toronto she was reluctant to talk about her own work. Her attitude was "The films were made. They speak for themselves. Who on earth can remember what it was all about and what one felt . . ."*

*Since 1977 Fox's main work has been for the National Film Board of Canada as executive producer on a number of documentary dramas. Generally she seems to be moving away from documentary and into the fiction film. At the moment she has a feature film in progress called* Surfacing, *but no details are available.*

Q. What was your background?

A. Working-class Socialists, North Winnipeg. I dropped out of high school, worked in factories, then eventually went back to school and finally graduated with a B.A. in history. After that I worked with emotionally disturbed kids, taught horseback riding and also sold lingerie, and so on. I ended up at the CBC as a script assistant. One day I volunteered for an impossible job with a man who had the reputation of being a workaholic. The person I had to work for turned out to be Douglas Leiterman. He was a hard taskmaster, but he had a nose for talent and enjoyed bringing people along.

Q. What year roughly are you talking about?

A. 1959.

Q. Were there many women in the CBC then?

A. Not in creative jobs. At that time women were script assistants, research assistants, secretaries. No one thought of going beyond that. On the film *One More River* I was hired as a script assistant, though in the end I did a lot of the directing. Even so the CBC wouldn't allow me an assistant director's credit. Actually I directed the early filming with Richard Leiterman, set up interviews, surveys, and so on, and then Doug completed the balance of the filming.

The next year I directed *Summer in Mississippi*. That one was more difficult as we were trying to trace the path of the three civil rights workers who'd been murdered there and that got a little hairy at times.

Q. How did your career progress after these two southern films?

A. Ask me about the future . . . but if you ask me to go back twelve years into my personal history it's so irrelevant. And who can remember?

Q. I understand your feeling, Beryl, but I do want to press you. What *are* some of the key films that stay in your mind? And why?

A. *Summer in Mississippi*. Because I cared and because I took risks for other people I wouldn't have for myself. And the Vietnam films.

228

Q. You made three films on Vietnam. How did you get into that?

A. I was working for the CBC at the time on a program called *This Hour Has Seven Days*. Doug wanted a report on Vietnam. I had just read David Halberstam's book and I wanted to go there. I told Doug that the major thing that interested me more than anything else was how civilizations are affected by wars. Also from my studies in history I had a very specific attitude to soldiers who are not mercenaries. I like them and feel that they too are victims. So I said I'd like to show all this . . . that the soldiers as well as the peasantry are suffering. Doug liked my ideas and fought with the CBC brass to send me.

Q. Had you been involved in a war before?

A. No. Though the South was a kind of war. In many ways it was more dangerous than Vietnam, I thought, because you never knew who had a gun, or if they were friendlies. In Vietnam, if you stayed with the U.S. troops you were at least covered. But of course, if you stayed with the troop concentrations you'd never get any good footage. For action you had to go off with small patrols and take your chances.

Q. Did you do much reading and research before you went out?

A. Yes, a lot. In addition, I spent a lot of time traveling with Bernard Fall. Where Bernard went I followed with a camera. By following on his coattails I got a lot of interviews I couldn't have got any other way.

Q. Did you have to write an outline proposal before you left? For Doug or for the CBC?

A. There was a bit of a memo before and after. There were also sparks at the CBC over sending a woman. I had to compile lists of all the women who were in Vietnam and all the women who had covered wars to prove that it could be done and that I could do it. Then, when I brought the footage back all the old Asia hands said, "Well, she got it all wrong. It's not like that at all." Vested interests are hard to change.

Q. Before you went, what was the thrust of the film as it appeared in the outline?

A. Basically about the appetites of war and the little people who suffer, including some fine young men who happen to be soldiers.

Q. Who was your photographer?

A. Eric Durschmed, who considered himself an old war hand and probably was. Eric once stopped me from walking into a helicopter jet blast. I didn't know that there were jets on helicopters. He pulled me out of the way and then called me a dumb cunt at the top of his voice in front of 10,000 men. Very annoying. Eric left after two weeks on another assignment and I used pick-up cameramen and also did some shooting myself.

This was harder, but by traveling alone I got way out in front. I traveled with small patrols. And out there where there hadn't been TV crews or army PR men the officers and men were rock honest and related in the incredible powerful way men do under fire.

Q. Did you have anything to do with the American Government Press Office there? Were any restrictions placed upon you as a film journalist? What you could film . . . where you could film?

A. Sure. The same restrictions as on any other journalist. We were also given all the usual handouts by the press officers and subtly pressed to show the government view. No one actually put a hand over my lens or tried to stop me filming. A few times the officer in charge was very nervous of the camera and got me out of there as fast as he could on the pretext that it was no place for a woman, but actually it was no place for a camera.

Q. What were the changes in your perception of the war when you got to Vietnam?

A. One can read again and again about death and hardship, but you can never prepare yourself for the reality of it all. After a time, however, I got hardened to the point that a group of refugees waiting for a helicopter airlift as their village burned behind them became for me a problem of focus and framing. Only at the end of the day do you perhaps allow things to reach you. You recall the face of a child or a small incident that gives you nightmares.

Something else on this subject. I had read a lot before coming, on Vietnam and on wars in general, but I had read nothing that prepared me for the spectacular courage and the exquisite camaraderie between men that takes place in battle. That measure of a man's worth has stayed with me.

Q. You say you weren't prepared, but camaraderie is one of the things that comes up in almost every feature film about war.

A. Yes, but that's bullshit. You don't know what it's like till you're pinned down under fire . . . a very small patrol . . . and you're ready to move out. The tanks have come in to get you. You're pinned down but you haven't lost anybody and you're dying to get the hell out of there. And no one will leave because Kelly is lost. No one will move without Kelly. Or you watch a kid you like who was a hairdresser in New Jersey literally dodging bullets to pull somebody out. They didn't have to do that. Nobody *has* to do that. I think I learned to love men in Vietnam. Not mankind but men.

Q. Was there anything you hoped for before you went to Vietnam and then realized you just weren't going to get, or a particular path which you realized you couldn't pursue?

A. I knew that whatever I was filming, there was material out there a thousand times stronger that I couldn't get to for one reason or another. Lack of time, lack of money, deadlines. I just couldn't stay until I felt I had the story and show what it was really like.

Q. How long were you there?

A. Three weeks, the first time.

Q. Do you remember any of the problems in shaping the film, or issues between you and the executive producer?

A. Doug was the producer and gave me a very free hand. He saw the rough-cut and worked with me on the narration, and other things. But basically it was between me and the editor, Don Haig.

Q. What was the reception of the film, particularly among the left wing?

A. After being shown on the CBC it was run on the BBC, introduced by Morley Safer who was then with CBS in London. Safer said that the film maker got carried away. It was subsequently run several times on NET, prepackaged with an apology, because people felt it was too way out. Now, of course, it's quite old hat. NET had Bernard Fall and S.L.A.M. Marshall introduce the film. Marshall called the film corrupt and emotional. Bernard said, "No. It's just right."

Some years later I met an American woman who told me she'd seen *Mills of the Gods* at a time when she was trying to make up her mind about the Vietnam war and trying to figure out how to relate to her own country. After seeing the film she and her husband decided to move to Canada. When I heard that I thought "My gosh . . . to have that kind of an effect on people's lives is the ultimate. That's what people make films for. That's what it's all about."

# 13

# Sad Song of Yellow Skin
## and
# Waiting For Fidel
### Michael Rubbo

> You must begin from where the audience is. You must
> respect their position and starting from this you may try
> to take them elsewhere.
>
> MICHAEL RUBBO

*The secret of Rubbo is in the personality. Open, relaxed, mischievous, warm,
smiling. Boyish in spite of the thick beard. It's all true, and yet it's all deceptive
because under the seemingly couldn't-care-less-let's-go-play-frisbee exterior lies
one of the sharpest and most penetrating minds in documentary today. And also
one of the most interesting stylists.*

*Style comes to the fore in any discussion of Rubbo's work.\* Most of his films
are cast in diary form: we travel through the Far East or Cuba. At first the
films seem to lack focus—to be too subjective and impressionistic—but the subtle
focus is very soon evident.*

*Unlike most other documentarists Rubbo appears in a great number of his
films either giving a low-key commentary* (Sad Song of Yellow Skin *1970*)
*or as an actual presence* (Waiting for Fidel *1974*). *But the voice is not the
usual voice of authority. Instead Rubbo's voice gives vent to feelings, impressions, doubts, musings. It's a voice that raises questions and involves the viewer
in the answers—a voice open to dialogue.*

*A third element of Rubbo's style and approach is the refutation of expectation.*
Sad Song *was shot in Vietnam in 1969. Instead of the usual army patrols,
helicopter attacks and naval raids—the familiar routines of TV coverage—we
see the street children of Saigon, the young writers of Dispatch, a strange peace
island, and a young Vietnamese soldier visiting his family under an officer's eye.
There is a sense of place, texture, and smell, and watching the film we realize
we have never thought about Vietnam or the Vietnamese this way.*

Waiting for Fidel *presents a strange trio visiting Cuba in 1970 to interview Castro. Along with Rubbo, the specially invited film maker, we meet
Geoff Stirling—a millionaire owner of radio and television stations, and Joey
Smallwood, socialist ex-premier of Newfoundland. Although the film, which
incidentally is very funny, presents a number of views of Cuba, its real center
is the exploration of the characters of Stirling and Smallwood.*

---

*For an interesting analysis of Rubbo's work see Piers Handling: "The Diary
Films of Mike Rubbo," *Cinema Canada*, October 1977.

Fidel *is one of the best examples of Rubbo's attitude to film making. There are no preconceptions as to where the material should go, what should be shot, or what form the film will take. Instead there is involvement, openness, a watchful eye, and an elastic ability to jump anywhere. Thus when Castro failed to materialize, Rubbo managed to refocus brilliantly on the interactions of Stirling and Smallwood.*

*This technique of nonpreconception and nonplanning looks deceptively simple from results but as any film maker knows is horrendously difficult in practice.\* It requires a sureness of ability that would daunt most film makers but Rubbo pulls it off time and time again. Yet Rubbo's films are not simple diary tourist statements but very complex political and cultural observations.*

*Rubbo is an anomaly at the Canadian National Film Board, which has sponsored most of his work. Australian by origin, he works for a Canadian corporation and makes films about Australia (*The Man Who Can't Stop *1973),* Indonesia *(*Wet Earth and Warm People *1971),* Cuba *(*Fidel *and* I'm an Old Tree *1975) and* Vietnam *(*Sad Song *and* Streets of Saigon *1973). His Canadian-based films include* Persistent and Finagling *(1971) and* I Hate to Lose *(1977).*

*Rubbo's formal film education was as a graduate student in Stanford's film and communications department in 1965. This was the time of burgeoning campus discontent and the beginnings of the free speech movement. A lot of this is captured on Rubbo's M.A. thesis film. Ostensibly about Stanford University, it also managed to provide a glimpse of major currents of feeling among California students in general. Eventually the film was adopted as the official record of the university in place of a much more expensive PR film which had already been made.*

Q. When you finished at Stanford did you think of going back to Australia? What was in your mind at that time?

A. Frankly I was looking for an excuse not to go back, and was saved as it were by the need for a few months of practical training before qualifying for the degree. I sent one of the few prints of *The True Source of Knowledge*, my rather silly release title, to the National Film Board of Canada and waited. We had been drooling over NFB films throughout the course, and Henry Breitrose, my professor who'd kept faith during some dark moments with the film, was prepared to write me a glowing letter of introduction.

\*I fully acknowledge the problems of many standard documentaries and *vérité* films but think that many of these have, in essence, an almost "found" structure in regard to crisis coverage, story, time parameters, and personality coverage. Rubbo, by contrast, tends to deal with very amorphous material totally lacking in obvious story or shape.

Time passed, and no answer came. Finally I left for Canada, rang the NFB in Montreal and was told to report the next day if I wished to see Tom Daly, to whom I'd written. I got to the Board just as they were viewing my film and in fact was ushered into a darkened theater just as everyone was looking at the film. It was unnerving. The work seemed so bad, so rough.

The lights came on and they filed out. Rather serious-looking men in suits. Public servants making some wonderful films. There was Wolf Koenig, Roman Kroitor, John Kemeney, Tom Daly, and some others. Anyway, they were sorry they could not have me as an intern, but if I was to assume that I was already trained, which I seemed to be from the film they had just seen, they could give me a job.

I later found out that the Board was feeling agonizingly out of touch. The campuses were erupting and they had nothing programmed. And then suddenly here was I walking through the door from one of those explosive campuses and with a film about youth to boot. I had no idea how attractive I must have looked. Later I turned out to be something of a disappointment. I was a disappointment in what I did in those first years, but not in the way I was. I think I was attractive to the Board, frankly, because I am incredibly enthusiastic about almost everything I do. A sort of elation in action that is not put on, it's just me. I was enthusiastic but I did not have the answers on the future of youth, and also I seemed to lose that voice I'd been developing.

Q. What films did you make in those first years?

A. Well, the status of fully-fledged director was dumped on me immediately and I was sent off to make a film about long-distance trucking to make kids appreciate the complexity of filling the supermarket with all the things we take for granted. I chose shrimps leaving Mexico, from the town of Guymas, and arriving in sub-zero Calgary four days later. I found a cooperative company and some sympathetic drivers, but did not touch on any of the more sordid aspects of long-distance trucking. During the editing of the truck film, I had some fights with my producer Kemeney, and he virtually took the film away from me and got Stanley Jackson to do the commentary. I was off to a bad start. Stanley is a master, but somehow the words did not fit too well with my style and my line.

Q. Was there any accepted way or style of documentary film making at the Board at that time? How did you evolve your own style?

A. It took me years to develop my own style. The main style leaders were the *cinéma vérité* films like *Lonely Boy*, and the intimate personal studies like *Paul Tomkowitz*; there were also the workmanlike sponsored films some of which soared to the level of real art, like Brittain's *Fields of Sacrifice*. As for myself, I wrote hundreds of proposals and made few films. Somehow I got into children's story films and ended up making some with animals which were quite successful. My most successful film in distribution terms remains a ten-minute thing about a courageous mouse. But I'd prefer not to think about that right now.

Q. If it was a matter of do what you like, can you, in thinking back, see what you wanted to do?

A. I had started at Stanford using my story-telling abilities to treat sociopolitical themes. But it took me a long time to get back to that. A loss of confidence, I suppose. I knew I wanted to be a persuader, and I knew I was not a shouter. But it was really not till I made *Sad Song of Yellow Skin* that I began to function in that way. In that film I became the rather subversive persuader I have remained till recently.

Q. That technique certainly comes off in your Vietnamese film. Is there any other film which is a good example of that?

A. I think almost all the one-hour documentaries I've made try to be subversively persuasive. They try to get under the skin of the viewer. *Waiting for Fidel* tries to get people to take a fresh look at Cuba without beating the drum. *Wet Earth and Warm People* tries to persuade you that it's really rather impossible to relate sensibly to Third World countries in a nonpatronizing way.

Q. In *Sad Song* we have an Australian film maker who studies in the States who's working for the Canadian government making a film about Vietnam. The mind boggles. How did the film come about?

A. Well, there was a feeling of unease around the NFB in the late sixties. A number of us were very upset about Vietnam. We felt guilty for Canada was supplying essential weapons and materials to the U.S. But could we do anything about it filmically? Our mandate was to interpret Canada to Canadians. Just to get into the situation and to relieve this sense of anguish, I proposed a film about the Foster Parents Plan and the Vietnamese children who were being sponsored by Canadians. That was the Canadian connection. I was going to interpret this humanitarian concern shown in sponsoring children in a war-ravaged country. It seemed to just fit into our mandate. I got it programmed and began by filming some interviews with families in Montreal who were sponsoring kids, asking at the end of each roll what they thought about the actual war. It was touchy.

Q. What did you have to present to the Board before you went to Vietnam?

A. A written proposal of perhaps ten pages. It was all about the Foster Parents Plan. This was passed by the Program Committee which includes management and film makers. So I left for Vietnam, and was accommodated in Saigon by the Foster Parent people and a magnificent Canadian lady called Elizabeth Brown. I had no doubts about their goodness or sincerity, but when I got into that war-torn country I started to find it harder and harder to justify to myself a film on this upbeat humanitarian effort. So I began to look for alternative subjects, cabling my doubts back to Tom Daly. He replied, "I have faith in your judgment. Go ahead." That must be one of the most amazing things about the Board. That he just trusted me to go ahead into who knows what.

Q. So in the middle of the film you were allowed to completely change directions? By the way, had you seen other films on Vietnam before going?

A. Not too many. I had seen Beryl Fox's terrifying *Mills of the Gods* with its famous fighter attack sequence in which a pilot jubilantly talks you through a napalm raid on a village, exalting in his hits, the running ants below and the toy grass houses going up in flames. I had seen some of the more *parti pris* films of Joris Ivens, and of course the nightly TV news. I knew I did not want to do any of those things.

Q. Now did you have a suspicion before you went to Vietnam that this might happen, that an entirely different film might come out?

A. Maybe, but I was not being tricky. Being a soft sort of guy I knew I was not going to make a film on the war itself, and the Foster Parent Society was the sort of humanitarian thing that interested me. I've since come to value my tendency to plunge in. And these days I even make a virtue of being unprepared. I like to say that the documentary film maker of my sort is a victim. You go out with vague ideas about what you want and then just let things happen, trusting in your good instincts. I know it sounds dangerous, but life will inevitably serve up much better stories than you could ever think up beforehand. The trick is to get involved, to get in.

Q. Did you have preconceptions about Vietnam?

A. I had made my analysis. The war was a civil war. America had sided with the nondemocratic corrupt Thieu regime and its successors. The other side were on the whole more admirable, more honorable. And finally it was just wrong for the richest nation on earth to be spewing its wealth in the form of bombs on this little pocket of Asia.

I still felt that when I got there, but somehow it was much more complicated. One saw all the Vietnamese who were in a sense thriving on the Americans. One met people who really feared being regimented into some society that might be like Czechoslovakia after 1968. The situation was soft and the soft guy was feeling very lost. It did not help to run into the established foreign correspondents, the old hands, and to be patronizingly treated like a new boy who would not last a week. For example, I was taken out to dinner by a very urbane correspondent for ABC news who seemed to feel sure it was my farewell meal.

Q. How did you begin to move into the body of the film after you had decided you were not going ahead with the Foster Parent film?

A. Well, I was very struck by the street kids. They were tough, theatrical, lovable, nasty, dangerous. Not kids really, but premature adults housed in tiny bodies sometimes burnt, sometimes deformed. Then I found Dick Hughes, the young American who had been drawn to Vietnam not as a soldier but rather like myself. He has a good line in the film. He says: "If you are concerned about something, my way is to go to the center of where it's happening and find out," and that center was Vietnam.

Dick had let his apartment become a haven for these kids of the street, and was giving the kids, as best he could, love as well as a safe place to sleep. Dick was also the prototype for a character I've used again and again, the acceptable go-between. The guy middle America could not help but like as a person, even if they had trouble with his opinions.

There was another side to these young Americans, I'd found. They were journalists outside the mainstream, writing for student newspapers and a few periodicals, doing in-depth stories in the New Journalist style of personal involvement that Tom Wolfe writes about. They were living the stories they were writing, and they were willing to let me live them too. And frankly they were a colorful bunch, and included John Steinbeck, the son of the author, who had been there as a GI and had come back to be a sort of a temporary monk on the strange Island of Peace which features in the film.

They were what any documentary film maker needs, namely interesting people doing interesting things. So through this bunch I got to know the kids, the dust of the streets they were called. And by the time Martin Duckworth, the cameraman, and the crew arrived, I was pretty much ready to go. Martin was pleased, except with the Island of Peace which he found phony. He gave me a lot of trouble over that. Sound was taken by an assistant cameraman, Pierre Letarte, who recently confessed over a few beers that he found me almost impossible to work with on that film. Completely insensitive to the crew's feelings, he said. It may be partly true. When I work I become obsessed. The fourth member of our crew was Trong, a Vietnamese cameraman who acted as a location manager and who was invaluable. He had a finger in every pie and could make anything happen that we wanted. Choosing good local people is perhaps one of the most important parts of making good documentaries away from home. The danger now became that there was too much to shoot, even limiting myself to the people of Dispatch (the little news agency they had formed). Knowing when to stop and start is one of the hardest parts of this role of the documentary film maker as the victim.

Q. Do you remember how much you shot actually?

A. I think it was a little less than 30,000 feet. That's about 15 to 1.

Q. Here we come to this business of knowing when to stop. At what point did it become apparent to you that you had enough?

A. Partly it's a question of exhaustion. You get exhausted, you can't take any more. That film put us all through the emotional ringer. Especially the final sequences with the death of the opium lady. She was someone who lived in a disused cemetery that Steve was researching for a story. We had got to know her quite well and had planned to interview her about her life in Hanoi during the French period when, we were told, she had been the mistress of a prince, and later a plaything for the French soldiers. In her frail body were thirty years of war. But she had TB as well as her addiction and before we could film her she died in her little cupboard above the tomb that was her home and that of her two tiny daughters. It was very pathetic.

For some reason we found ourselves filming her funeral, except it was much more sordid than a funeral. Her poor thin body was lugged between the tombs like a sack. Perhaps that scene was a terrible invasion of privacy. I justified it to myself in saying that that was Saigon, a place without privacy. But I wonder about the ethics of it. It seems that I am prepared to go quite far after material, though I never think of myself as a sensationalist.

Q. Were there any key scenes that you shot which did not get into the film?

A. Well, we followed several families and individuals in the cemetery area. There was one woman who lived deep in the slum, but in a very opulent house compared with the shack of her neighbors. It was said that her husband was an important racketeer. We were scared to press our questioning too close to the bone because we were hundreds of yards from the public streets in a maze where, if somebody was to take a dislike to us, we might simply never be seen again.

Then there were quite a lot of interviews that I shot with various cemetery people which like most interviews were the first things to hit the cutting room floor. For the rest it's more a matter of having a lot more of what is already in the film. We had a great deal on Wei, the tiny seventeen-year-old who was the chief hustler of Dick's house, and who flips his hat so disarmingly. Wei was hard to stay away from.

238

There was also a lot more introspective stuff which was a bit thin to put in or which we just couldn't find room for in the hour.

Q. Some film makers work to a very rigid structure. You are very loose. Does that bother you, the loose feeling to your material? Do you have a sense of structure as you are filming or is it just an innate sense of what is right, and the knowledge that you can build a film on the editing table?

A. In Vietnam I was running away from the tight structure of the nightly news. I also felt all the time that Saigon, where I did most of the filming, was a truly chaotic place which would be misrepresented if too tightly organized in a film. It is also in the nature of the picaresque film I was making that the main structure will be time passing. The time passing element is the nature of most of my documentary stories, though recently they have had clearer ends, such as when the VIP's leave Cuba without having seen Fidel in *Waiting for Fidel*. Strong structure is often achieved with a dominating voice-of-God commentary which I never use, or with an on-camera commentator who tells you what to see and think. Strong structure also comes from a clear analysis of a situation, the boiling it down to its tangible truth, which I freely admit I am incapable of doing. So I leave that to the BBC.

For me, structure will be clear to the extent that the events which are happening to me are clear. *Waiting for Fidel* has a very tight structure because Cuba is a tight, well-organized little country, at least for the foreign VIP, and because I had a tight neat cast of eccentrics almost fully under my control—at least in the sense that there was actually a written itinerary of the things they were going to be shown. How their arguments about the communism they were seeing would go, that I had to guess. Also how long the battle of nerves between ourselves and our unseen host would go on, I also had to guess and spend my footage accordingly.

In the editing structure is rhythm, the way you mix elements and moods. Up till recently I have had a tendency to go for more hectic material. If things were moving in the frame, I tended to feel happy. Now I've learned the value of silence and stillness. The chairs gently rocking by themselves for instance in *Waiting for Fidel*. The girl on the roof top in the late afternoon in *Sad Song*. Who is she? I'll never know. And the plane that passes as a speck behind her. Was it going to bomb her people? These are the pauses in which you can think whatever you like. I must put in more of them. I am getting less hectic.

Of course, the problem for most film makers is that unless you have a tight structure down on paper, nobody is going to give you the money to make the film. And if you start to deviate during shooting, chances are that the money men have their spies out who will tell tales on you and get you straightened out. We don't have that problem at the Board. And for that alone I'm extremely grateful.

Q. You said something about looking for go-betweens. What do you mean by that?

A. That may stem from a principle they taught us at Stanford. Namely that the way a message is received depends in part on the credibility of the source. The same information coming from a child or from the family doctor may be viewed quite differently especially if it's information which goes against your current beliefs. Thus I have tried, when I wanted to persuade people, to build into my films informants who seem credible and likable. It's as simple as that. Sometimes it's rather a matter of having an opinion represented. In *Fidel*, for instance, Geoff Stirling represents, and is, the capitalist, a millionaire, the capitalist par excellence. I must admit I did not put him there. He was just part of that crazy adventure. Perhaps I would not have started to make the film about the socialist and the capitalist arguing about Cuba while waiting for their interview, if I had not felt that these characters fitted into my idea of good go-betweens.

Q. There is a great deal of you in the films I've seen. Do people like your participation?

A. Some people like it. Some people are driven up the wall or out of the theater by it. For people used to so-called objective TV reporting there is something quite disturbing about seeing the film maker come from behind the camera. My trouble is that I am not a particularly fascinating person, so that my appearance is not immediately accepted on the power of my personality. I have to be accepted for other reasons, namely that it would seem natural that I am there. It tends to bother other film makers more perhaps than the public. It can be pretentious. It can be beside the point, and sometimes I wonder what I'm doing there too.

Actually in *Waiting for Fidel*, I just could not keep out of the first argument. I found what Geoff was saying about high schools in Cuba being sweat shops so absurd. After the take, I asked the cameraman, Doug Kieffer, "Am I in the shot?" "Are you in the shot," he said, "my God you are all over the shot." "Well, maybe," I replied, "we should keep on that way." "Yes," he said, doubtfully. But it worked out because in this case I am a new element. I am the in-between of the go-betweens. Whether I will become in the future hooked on having in-betweens between my go-betweens, I don't know.

Q. The subjects of many of your films fall into the realm of public affairs. The general network feeling has been to keep out the personal feeling, the personal statement and the personal emotions of the journalist in these kind of programs. Obviously you would disagree with that?

A. There is a lot of talk about the journalist's responsibility to protect the public from loose opinions. In fact it's not the public who is really being protected. There is no need to protect the public from personal opinions. Firstly because there is or should be access to a range of conflicting opinion. Secondly because no propaganda machine of the harmful sort ever used the personal approach to distort the news except maybe Axis Sally and Tokyo Rose in the war. But such blatant cases can hardly be taken as justification of continual depersonalization now in times of peace. No, the reason for the objectivity is to protect the management of the TV enterprises, the bureaucrats who would find it much harder to deal with opinionated individuals.

The irony is, of course, that when the CBC pulls out its bits of memorable coverage for some sort of review of their journalistic achievements, what do they show? Those occasional lapses of course when the reporter became, if ever so briefly, a human being. In most cases the circumstances are extreme, such as war. And then the big brass looks the other way, and is in fact proud of the piece.

I'm another case entirely. In the most innocuous situations, I use the word "I." I personalize things without those extenuating circumstances that would make a block of wood cry. Hence I am much disapproved of by the pros. And this is all a bit ironic. I have just been looking over some forty clippings from papers around the world about *Sad Song of Yellow Skin*, mostly from the result of a BBC screening. Not one reviewer seems to object to the blatantly personal style, and yet they are the arbiters of public taste.

Q. Your films look very artless, very loose, yet when I look closely I find them subtle, very pointed, especially in the use of sound. The Nixon scene for instance in *Sad Song*.

A. Well, we were in a street bar one night and they had a TV playing in the background and I knew that one of Nixon's fatuous speeches which was being broadcast in the States was going to be carried there in Saigon on the American Forces Vietnam network. As we were shooting some excerpts of the speech, it struck me how incongruous it was that this man, who had the destiny of this tiny country in his hands, was being received in a Saigon bar where almost none of the customers knew what he was talking about. So in the editing I fiddled around with it so that it appeared that they were partly ignoring him, which was true, and partly indulging in some ironic applause for his remarks. This was all done with overlapping sounds. Nothing very

241

special about it, I think. I like better the weather girl, Bobby, who comes on next to assure the boys out there that the weather is fine back in their home towns, and even here in Vietnam where the bodies lie rotting in the sun, it will stay fine.

Q. How do you tackle the editing?

A. I do it myself, and first tend to attack the material in the simplest way possible. Paring it down, seeing if it means what I thought it meant. Then, when the basic line is clear, I will start to play around with the material to see how I can make it more powerful than it actually is. That's what I was doing with Nixon. I wondered what would happen if I intercut the people in the bar with the TV bits. Would it make you feel how remote he was from their lives, and how little he understands or cares what they might think? So I tried it and it worked.

Q. How was *Sad Song* received by the pro-North Vietnam left and the radicals?

A. Most of them didn't like it. It's too soft. Yet because in the early seventies there were not too many Vietnam films around that could be borrowed by organizations, it had a wide use.

Q. The film ends on the Island of Peace. Had that structure been there from the beginning or did it evolve in the editing?

A. No, the way to include the Island of Peace material was something that I worked out with Tom Daly's help. Tom is a marvellous producer, someone who does not tell you what to do but plants the seed of an idea. I had all the material at the end of the film, a great solid lump. It was really like starting another film. So Tom then suggested that I salt the subject throughout the film. Tempting tidbits earlier on that would want to make one ask for more. Facts like: "They called him the coconut monk because he once spent seven years in a coconut tree, vowed to silence praying for peace." Would you not want to see more of such a man? Also, this allowed the island to build as a metaphor well interspersed as it was with the decadent street life of Saigon. At the end, the full story of the island is told just when you are ready for something peaceful to finish with.

Q. Can you tell me about the beginnings of *Waiting for Fidel*?

A. Well, Stirling the lanky splendidly preserved millionaire came to us with a proposition. He was off to Cuba with his pal Joey Smallwood, a very well known Canadian political figure, who had recently been defeated after having been Premier of Newfoundland for twenty-three years. They had an interview lined up with Fidel which might change the world. Would we like to go along, film the interview, and give the whole thing respectability? Stirling had seen *Sad Song* and was

242

especially asking for me. The private jet was leaving in a week. We could be on it if we liked. We did and we were.

And that's how I got mixed up with the two craziest characters I'm ever likely to meet. Opinionated? One couldn't meet a more scrappy pair. There was Stirling, 55 looking 35, and Joey Smallwood, 74 acting 44. And there was Cuba all laid out for us with tours here and there to schools and mental hospitals while we waited for Fidel to drive through the gates of the mansion in which we were lodged. Within a day I knew that life could have not handed me a more intriguing little drama. So Fidel or no Fidel, I began to film our antics, and when Fidel finally decided not to show, I really didn't care that much, though I was sorry for Joey and Geoff. I think that this film came at just the right time for me. A year or two earlier and I would not have had the confidence to go out on the limb as I did. Once the decision was made I felt quite relaxed about it all and merely had to think of how to best tell the story of the waiting VIP's who don't have quite the clout it takes to get to see the chief. It was not what I was supposed to be doing, but it felt like a good film.

Q. At what point did they realize the whole emphasis of the film had changed?

A. Well, they considered that I was filling in time till the interview took place. Getting illustrative material. Then towards the end of the week Geoff began to realize that I had shot a lot of film, film that he felt he was going to have to pay for. That's when he and I began to fall out.

Q. There's a scene in which Geoff actually explodes in front of the camera because you have been shooting 20 to 1 instead of 3 to 1. Is that something you deliberately induced? I mean it works very well in the film.

A. It's fairly natural. I shared a bedroom with Geoff, for though we were billeted in a mansion, it was a mansion with few but enormous rooms. So he was at one end of a huge bedroom, I at the other. Lately I would wake up to find a cassette player and tape beside my bed with a note saying "play me" attached. On it would be a tirade against me as some sort of pinko idealist who was wasting film on all the wrong things and had no idea of the rules of this game, which was to get an interview that could be sold to NBC or PBS. This happened once or twice, and I got a bit worried that he might be ringing the NFB in Montreal and putting the same idea across. So I said: "Next time you do that we'll have it out in front of the camera, and then *I'll* have a record of how you are treating me. OK?" "OK," he said, for at that moment he was in a better humor. So that's how that little argument got to be filmed. Not initially for use in the film but as protection for me.

Q. You said to me a few days ago that you came into film to say certain things. What do you still want to say?

A. I'm not a true believer, and am becoming less of one every day. I distrust more and more those who say they have the answers. The idealists and the utopians. I tend to want to be a weakener of strong positions where blind strength and dogmatism go together. I want to say hold on now, there's another side to that question. I want to sabotage the sloganistic response to life. I am more skeptical than I was of societies that say they are trying to create the new man, like Cuba. I think these things appear in most of my films and will probably go on appearing in them in the future.

# 14

## Action: The October Crisis of 1970
### Robin Spry

*The Canadian National Film Board has known varying periods of greatness, particularly in the early forties and late fifties. The sixties in turn brought forward a new crop of film makers which included Don Owen, Mike Rubbo, and Robin Spry among its best talents. Many of these newcomers tended towards social documentary rather than the old NFB descriptive documentary, with the occasional director being very politically focused indeed.*

*This is certainly true of Robin Spry. Power and the politics of power appear as the themes in many of his films including* Prologue *and* One Man. *However his most politically significant film is* Action, *a look at the desperate days of October 1970 when FLQ (Le Front de Libération de Québec) kidnappings brought turmoil to the streets of Montreal.*

*In October 1970 Pierre Laporte, a Quebec cabinet minister, and James Cross, a British Trade Commissioner, were abducted by the FLQ. A swift War Measures Act was passed, many civil liberties suspended, and the Canadian army seemed to take over Montreal in its hunt for the kidnappers.*

*Robin Spry's film puts the crisis in perspective. In very clear terms it relates the long history and nature of the French resentments and aspirations, and the immediate events of the crisis itself which ended in the murder of Laporte. Though Spry's sympathies seem fractionally to lie on the French side he is absolutely scrupulous in his treatment of history, political views, and rival personalities.*

*Although he was born in Canada, much of Spry's formative background can be traced to England. His filming began as a part-time activity while studying engineering at Oxford University, and continued at the London School of Economics where he got an M.Sc. in economics and politics.*

*Spry's introduction to the NFB was through a summer student program which gave him a chance to work as assistant to Don Owen on* High Steel. *In 1965 he joined the NFB full time commencing with classroom films such as* Change in the Maritimes *and* Miner.

*Besides* Action *Spry's most noted documentaries are* Illegal Abortion *and* Flowers on a One Way Street. *Abortion had the dubious distinction of being locked up for a year by the NFB before being shown in a truncated form on the CBC network.* Flowers, *about a hippie and student protest in Toronto, had a happier career being shown on the CBC and NET, and winning the Blue Ribbon Award for social documentaries at the American Film Festival.*

*Although Spry has a fine reputation as a documentarist his ultimate inclination seems to be towards the dramatic feature. His first feature,* Prologue, *was made when he was twenty-nine and, like* Medium Cool, *was set against the 1968 Chicago Convention riots. Another long feature,* One Man, *was completed in 1977 and dealt with the issue of industrial pollution. When I talked to him he was just shooting another fiction piece,* They're Drying Up the Streets, *which was due to be run as a television feature on the CBC.*

Q. Was there any specific direction to the National Film Board's documentaries when you joined in 1964?

A. It was pretty open. I arrived at the NFB just after the peak of the Unit B era when Tom Daly, Roman Kroitor, Wolf Koenig, Colin Low, Terry Macartney-Filgate, John Spotton and others had been breaking new ground in candid documentaries. Largely because of the inventiveness of these people, both at a technical and at a film-making level, candid shooting had become part of the accepted vocabulary of the documentary. So when I arrived I found myself lucky enough to work with the people who were responsible for the best work coming out at that time.

Q. Did you find yourself going into films on social or political change or were you trying everything?

A. Initially I was assigned two films. Both were educational. One was on the maritimes, and the second was about mining, and both had to meet curricula requirements. But in both cases I found myself very interested in the social aspects of the subjects. In the case of the maritime region film I found a conflict between the lifestyle of the fishermen and the planning aims of the economists. The planners wanted big modern impersonal cities which they felt would solve the economic problems of the maritimes whereas the fishermen just wanted to stay home and catch fish and keep their old ways of life going. The mining film was about how a man comes to be obsessed by material goods because his parents had such a rough time in the depression. In both films the social concern was rather vague because I was unclear about a lot of things at the time, because I had to fulfill the educational aims, and because I was putting most of my energies into just learning the basics of film making. It was a full time for me.

Q. In *Prologue* you got involved with the Chicago scene. How come you as a Canadian working at the NFB would touch America?

A. Well, it grew out of some experiences of mine in the Haight-Ashbury district of San Francisco, and a general interest in what was happening in America in the sixties—a sense that there was an up-heaval of my generation going on. Furthermore I was only recently back in North America so I really wanted to catch up on what was going on. And it all had its equivalent in Canada. In fact, *Prologue* is partly about the question whether a Canadian should go down and get involved in activism in the States. Canada is not exactly a cultural threat to the existence of the U.S., but the reverse is all too true and what happens in the U.S. almost always affects what happens in Canada. Anyway, going down to Chicago was pretty unpopular in some quarters. *Variety* published an angry article about *Prologue*, and questions were asked about it in the House of Commons in Ottawa. But somehow that only helped because *Prologue* sold all over the world and won a number of prizes.

Q. In *Prologue* you intermix straight documentary footage and drama. I know Wexler was doing it at the same time for *Medium Cool*. Did you know about his work?

A. In a way. Wexler and I found ourselves shooting side by side in the Chicago battles but neither of us was aware of what the other was doing, and then *Medium Cool* and *Prologue* opened the same day in London! I am sure that people had mixed drama and documentary footage before although perhaps what was new was to put actors in the middle of documentary situations which were completely out of control, such as a police riot, and then ask the actor to say written lines while he was being chased or gassed or whatever. And that's what we did in Chicago.

The decision to do that came about because I wanted those events in what was essentially a dramatic film. We did in fact have a script which had been written around what had happened at the Pentagon the year before. We told the Film Board we would shoot rear projection with stock shots from the Pentagon but at the last minute we were able to get down to Chicago and shoot the real events. I chose to do that partly as a bridge from documentary to drama, and partly because we were trying to make a feature film with very little money. We couldn't afford 15,000 extras but there were 15,000 people already in place in Chicago. The final budget of the film was under $140,000.

Q. You were filming in the middle of riots and police violence in Chicago. Did that get hairy for you at times?

A. Yes. We got gassed and chased several times. There was a night when we were hiding in the crowd after all the big TV cameras had been chased off the street outside the Conrad Hilton, and the police were beating up a lot of demonstrators. We had an entertaining time bouncing out of the crowd, switching on our sungun light, filming a few seconds of the police violence, and then when the police started to run towards us to get our camera, the crowd would open up to allow us to hide back inside it. We filmed nonstop for three days.

It was an incredible experience for me and I think for the whole crew. There was a sense of "God damn media" from the demonstrators when we first appeared. But by the end of the three days most of the demonstrators seemed to accept us as being on their side. This was partly because we were almost always on *their* side of the police line, filming from *their* point of view and being attacked when they were attacked. Eventually we were able to sit in the middle of the victorious sing-song opposite the Conrad Hilton and film, with the crowd more or less with us in whatever we did. It was an extremely joyful experience on many levels and there was a lovely simple sense that for once good was resisting evil. But it was also extremely frightening, very frightening indeed.

Q. I myself lived in Canada for a couple of years in the early seventies and at that stage it seemed Canada was getting very politicized. There was a lot of national consciousness in regard to Canadian-American relations. The question of an independent Quebec was also coming to the forefront. How did the Film Board generally mirror this kind of turbulence? And how did you begin *Action*?

A. I don't think the Film Board did mirror it very much. The Board is an odd place and essentially it is made up of an accumulation of personal interests. For the most part there are no general policies being constantly imposed on everyone, saying this year we will make films about this or that. Somehow the films that are of interest that come out of the NFB are usually nothing to do with the policies. They have to do with personal obsessions.

*Action* came about while I was trying, as usual, to do another feature film. I've travelled quite a bit. I've seen Eastern Europe and various police states, and suddenly one day there were soldiers standing on the streets in Montreal. It looked as if I was now living in a police state and I knew that whatever was going on had to be filmed. That was October 1970—the Friday that the War Measures Act was announced by Prime Minister Trudeau. I saw all the troops, rushed back to the English Program Committee of the Board and said, "We've got to cover this even if it is just for archival purposes." And they said, "No, it's impossible."

Fortunately the French Unit had received the same suggestion and had said "Yes." Then the upper management of the NFB, that is, Sydney Newman, said "OK, you can shoot it for the archives, provided you have an English- and a French-speaking component." So I became the English component of that archival shoot and we shot the events and also how the English-speaking Quebeckers were reacting to the crisis. This latter material, which consisted of groups of intellectuals, immigrants, children, artists, businessmen, poor people and others discussing what was happening to them became a film called *Reaction: Portrait of a Society in Crisis*. It's an examination of how groups up and down the social ladder react to essentially the same circumstances. Needless to say, the richer the group, the happier they were to see the soldiers, although there were exceptions in every group.

While we were shooting everything we could, two Francophone crews were shooting a lot of other material with the agreement right from the start that we would all pool our material for an eventual film. In fact two years went by and nothing happened because the NFB did not want a film coming out while the court cases involving the kidnappers were still underway. However, eventually I got permission to make *Reaction* and while making it decided to add a five-minute stock shot introduction so the people seen talking in *Reaction* would be in context. And that five-minute introduction ended up as a separate ninety-minute documentary feature which is *Action*. This was to be the full story, or as full as possible, of the October crisis; the removal of civil liberties, the kidnappings, the killing and the whole battle between the Canadian government and the FLQ.

Q. Was that the first major film to analyze the events of 1970? Hadn't the CBC done anything?

A. We'd shot in 1970 and I started work on *Action* a few years later. In between our shooting and the time we started editing Ian McLaren had done a film for the CBC which was called *October Plus One*. It was about forty minutes on the crisis and about twenty minutes on Trudeau. It's a good film but as it was made fast it didn't have the whole story. I think that they had to close off before everything had clarified itself. And then while I was finishing *Action* and *Reaction* Michel Brault shot *Les Ordres*, a fictional feature about the victims of the War Measures Act. In fact the day before Michel started shooting he looked at an almost final-cutting copy of *Action* to remind himself of what had happened at that time and how it had felt.

Q. Can you explain in more detail why you had to wait so long before starting on *Action*?

A. The Film Board quite simply stated once we had finished shooting that the situation was *sub judice* and no one was to use the material. After two years the French unit got permission to look at all the material and decided that there was no film there. At about the same time a film maker called Yves Dion was trying, using both the NFB footage and the CBC-TV footage at Radio Canada, to do a film at the Board.

In the end Radio Canada would not give him the material so he too was blocked. He did a lot of research and helped us with *Action* once it was clear that he was not going ahead.

At that point I began to feel that nothing would ever be done so I proposed *Reaction* which seemed to the Board to be relatively harmless. It was accepted because it was just people talking about, or rather fighting about, what was happening as it happened. But in making *Reaction*, I also found myself making *Action*. And without really intending to I ended up with two films, *Action* being actually about the events and using stock shots, stills, the material shot by our three crews during the events, and anything else we could get our hands on.

Q. In *Action*, without particularly supporting the FLQ, you are fairly critical of the Canadian government. How does a film like that work within the context of a government-supported agency? Did the Film Board know the kind of film you were going to do?

A. More or less, but I didn't know that *Action* would be a separate film until suddenly there it was. All the people in English production knew roughly what was happening. At the end it simply became a matter of showing *Action* to Sydney Newman who was in charge of the Board and saying, "Here it is, it's done." It wasn't exactly what we said we'd do, maybe it was something in addition, but there wasn't any intentional deception involved and Newman either had to lock it up or buy it. To his great credit he bought *Action*, then went to bat for it. He showed it to the Secretary of State for his clearance. The Secretary bought it, nervously I'm told, but he bought it, and I'm sure that this was largely because of Sydney Newman's support. It was then shown to the Board of Governors of the Film Board who are the people who theoretically represent the people of Canada in the overseeing of this place. They also bought it, but by then there were a number of people feeling rather edgy about it.

Eventually I was told that the film could be released provided we took out a few things. These included the final line of commentary which was "The question remains; will Quebec separate?" Evidently, recent history to the contrary, this apparently was not seen as a vital question. I was also asked to take out something on Drapeau, the mayor of Montreal, and something on the NDP, the socialist party which opposed the War Measures Act. What exactly came out was left to my discretion and I took out a few seconds of each. By then, six months had gone by between the completion of the film and this tiny re-editing, and I was actually able to strengthen the film because I was a little removed from it. But I was sorry to lose the commentary line that came out at the end. The fact that a film like *Action*, which is somewhat critical of the government, can be made at the NFB, which is a government department, is one of the things that make the NFB special.

Q. In *Action* you were dealing with the most explosive situation in Canada in the last twenty or thirty years. Especially at the time of making the film the situation was extremely up in the air and you must have been conscious of walking over baskets of eggs, treading very carefully. So what were the guidelines which you set yourself? As a historian and as a documentary film maker. What did you see as the possible traps you might fall into?

A. At the time of shooting everything was fairly simple. My idea was to accumulate as much material of what was happening as possible. And there were no guidelines whatsoever. We had three crews going and we went as fast as we could. Things were happening all over the place and it was just a matter of covering as much as we could. However I did decide that my central lines were to be the behavior of the English-speaking community and then the events. Another crew was covering the media and the events and another was covering the Francophone reactions and the events. We all covered the events as best we could. There were three full-time crews and there were other people coming and going all the time.

It was only when the shooting was over and we sat down to look at the material that we started asking ourselves questions about guidelines and how to handle history and weighty things like that. And certainly the excitement of shooting under those conditions was so strong that any attempt to remove oneself from what was happening and say, well, I'm working according to this guideline or that guideline was out of the question. It was just a matter of going flat out, as it had been in Chicago with *Prologue*.

Q. What guided you a year or two later in editing?

A. I was very much guided by the material and the experience of 1970. I also had two of my editors, Shelagh Mackenzie and Joan Henderson, keeping an intelligent eye on me, to say nothing of Tom Daly, the producer. I found as we went along that there were whole areas where we didn't have what we wanted. So it was a matter of story telling at a certain level. For instance, I felt it absolutely essential in terms of story and in terms of history to include the FLQ manifesto which the government had allowed to be read on CBC television. Getting that was quite a problem. The CBC wouldn't give it to us but finally we managed to get our hands on an illicit half-inch tape which someone had recorded and which we then transferred to film. I also

251

used the advice of a lot of people who had been involved in the events we were dealing with.

To say how exactly I arrived at a particular historical perspective in the film is impossible. With the 1970 material I tried as far as possible to get down my own subjective feelings of my experience of those days because in the filming of the crisis we probably lived it as fully as almost anyone not directly involved. Apart from that I couldn't say that there was any method other than trying the unfinished film on people and trying it on myself. There was no sort of prior attempt to set up real guidelines. I was constantly reading about the different elements and comparing what I read with what we had. We kept trying to find out what was missing. Trying to find where we felt there were real holes and supplement our material with either TV stock shots or videotape or stills or whatever. It was like a jigsaw puzzle with a lot of pieces missing to begin with. But we kept putting the pieces in place until eventually we began to feel we had a whole—as opposed to nothing but holes.

Q. The film really splits in two. First it's about the whole history of the separatist movement in Quebec. And then it's about the rights and wrongs of the War Measures Act and the other acts of the government of 1970. Now in the earlier part where you're discussing separatism there's a very clear argument in favor of French Canada separating. Is that you *personally*, or a historian providing a history of a movement?

A. There is a distinction here. There *is* a strong bias in favor of French Canada. But I would not say there was a strong bias in favor of me, personally, wanting a separate Quebec. That's perhaps a subtle distinction for someone from outside of Montreal but, living in Quebec, and as someone who spends a lot of his life in French, I feel enormous sympathy for most of the aspirations of Quebec.

On the other hand, as an English Canadian I feel quite unsettled about Quebec separating even though I can see that if I was a Francophone Québecois the chances are I'd be a separatist. But I have been brought up in a strong federalist context with strong federalist ties and lots of friends all across Canada, which allows me to simultaneously draw on and participate in two rich cultures. So for me personally my life is going to be fuller if Canada stays both English and French. But at the same time I see that English Canada has done some terrible things to Quebec and as a result I'm very sympathetic to Quebec's anger and if Quebec does separate, well that's democracy . . . and I'll probably stay here anyway. So there is an uneasy ambivalence in my attitude which is in the film.

252

Q. In the early parts of *Action* you go into the social climate in Quebec. Did you research alone or did you have advisors or research assistants?

A. Well, there were no specific historical advisors in the sense of a team of academics peering over my shoulder. I read numerous books and I showed the film to people who were or who had been involved. It was an endless process of cutting in everything that we had, then showing it to see how people reacted. Then reading more about it and going out and looking for more of the missing pieces.

Q. In the film you work with the straight voice-over narrative explaining historical events. Had you considered any other kind of form?

A. Yes. But the bulk of the film is about the October crisis; that was what I personally was involved in and that experience is the core of the film. Therefore I wanted the historical perspective dealt with as fast as possible. For me, anyway, the most economical way of doing this was to skim through things very fast and unify them with a voice-over commentary. I think that had I gone the Wiseman route of avoiding commentary I would have ended up with a three-hour movie just on the historical lead-in. Leaping through decades of history needs more explanation than, say, an interpersonal exchange in a well-established context. Anyway *Action* had already shown a tendency to go on forever and there was also the question of the volume of good historical material that had to be stitched together, so I think I was almost forced to use a linking commentary.

There was also something else in my mind. I wanted *Action* to be, as far as possible, the expression of my personal feelings and views about the October crisis as I had experienced them in 1970 without any sort of hindsight. I did *not* want *Action* to come across as if it were the definitive God-like NFB version, you know, "This is really the official history folks!" I wanted to give it a certain fallible personal element and I decided to use my own voice to do that. So there were a number of reasons why I went with commentary.

Q. In *Action* you use a lot of material from other sources, like the CBC. As you went over this material were you aware at any times of any radical differences between the totality of the material in your possession and a limited or emasculated version seen on television? Or didn't that happen?

A. Very much so. One of the main things you are referring to is the Trudeau interview outside the House of Commons which runs as an uncut ten-minute interview in *Action*. If I had shot that myself I would probably have edited it slightly. But the interview had been on TV edited down to a very short distorted item which made Trudeau look like a blind raving fascist which wasn't true of the original. Although I am not in favor of very much of what Trudeau did in 1970 I do think that he is a strong, determined, and thinking man and that he, like everyone else, should be dealt with honestly and accurately. Because of that we ran the whole interview so the people of Canada could see what had been done to Trudeau in the truncated TV version. The interview was of course also very important because it was about the only time Trudeau explained informally what he was thinking at the time and why he acted the way he did.

In general the television material, as we found it initially, was pre-edited with television's demands of time and television's own political bias built in. We then went on to try and get at the original uncut video tapes. And that took me six months of writing letters to the CBC. Finally I got in by the back door to see four hours of video tapes which I had selected from library cards.

Besides the Trudeau interview there were other things which I left contrary to what I would consider normal pacing demands, such as the FLQ Manifesto. I wanted to have this in the film to ensure that as historical material it would be around, at least for a few years, and even then we did end up cutting out one section because the references in it were so local. There is always a danger, even a likelihood, that something like the FLQ Manifesto will be erased by Radio Canada, intentionally or otherwise. After Chicago when I went looking for stock shots of the riots I found that even just weeks after the events someone or some persons had been spiriting away a lot of material, editing history into oblivion.

Q. Has *Action* been shown on television?

A. It was shown on the CBC in English and on Radio Canada in French the same evening and it had a record public affairs audience: something close to five million people, which means that close to a quarter of the population of this country watched *Action* in one evening.

One of the reasons that *Action* had such a big audience, apart from the natural interest the subject has for Canadians, was because the CBC had told us for six months that it was no good for television. They said nobody wanted to see it and that therefore they did not want to run it.

Q. Were they scared of the contents?

A. It's hard to tell because of the different levels of bureaucracy at the CBC. Who knows who actually decided what and why? Eventually a guy called Peter Herndorf came in and took over the CBC public affairs department. He saw *Action*, liked it, and put it on the air. But prior to that we had a real battle which in fact began to involve the

media, and I found myself having to go around Canada screening
*Action*. We had a big and successful screening in Toronto at the St.
Lawrence Centre, with the result that journalists started calling the
CBC and asking why they weren't running it on television. This built
up pressure on the CBC and finally it became so great that they agreed
to air the film. Meanwhile the battle had created a lot of interest, which
partly explains why we got such a huge audience.

Q. Have most of the people you've come across taken *Action* as a fair
film? Did you get what you considered any adverse comments?

A. I was extremely gratified by the good reaction because I was
treading a very thin line between being called a separatist by the English Canadian audiences or being called an English Canadian bigot by
the Québecois. The screenings in the St. Lawrence Centre in Toronto,
and, say, the Outremont Cinema in Montreal were both, for the most
part, friendly and enthusiastic. At the St. Lawrence Centre I was attacked by both the extreme left and the extreme right and in both cases
the audience came to my defense. I've had criticism from the extremists
on both sides of the fence, and I feel quite happy about that because
it satisfies my sense of balance. I knew when I was making *Action* that
I was going to get flak from both sides. My feeling, judging strictly
from actual audience reactions, was that the film came out of it all in
a correct way. It wasn't seen by the bulk of the Québecois as some sort
of blind federalist propaganda. Equally, English Canada, for the most
part, felt that it was a fairly accurate portrayal of what they too had
seen happen.

Q. You've now had over ten years at the Film Board. What have you
seen happen there in regard to the making of controversial or socially
conscious films outside of "The Challenge for Change" series?

A. There is a rough rule of thumb at the NFB that if you're doing
a film that is on a difficult and touchy social subject and you don't at
some point in the making of it have trouble, then you're probably not
exploring the subject fully. I don't consider myself to be that political
or radical or anything extreme, but I find at the Film Board that I'm
sometimes bouncing along the ceiling of what is permissible, but the
ceiling is high enough for me to do most things that I want to do.
However, if you want to make a film to advocate violent revolution
you probably won't get it made here, or you will get it made and then
it will be locked up. But I think that it is remarkable, in spite of the
place being a government institution, how open the Film Board is to
films which criticize the way our Canadian society is working and even
the way our government is making out. So although I could criticize
the NFB at length about all sorts of things I still think that it is a

marvellous place and I'm very grateful for everything I've been able to do and learn here. And I do think that the NFB does have a very real role to play in the development of our society, a role it could play much more fully, but nonetheless I think that to a certain extent the NFB does actually do that.

Q. You said before we started taping that you were drifting towards drama. Can you explain a bit more about that?

A. Well, I wouldn't say drifting. I've been struggling tooth and nail for 15 years towards drama. And certainly at the Board, where the tradition is all documentary, it's quite a struggle. One of the reasons that I seem to find fiction more satisfactory is that I suspect that there is an element of the lazy parasite in all documentary film makers. As a documentarian you are dependent on somebody else's pre-existent reality. And if that is a private reality, it bothers me. I don't like invading people's personal lives with a camera crew. Most of my own documentaries, at least recently and where I've had control over the subject, have tended to be about public figures and public events. And where there has been a private element I've tried to give the people involved in the film the right during editing to say, "I no longer want to be in your film." The right to see what they look like after the editing and the right to pull themselves out of the film if they do not like what they see.

Q. Did you bring the participants in to see *Reaction*?

A. In *Reaction* most of the participants were private individuals in intimate surroundings and I think, with perhaps one or two exceptions for logistical reasons, everybody came in and saw the final cut. And without exception they all said "Yes." I think that's because of the fact that they were given that right.

Now someone like Trudeau, who is a public figure and who has made the choice to get up there in front of the world and behave publicly, is fair game I think. But that only applies while he is in the public arena. In fact I think one of the most important jobs of the documentary film maker is to analyze and dissect powerful public figures to see what makes them tick and to show us clearly what they are up to. So I would not show Trudeau a film he was in and ask him if he minded.

It is the private person I worry about in documentaries, and it is at that level that I think documentaries can be dangerously parasitic. But I also know that documentaries are often at their most moving when touching on intimate details, so there is a dilemma here. In documentary I'm constantly aware of the fact that I may be hurting someone with my material or my editing, and even when you have checked out everyone in a film there can still be problems.

256

In the case of *Reaction*, six months after having shown it to everyone for their approval I got an unhappy letter from one of the people in one of the sequences. He said that his friends at work had seen the film and found him to be, whatever it was, too this or too that. His peers and colleagues had reacted in a way that upset him. And so well after he'd said "Yes," and well after the film had been finished and a lot of prints had gone out he now wanted to be taken out of the film.

I went through a long and painful correspondence with him saying that if you really insist we will take you out of the film but it is going to cost a lot of money. It means that the film will be withdrawn for several months and it means that all the prints will have to be recalled. Eventually he said "OK, forget it and leave me in." But in the final analysis I hope I would have taken him out if he had insisted—but I also know that this sort of moral luxury can only be afforded by a place like the NFB. And I also know that because I did not want my film held up or shelved I talked someone into accepting a public version of himself that he did not like. But apart from all that potential for pain and harm in documentaries I still find fiction more interesting simply because you have to create the reality before filming it. And it is this act of imagination, with all the work that it entails, with scripts, actors and all the other story elements, which keeps me going.

*Personal Passion*

# 15

# My Homeland
### and
# Nine Days in '26
### Robert Vas

*Robert Vas was born in Hungary in 1931. His adult years were spent under Stalinist repression. After the collapse of the 1956 Hungarian revolution he came to Britain and in 1958 directed his first film,* Refuge England. *In the next two decades he made thirty-four more films. He died on April 10, 1978. These are the bare facts, and they say little about the man or the qualities which made Robert Vas such a unique and important figure in the history of documentary.*

*To my great sadness I knew Robert only very briefly. We met just four times, but that was enough for me to be overwhelmed not just by his films, but by the man himself. He shed a warmth and a passion. Certain things had to be said. Certain films had to be made. And certain things had to be done.*

*In his twelve years at the BBC Vas made films on an immense variety of subjects—his homeland Hungary, Bruno Walter, Arthur Koestler, Alexander Solzhenitsyn, and the '26 General Strike. All were made with consummate skill and brilliant film construction. He told me Humphrey Jennings was his idol and key influence, and made a film portrait of him called* The Heart of Britain. *In the end, however, he expanded Jenning's style into something far broader and richer. Writing about Robert Vas in* Sight and Sound *Barrie Gavin said that he invented a kind of personal documentary which has no parallel.*

*The key to all Vas's work was his moral fervor. Concern, commitment, passion—there were the words he used over and over again, and which guided him. Plus compassionate understanding, which was the force that bound everything together.*

*Television, particularly in America, tends to avoid issues. This was never Vas's way. During the seventies he brought all his filmic skill to focus on issues which he thought needed exposure, and on which other people were silent. Thus emerged his brilliant films on the legacy of Hiroshima, the forcible repatriation of Russian emigrés after the war, and on the myths of the 1926 General Strike.*

*What troubled Vas was the abandonment of a heritage. He saw the BBC of the sixties making a certain number of dynamic personal and committed films.*

*By the seventies this legacy had almost disappeared with epic documentary series being the order of the day. Against this background Vas stood out as someone different—a lone figure, both tolerated and admired by authority as the conscience of the BBC.*

*When Vas died after just finishing a film for the Queen's Jubilee, he was customarily in the middle of a mass of projects. There is an unfinished portrait of Bertolt Brecht; research on a film about the political abuses of psychiatry; and a projected adaptation of Solzhenitsyn's* The Gulag Archipelago.

*For years Vas had worked as a free lance, existing from film to film, and was only put on BBC full staff in 1977. A few days after the event he wrote to me "I can now fully make use of this creative freedom. I want to make more personal films but the thing is not to talk about it, but to do it."*

*As I said, we only met a few times, but that was enough for me to like Vas immensely and to want him as a friend. But that was not to be. And if after such a short acquaintance I could feel his loss so deeply I could, because of that, well imagine the immense grief and emptiness felt by those who truly knew him and loved him. One of those people was documentary film maker Barrie Gavin who wrote this in memory of him:*

> *His true legacy is the standards by which he lived and worked—precision of execution, seriousness of purpose, clarity of personal expression and fervor of commitment. The responsibility to keep those things alive now rests not only on those who were close to him during his life but with all who make our television.*

Q. Can you tell me a bit about your background in Hungary?

A. I started by playing about with a projector when I was five. Bits and pieces of film. I had snippets of German newsreels, an old Tarzan film, bits of an old Douglas Fairbanks movie. I had these in my cupboard and I started with my mother's nail varnish remover to join these things, and got a real spark out of it. Somehow it all started as a love affair with the stuff itself. Touching it. Winding it. I put on shows. It was an infatuation with putting pieces of film together, and somehow this rather childish feeling remains with me up till now, because I am mad about editing. I feel it's in my blood. I conceive and do my films in the cutting room. I put the material together and there is that spark—when "A" and "B" become *more*, become "C."

I've been thinking about this quite a lot since coming to England, that this act of putting small bits of things together stands for a great many things in my life. My life has been broken like a piece of film and all my attempts now are an enlarged version of this small act of joining it all together. One piece is the past. Another piece is the present. Another piece is the future. One part is communism. One the

East, the certainty of the dogma. Another is the West, with its schisms and confusions. And what I am constantly trying to do through these pieces of film is to build a bridge. And I want you, the viewer, to *know* I am trying to build this bridge. That it is inevitable for me to build a bridge. Ultimately it all comes back to joining bits of film, that I started during my childhood and which I nurture and cultivate, because it is fundamental to what I'm now about.

Q. What happened to you in the war?

A. I had a very difficult time during the war, under Nazism. I am Jewish, and I was in a ghetto. But even before the war there was this atmosphere of fear, of approaching Nazism, of the first bombing raids—and a lack of security, because my parents were constantly in a state of divorce. It was a kind of Kafkaesque feeling of fear and insecurity which burst out even more in the ghetto years.

My parents had obtained a Swedish "Schutzpass" which saved me from being taken to the official ghetto, and to possible death. Instead we were in a kind of "privileged" ghetto. It was near the Danube. After a while the Germans wouldn't accept the pretense that we were Swedish citizens, and a great many inhabitants from the neighboring houses were herded to the embankment, shot and thrown into the river.

One can't forget these things—that 90 percent of Hungarian Jews ended in Auschwitz. And the fact that I am alive and survived made me a person who has a lot of obligations to speak about it. I cultivate this feeling. I strive for it. I have no choice.

My mother died tragically after the war, when I was seventeen, and that was about the time I started developing some kind of social, political consciousness. I had lots of conflicts with my father who was a rich man, and I had nothing to cling on to. There was, of course, *the system*. This youthful joyous communist system which all my youthful petty bourgeois friends had subscribed to, and like them, I found myself marching, and believing, and holding the flag—and not questioning. Then my father escaped from the country and went to Australia, and I was completely left on my own and had to hold on to something. That something was the communist youth movement.

However the fact that I had a father in the West automatically meant that I was an "enemy of the people" and because of this I had an enormous amount of trials and tribulations. I wasn't put against the wall, but my life was made hell. At one point I had to go into the army for three years and arranged to become an army projectionist. And then seeing all the Soviet films of the twenties and thirties my old dream came back: "to put on a show." I had an unbelievably vast open-air cinema, for three thousand soldiers, and I was playing movies for them. One day I was showing *The Young Guard*, and I put the volume way up to make a real impact. Then everything blew, and there was no sound. So the political officer comes waving a revolver and says, "You are sabotaging the showing of the masterwork of Soviet cinema! Get out of here!" I had a very difficult time. I finished up in an army psychiatric hospital, and I owe my marriage to the fact that I was released for a small holiday when I met my wife. That was twenty-four years ago.

Q. I know you were a trainee script editor at the National Theater in Hungary, and also wrote a lot of radio plays—but what about your entry into film?

A. I tried to be around movies but it was impossible. It was a closed shop. So I settled down doing manual work during the day and working as a projectionist in the evening, and that took us right up to the 1956 Revolution. We had a child. I lived one place, my wife somewhere else, because we couldn't manage to find a place together. Gradually, with one bitter experience after another, it dawned on many of us of my generation that this was a shattering regime and there was a devastating abyss between the things we were being told and the things that happened to us—and not only me, but my whole generation, became opposed to the regime. Then, after Stalin's death and after the Thaw, the writers tried to put all this into words and from then on, no one could put a stop to it. We found ourselves on the streets in the middle of the Revolution.

On that day, October 23rd, 1956, I had a show in the cinema in the morning. I stopped the projector at two o'clock, went out into the streets and never went back. The news came, "The students are demonstrating." I knew my wife who was a fourth-year student was there and went out to find her. We both worked together the next few days among the students, printing and delivering leaflets. The unbelievable had happened: the Revolution was victorious. We had the incredible experience of a few days of a democratic socialism. And then the Russians came and the tanks. We had nothing to stay for. And taking a tremendous risk we left the country about two weeks after the crushing of the Revolution.

I came to an England which seemed to be alive and sparkling and looking for something, and I found a great affinity between the excitement which I found and the excitement which I left behind. Great things were happening in drama, literature, cinema, social movement. I felt like a bird of paradise. Lindsay Anderson talked to me, and Karel Reisz and others. It was just about the time that "Free Cinema" took wings, and they said, "Why don't you make a film?"

Q. Where did you get the money and the backing for your first film, *Refuge England*?

A. Well, there was the British Film Institute's Experimental Film Fund which was just starting, and I was told about it. Anderson and Reisz urged me to try, and it seemed inevitable that I would make this film about the arrival in England of this "bird of paradise": the experience of my first days in London. I wrote a short story which served as the synopsis. I needed very little money: I think it was under £1000. Walter Lassally, who sympathized with the cause of the Hungarians, offered to be the cameraman for expenses. I had an actor, a Hungarian refugee, to play the refugee, and it all just came about very quickly. The late Sir Michael Balcon, who was head of the committee which gave the money, was very helpful in getting the idea passed. And the film was on its way. What really surprised me was that I suddenly saw how all my life I had been preparing for this. When I sat down at the editing table, it was OK—it clicked.

Q. At that time you probably could have gone either into features or documentary. What pushed you along the path of documentary?

A. I was working for a while at the British Film Institute, in the Information Department. A nice little job, reading and cataloguing all the world's film magazines. And the great fringe benefit was that I could go to the National Film Theatre every day, for nothing. The second advantage was I could go down into the basement and look at all the films distributed by the Institute, or borrow them. And at home I went through all the Eisenstein films, all the classic documentaries and all the films of Humphrey Jennings. The Jennings films were a kind of initiation not only to England, but into the idea of a particular sort of subjective poetic documentary.

As a new citizen of this country it was essential to me to understand what England was all about; and it was these films which gave me the understanding, mainly through the language which Jennings used, through the imagery, through sounds, through the juxtapositions. It made me feel that documentary films, or that kind of documentary films, were the films I would like to make. They would help me to strike new roots.

As I had no English experience, I chose subjects in which I was, in a sense, at home. A refugee's first day in London. A Jewish street in London (because my Jewish experience helped me to understand that, or at least see it in a particular way). Then in the first BBC film I did I went back to the Iron Curtain, to the place where I had left my country.

In other words I was trying to work out a language for myself, but using the places and experiences I felt at home in. I've brought with me from the other side a "baggage," a great many things to talk about. I see myself as a self-appointed professional survivor. I was scarred by two shattering events: the Nazis and 1956—and the baggage, the message, that nobody asked me to speak about, is absolutely central to me; I can't exist without it. I must talk about it. And I must talk about it to an *English* audience which never experienced these things directly.

Q. How did you get into the BBC? And what was your reaction to this most British, possibly, of all environments?

A. I arrived when the television was just starting to expand and there was terrific excitement. There were personalities. There were impresarios. There were a lot of possibilities for personal expression. The BBC then was much smaller and much more intimate. I had already made one film. Another was being financed by the Fund. So I had something to show, and there were people to whom one could show them, people working on *Monitor,* the arts program, and so on. And they said, "OK, we'll give you a hundred rolls of film (that's ten thousand feet) and a mute Bolex. Now go back to the Austro-Hungarian border, shoot your film, and we'll see what happens." And that was my first BBC film, in 1963. A long time ago. I remember running out of stock and getting Peter Watkins* on the phone, who sent a few rolls after me, so I could actually complete my film.

Q. Did you find the BBC very free, very open to ideas and personal impressions then? Do you think it has changed much over the years?

A. I certainly found it very open to ideas and to the possibility of breaking in. Then the BBC needed new people. Today this is much less so. Then you could discuss with top executives for hours where exactly within the frame the title should appear; it was possible to discuss tiny details and major principles. A few years later many of these people of high quality who were responsible for the effervescence and excitement, and who brought in myself and many others, became removed from us to a third or fourth degree at the end of a long chain of command.

When I came in there was a need for people with a personal eye making personal statements in visual terms, in "one-off" films. And this kind of thing is almost a dead species in documentaries. I'm not saying it's impossible to make individual sparks within the framework of a series, but everything is seen now in quite different terms: large productions and large series—where one's approach has to fit a whole series like the Cooke or Bronowski series, and the film maker merely provides visual backing material for these people and their ideas.

And this is what is so sad at the present time. In the past you knew that if your talent is limited and you're able to formulate only a small segment of the truth it didn't matter that much. Because what *you*

*Director of *Culloden* and *The War Game.*

didn't say, other film makers would say. In the atmosphere then it was almost like being in the front line. There was discussion, action. And it was marvellous if someone could make a film better than you could, because there was a possibility to follow that up, and live up to it and outdo it. There was even a magazine called *Contrast* which is so badly needed now. I don't want to present it as some form of a lost paradise, but the fact is that what was so dear to us, that personal kind of film, was not only tolerated but promoted. Television was the only showcase for this kind of films and gradually one was educating the viewer to understand, to read between the lines, to *see*. I've experienced what happened in Hungary before 1956 when four people sat down behind a coffee table, and it would be inevitable that they would emerge with an enthusiastic resolution: "We must make a film about our story. We must tell it all." I loved that atmosphere, and I cherished it—and I found it again in England. But that was only in the first few years; then it changed.

Q. This kind of film—the personal statement—is almost unknown on American television, but like you I remember it blossoming in England. This personal vision, this willingness to say "I see the world in such and such a way," is absolutely fundamental to your work. And of your films the one which comes most to mind on this score is a 1976 film, *My Homeland*, about the 1956 Hungarian Revolution. Can you tell me how that came about and what relationship was with the BBC during the making of that film?

A. The BBC accepted and respected that I went through the Hungarian experience, and that I had something to say about it—and moreover that it was *essential* for me to say it. They knew it might be an expensive way of saying it, but were willing to give me the opportunity to talk about it. Now the editor of the "Omnibus" series, where it appeared, may have been of a different political viewpoint, I'm not sure, but he had no hesitation about giving me an absolutely free hand. The BBC was willing to take the small risks, political and otherwise, because they felt it was necessary for me to make the film.

I had a completely free hand. I had been talking about the experience for about fifteen years and wanted to use the opportunity to express something wider than just the history of the revolution. And at the BBC they were willing to sit back and see what I came up with. They then approved it on the spot.

Q. Did you have to give the Executive Producer or whoever was over you any outline of your film, or were you totally free?

A. In the making of this one I was totally free, because it was my experience and my life, and the inevitability of me wanting to say that and they just waited to see how I was going to say it, and how effective it would be. There were slight conflicts on me overshooting, and so on, but that can always happen. No. That was one of the few films where they just waited and approved it.

Q. How did you approach structure and form on the film? You obviously had the possibility of doing just straight reportage, or straight analysis of the events, but in the end you chose a fusion of very emotive poetry, plus the events of 1956 gradually being threaded through the program. Did you come to that fusion easily, or had you thought of it as straight reportage, or straight poetry at first? I really would like to get into this question of preliminary structuring of the film.

A. Well, the film was a visual anthology of poetry (like Jennings's *Words for Battle*), and the tone of the film took its key from the forcefulness, the intensity of the poetry. I knew I wanted to end up on the long poem by Illyes, "A Sentence on Tyranny."* The structure of the anthology was really suggested by the chronology of events of

*The following is an extract from the poem "A Sentence on Tyranny," written by Gyula Illyes and used by Robert Vas in *My Homeland*. While the poem is being recited by Judi Dench, we see general shots of the 1956 revolution on the screen. Illyes wrote the poem in 1950, but the only time it was ever published in Hungary was in the middle of the revolution.

Where seek out tyranny?
There seek out tyranny,
Not just in barrels of guns,
Not just in prisons,

Not in the cell alone
Where the third degree goes on,
Not in the night without
Challenged by sentry shout,

Not where in deathbright smoke
Prosecutors' words provoke,
Not just in the emphasis
Of wall-tapped Morse messages

Not in confession told,
Not in the judge's cold
Death sentence: 'Guilty'

. . . . . . . . . . .
It is in the plate, the glass,
In the nose and the mouth,
It is in the cold and the dark,
In the outer air and in your house:

Talk to yourself and hear
Tyranny your inquisitor:
You have no isolation,
Not even in imagination.

. . . . . . . . . .
Where seek tyranny? Think again;
Everyone is a link in the chain;
Of tyranny's stench you are not free
You yourself are tyranny.

Like a mole on a sunny day
Walking in his blind, dark way,
We walk and fidget in our rooms
Making a Sahara of our homes;

Because where tyranny is,
Everything is in vain,
Every creation, even this
Poem I sing turns vain,

Because it is standing
From the first at your grave,
Your own biography branding,
And even your ashes are its slave.

"A Sentence on Tyranny" was translated by Vernon Watkins. It appears in *A Hundred Hungarian Poems*, ed. T. Kabdebo (Manchester: Albion Edition, 1976), and is used by kind permission of Mr. Kabdebo.

the Revolution. What I set out to do was tell the almost factual story of a few glorious and bloody days, expressed through means of news-reels, photos—and by seven hundred years of Hungarian poetry. To tell the *spiritual* story of the event. To show that this short, violent outburst for freedom was always present during those seven hundred years and it was the writer and the artist who have helped bring it about. On the one hand, then, you had the events of those few days and on the other hand you had the overwhelming power of poetry and art for so many hundreds of years commenting and bringing to life what the revolution was all about.

Now that, as I say, outwardly suggested a straightforward chrono-logical structure. Less easy was the recognition of the fact that the story for me carried such an enormous emotional charge. From the word "go" the making of the film became a personal search for what my country, Hungary, really meant to me. Its language, its landscape, its brutality, its spirit, its history, everything. And I was trying to for-mulate this for myself and an English audience, from a distance of space and time. And I was digging into this search by reflecting on this extraordinary event, the revolution, which, I can now well see, was a turning point in my life—the event by which I am living for the rest of my life.

I haven't been back for twenty-one years, but the distance has helped me see my country in a spiritual sense. In exile I have discovered her literature and her poetry which at home I took so completely for granted. Suddenly they've said great, tremendous things to me. They are unique pieces of literature. I discovered the country's music. Bar-tok. Folk art. From a distance I discovered beauty of a landscape. I cherished and nurtured this precious feeling, and after a time I felt that somehow I must try to express it in a film.

So I called upon these writers and poets of the past 700 years and enlisted them to help me, to put it all in words for me. Through them I wanted to say that the country is ultimately uncrushable because it is able to express its own predicament in such powerful, enduring ar-tistic terms.

Q. How did you prepare the script?

A. I felt that the power of that historical event could be well captured through faces. Through motionless faces on still photographs. Through the faces of those who've brought about the event, who've carried it in themselves but in a repressed, frozen way (as on a still), waiting to come to life again, relive the experience, speak about it. That was really the first visual motive: who was going to bring those faces alive? The photos were there (and the animation camera can do wonders with this sort of material). The poets were more or less given, and somehow they began to fit in with each other.

One of the first-ever Hungarian poems, a funeral oration from the fourteenth century, seemed almost to have been specially written to accompany the shattering photographs of the funeral of 84 victims of a secret police massacre in a small town during the Revolution. In a film library I found some very long held, tremendously evocative, almost musical, shots made from a car rolling along the rainy, empty streets of Budapest in October 1956. They were outtakes, never used in any newsreel: they became a kind of visual leitmotif, speaking about my search.

Through such finds, such recognitions, it became in the end a sort of inevitable film. It seems now in that state of mind *this* image *had* to meet *that* word; and to fit *this* event of the Revolution to *that* folk song, or to find this shot working against that line of text—all these were somehow parts of the inevitable, painful and exciting search which is really the subject of the film. To find my country for myself. I don't know how the film works, but making it was like writing a poem somehow.

Q. Where did you get all the actuality newsreel-type material of the Revolution itself?

A. One of my most precious memories of '56 is standing in the huge square in front of the Parliament shouting together with thousands of people in the crowd: "Switch off the lights! Switch off the lights!" What we meant was the red star on top of the Parliament building. And the regime replied with switching off all the street lights in the square itself. We were standing there in darkness, our anger mounting. Without a moment's hesitation torches started to burn and I saw there were two cameramen from the State newsreel company starting to roll, and people were shouting to them "*This* is what you should film! *This* is what you should have been filming all the time!"

There is quite a lot of material available of Hungary in '56 and it's fairly easy to get hold of it. So I viewed and viewed. Pictures suggested lines in poems. Poems suggested shots in the library material. And somehow, without predetermined construction, half a dozen basic visual parallels and ideas emerged, good enough to serve as a backbone on which to build a body. Or hold up the building, even though, like scaffolding, they may fall away eventually. But they help to formulate for you the essentials in the early stages.

Q. There is a motif of shots which runs through the film, of stallions in black and white symbolizing freedom or the desire for liberty. In the end of the film you actually see these stallions hobbled and shack-led. Was that link motif there in the beginning? Was it an idea which arose when you were well into the film?

A. The idea arose during the viewing of a lot of library material from Hungary, mainly tourist films about attractions of the country. Films about folklore or nature. There were some nice, neutral images of horses running in a film about breeding stallions. I simply put these images into a more heated, more committed context. Then I found a nice film about a peasant family who live in the country but then go to an industrial town and become new socialist people. It started off with the chained horse and ended up with the horse free from the shackles. But once I saw these beautiful shots they somehow stood for the essence of my film: the free horse enchained. I only wish my film could have been made in Hungary. It was a Hungarian film. If I could make such a film in Hungary I would go home without a moment's hesitation.

Q. The film ends with a very powerful long poem whose refrain is "Where seek out tyranny?" And you set this against pictures of tanks, pictures of life in Hungary. There are also shots of a statue of Lenin and a statue of Stalin. I assume you want that to be understood as a general as well as a particular statement?

A. I don't think it is a clearly defined political statement. Like the poem, it is a lyrical statement against *all* tyranny. Illyes's poem deals not just about particular regimes, but about bureaucracy, about an enormous machine towering over people, eating itself into every human situation and making life impossible. I hope my film was profoundly political, but I also hope it made a more subjective and universal statement.

Incidentally a friend of mine who happened to be at the Hungarian Embassy the day after the showing of the film told me that the Embassy people were apparently enthralled by the film. "Every word of it was true," they said, "but this was a film made by the enemy."

Some while ago I made a program about Solzhenitzyn, at the time when very little was known about him. Members at the Russian Embassy saw it and said "He's a very great writer, but why do you have to make such a fuss about him?"

The Hungarian film was a statement about the importance of the spoken and written word. Solzhenitzyn has put that into words, in his Nobel Prize speech: that it is the *writer* and the *artist* who record and formulate history, that once an artistic truth—a line in a poem or in a novel—is actually put down on paper it cannot be undone. And it

271

can work miracles. That's why in the Hungarian film I have a close-up of all those hands reaching for the falling leaflets, scraps of paper. They are reaching for The Word.

Truly, one of the things that bothers me most is how the artist is such a con-man, such an entertainer, in the West. I find it unbelievable that such a person as say Osbourne and others, people who formulated the credo, the ideas of a generation in the fifties, how *dare* they not live by the ethics, the morality of their own words, for the rest of their lives. I know that this is impossible and perhaps too romantic a wish. In my film I mentioned that the average lifespan of a Hungarian poet was about thirty years. These people actually wrote poems in the last seconds of their lives before they were shot or committed suicide, because they *wanted* people to know what befell them and their nation. And now to come to a place where there is real freedom of speech and expression and to see that the spoken and written word and the picture on the screen means so little and does so little—it hurts. I don't want to generalize too much but one sees art and culture here as a pastime of the "eggheads." It doesn't become life and blood. This is really what the film is about: to show what poetry and art can achieve in changing history; how it becomes a chronicler of the times in ways which no standard historical chronicle can describe.

Q. What amazes me and moves me again and again is the way you work from the inside, from passion and from personal feeling. However, one of the most famous and well known films that you've done was *Nine Days in '26* which deals with the General Strike in Britain of that time. I am rather curious as to how you, a Hungarian, came to deal with a subject so centrally British?

A. I didn't set out by saying, "Now I am going to show the English what their history is about." The reason why I like and chose documentaries is because there are so many roots, so many uncharted territories, so much that you can explore. Take library film, which I like so much to work with. You have what appears to be "factuality," a record of an outward happening, revealing a fact; but what you should really aim at is to find new meanings, personal interpretations of that fact almost as if the event would take place inside. I feel, for instance, that history, library material, outward events ought to be constantly reinterpreted in psychological, spiritual and personal terms like the Rossif film on Spain or Marcel Ophuls's films. The historical facts, constantly re-evaluated and re-interpreted, should be seen from different viewpoints, an internal one, a meditative one, a thoughtful one, a personal one, a lyrical one.

Now coming to the General Strike, I was disturbed to realize that this particular segment of British social history, with which I socially and humanly felt much affinity, was constantly and repeatedly seen from only *one* viewpoint: the viewpoint of the middle class. A cozy consensus viewpoint which ignores the real price in human suffering, and the complexity of ideas and beliefs that went on behind the strike. Instead this middle-class viewpoint dwells on a certain myth of the strike: how the nation was strong enough not to be broken, and tells it again and again.

For example I found some library material which reinterpreted the story of 1926, which took place in the midst of the darkest social slump of the postwar decade, in the most cozy and comfortable way, almost like a Boy Scouts story of how marvellous we are to survive such an ordeal. I felt there was a need for another, perhaps different interpretation of the same truth using the same material. I set out to find it.

I mentioned to you I am doing these things because I want to re-root in England. In one sense I want to achieve this by trying to explain my own past experiences to a British audience. And in another sense, as a film maker, given the privilege and opportunity to communicate I somehow see it as my duty to get to the point of what is happening in this country today. I believe in continuity in history. So I tried to use the historic parallel to show the various social and political forces that were present in the country at the time and their equivalent now, so that today we can learn from that experience.

Q. The normal or standard BBC practice, or quoted practice in their guide to documentarists put out some years ago, is to aim for strict objectivity. Your film is very objective and at the same manages to be very compassionate towards the miners' point of view. It demythologizes the middle-class view and I personally happen to agree with you on this matter. However, in your making of the film some of the types you take to represent the aristocratic or the middle-class point of view seem very set-up, caricatured types. There is, for example, one rather aristocratic woman for whom the whole thing was a game. Were you conscious of this bias in selection?

A. Well, as far as the choice of people is concerned, everyone in the film, the aristocrats *and* the miners, came to us via the same methods. We advertised in various newspapers for people who had something to say about their experience to come forward. We had a tremendous response because this was a crucial event of social history. I certainly didn't go for distortion. I strongly sensed that there were different sides to the same truth. I felt a genuine anger against the sort of bias in the

273

way this historical material was treated in the films of the thirties and forties, purely from the middle-class viewpoint. There was an aim to illuminate the present through the experience of the past. But having said that, the rest was a process of discovery.

Together with my co-producer I went to see these people. We had a tremendous response and by selecting twenty-five people after visiting and talking to at least 150 during the research, we gradually realized the enormous conflicts, the gulf between the attitudes, the tension, the charge of this whole situation. And it's possible that as this feeling and anger and relationship to our story grew, that perhaps we were ending up with various polarized contrasts. But it wasn't that we tried to find a "funny lady" who is sending up the upper class which we can then contrast with the miners who speak about their tragedy. It may appear like that—but this is not the way I'd approach a subject. The essence of making the film was a process of discovery.

Q. The BBC is sometimes referred to as "Auntie." In other words it is seen as stating the accepted middle-class view and as endorsing the status quo. Given this background, did you have any difficulties before the film was made or after the film was finished? Was it easily accepted by your senior producer?

A. It wasn't at all difficult to bring about the film. I knew and read about the subject. Then, about October 25th, 1972, a very good book was published on the subject with much new material. So I put the subject up on October 26th and it was accepted on November 1st. Instantly. And for the next six months no one asked a single question as to how I was going to treat this material. No one asked me what my viewpoint was. At that time I didn't have a developed viewpoint. I felt what I was after, but the viewpoint was slowly developing in the process of the research. Although I was a foreigner, I got a totally free hand to treat this utterly controversial segment of British history. Perhaps it was taken for granted that whoever touches this subject would treat it in the same way it has always been treated. No one asked me any kind of question. That was kind of horrifying and it was also marvellous.

Q. As it happened the projected showing of the film coincided with a threatened miners' strike in England. The BBC decided to delay the screening three months, and to my mind—and in the opinion of a lot of other people—this was a wrong decision and made the film lose its very pertinent immediate relevance. This must have made you pretty sick as well.

A. What bothered me most is this. I was talking to you about patriotism. About the role of the artist. About the artist as a catalyst.

274

How he can bring about events. I didn't want to become famous, or sensational. Or be in the center of events. I just felt that, unknown almost to myself, and together with my colleague, Tom Scott, we achieved something that was relevant and responsible and for which we cared. And we felt if you show the film at that particular moment to the people for whom it was intended, that could be a starting point for a sane, helpful, constructive discussion about the state of the nation. I do not think that any broadcaster or communicator can hope for more than to be of help in a given difficult historical situation.

I wouldn't have minded if everybody on the discussion dissected the film and said it was absolute rubbish and factually untrue. At least I would have had my voice heard. The fact that this didn't come about at the time when it was most needed and when it could have been of some help has hurt me tremendously because I felt that my word was not valid. It was a possibility to use my capacities in a useful way in my chosen country, and it bothered me enormously that it didn't come about. I felt if you have freedom you must be able to have the courage to look into the face of history. I hadn't set myself up as passing judgment. Nothing of the sort. I just wanted, as a communicator, to *communicate*, to be relevant. Instead the film was shown a long time after the strike had ended, and late in the evening. I was deeply upset.

But having said that, I must reiterate that the film was *made* and I had complete freedom in doing it. And that, ultimately, it was *shown*. But if they *had* allowed it to be made, why weren't they proud of it? Why didn't they uphold it? And when in 1976 there was the 50th anniversary of the event, why didn't they take it off the shelf and say to the viewer: "Look here: this is what we have and we're showing it even if we don't quite agree with it. But it may well be a valid view of history and you should see it because it might interest you."

# 16

# Dreams and Nightmares
## Abe Osheroff

*During the Spanish Civil War 40,000 men from over 20 countries joined various International Brigades, and went to Spain to defend the Republic against Franco and against fascism. Abe Osheroff, then in his early twenties, was one of those who joined the Abraham Lincoln Brigade and went to fight. Thirty-five years later he returned to Spain and out of a short visit grew the idea and the necessity of* Dreams and Nightmares.

Dreams *shows Spain seen through Osheroff's eyes. It is an intensely personal statement about the Spanish Civil War, contemporary Spain, and American foreign policy vis-à-vis Spain in the Nixon era. It's partly autobiographic, partly historical, and partly an antiwar and anti-Franco piece of pleading.*

*The film starts with Osheroff talking about his early life on the Lower East Side of New York and sets up the emotional and social conditions that led Osheroff to join the Lincoln Brigade. The film then goes on to combine newsreel footage (a lot of it new) of the Spanish Civil War with contemporary footage shot by Osheroff. In addition to interviews shot with anti-fascist dissidents, Osheroff also uses a lot of underground footage smuggled out of Spain showing mainly student riots of the late sixties. The civil war footage is fascinating but Osheroff wants to go beyond yet another historical re-examination.\* His main point is that the U.S. Spanish bases are props for the (then) Franco regime rather than democratic bulwarks against Soviet threats.*

Dreams *is full of passion and judgments. It's the civil war from the inside as felt and experienced by one human being, and totally different from the coolness of Rossif's* To Die in Madrid. *It's a film from the gut, slightly ingenuous and yet still intellectually appealing. As Wayne Johnson wrote in* Film Library Quarterly,† *"The film is an odyssey by a thoroughly decent committed human being. It's this quality which gives the film its piquancy and depth."*

*I met Abe for the first time a couple of years ago at a film seminar in Boston. You couldn't overlook him. A very well built older man with a mane of waving grey hair, always dressed in carpenter's overalls. And passion bursting from the seams. A refugee prophet from some Bible picture.*

---

\*Of recent films about the Spanish Civil War a very interesting example is Albert Kisch's *Los Canadienses* which tells about Canadian volunteers in the International Brigade.

†*Film Library Quarterly*, Vol. 8, No. 3/4, 1975.

*He'd come from a radical Jewish background in New York and while working as a carpenter had taken time off to become very involved in political action throughout the forties, fifties and sixties. This kind of action included both field work in union organizing among the steel workers and coal miners of Penn-sylvania and protesting in Mississippi. Then, at the age of 59, overwhelmed with disgust at American foreign policy, he'd decided to act in a different di-rection. To make another political statement—but this time on film.*

*The beauty of the seminar was that you could talk and explore. So for a week Abe, myself, other friends and other film makers all talked, and Abe's message was always the same. "What's this crap you're doing for TV—plastic docu-mentaries! If you believe in something then go out and do it. Don't plead the organization or your family. If you really believe then go and do it."*

*Since then we've corresponded intermittently. Only a few days ago a letter came from Abe. He'd been stirred up by the NBC film on the Holocaust but was left with a "burning desire to do something different . . . maybe a film dealing with the nature and scope of Jewish resistance."*

*Abe has become a kind of beacon for me. I don't go with him all the way but like very much what he says at the end of the interview: "In a world that takes power away from individuals I have exercised some control, some power over my life. I know where I'm going to be when I'm eighty because I'm going to make it be."*

Q. You've been working for many years as a carpenter. During this time you also carried on parallel political involvement. What was the key thing that moved you to do a film on Spain? It seems amazing to move from years of carpentry and suddenly go out and raise money for such a film.

A. In 1971 I returned to Spain for the first time in thirty years or so, primarily for nostalgic reasons. I wanted to walk leisurely where we had run and crawled. My visit was limited to retracing all the steps I had made when I first went to Spain. As a matter of fact, I started my tour at precisely that point where I had swum ashore after being torpedoed, and I followed the route right up to the point where I was wounded and shipped back. Then I came to one site that moved me to tears—a town called Belcite, which is now a ghost town which Franco preserved as a war memorial of "the atrocities of the Reds" and "the heroic defense of his crusaders against the communist hordes."

In 1971 that town looked exactly as I remembered it from my time there: deserted, barren. Standing there in the ruins of Belcite, I was just overwhelmed emotionally, and I saw passing in front of my eyes almost all of my life that led me to Belcite. I lived through an expe-rience of flashbacks one after another, and I had this enormous urge to tell everybody. My companion, a very bright young lady, listened to some of my ideas about writing some articles to the press and said, "That's nonsense. If you want to do a project on a serious level and reach people, it has to be visual."

Q. At that time, you were thinking about the past. But the major part of your film deals with Spain in the present and *not* just your experiences of Spain in the past. At what point did you start thinking about Spain today and trying to say something about that as well?

A. When I went to Spain on that trip I was already very much involved here in the United States fighting against the American support of Franco, against the pact with Franco, against the American presence in Spain and economic help to Franco. But when I went to Spain for what was a nostalgic visit that had nothing to do with politics, it all came together for me. I had this enormous need to tell people of my country a couple of things: one, why young Americans went to fight as volunteers in 1937—and remember this was 1971 when other young Americans were refusing to go and fight in another kind of war in Vietnam—and I thought there was a link between the two; two, I wanted to explain why I was now taking a position of tremendous resistance to the foreign policy of my government which was supporting the regime that I had fought against.

Well, the whole idea of making a film overwhelmed me. I became possessed. That's the only way I can describe it, and it didn't matter that I'd never made films and didn't even take still pictures. I couldn't get the idea of a film out of my system.

OK. So I didn't know anything about film, but I did know I was a capable organizer. I have a lot of energy and I have a capacity for raising funds when I am deeply committed to an idea.

I then took my idea, called a meeting of friends in Los Angeles and said, "You guys have been peace activists for years. You've been resisting America's position in Vietnam. One of the weaknesses of the peace movement is that it always gets involved *after* the thing gets started. I have a concept which may be contributory to stopping a war *before* it gets started. I want to deal with American intervention before it gets serious."

The response was terrific. A couple of people gave me a few thousand dollars right then and there. I also had the good fortune to run into an old friend who had been in Mississippi with me, who was quite wealthy though I didn't know it. She became involved with the idea and said, "I'll help you." I said "OK, I need large sums of money," and she gave me some very big seed money.

Q. Did they query your capacity to make the film?

A. Yes, nearly everybody did. But my answer was "All I can guarantee is that I will make a major effort." My track record is very good. Most of the things I've undertaken I've pulled off. I built, for instance, a community center in Mississippi in 1964 despite the fact that I was the only white man for many miles around, and that the Ku Klux Klan was really gunning for my ass. I raised the money for that and I built it together with local blacks, although they said it couldn't be done. Some of the same people gave me money for the film.

I got the seed money together, and then I went to certain progressive and left-wing elements in Hollywood for help. I don't want at the moment to go into the names of these personalities, but they were the better known actors, writers, and directors who have always associated themselves with progressive forces. They all had one thing to say, "Carpenters don't make films, and if someone did make such a film, he would not get it shown." A real negative reaction.

Now I was doing some carpentry work for a small film distributor—Churchill Films—and I went to this Mr. Churchill and told him my dilemma. I said, "What I want you to do is introduce me to some young film makers who will at least hear me out." And two or three down the line one young guy called Larry Klingman got excited. I spelled out my ideas and for many reasons, including some personal ones, he got into it, and in fact became my guide, production manager, and editor. Then I wrote a rough script for the film and pulled together fifteen thousand dollars in order for us to begin.

Q. Can you tell me about the rough script? I am interested in how it changed as the picture developed.

A. The idea was to stop a war before it starts. In other words, the time has come to put an end to conducting major policies of the country by secret executive policies of our president. The president then was Nixon. I wanted to make a statement that shows that the volunteering of young Americans in 1936 and 1937 to fight in a foreign war was part of the same moral pattern as the refusal of young Americans to fight in Vietnam.

Q. How did Larry react to that concept?

A. Well, the big problem was that he was not politically in the same place I was, neither was he as interested in the subject as I was. Later he said the main thing that brought him in was my energy and my enthusiasm. He thought I had something. I also guaranteed him the same salary he was getting, and that was quite a problem as we were working for two years. So he had me put together a small team which consisted of him, Steve Larner, who became the cinematographer for

279

*Roots,* and a young Canadian woman of Spanish extraction to serve as the guide, contact woman, and translator.

Q. What was your first move?

A. I went over to Spain myself and contacted the underground. I told them about my project and they got very excited about it. They would do anything they could to help. They wanted *their* story to be told, and saw that one of the elements of the film would be what is happening in Spain today. I came back with that connection and was then able to raise more money on account of those meetings. In fact I took some of my recordings and did a number of shows for radio. The response was great. People sent me hundreds, fifties. One woman sent me three thousand dollars—a little old lady from Los Angeles.

Q. You went into Spain to make a film against the regime. I assume you must have had a certain cover there, like saying you were doing "X" with the crew when in fact you were shooting "Y."

A. It was pretty evident that such a project could run into very serious difficulties, so I thought it through carefully and established certain procedures. The first thing I did was pick up insurance policies for the crew—about a quarter of a million dollars for the two principals. I was only able to make one payment because I knew it was a one-shot deal. The next thing that I did was to work out meticulously an itinerary for the crew. Where they would go, to whom they would talk, what they would shoot.

When we finally got ready to go into Spain we established a pretty disciplined procedure. I was never with them during the course of the work. The crew chief, however, was to report back to me periodically. My thinking on this was that if we got caught and we were all together it would be very, very serious. Then, through a mutual contact in Madrid, we set up a phony film company called AO Productions (those are my initials) and got a license to make a film in Spain called *Winter Vacation in Spain.* And with that, the crew went in.

It was winter, so *Winter Vacation* seemed right to the Spanish. However, when the crew was caught by the police, they were going to a church meeting with striking workers, and were nowhere near the ski slopes. We don't know all the reasons they got caught. Maybe there was some sloppiness. Maybe the phones were tapped and that's how they got caught. When the crew chief did not report to me on schedule I left the country quickly. I went back to Paris and was able to confirm my suspicions that they had been busted through some people in the committee in the area. The American embassy would not have helped. A telephone call quickly established that this woman was in jail, held by the security police in Madrid, and that the two crew men were being held under house arrest in the hotel.

The woman was expelled from the country after a severe interrogation: she was physically put on a plane and expelled. The crew was forced to drive from Madrid to Barcelona and across the border, exposing all the footage they had left while the police accompanied them to the border.

Q. What happened to the former footage? Did the police try to take that away or was that footage already with you?

A. They couldn't take it away because every time some footage was shot a crew member would go into a department store, and because it's that kind of a country, make a purchase, put everything into a package and mail it off as a gift. So the only thing they confiscated was the last little bit of footage.

Q. In your film, you have a lot of shooting with the Spanish underground. How was that done?

A. Well, the part of the film in color we did. Some of it was done in Paris where some of the people we interviewed had been living as exiles. One or two however came across the border from Spain to be interviewed, such as the young Basque who appears in the film. All of the black-and-white footage of the underground that appears in the film was shot for me by the Spanish underground after the police had busted the crew.

After the arrest I realized that I didn't have enough material to make a picture of underground activity. I had no footage of strikes, demonstrations, student activity, so I went back to Spain illegally. That was the third time in regard to the film. I met the underground, told them of my problem, and they said, "We have been taking footage and will take some more. You have to understand our footage is real underground. It's cheap Super 8 and it's all on black and white." And I said, "It'll work even better." So I made that arrangement and went back to Paris. A few weeks later a representative of the Spanish underground delivered a whole load of footage to me. And even after that some was sent to me to the United States.

Q. You hadn't made a film before, but you knew politically where you were going and what you wanted to do and say. However, you were working with a group who had made films before. Was there any tension of you wanting to go one way and your crew demanding or saying that artistically it has to go another way?

A. There was tension from the word go. Firstly these people were used to a standard of living and comfort that I couldn't provide them with. That was the first thing that happened. They came, checked into a big hotel and gave me the bills. And I said "No." I quickly straightened that out. They understood and backed off.

The bigger problem was they would not accept my direction. It even shows in the credits where Larry who handled the technical aspects of the job stuck himself on as director. I didn't make an issue of this but it was ridiculous. Anybody who sees the film knows whose film that is. He edited it excellently, but also under my control by the way.

So there was an ego problem involved, and it had a concrete effect. When they went out into the field I gave them a schedule of what I wanted and there were things that they actually refused to do, because they said it was corny—unprofessional. Let me give you an example of something that's missing in my film that pains me to this day.

I said "I don't want the audience just to see the war by showing them the battle zones. I want you to do it a different way. I want a living camera to be careening through a crowd in Spain and noting that there is an absence of men of my generation. The dialogue accompanying the shooting helps to explain that. You see young people, very old people, but you do not see able-bodied men of sixty, because there were so many casualties. And then I want the camera suddenly to discover the man of 1936. For example, the camera bumps into a pair of hands holding a little box with some cigarettes and matches. The camera bounces off this collision, and what you see is a guy who is two feet shorter than the rest of us. He's standing on a pair of stumps and he's a beggar—in the streets of Barcelona."

I wanted that shot and I found these beggars. I knew what I wanted which was an oblique but very powerful reference to the human cost of the war. But they just laughed at the idea. They finally agreed to do it, but then just didn't. It was "cornball." They didn't do it because they were pros, and I was a carpenter, and they never forgot that. I was an organizer. I was a doer. But I was *not* a film maker. Well, quite frankly, I think my judgment afterwards was corroborated. But this matter of control was a central problem right through the film.

Q. Towards the end of the film you have a lot of footage where one sees American strategic bombers and American officials landing in Spain. And the footage is very effective in the context of the film. How did you get that footage, which I assume the authorities would be reluctant to release for an anti-Franco film, not to speak of an anti-American foreign policy film?

A. I set up a little dummy corporation in Los Angeles to make films. I then wrote a very powerful anti-communist script which was designed for college level to teach people the need for the American presence in Western Europe. I then sent the script to the Pentagon and told them that to do this anti-communist film well I needed footage to show some of these things. The people at the Pentagon were delighted with the script and gave me clearance to go to Vandenberg and other air bases where there are stores of information. They said I could see everything except "highly classified" information.

Now, on the letter telling us we could go get the footage it was stated very clearly that the use of any of this material for purposes other than those set out in the script was subject to imprisonment and fine. I didn't give a shit about that. I was too deeply into my film to care.

So we went up there and then it became a very complicated problem for me financially as I couldn't just go in and get the footage on Spain. That would have given the game away. So I had to buy a whole lot of other junk—Germany, Italy, wherever we had bases—and have it copied. And the copying cost a hell of a lot of money. But I came up with shots of American missiles, submarines, most of the things I needed. So the Pentagon *did* help me with this film.

As a matter of fact I wanted to use them again, but they wouldn't bite the second time. I figured if I got busted that would make the film. How else could I get publicity? So I baited them and tried to get busted. But there were some intelligent people there, and nothing happened.

Q. But it was quite clear to them that you had taken material for one purpose and used it for another, and they just did nothing.

A. For once they used intelligence. I wanted them to bust me. I had already got commitments from the Civil Liberties Union and *The New York Times* to treat it as a minor Elderberry case, because my position was that this information belongs to the American people. But they did nothing. Anyway, that's where I got that material.

Q. You got some material via the Pentagon. Where did you get other dupe material, material for example which doesn't appear in *To Die in Madrid* and films like that?

A. In a number of ways. There was first of all a large amount of material on the subject available in American film archives. When they found out I had some interesting original Brigade footage they were more than happy to let me copy some of theirs. It was a trade-off. The other way was I had a few friends—names and specific occupations in the industry unmentionable—who were in a position to make contact for me with librarians and large corporations. This way I was able to get my hands on some interesting documentaries. I couldn't get them

printed and copied in an ordinary lab because you have to account for
your material. But some of the porno houses in Los Angeles couldn't
give a damn what they print. So we could take them there, rush them
through at night, and have the films back in the files before dawn and
I would have copies of the stuff. I also picked up some odds and ends
running around Europe, in Paris, in Italy, and so forth.

Q. How long did you work on the filming by itself, apart from the
editing?

A. The filming itself was unfortunately too short. We had planned
to spend about a month and were busted in the second week. When
I went back to France I still did not have my story. That's when I
contacted the underground and got all that black-and-white footage,
then went back to the United States.

Q. Were there many changes you made in the editing? Things that
had happened in the shooting that you now had to reassess and incorporate into the film?

A. Yes. The original outline that I had written underwent a great
deal of modification. The final script that you hear me and a young
woman narrate went through, I would say, fifteen or twenty rewrites,
always dictated by the nature of the material and the way we were
organizing it, though the narrative is still very basically the story I
wanted to tell.

Q. How did the difficulties between yourself and Larry affect the
editing?

A. We'd agreed that Larry would do the actual work of editing, and
I would respectfully listen to his judgment. He is a very capable film
maker. But I had to make the ultimate decisions, and he agreed with
that. Implementing this, however, turned out to be something else. We
had different reasons for being interested in all this. I didn't care if the
film made a million dollars. That was not important to me. Neither
did I care whether it advanced my film career, because I'm not a film
person. But I can understand that he did. He's a professional film
maker with certain standards in the way he makes a living. And this
became a problem from time to time. So we had plenty of arguments,
and I gave in on certain points, and he gave in on others.

Q. The film is very personal, and seeing you here and there in the
film helps very much and makes the film different. Was that person-
alization in from the start?

A. I resisted the film being a personal document, and I want to say
to Klingman's credit that he was the one who forced the change. The
film was practically all finished and cut and didn't have the introduction with me as a carpenter which starts the film and didn't have the

ending where I appear again. I very much resisted because I was a little scared, and felt very vulnerable, particularly since I had to deal with a lot of audiences who were my friends and comrades in the struggle who I knew would take different interpretations of the film from me. It was Larry (and Steve Larner and a few other persons) who insisted that the personal way was the way the film should go.

What I then did was I took the film before it was finally cut and I showed it to groups of young people—and it fell flat. And I realized the only way it could be made workable was to humanize it. So not only did we change the filming to shoot myself, but there are two spots in the film where I consciously tried to humanize the film. I wanted to make people feel this could happen to them. One is where I say, "I wanted to go but I had a beautiful girl friend, and I was in love with her, and so I hesitated four months," and the other is when I get wounded in the film and say, "I felt a tremendous sense of relief." I felt a certain shame from that feeling. These are the things you're not supposed to say—and yet I did.

Q. While you were finishing the film you must have started thinking about distribution—where it would go, how it could best be used.

A. The first thing I did with the film was to rent a theater in Los Angeles for an evening. Then I got on the telephone and 1200 people came to the opening. Straight after that, still full of enthusiasm, I took the film to New York. I went to ABC, NBC, and CBS, but I couldn't even get them to look at it. They turned out to be pure chickenshit. I couldn't even get PBS to look at it. NBC and CBS told me that they wouldn't do it, because when they wanted to deal with a subject they have their own people do the documentary.

When I went to see a guy at ABC he threw three letters on the desk. He said "You can read these but don't touch them." They were three letters from three major oil companies, which gently threatened ABC and said that if their stand towards the oil companies was not modified they would have to reexamine their business relationships and so forth. That was the atmosphere in which he worked. He told me he liked the film very much, but said "You'll never get it on a major network." He was right.

I went to a number of distributors, but they wouldn't look at it. Finally Dan Talbot of New Yorker Films saw it, loved it, and said "I'm going to show it." I went back to Los Angeles, but then I got a letter from him which said, "From a business viewpoint I've thought it over and I'm sorry I have to withdraw." I wrote right back and said "Dan, you can't withdraw, because you have a commitment. You liked that film, not only as a work of art, but also because you happen to

agree with what it says and you share the responsibility for that statement being made." I phoned him right away, and his next letter was,
"You're absolutely right and I'll distribute the film."

Now in actual distribution he didn't do that much of a job, but using
his name and prestige I was able to lever my way up. I knew I couldn't
get off the ground by showing it only in the United States. So I said,
how do I get this film over to Europe? Then a guy called Gordon
Hitchens saw the film here at a small screening, liked it and said, "I
want to take this film to the Leipzig Film Festival and one or two
others."

I wasn't too excited. Leipzig—what the hell. Gordon said "This festival crosses borders and has influence beyond Eastern Europe—tremendous publicity." So I took it to Leipzig and it walked off with the
major prizes. I couldn't believe it. All of a sudden I was somebody,
and I started to get invitations to show the film, East and West and the
Soviet Union.

With that I came back to the United States and consciously organized the kind of showings where I could get press coverage. I got
favorable reviews in the Los Angeles press and the San Francisco press,
and so on. Finally the film was entered in the American Film Festival
in New York, and won an award and that made it kosher.

By now I had two distributors and various awards. I then made a
very impressive-looking brochure and mailed it all over the damned
country. Every possible address. Everybody in the Spanish and Por-
tuguese Historical Society, American Historical Societies, professors
all over the campuses and so on. And I began to get something of a
response.

Q. How did your old friends and comrades in the Lincoln Brigade
react to the film?

A. Initially half of my old friends took a negative attitude, and some
of them were very vociferous. One of the accusations was "ego trip-
ping." Another was, "Why should we help a venture which is turning
out to be a commercial film, and is being shown in big centers with
distributors charging money?" But the big thing was, "How dare anybody make a film of the Spanish Civil War and not point out both the
heroic role of the Communist Party and how it helped organize the
International Brigade, and the enormous aid that the Soviet Union
gave."

I was finally driven into taking the offensive. I didn't just defend
myself. Starting with the last question first, this is not simply a film
about the Spanish Civil War. That is just *part* of my film. This is a
very personal statement about my experiences of that situation. And
I never wanted to get caught in that trap—I was making a film for

American audiences primarily—as to whether or not the Soviet Union helped the Spanish people, but rather asked why didn't the American government help the Spanish people. This is a much simpler question, and this is what I wanted to focus on.

Q. There has been a terrific change in Spain since your film was finished. Franco has died, there has been a certain movement towards a different system. Has your film, following this climate of change, been shown in Spain?

A. Yes, I was in Florence last year for the fortieth reunion of the International Brigade, and I had my film with me. I had decided to try and take it into Spain. But how was I going to get this film into Spain? The Spaniards told me, "Cut it into sixteen pieces," but I decided that wasn't the way to do it. I took the film can out in the open and walked out through the customs. The guys with me thought I was out of my mind—crazy. But I just walked right through the customs. It didn't occur to anyone somebody would bring in controversial material that way.

I then showed the film in Barcelona to a group called the Catalan Assembly who appear in my film, and there were people recognizing themselves on the screen, because I had put their very first illegal meeting in the film. They loved it, and introduced me to the rightist director of Filmoteca which is a national film organization. He saw the film. He was a Francoist and his assistant was a leftist—it's a crazy country. The young guy got very excited and the older guy said, "Well, it's very interesting and certainly belongs in our archives." So they bought it. I then turned to the leftist, who had just said goodbye to the older man and said "What's with this fellow?" And he said "This guy wants to keep his job, and he knows where things are going!"

Q. You showed your film a lot in Russia and Eastern Europe. Were there any questions or reactions there which really shook you?

A. The question which most fascinated me in Eastern Europe was, "Are you really a carpenter?" And I said "Are you really Marxists?" They said "What do you mean?" I said, "You guys are supposed to think the working class are the salt of the earth and can do anything and innate in us is infinite intelligence and skill just waiting to come out. Well, I got tired of waiting and I liberated myself."

Q. I would like to know how you feel about your actions in the thirties from today's viewpoint. What I want to do is distinguish between the romanticism with which we see the Spanish Civil War and the realities of why one went.

A. Of all the serious decisions I've made in my life, some of which I regret, going to Spain is one I've never regretted. And the basic reason I don't regret it is I got more out than I put in. Not simply learning lessons historically, not just experiencing a people who at that time I considered noble, and watching them in action, but in a very personal sense the experience of Spain helped me integrate myself as a human being. I was a person of social convictions and actions, and when Spain came up it stood before me as a test at the right time. For me not to have gone to Spain would have been to fail the concept I had of myself as a person and human being.

I am happy to this day that I went. It was an accident, but at the right time. There were a lot of pressures not to go but in the end it brought me together as a whole person. Finally there was a correspondence between my ideology, my words, and my conduct. I have a number of good friends who faced the same decision at the same time and for whatever reasons, not that they are lesser people, decided not to go or could not get themselves to go, or were pressured into not going, and to this day they regret that decision.

When I hear people say, "I went to Spain because I hated the fascists," it blows my mind. Because it's an abstract political concept made by somebody who doesn't know what fascism is. I didn't know what fascism was, but I went to Spain. Yes, I was motivated by the fact that Italy and Germany came in. That provoked enormous responses in me, but the essential reason for my going was a personal decision as to where I was at the time.

Q. You've made one film on Spain and your beliefs in and around the situation of Spain and America today. But what moves you now?

A. I'm doing what I would loosely describe as a radical film on aging. It's sort of chic now to talk about aging, and I'm nauseated every time I turn on the television and see programs that say, "Now be nice to them, the old folks, because you too will soon be one of them." "Use it before you lose it," or all these geriatric approaches: "Be kind to them and understand them," or "They are a large section of the population and we have to deal with them." All this nauseates me. So I want to make a film which is addressed to young people about aging and which takes a totally different approach to the question.

I want to talk about spiritual aging. I want to talk about the fact that many people are finished at the age of sixteen. I have met many dead people. Every day I see dead people in the streets with burnt-out eyes and with walks that indicate they've had it. If they once were, they no longer are. And every once in a while you meet an older person who still is. And I want to talk about aging from the viewpoint of that point at which personal development and growth stops. At that point you have begun the aging process, and you could be two years old. I want to talk about the process of socialization where we are so anxious to get rid of childlike behavior that the child is often wounded or murdered in the process. And I want to talk about raising that to a conscious level. And I want to talk to young people about keeping that childlike quality alive and never surrendering it to anybody.

Now all this I want to do in a personal way, because I'm conducting a revolution in my own life and I want my film to be an example of what I'm talking about. I'm trying now to make a major leap in my own development. I'm 63. I want to start a new career. I don't want to buy condominiums. I don't want to get involved with investments, battening down the hatches, preparing for the winter and all that shit. I want to become a promising young film maker.

And the other thing I want to do is break the rules, because my film is going to urge people whenever in doubt to break the rules. All the rules that society implies, all the role-playing. Men are supposed to be this, women that, children this, and old people that.

I live with a woman thirty years old. My friends, with a disgusting lewd kind of look, say "When are you going to start acting your age?" And all I can respond to them is to say, "You jealous bastards. What do you mean my age? What is my age? I have no age." In the deepest sense of the word I am younger in the last five years than when I was twenty-five because I am on my own—I run my own life.

In a world that takes power away from individuals I have exerted some control, some power over my life, and I know pretty well where I'm going to be when I'm eighty. I know because I'm going to *make it be*. That's what I'm trying to say in my film. I know what I want to be. I'm not going to search for my identity—find out who is Abe Osheroff. I'm going to *make* Abe Osheroff because what I'm going to be twenty years from now is whatever I am now plus whatever I do. And what I want to do is make a very successful film. What I want to do is at the age of seventy go back and teach in a university after everybody else is getting retired. And for me this is not growing old—to me this is resisting aging.

Robert Vas [Photo: National Film Archive]

*My Homeland*, by Robert Vas. The 1956 uprising in Hungary.

*My Homeland*. Popular control of the streets of Budapest.

Abe Osheroff,
director of
*Dreams and
Nightmares*.

Cinda Firestone's *Attica:* A prisoner expresses his rage.

Barbara Kopple's *Harlan County U.S.A.:* conflict
between miners and company reaches the lethal point.

Richard Cohen's *Hurry Tomorrow.*
Patient is tied down in institution bed.

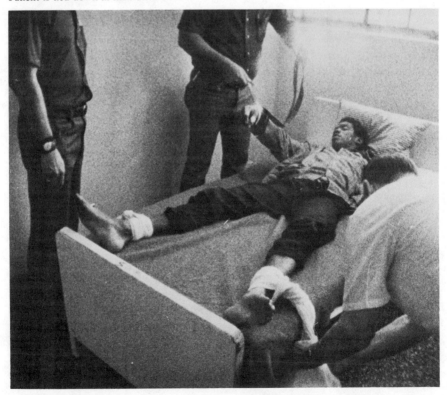

Sylvia Woods, Kate Hyndman, and Stella Nowicki in *Union Maids*,
by Julia Reichert, James Klein, and Miles Mogulescu.

Jill Godmilow's *Antonia:* Antonia Brico conducting.

*Grey Gardens*, a film by David Maysles, Albert Maysles,
Ellen Hovde, Muffie Meyer, and Susan Froemke.
Edie Beale and Mrs. Beale.

*Nana, Mom and Me*, by Amalie R. Rothschild.

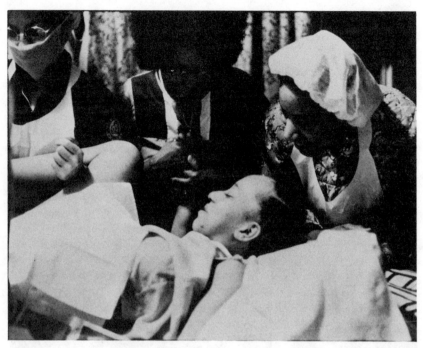

*The Chicago Maternity Centre Story*, by The Kartemquin Collective.

*Men's Lives*, by Will Roberts

*It Happens to Us*, by Amalie R. Rothschild.

*Radical Fire*

# 17

# **Attica**
## Cinda Firestone

*Attica is an outraged recollection of the September 1971 rebellion against their conditions by inmates of New York State's Attica prison. For four days the inmates controlled the prison yard and thirty-five hostages while they argued for improvements in the prison. In the end the rebellion was crushed by the state authorities and Governor Rockefeller in one of the ghastliest shootouts in American penal history. The final assault by state troopers to retake the prison left thirty-nine dead, including nine hostages, and over two hundred wounded.*

*The first part of the film explores conditions inside Attica, the grievances of the prisoners and the demands for reform. A lot of this is covered by some extraordinary footage shot by two black camerapersons, Roland Barnes and Jay Lamarch. The film then moves on to the refusal of the demands and the brutal retaking of the prison. Most of the bloody sequences of the assault were in fact shot by the state troopers themselves and are covered by voice-overs of the surviving inmates.*

*The second part of the film presents extracts from the videotaped McKay Commission where the duplicity of the government appears to be quite clear. However, in what looks like a peculiar replay of Kent State, no government officials are charged while sixty-one indictments are handed down against prisoners. To wind up this eighty-minute film we hear surviving inmates talking about how the rebellion changed their lives and their thoughts on society in general.*

*Attica is a painful, searing, bombshell piece of advocacy. It came out in 1973 and was twenty-five-year-old Cinda Firestone's first film, though she had worked for a while as assistant editor for Emile de Antonio. She had graduated a few years earlier from Sarah Lawrence College and after a brush with the Newsreel group had started writing for the Liberation News Service, a newsgathering collective for underground and campus newspapers.*

*From the interview it is clear that Attica is a film that evolved without an overriding guideline. It took two years to make, with Firestone's family providing much of the financial support. In the end the film that emerged is not just a tribute to Firestone's talent and skill, but a film that also gives proof of Firestone's determination, tenacity, and refusal to take no for an answer in many difficult situations.*

*At the time of the first major release, April 1974, most reviewers reacted favorably. Vincent Canby called* Attica *"a superior example of committed film making," and "exceptionally moving." Some critics, however, were deterred by Firestone's partisan qualities. Thus Jerry Oster in the New York* Daily News *damned the film for being "a far from objective historical account" and complained that Firestone's sympathies were clearly with the prisoners.*

*As Firestone relates, the film had difficulties in finding a place even on PBS. Once again one sees the problem of the networks, striving for "objectivity," "balance," "fairness," and "impartiality" being faced with an impassioned film that fits few of the accepted rules. The arguments on both sides are discussed throughout this book.*

*On a personal level I like the film but I am still left with a few nagging doubts at the back of my mind. I find there is a tendency for the prisoners to be presented as blameless saints, which I don't think they were. I find the chronology confusing, and I would like to have heard a little bit more from the other side when not under commission pressure. However the balance on the credit side is overpowering.* Attica *is a shattering film that will be remembered for a long time.*

Q. After *Attica* was first screened you were interviewed fairly widely, including national television. How did the media portray you?

A. As a sort of typical sixties radical young woman, who comes from a fairly wealthy background and is rebelling against all that. And to a certain degree that was true. But it was irrelevant and that approach bothered me because the things I was trying to deal with in *Attica* were on a much deeper level than just this sort of superficial protest. I felt that *Attica* represented some very basic things about American society and I was not just making it as a simple protest.

Q. The Attica tragedy happened in December 1971. How did the film start generating in your mind?

A. Well, it did not start as a film at all. I intended to do a pamphlet for the Attica Defense Committee. A friend of mine had already done tapes but wanted pictures for a pamphlet, so I went up to Attica mainly to do the photography. However, I was so impressed by some of the men and their eloquence that I thought, well, maybe I can make a little three-minute movie, just using their voices and pictures of them on the screen.

Q. Were these men you were talking to in ordinary custody or in special confinement?

A. At the time they were in solitary confinement. The authorities had picked out 100 or 150 men, decided these were the ringleaders, and kept all of them in isolation. So a lot of them had just been sitting there with nothing to do all day but think about what had happened. What they had to say was very moving. I think being confined so long intensified their feelings about what had happened in Attica. And it was after talking to them that I began to think a short movie was possible.

Q. What had been your film experience up to then?

A. A Super-8 movie course at college and then teaching film and photography. I had been a photographer and writer for a news service and then worked as assistant editor for Emile de Antonio. So I was planning on getting into movies, but I did not really plan on doing it that way. And then what happened is the movie just grew.

I started working on this little three-minute movie, and then someone called me up, and said "Did you know some of the men who were in Attica have gotten out on parole, and you can actually interview these people on film if you want." I had never done any interviews on film and never shot on 16mm, but just rounded up a couple of people that I knew could do that, and went off to interview these people.

Q. At that stage, was it just setting an interview against a picture, or were you already interested in the wider issues? Had these wider issues become defined in your mind yet or were you just inching along?

A. The wider issues were *always* defined in my mind. It had really shocked me, the way troopers had been sent in to Attica, and police. And they had killed not only inmates, but the hostages as well. I was overwhelmed by the massive amount of firepower and destruction. It just seemed a really brutal side of America that had to be exposed, which was why I really wanted to work on the pamphlet in the first place.

Q. What did you specifically see as these wider issues?

A. Incredible violence unleashed by structured society, establishment or whatever; then the covering up by the establishment press; the fact that the officials at the prison have been able to say, "Oh, well, we did not kill the hostages, they had their throats cut by the prisoners." And that was believed and reported by the newspapers, and no one, except the coroner, said "Wait a minute, this is a lie." This could have gone on the record as being the truth, and I found that very scary, that not only could an atrocity occur, but that it could be covered up so easily.

Q. What happened after those first interviews?

A. As I mentioned, I found out that some of the prisoners who had been involved in Attica had got out on parole, so I filmed interviews with them. Shortly after that our public TV station in New York showed the hearings of the McKay Commission. The film was fascinating, full of officials trying to explain their actions with the strangest kind of rationalizations for what they clearly knew was wrong. That came across very strongly in the McKay hearings, so I thought now I should get hold of that and cut it in with what I already have.

I called up NET, asked them for the footage, and was just given this incredible runaround. I called them every day for three months and finally they said, "All right, you can have the footage but it will cost you $1,000 a minute." I had absolutely no way of paying that money, but said, "Ok, fine, send it over. I'll get it duped and then send it back to you. Send me the bill later." So they did that. I had it transferred, and never heard another word from them.

Q. You had your hearings and you had your interviews . . .

A. I had the McKay Commission report. Then there was all this footage shot in the yard by Roland Barnes. He was in rather a peculiar position regarding the footage because he was on assignment for a TV station in Buffalo to do something else. He'd said, "I would really like to go to Attica and film," and they said, "No, no, it's not important," and asked him to go to a cornerstone laying, or whatever it was. Anyway he disobeyed the station and went off to film Attica.

The inmates then let Barnes inside the prison during the days of negotiation and stalemate. Before that Russell Oswald appeared to be saying one thing to the inmates, and something different to the outside television crews. The inmates were watching television, saw Oswald apparently lying and said, "There has got to be a camera crew in the yard, otherwise you will tell *us* one thing and the television and newspapers will hear something else, and we won't be able to do anything about it." So Oswald gave permission for Roland and his crew to go inside.

I wanted Roland to sell me some footage, and harassed him for about nine months. He kept saying he was going to give it to me but didn't. The color footage of what happened was actually among the last stuff I got for the film.

Q. Had a full-length film crystallized in your mind while you were talking to Barnes?

A. Well, I never really knew how long it was going to be. It just sort of grew. At one point *Attica* was four and a half hours and then I cut it down.

Q. While you were working on the movie, did you go back and do any more interviews?

A. Yes. I did a lot of interviews. I went to Attica three times. When the hearings against the inmates began I went back up and interviewed people about how they felt having murder charges brought against them.

Q. Did you think, at any stage, of interviewing Oswald or Rockefeller? Did you try?

A. Yes.

Q. What happened?

A. Just flat rejection. But that didn't worry me too much. I didn't think it necessary to be fair to both sides, and in any case Rockefeller and Oswald had had ample coverage to show their side. What I really wanted to do was to interview the new head of the prison, and what he kept saying to me was, "I cannot give you an interview now, but come back in four or five months and I will give you an interview then." He assumed I would not be around in five months. Then I would come back, and he would have another excuse.

That was really frustrating to me because all I really had was the prisoners' side and the McKay Commission hearings, and I very much wanted to interview the guards. But it seemed as if there was an unwritten agreement not to speak to the media after all the bad coverage they had had. One guard was willing to talk to me—the young white guard who is a hostage in the yard. I wanted to get his view as a hostage. He was all set to talk to me, and then very peculiar things happened. He and his wife would get very upset when I called, and finally he just said he could not do it. I really got the feeling that he was under pressure by his friends or fellow guards not to talk to me.

Q. At a certain stage it must have been clear to the prison authorities or to Rockefeller that you were doing a full-length film on Attica. Did anyone say anything to you, or try to interfere with what you were doing?

A. No, I had no harassment at all. But I got very paranoiac towards the end of the movie, because when you have been working on a film you know how fragile it is. I thought all someone had to do was just come in here and destroy my tapes, ruin my track or wreck my negative, and I have had it. But no, I wasn't really harassed.

Q. What interests me, as a film maker myself, is the length of the process where over a year or two you're adding bits and putting it together. At what stage did you sit down and try to define the basic structure of the film? Did you ever do that, or was it evolving the whole time?

A. Totally evolving the whole time. I just do not plan. The way I make documentaries, I never really know what I am going to get, so what I get determines what else I do. *Attica* was predictable to a certain extent. I knew to a large degree what people were going to say, but then people would say things just a little differently, or I would look at them and the footage again and I would think, well this is really more important than that. So while I had my ideas of what happened, my attitudes were changing as I was working on the film and talking to people.

Q. What attitudes? To the film—to the situation?

A. Both really. I don't really research first, and then film. It is more that I do both at the same time.

Q. As you look at the film now it has a pretty clear structure. You say these are the conditions, and you start off with a comment of the guards to the effect that they are just pigs, not human, or something like that. You set the conditions, then you come up with the riots commencing, then the sheriffs and the police and the guards come in. You set up for the confrontation and for the hearings. There is a very clear chronological line.

A. Well, *Attica* is really an editor's movie. I mean it was edited more than anything else. I learned about editing from Mary Lampson. She's edited almost all of Emile de Antonio's movies and she just finished editing *Harlan County*. The way Mary edits is to put things together so that they work. That "does it work" idea guides me more than rigid structure. Often I would have a very good idea of how to structure *Attica*, would put it together, and it would just be terrible, for no logical reason that I could think of. It just wouldn't look or feel right. Then I'd alter it and gradually some emotion would come through.

Q. Can you think of a conceptual idea that did not work on the editing table, and that you had to change?

A. I wanted to begin with the conditions leading up to the riot, what is now the third reel, then show the riot and the aftermath. I wanted to keep it very simple, but that structure was very static, very boring. It just had nothing. There are parts at the beginning of the third reel I am still not happy about. It doesn't move well. It was not the way I had in my head to do it, but it was the best way I could work it so as not to fall asleep looking at it.

Q. Who else helped you on the film?

A. Oh, a lot of people. I only had one full-time person that I paid. That was a guy who had just graduated from high school called Tucker, who became indispensable to me. In the beginning we were working really crazy hours, because we were using the editing room of a friend of mine who worked at a television station. She would let us in secretly every night after everyone left, about six or seven, and we would work all night. At five in the morning we would put everything away or hide it behind editing tables.

Q. Emile de Antonio is listed in your credits with "special thanks." How did he help?

A. He was great. I had a lot of doubts about making the film. I am one of these people who, if I really want to do something, just plow right ahead and do it, no matter if everyone in the world says it is wrong, but I get upset when everyone in the world tells me I am wrong. So here I was. I had never made a movie before, I did not know very much about anything I was doing. I was learning as I was going along. I had a seventeen-year-old assistant who had never worked in movies, and there were a lot of things in the movie that seemed, to me, a little strange, like all those stills. We thought maybe this is going to drive people crazy, just seeing a collection of stills—maybe this movie does not make any sense, because it does seem to jump around. And I had a lot of sorts of producer types, middle-aged men who would be like father of a friend, or something, who would come in and say, "This is a great idea. This could be a good movie, but obviously you do not know what you are doing. If you would just sell out to me, I will show you how to edit it so that it will be terribly successful."

One producer came to me and said, "This will be really great if you will just let me get Paul Newman to do the narration." I said, "I really do not want any narration." And he said, "Then nobody will understand this movie. It will never sell." I heard that a lot, and de Antonio, "De" as we call him, whom I respected a lot, would come and look at these horrendous rough cuts, and just tell me that he really thought they were good, and he could see the potential. He would not tell me how to edit it. He would say, "I can see this is going to be terrific, keep going." And that, coming from someone who I knew was a really good movie maker, was very important, because I had a lot of doubts. He also did things like call up the labs and say, "My friend Cinda Firestone is coming over. She's great and you've got to give her total credit. Don't worry, she is very responsible."

Q. Where was the money coming from for the film?

A. I have a trust fund, but it is a very tight trust fund, so I was going through a battle with my family to release money to make the movie. In the beginning the money was fairly tight, but by the end of the movie I had much more.

Q. Were your family supportive in this?

A. Well, my family consist of my brothers and sisters whom I get along with, and my mother who is very conservative and has always disapproved of my radical activities. I was in SDS in school and was in jail twice, once in the Columbia protest, once as a reporter for the Liberation News Service. My mother did not approve of the Liberation News Service either, and as she is my trustee it was sort of a sticky situation. However, a year ago my mother finally told me that she liked the movie, but that was after she saw me with Mike Douglas on TV. She read the reviews and I guess she decided that after all it was not so terrible, but in the beginning, I think she said to herself, "Oh God, another one of Cinda's radical projects."

Q. It is now over three years since the film came out. When you look back on it now, are there things you would like to change?

A. Sure, there are things that bothered me then, that bother me a great deal more now. There is a part of the film that I rushed, with the idiotic idea that I would finish it in time for the Moscow Film Festival.

Q. What part is that?

A. The part where they are talking about the indictments of the inmates in the riot. I look at it, and the rhythm does not seem right. The workmanship seems to be very bad. That bothers me a lot because I know I could have done it better, and I skimped on it.

There is also a part where the roll title goes down with people's names which I did myself on a sheet of typing paper. To do it right I would have to have paid a lab $1,000 and that just seemed like such a huge amount of money. But now I feel I could have gotten that money together somehow. Both of these things bother me, because I know I could have done them differently. There are parts of the movie that I don't like, but that I still do not know how to remedy, like talking about conditions in the prison. That part seems dull to me, but I still don't know how to remedy it.

Q. There are a number of very moving scenes in the film where you have the inmates talking about brotherhood and understanding. In fact the film ends with more or less that kind of message. Now there is no mention in the film of what the inmates were in for.

I myself am not an American. Before 1970 I knew little of Attica and its inmates. I would assume, however, that most of the inmates were in prison for committing fairly violent crimes, which may be their fault, which may be the fault of society. Has anyone commented on your failure to mention the criminal background of the prisoners, because any person looking at your film and not knowing Attica is really being told (and I am not saying that this is right or wrong) "You

300

are fine men, suddenly inside and being totally brutalized." Do you think mention of their crimes might have dampened that nobility and sympathy?

A. Well, I do not think that anyone starts off with that feeling, because everyone knows what people go to prison for. You know there are some people railroaded to prison (probably more than people think) but nevertheless most people in prison are there because they did something pretty terrible. There were people in the film who had done relatively minor things, but a good majority of the people are in for things like robbery, and everybody knows that.

What I was trying to do in the movie was to make people forget that in a way. I wanted to say that whatever these people have done, they are human beings and do not deserve to get shotguns fired at them. That was one of the things that really struck me. I felt if people can only see these people as *people*, real people, not just 42 people who got killed. If you could see them in flesh and blood, people would have a different attitude.

The one thing I feel the movie does not do adequately is show the position of the guards, and we've talked about that. I have seen how racism works, and I have seen how prejudice works, and I know how you can rationalize to yourself about killing people, "Oh, it is just one of these black criminals, they are brutal, they don't really deserve to live." But I never quite understood how the people who had gone inside shooting had rationalized killing the *hostages* who were after all guards like themselves. I really wanted to interview a guard who had participated in the raid, and ask how he felt about killing his fellow guards. They killed so many of them.

Q. When the film was finished, what did you do with it?

A. I did not have any real distribution for about nine months. I gave the Attica Defense Committee about eleven copies, and they showed it to raise money for the defense fund. I thought I should really open the film in movie theaters, and got a lot of offers from various distributors, but no one offered me an opening in a movie theater. In the end I opened it myself.

Q. Did the networks view it?

A. Yes, I sent it to all of them. They just sent it back and said thank you. It was almost a formality, because I knew they would never put it on and they knew they would never put it on, but I felt I had to try.

Q. Thank you, but it is not commercial!

A. Well, it wasn't only that. PBS was going to show it, and I only found out a while ago what happened. They were going to put *Attica* on to start off a series of documentary films, but had to show it to the

301

sponsor. I cannot remember who the sponsors were, but they were horrified. They felt it was too radical, too controversial. So they not only dropped *Attica* but also the whole series. So even on PBS I could not get it on. But you know I am not unhappy with the distribution. It played in about four small theaters in New York, Boston, San Francisco, and it played a lot of colleges.

Q. When you are playing in the colleges, you are already playing to the converted in many ways. Do you see any way of breaking that system—of getting out to the middle-American?

A. The only way that *Attica* has really done that at all is by being rented by church groups and high schools. But that is really about all.

Q. What are you working on now?

A. I have just finished three movies about old people, one about old people in Florida, one about retirement communities, and one about old people in West Virginia. These are films about people's feelings more than facts. They got less and less factual as I went along. The first was more factual in the story, the second was less so, and the third, West Virginia, was much more sort of slow and rambling.

Q. These films, *Attica* and the ones on age, are outside you. Do you see yourself making any films inside, about the way you are, or your concerns? I mention that because many of the people I have been speaking to recently are using film to define themselves, as a woman, as a black, or as a Jew or something like that. Do you see yourself doing that, or is that outside your concern?

A. Well, I have begun working on a script for a fiction movie, which is not totally about me, but it is about a radical woman and the problems she has, not all that similar to my life, but similar enough that I can identify very strongly with her. The movie I plan to make after these movies are finished is going to be, if all goes well, on Louise Nevelson. She is a woman sculptor, and she is seventy-six. There is a lot of the way she is, wanting to do something very much and being determined to do it, and living her life the way she wants to live it, that I identify with. So perhaps I *am* moving in that direction.

# 18

# *Harlan County, USA*
## *Barbara Kopple and Hart Perry*

Harlan County *was made between 1972 and 1976 with money raised from foundations, various church groups and individual donors. It was Barbara Kopple's first major film as a director and began as the documentation of the fight against the old guard inside the United Mine Workers Union. Later, when the miners in Brookside, Harlan County, went on strike in July 1973 seeking recognition of the UMW as their union, the film began to change direction. At that point Kopple went down to Brookside and lived with the miners for the 13 months of the strike.*

Harlan County *tells the story of a Kentucky community with a legendary history of strife and warfare against the bosses. This is a community in which the question asked by the song* Which Side Are You On, Boys? *represents the key question of life.*

*The film celebrates the collective action of the miners, from whose point of view the issues are seen. Barbara Kopple makes no pretense of neutrality. The miners and their wives are the heroes and the bosses and the Duke Power Company are the villains.*

*The action is beautifully photographed by Hart Perry who documents the quiet, intimate moments of the community as well as the violence and the clashes. The direction is low-key and it is obvious that Barbara Kopple managed to establish a deep rapport with the miners and their wives. So, while the political events unfold, we are taken into the homes and lives of the miners till we know what it is to eat, feel, and suffer with them.*

*The dangers of such a film are many. It is easy to overdo simple aesthetic shots, to over-emotionalize issues, and to set up symbolic heroic types. Kopple and Perry avoid those pitfalls for the most part. And if the editing is a bit jumbled and some of the issues unclear this doesn't matter much in the overall view. What is important is that real people are presented to us in a very straight way, from the gun-toting chief of the strike breakers to the old man dying of black-lung disease. And when a miner's wife says, "If I get shot they still can't shoot the union out of me," she embodies a whole side of American life that seldom appears on any screen.*

*The film shows key issues, but leaves you with much more: a sense of admiration for the miners, and for a community whose members can live their lives with dignity in spite of tremendous suffering.*

*For thirty-year-old Barbara Kopple the film represents four years of unrelenting dedication. Previously she had worked as editor, producer, and soundperson on various films. She was also very involved in the making of* Hearts and Minds, Winter Soldier, *and* Richard the Third.

*When we met it was for a brief interlude in between her rushing around the country and talking on behalf of the miners and other groups. Somewhere on the horizon, so she said, there was the vision of a dramatic feature about the struggle of Southern textile workers to unionize the J. P. Stevens mills.*

*The occasion for seeing Barbara Kopple also gave me the chance to have a word with Hart Perry. Between Perry and Kopple exists an obvious rapport and understanding which would account for much of the fine quality of the film. Most of Perry's experience has been in making films for TV. He was one of the camerapeople on* Woodstock, *staff cameraperson for "The 51st State" and also shot* Carole King. *He has won five Emmies for photography, including one for a segment of "The Great American Dream Machine." His own films as director include* Veterans, Convention, *and* Stephen Sondheim.

Q. You spent a couple of years involved with the film—which just grew. How did you come to the subject in the beginning? I assume it must have started off as a much shorter, more specific project.

K. In the beginning the idea was just to film the Miners for Democracy movement. After Yablonski was murdered there was a whole siege within the miners' movement. They were sick and tired of dictatorship and wanted new leadership. A leadership which they said would really represent them. They wanted the right to ratify their own contracts. Things like that. And that was how the film began. We wanted to record that moment, that turmoil. I thought it would be incredible to hear three men, one of whom had worked 26 years in the mines and was disabled with black lung, running up against Tony Boyle. Plus there had never been a real election in the United Mine Workers Union.

Q. Where did you get the money for the film?

K. Funding was difficult. We were given a loan of $9,000 at the beginning with the promise that the person would put up the money for the entire film. When I got back after the first shoot I made the mistake of showing rushes. And then this fine gentleman decided that a twenty-six-year-old woman couldn't possibly make a major political film and decided not to fund it. So here I was, after traveling for a year in the coal fields, meeting people who were dying with black lung and living off oxygen; meeting widows of miners killed in the coal mines; listening to old timers talk about the thirties and bursting into original song, and I just wanted to continue. I really felt very strongly about what I was seeing and what I was feeling.

At that point I started learning about foundations. I learned you had to be non-profit tax-exempt. You had to give these incredible proposals that answered everything from where you were going to distribute it, to exactly what you were going to shoot. They had boards of directors with the most incredible minds you could ever want to meet. Labor historians, economists, whatever. And I thought, "If that's what they want, better try to do that." So I did it. I reckon I must have applied to hundreds of foundations. I got rejected by a great many of them but would do all sorts of things to keep the process going.

For example, I'd go into banks and say, "Hey, you want to invest in a film on coal mining?" They would think I was crazy. Then I'd say, "OK. Well, can I use your Xerox machine? Can I use your stamp machine?" And I'd sit there and I'd xerox 117 proposals and then stamp them all. Collate them all over the bank's floor. This continued for the entire four years of making the film. At the end of the film I was $60,000 in debt.

p. Barbara developed one technique which I've borrowed and found very useful. Barbara would get a load of rejections and they would pile up, but she would call them up and ask why she was rejected. Then she would find other foundations to apply to but would first correlate and use her rejection information.

k. I would also apply year after year to the same foundation. So some of them, after three years, would finally give me a grant. As to the ones that did reject me, I'd call them up, ask them why. Then I'd invite them over to see footage and then ask them for a list of other people who they thought might help. So I started becoming somewhat of an expert on foundations.

q. What were some of the reasons for rejection?

k. I got one letter which said they only sponsor birds and trees because they don't talk back. Most of them went, "You don't fit our guidelines. We only support gun control," and whatever. The letters are marvelous to look at. I can laugh at them now but I used to get very upset.

q. What were your impressions and what were the miners' reactions to you when you first arrived in Harlan County?

k. When I first came to Harlan County I was lucky, because a lot of the people who were organizers had fought for the Miners for Democracy movement. Since I had just been doing that for a whole year

305

I knew people. I remember the first morning that I got to Harlan County. We left Tennessee very early and got to Harlan about 4:30 in the morning and I went and saw one of the organizers and asked him, "What's happened?" He said, "Go down the road. Go over the bridge and you'll see the people on strike. The state troopers are there as well." So we did.

We drove across the bridge and saw the women with switches and state troopers with clubs. And I figured I can't just get out of this car and say, "Hi, I'm a film maker from New York. I've come to film your story." And while I was thinking the other people in the car were saying, "Why don't you get it together," and things like that. Then I went back across the bridge and said to one of the organizers, "Introduce us." So he introduced us, but the women didn't trust us at first. They gave us phony names—they said they were Martha Washington and Florence Nightingale. It took a week of us just being there on the picket line all the time to get some kind of acceptance.

We got in a big car accident about the third day we were there. The car was all battered and our equipment all broken but we came to the picket line anyway. And they thought we were out of our minds and then they really opened up to us. We lived with the miners in their homes. They fed us. I used to bring films down to show them like *Salt of the Earth* and *The Inheritance*. We did everything from butchering hogs with them to starting a newspaper called *The Harlan Labor News*. It was a matter of really engaging in that life.

I lived there for 13 months and after a while people didn't recognize us without our equipment. I remember Lois, the heavy-set one who pulls the gun out of her dress in the film, saying to me, "OK, Barbara, you can be on the picket line." And I'd say "Shush. We're filming you. You're not supposed to say that." And she'd say, "I know. But I have to write your name down. You've just got to be there." They just forgot. I remember the morning she said that because it was really scary. All the miners had guns. We knew there were going to be a lot of problems and we had just been machine-gunned the day before. So everybody was really nervous, including me.

Q. Were you ever in fear for your lives?

K. Yes. The scabs and gun thugs told us that if we were ever caught alone we would be killed and during the last couple of weeks of the strike the violence started to intensify and we carried weapons. But only at night because we didn't want to be caught with them during the day because that would be an excuse to kill us. I could just see it. "New York film crew found dead. Woman holding .45 revolver."

Something like that. One night they were shooting at the homes of the miners down below. I was in the house and had to go to the bathroom, but as they had no indoor plumbing we always went outside on the "buddy system." So Hart was nice enough to accompany me. Hart had an M-1. I had a .357 Magnum. And this was just to go to the bathroom.

P. They were shooting at the house down below.

K. So I was sitting there listening, and hearing all the gunshots, and we are at a spot that seems pretty safe. Then we hear a rustling in the bushes and both of us pull out our weapons and a dog runs out. That's how scary it was. It was about 4:30 to 5:00 in the morning and there were mostly women and the film crew on the picket line. Then from out of nowhere came shots and tracer bullets. We didn't know where they were coming from. Whether they were there to kill us. Whether they were aiming at waist level or over our heads. We didn't know what was happening.

Then the strike breakers pulled up and the head strike breaker started pointing his gun—all he had to do was pull his little finger and one of us wouldn't be here any more. It was pointed directly at us, and at Hart in particular. They went over the bridge and then they came back. I felt them coming and knew they were coming for the film crew first. Hart was in front and the person doing the lights was further away. I was doing sound and figured, stupidly, "Well, they are not going to hurt a woman as much as a man." They walked up in front of Hart and they got me, got Hart, got Ann. Took each one of us individually and beat us up. I was pretty lucky because I was largely covered by the tape recorder and I had a long aluminum fish pole with the mike on the end of it and just started beating them back.

P. In a John Birch paper one of the gun thugs described this incident. He said he was beaten by a woman sound recordist who was better armed. It was a very confusing scene. It was certainly strange and terrifying. You're not getting pistol-whipped every day. But we continued filming. The camera was battered but it still worked. It's probably one of the most dramatic scenes in the film but is underexposed because it all happened at 4:30 in the morning.

The head gun thug stuck his pistol in a miner's stomach. I heard a gun fall. The miner had some pistols in his back pocket. One fell but he stuck the other in the gun thug's stomach. Then another strike breaker came up and pointed his pistol at the miner's head. I was around ten feet away at the time and I recorded it. I guess that's just one of the realities of documentary film making. It was a strange situation. Filming it I wasn't sure whether I should take the camera and smash the guy over the head with it or record it. It was a very confusing disturbing experience.

Q. In the film you tell one of the thug drivers that you had press credentials. Did you have them? That was obviously to make him back off.

K. Yes. We had loads. But we did that because we figured maybe they wouldn't kill us if they figured it would be bad publicity. But really we were just three people without a penny to our names or any support whatsoever, so we tried to get something that would make us seem a little more credible.

Q. Did the police ever bother you?

K. No. The first day I came into Harlan County I was introduced to the head of the state police and had some pretty interesting interviews with him. He felt that murder in Harlan County wasn't a crime. It was a crime of passion. The real criminals were the burglars and the robbers.

Q. How did the sheer length of time you spent on the film affect the quality of what you shot? Such a huge time span must in many ways have been very beneficial to you as well as frustrating.

P. The time period for the filming was extremely important. We could get particular kinds of shots. We could see things develop over time. It gave us the chance to take care over a particular kind of lighting. It gave us a chance to discover what we were doing. It gave us a chance to establish a real relationship with the people. Time was never at a premium. There was no producer, no budget. And all that meant a certain amount of freedom.

Q. You must have gone into that situation with very human preconceptions of how miners live, work, act, and think. Preconceptions from the media and from your education—how unions work, how management works. What preconceptions had to be readjusted?

K. As I went through the coal fields I just started learning things from a very different perspective. In a situation that I don't know much about, I tend to just flow with whatever happens and not be shocked by anything and just go through it. I'll go with whatever anybody wants to lay on me, whether that be good or bad, just to see what it's like. We did some pretty crazy things when we were there and I guess all the things that I thought about academically as far as what trade unions were about were totally different from what I saw and felt and experienced. I got much more politicized. I started to learn who was the enemy. How you fight the enemy. I learned a lot of different things I never knew before.

Q. The crew appears in the film and asks questions and one feels the crew is part of everything and very concerned. Did you have mixed feelings about keeping the crew in?

K. I tried to get the feeling of the crew out of the film as much as possible, because sometimes people find it easier to identify with the film makers than get to grips with the real issues of what's happening. And it was very important to me that people really dealt with the struggle and what was going on. So I really tried to minimize the sense of the crew as much as possible.

P. Stylistically we tried to let the people develop as characters. It wasn't the documentary situation where there is a formal interview. We watched behavior, nuances of behavior, and tried to be aware of scenes as they developed.

Q. Where did the scabs and the strike breakers come from?

K. Some of them were local people. Some of them were imported from the local prison. The company got them out and told them they were going to be rehabilitated. There were people who were convicted murderers. Some of the strike breakers actually lived next door to the coal miners and I was always wondering why that was. Then one of the miners told me that in the thirties when they had all these struggles, if your grandfather was a union man then you were a union family. If your grandfather was a scab then you were a scab family.

Q. How did you get permission to film at the jail, at the stockholders' meeting and in the courtroom?

K. In the courtroom? Well, I used to use a radio mike whenever I thought I couldn't be somewhere where I wanted to be, and I wanted to tape it and know what was happening. So I put the wireless mike on a defendant in the courtroom. There was a terrific amount of commotion and confusion in the courtroom. Everyone was getting up and saying different things to the judge. Hart saw all this confusion, opened up the back door to the courtroom (not being inside), filmed and pushed the film two stops. In other words he filmed from the outside.

In the jail we just walked right in. We followed the people who were going to jail, smiled nicely at the jailer and just walked right through and did it. At the stockholders' meeting they would only let one of us in. Because I didn't think they would let either Hart or myself in I had already miked a miner. So we looked sorry and said, "Oh, all right, we'll just have the camera go in." So I stayed outside, Hart went inside, and we got the sound from the miner.

P. We were worried in the courtroom shooting because the mike was on one of the defendants and we were afraid he was going to get sentenced and we would never see the mike again.

309

Q. Can you tell us a little about the editing?

K. The editing process was one of the most supportive times of the whole film. There were five or six people who worked on the editing. Nancy Baker was prime editor and she really worked incredibly hard and was committed to the entire thing.

We screened maybe ten and a half hours of rough-cut material and then we'd sit around a table and discuss it. And you couldn't say, "Well, this doesn't work because it's boring," or "It has no flow, no rhythm." You couldn't say that. What happened is people had to really figure out politically what was being said. If they had criticisms they would say so. They would try to make connections and also offer alternative ways of editing. Some of the people had never worked on film before and wanted to learn it and were really politically committed.

The film was really a monster to put together because there was so much stuff going into it. There was stock footage, black lung footage, mine safety, working in a coal mine, national safety, national coal contract, production. *Plus* the whole story of Harlan. Plus the music. Putting all that in so that it worked and had shape was a really monstrous job. We got almost everything in that was shot except strip-mining. That was a whole other bag of worms and there wasn't a place to fit it in.

P. When we were shooting the film we had in mind a general structure. We were telling the story of Harlan and developing characters. We then dealt with other issues as a kind of parallel action.

K. That makes it sound too easy. We had a rough line but we didn't know whether history would all come first and then the story of Harlan or vice versa. All that was worked out in the editing. And of course things you shot and thought would really work would totally fall apart in the editing.

Q. You've discussed the cooperation in editing. How cooperatively did you work in direction?

K. I started the film in 1972 and throughout the film a lot of different people worked on it because it was really rough to get a continuous group of people to come away for a long time. My own role was in raising the money, figuring out who to shoot and where to shoot, how to shoot and what was going on. I went up to the leadership to find out what was happening to the organizers. Loads of people helped but I was the only one who was through it from day one to the end. Other people would come in and devote tremendous energy and support and really work hard to make the film what it is.

P. Barbara had the vision of what the overall project was, which was the important thing to everyone who worked on it.

310

Q. And you managed to contribute that vision successfully to all the different people you worked with?

K. That wasn't really necessary. The people around me were people I'd known for many years and already worked with. Hart and I have worked on a lot of things together, and this is true throughout the crew. The person had to be very right to come down and work through that situation. It was also very important that the people working on the film were politically committed and knew how to react in the face of danger. There was no one who went down there whom I hadn't known and worked with for a very long time.

Q. So the direction was team work rather than a specific person.

P. Yes, as far as I can understand it.

Q. You said when you first got there the strike was on and the state troopers were out. Now you open the film with these lovely shots, incredible shots, of the miners jumping on the conveyor belt, whizzing down the hillside and then entering the mines. And then you have other shots inside the mines. When did you get those? And how did you get permission from the company when you had just been out there with the strikers?

K. That scene was shot in a different mine in Harlan County. It wasn't the Eastover Mining Co. What we are trying to show there is low coal. In that particular mine Hart met the mine foreman while he was in a store and got into conversation. We told him we wanted to film and got to meet the man who owned the mine who was rather young and egotistical. We talked him into letting us film in that mine so that he could show his grandchildren how happy the miners were, and how good the conditions were and what he did. That kind of thing.

The last coal mine that you see in the film is Consolidated Coal. I went through the usual thing of writing them a letter and asking permission and of course I was turned down. That was the time the national coal contract was just about to begin and the local union in that area were really good friends of mine. I'd known them since 1972 and they put on pressure. They said, you know, it will make it a lot easier during the strike if you let these students go down the mine, they want to do a little filming. They're from New York, and there's no big industry in New York. That kind of thing. So we went down and filmed.

Now I'd spoken to a guy on the phone and I guess my voice is really recognizable because Phil did that part of the film, and he slipped a couple of times because we made up different names. When we were talking with this mine official he forgot to call me Suzy and called me Barbara instead. And at the end of the day this guy said, "You're not that Barbara Kopple who's doing the film on the coal mines, are you?"

311

Then he got very excited and they got some big thugs to come out and try and get the film from us. So I gave them about ten rolls of unexposed stock and then we just beat it.

Q. What did the miners get in that contract? What did they achieve after a thirty-month strike?

K. Wages were increased to $57 a day. Vacations went from five days to ten days. Pensions were increased to $250 a month instead of $150 a month. They lost the right to strike but supposedly they were getting a grievance procedure.

Q. Did you ever consider putting that information in the film?

K. Well, I thought the miners in the line were talking a bit about it. They were talking about ten days being enough to get all the coal dust out of your lungs. And they were complaining about the steel workers getting thirteen weeks. So I thought people would get the general gist of what the contractual thing was.

Q. When you made the film did you consider at all the fact that many people watching it would have no knowledge, no experience, no sense of history at all of these incidents and these patterns? That for many of them Harlan County and all the mining problems were happening on another planet? Did you consider that kind of audience when you made the film, and did it affect at all the way you shaped it?

K. This may sound terrible but I never really thought about it. When I was filming in Harlan I didn't even really care if a film never came out of it. I think I was maybe more engaged in the struggle and using the film as a vehicle to get through it. It was something that I was just doing. I was working and I wasn't afraid when things started to happen because sometimes you're like a dumb animal behind a camera or a tape recorder. You're there but you're not totally engaged in it, and you're kept occupied by the work you're doing.

I think for me the struggle was to keep going from day to day, to stay alive, to keep raising the money—and that was it. I just didn't think the film would ever be shown anywhere. I wasn't thinking of all those wider things. I thought, "OK. Maybe my friends will see it. Maybe the Whitney Museum will show it. Maybe the trade unionists will see it and the people in Harlan." I never expected it to go much further than that and am still amazed by its reception.

Q. What sort of ratios were you shooting at?

K. We shot fifty hours of film over a three-year period. We probably overcovered. We could make complete films on black lung, mine safety, and so on. But in the end it's not bad.

Q. Are you happy with your parallel film, which is really about the miners' political situation? Some people have said it's difficult to follow all the political threads if you haven't got a knowledge of mining politics.

K. No, I don't think that's right. I think the politics are well covered and well explained in the film. However, what the end of the film is trying to say is you can't trust leadership, no matter who it is. You can't trust the government. You can't trust the coal operators. What happens is you have to keep fighting and have something really solid from below to keep moving you forward. Just because you win one struggle doesn't mean you can sit back and relax. You have to keep going on to the next struggle. For me the film was trying to be more what it was like from below. It was about the rank and file rather than the leadership.

Q. Are you getting any distribution by the unions?

K. Many of the trade unions are using the film at benefit showings. And it's showing at conventions. It's showing at local unions for fund-raising. It's being used a lot in the mine fields. The miners have their own prints.

Q. How has it been received by top union officials?

K. The union bureaucrats don't like it because it's not too favorable about leadership. So they are not using it. The rank and file are the ones that are requesting it and using it.

Q. I believe you finally got a commercial distributor. What is the basis of your agreement with the distributor? Is there any conflict between your social and political objectives for the film, and the distributing company's interest in a high commercial return?

K. I went through a long process of trying to decide whether to distribute it myself or to have someone else distribute it. Through the help of a lot of friends we were able to raise about $170,000 to do self-distribution. However, after a really hard painful struggle we decided against it because there wasn't anything to follow. I was really scared I would have to pay this money back with five and a half per cent interest, and if after a year or two years the film didn't do well, I might be $200,000 in debt. It would also make me into a business person which I'm not very good at and don't want to be.

Theaters tend to rip off independents because you don't have any more product to follow, and when you go to collect money they just say, "Sue us." So for many many reasons I decided against doing self-distribution for this film. However, instead of making a financial contract with the distributor I made a political contract with him. This enables me to have ten political benefits a year of my choice where he can't charge any money. Groups in Appalachia get the film for nothing and community groups (when it goes into nontheatrical distribution) get it for fifty per cent if they really can't afford the rental. People with union cards get a dollar or a dollar fifty off the ticket in a theater when they show their union card. All these kinds of things I was able to work out.

Q. What did you mean by a "political contract"? What does this mean financially?

K. It means I didn't struggle with the distributor as to how much money he is going to put in to distribute it, where it would be shown, that kind of thing. I just figured that he's a capitalist and is just going to do as much as he can to make a buck off the film. So instead of arguing I said, "Whatever you want to do go ahead. I don't care if you spend $20,000 to open the film or $200,000. I'm not dealing with that. These are the things I want." And then I outlined the benefit showings and the rest I told you about.

As to actual money: he gets 70 percent of everything that the film makes for fifteen years theatrically and nontheatrically. He also gets to recoup on advertising, prints, and those millions of costs that they invent. Then Cabin Creek Center gets 30 percent and we haven't even seen a penny yet.

Q. What do you know of the situation and the good and bad moments after you'd finished filming?

K. Well, the Ku Klux Klan went to Harlan County after the strike was over and the people who were the scabs during the strike then became members of the Klan. The coal operators were members of the Klan. Many of the state troopers were members of the Klan. So that fight's still happening. I can tell you many stories of how many of the people in the film became real leaders and what the Klan has tried to do to them.

The woman who sat up in the courtroom and said, "Laws aren't made for the working people in this country" became a real leader and was working with one of the communities down there who were getting evicted from their homes. Eventually she was put in jail for allegedly kidnapping the wife of a Klansman. During the time she was in jail, the Klan had paramilitary rallies and the principal of the local high school had the girls in the home economics class making gowns and hoods for the Klan.

The stories go on and on. A week after the film was finished I took it to Harlan County to show it to the people there and the Klan hung a goat right by the place where I was going to show it with the initials KKK in its belly. So the screening had to be an armed screening. Miners had to stand around with shotguns to make sure nothing happened. Before that they had called me up to tell me what was happening so I brought a film down called *The Ku Klux Klan: The Invisible Empire* that was made in 1965. I also brought down Leo Hurwitz's *Native Land*, and we showed these from house to house all over Harlan County.

We were showing it in Georgetown and two state troopers drove up and said, "What are those films?" and I said, "Educational, sir." And they said they wanted them. Then the whole black community just moved around us and the films and took us and the films inside. We were going to have a revival meeting the next day and the Klan told the guy who ran the revival center that if the meeting took place the place would be fire-bombed and burnt to the ground. So we told the people not to come. And a couple of black Cadillacs pulled up with high-powered rifles and just stayed parked outside the whole time. So the fight still goes on.

Q. What were your personal feelings, being among the miners?

K. For me, and probably for everyone who worked on the film, it was a great honor to be down there. These people really let us become part of the struggle and I learned so much from it. I learned that in making a film you don't do it by yourself. It takes a lot of committed people giving their time and energy and support all the time. In the strike, all the people were there every single day on the pickets although their lives were in danger. These people aren't victims. They are really courageous people who aren't afraid to fight back at a time in this country when sometimes people are afraid.

When I've been traveling around the country with the film, its effect has been to really open up audiences. They start to deal with issues in their own lives. For example, one woman in Dallas, Texas, stood up and said, "I've been a Republican all my life. I hated unions, but after seeing this I have to reassess where I am." Another woman in San Francisco stood up and told the story of how she fought against the American Nazi Party. The film is encouraging people to really feel, and deal with things.

Q. Was there a great demand for the film after the award in Hollywood?

K. No. It was the New York Film Festival more than anything else that really made people realize the film existed. The three days of that festival were the three greatest days of my life. Here it was. Working four years and having the festival accept it. And thinking, OK, there's going to be an audience of 1100 people. Plus the miners and their wives.

But I was also really scared. I remember picking up the film and thinking I spent four years of my life on this. I remember bringing it

315

over to Lincoln Center and being really scared. What if the miners thought I had exploited them? Or this and that wasn't true. They were going to speak on the panel. And what if everybody hated it? I was going through all these different things, but people really said good things about it and responded very warmly.

q. Do you still find it dangerous to travel around Harlan?

к. Yes. Because the Klan is in Harlan County. However I think one of the results of the film is that it provided in a strange way some protection for the people in Harlan County. It is going to be much easier now, when things happen there, to have a massive campaign of getting press in there doing a lot of publicity. We did big fund-raising things when the big floods came. We did a lot of stuff for Bessie Lou when she was thrown into jail. Telegrams came from all over the country. The jailer had never seen anything like this before. I think the film has possibly helped to serve a lot of those people's lives.

NOTE: This chapter was recorded at an open discussion of the film at the Flaherty International Film Seminar, August, 1977. Some of the questions are mine, but some are from other persons who are, unfortunately, unidentifiable.—A. R.

# 19

# Union Maids
## Julia Reichert and James Klein

Union Maids *is a modest film about trade unions in the twenties and thir-ties, and about three extraordinary women—Kate Hyndman, Stella Nowicki, and Sylvia Woods. In three separate interviews intercut with each other the women comment and reflect on their lives as union organizers and women work-ers. The film deals with the evolution of the trade unions but the basic message is one of the worth of cooperative social action. The second message is the strength and possibility of women's action.*

*The film looks deceptively simple. There are straight interviews, rousing union songs, and stills and newsreel dupes of the thirties. But the whole piece of oral history is beautifully edited and was rightfully nominated for an Oscar in 1978.*

*It's a political film but not a didactic one, and is the third major film of Reichert and Klein. Their first film,* Growing Up Female, *looked at the social forces that shape women as they grow up and move from nursery, through school, to become middle-aged housewives. Made in 1971, it was the first film really to explore the dilemmas of being a woman in modern America.*

*For their second film* Methadone, *Reichert and Klein spent six months around a midwest methadone clinic. The observations of life at the clinic create a devastating picture. The claim of the film makers is "that this is another example of how social services, designed to help, often neutralize those they serve."*

*One thread running through all the pictures is the obvious ability of the film makers to really get people to open up and have their say. This seems rule number one of any documentary and yet there is a dimensional difference between the usual network interview and the Reichert-Klein piece. The difference probably arises from the position of the film makers. Reichert and Klein give the impression of being truly part of and concerned with what they film. They are not casual observers just looking in but seem to be truly involved with the subject.*

*Both Reichert and Klein define themselves as radical film makers contributing to what they consider are the progressive forces of society. They claim, too, that the completion of the film is only half the work: the other half is sharing ideas* *in open discussions after the screenings. To forward this concept they helped set up an independent distribution agency, New Day Films,\* which is now one of the prime distributors of films on social change.*

*If an image has been created of two tense, heavy, beetle-browed and dour radicals then the image is very wrong. Both Reichert and Klein are utterly open and delightful people. And both are extremely modest. I believe their films and the distribution company are really important contributions to the documentary field and yet, when we talked, they were both anxious to stress their own limitations and how much they still had to learn.*

*Recently I had an invitation to their wedding. When I said "Well, isn't it time, after being together for eight years or so" they told me there had been so many other things to do, who had time for weddings! The two of them met as graduate students at Antioch College and have taught courses there on the political use of the media. Besides filming they have also spent a lot of time in radio broadcasting, general political work and in community organization. Their work in Dayton, Ohio, is typical of their involvements. For a couple of summers the two of them made slide shows for and about specific neighborhoods. The material for the shows was collected by walking up and down certain areas and just sitting down with people and asking them what they felt. When completed the shows were put on in the neighborhood parks with the whole populace turning out at night to watch.*

*Reichert talked to me about this, revealing at the same time much about herself and Klein: "They sit on the grass. It's a real community event and we've learned so much from that process about the real concerns of working-class people and what their lives are like. It's been a tremendous influence on us."*

Q. Had any of your previous films prepared you for *Union Maids* or set you along in that direction?

R. Our previous work and our previous life, both. It was important for me that I had made another film on women, *Growing Up Female*, and that I was part of the women's movement, and had a commitment to build that movement. I felt it was important for people to make films about different aspects of women's lives. Also, being a woman of working-class origins myself, that also makes me want to make films by, for, and about working-class women. That's an interest I had for a long time. There's another thing. In a film we made, *Methadone: An American Way of Dealing*, one part of the film consists of an historical overview of the problem of dealing with drugs in America. It covers about fifty years. I did the research for it and found the stills, and I found it tremendously interesting to do an historical overview that

*See also the interview with Amalie Rothschild.

318

pushed us a little bit in the direction of the importance of history in dealing with political questions of society today.

Q. How did you come to the three women in *Union Maids*?

K. We didn't come to the three women in *Union Maids*. Our collaborator Miles Mogulesco did. The women are from a book, *Rank and File*, which tells the story of twenty-odd rank and file organizers of the thirties in an oral history fashion. The book and Miles's prodding sparked the idea of the film and it seemed like a film that would really work, and would really be needed.

Q. Was it difficult for you to trace these women? What was their reaction when you suggested the idea of a film?

R. It wasn't difficult to find them at all because the author of the source book knew their addresses so we just called and then looked them up. They were pretty enthusiastic about the idea of doing a film. I don't think they ever imagined what it would finally be but they were certainly interested in sharing the experiences of their lives, and what history was about, with the generation to come.

K. I don't think they did have a real good conception what it would all be about. We were people whom they were very happy to talk to and give information to. Later when we went back to them for more material and for the narration, and they saw the film cut, they were very surprised.

Q. Did you define a structure before you came to them or did you get permission first and then think about the film?

R. We had a pretty good idea that this was going to be a story-telling film. It was going to be very simple. Just the three of them telling the story of their lives and then we would use it against some archival footage. So the structure was very simple. It was just a matter of finding the places where their stories would amplify one another, and picking out of a three-hour interview the most interesting and important stories.

K. After the interviews we more and more got involved in the historical material, archive material. And at that stage, as we were putting it together we had to go back and do a lot more research.

Q. When you say lots more research are you talking about your own knowledge of the history of that time or simple film research? Or research in the sense of collaborating and checking up on the authenticity of their stories?

R. Well, the first two were very intertwined. As we looked for stills, that took us to books, and we began to read more about the period. The interviews were the beginning of a process for us. At that stage we knew very little about the history of unions. We were pretty ignorant, which in some ways was OK and in some ways was a detriment to what we did. While we were doing the research we'd see this footage of workers being beaten up by the police and huge demonstrations and so forth. And we wondered—wow, what had really happened back there? So we really wanted to find out more about it and spent nine months just reading all about the period. That was partly to help us make sure that their stories were representative. But that was more minor. Really it was much more for ourselves—to follow up our own curiosity.

κ. Also, as we started to put the film together all sorts of problems would arise. New material, new themes. And we had to question and reexamine some of our earlier ideas. For example, what had happened to the unions since the thirties was not an issue we had thought about much before. We knew a little bit about it—enough to ask a few questions—but when it came to asking how did it affect the three women, we found we didn't have a perspective *ourselves* on what had happened. It was the same on the effects of the McCarthy period and repression. Were there things wrong with the organizing they did which led to a change in the nature of unions? What kind of internal battles were there in the unions? So we spent a lot of time researching very hard and reading everything.*

R. The question is very much posed by the film. You see these very militant women, you see masses of people in the streets, you see workers sitting down on the sidewalks. You see all this stuff. It happened in the 1930s and 1940s. And then you have the unions today, which many people would say are not a progressive force in society any more. So you wonder what happened. And that was a question we hadn't thought about very much and had to research.

Q. You were setting out the public life and maybe a bit of the private life of the women. Did they impose any limitations on you? Were they worried about limits of privacy?

R. The only limitation was that two of them did not want to talk about the fact that they had been Communists. They were willing to call themselves socialists or radicals but did not want to be called Communists. One of them in particular, because of her job now, was very worried that if she was identified as having been a Communist at one point in her life she would lose her job. So that was the only real limitation.

*The section of the film alluded to here deals with problems of the unions after the Second World War and during the McCarthy period. It also shows briefly the more left-wing section of the unions being ostracized by the main body.

K. When we were doing the interviews the women would occasionally say, "Turn off the tape and we'll talk about certain things." These were things they didn't want us to pursue in the interview, or didn't want to be shown in the interview. They weren't major points but were indications of their hesitancies. The other thing is that when we went back to work on the narrations, which were done while we were editing the film (we knew what was needed then for certain sections and could see also what was missing), Kate, the eldest woman, was very crotchety about us telling her or suggesting to her what to say or what area we were interested in.

R. We had written out narrations for them to say. We wanted them to expand on certain subjects.

K. Kate didn't want to have anything to do with this kind of thing.

Q. Did the women meet? Were you interviewing them together?

R. No. When we did the original interviews we did them on three separate days. In fact we didn't even know the women had known each other and had been friends. See, again, we were ignorant of a lot of things. That's one reason we had a photograph of them at the end, all together.

Q. One of the problems of historical films done first-person, and I am thinking of many Second World War films, is that the memory plays tricks—romanticizes, omits. Did you have this feeling at all with these women?

K. Sure. Some. I don't think they were off on basic issues like their careers and the basic organizing they were doing. But where there were shades or memory lapses it didn't really matter. We weren't trying to document three important people and what they did and what made them famous. We were trying instead to get in touch with a whole period and a whole group of people in similar positions.

Q. In the film you use stills and dupes of old film material. Sometimes this material illustrates very specific instances from their stories and sometimes there is a generalized use of the material to illustrate a whole period. Were you aware of any dangers of using a generalized picture to illustrate a specific story or happening? And what do you think of the rights and wrongs of such use of footage?*

R. Certainly we mixed the footage. For example, let's say one of the women would say, "Us women got together" and a picture comes on with a group of women looking into the camera with their hands on their hips. That's just one example. There're many throughout the film. Somewhere else one of them says, "I worked in a laundry," and

*See also the discussions with Kuehl and Vas.

321

you see women working in a laundry. Well, obviously that particular woman working in that laundry is not Sylvia who's talking, because they weren't taking pictures.

κ. That's a really important thing because there is so little material of working women, of people just doing things without glory at all. Without using these devices you would either have to give up the idea of covering the subject in a pictorial way that can help people to imagine what it was like or you had to work with material that was very similar though not 100 percent authentic or absolutely specific.

R. We were mostly trying to give a strong impressionistic feeling of what it was like, what the conditions were like, what people might have looked like. We tried very hard to get pictures of the same industry at the same time period. For example, hair styles change, dress styles change. And I got to know what dress styles look like in the early thirties as opposed to the later thirties. We wanted to make it as close as possible. And I was gratified when we showed the film to the women, that they were astounded at how similar the shots of their work which we put in the film were to the real thing they had experienced. Some of it is, of course, the actual footage and the real people.

Q. The film was shot on videotape. What were the advantages and disadvantages of doing it that way and then transferring it to celluloid?

R. I can think of nothing but disadvantages. The quality of the transfers was very poor. We tried for a long time to get better transfers. We went to a number of different places till we finally realized we are not going to get high-quality transfers. At one point we even considered not finishing the film because we thought it was going to look so terrible. The quality is the main disadvantage. The one advantage for me as an interviewer was that with video you can run tape for the whole interview and you can use two cameras. So I didn't have to be constantly thinking how much film was running through the cameras and how much money was being spent. I could just forget about those things, which was very liberating as an interviewer. But if we had to do it again we certainly wouldn't do it on tape.

κ. There was an advantage to video, which doesn't have to do with film quality but does concern the way we work. We like to work with people who are learning film making. We like to give people a chance to get experience and because we were working on video and I could be watching on a monitor what we were shooting, and could talk to them on intercom, we could work with people with hardly any experience. I could give them precise directions on their shooting which you normally can't do in documentary.

Q. How do you split up the work?

R. Most of it is done collectively in the sense of developing the questions together. I do the interviews, but we develop the questions and the concepts together, sit at the editing table together, and we argue together on every cut. A little bit of a separation of tasks developed with *Union Maids*, which turned out to be very healthy. There was so much research to be done, both in stills and reading, that I finished up doing that and Jim did a little bit more of the fine editing of the film. During the last two months of editing I was in the library most of the day while Jim was fine cutting, and at night we would work together and go over what he had fine cut during the day.

K. We've been making films together for seven years. In the beginning we thought we had to do everything together and had to have equal skills in every part of film making and had to develop each other and keep up with each other and not go beyond. Over time, as we've become more confident in our film making and less insecure about our own abilities to make films, we've seen that it makes more sense sometimes to split the roles.

R. I'd like to go back to the film structure for a moment. The way I've described it, it sounds very simple. As if we just threw it together. The reality was, once we got the basic idea down—a story-telling film with breaks for music—there were tremendous problems in making it work as a film and telling the story in an interesting way. Here's an example:

You may remember in the film that one of the climaxes is the story of the woman who faces the shotguns and who is helping prevent the evictions. After that we get the funerals of the men who are killed for doing unemployed organizing work. Now that was all problematical in the film. We knew it was one of our best stories but on the other hand it was about the unemployed organizing which historically happened much earlier than the CIO organizing—about 1930 to 1932, whereas the CIO was 1937 to 1940. But it was such a strong story that we couldn't have it at the beginning of the film, though that's where it fitted chronologically, so we kept that roll on the shelf and kept putting it into the film and taking it out for a whole year until finally we figured out a way to include it. There were many problems like that in the film.

Q. For most of the film you simply go along with the story of the three women, adding in the period background, but towards the end you raise almost three separate issues. First you discuss what happened to the unions in the early fifties. Then you raise the issue of the women's movement today, and then you fractionally touch on but don't go into where the unions themselves are at now. Had you thought

323

about going into these areas in more depth? Was it a problem of time? Did you really see them as three separate films?

K. No. We knew we couldn't go into them in depth because that would divert us from what we were trying to accomplish in the film. But they were issues which we wanted to bring up and discuss, even briefly. We wanted people to think about these issues. We wanted to put out a little bit of information. A little bit of knowledge and tease people so that they would think about it all. Think about historical patterns and social change and maybe think about preventing certain things from happening again. As to the women's movement, we knew we couldn't go into that in depth but by putting a little bit in about it we knew our audience would really key up and take off in discussions. Many of these points are there so that a skillful discussion leader or organizer can pick up on them.

R. One thing we do at the end of the film is to ask the women how they feel about their lives looking back on it all. Do they feel their lives were worthwhile even though the unions today are not what they had hoped for? And to me that's one of the most important things about the film. They all speak with a great deal of pride about what they did and feel they lived their lives correctly. And in many ways that's the most important thing the film can say. That someone can lead a politically committed life, and is active, and tries to work for changes for the better in society, and can say in old age, "I have no regrets. I'm glad I've lived as I have."

Q. How did you arrange the funding of the film?

R. That was fairly easy. We started out with a small grant of $2,500 from the Rabinowitz Foundation. Almost all the rest of the money came from money we were able to save from the making of *Growing Up Female*. So most of the money came out of our own pockets. Then right at the end we got another grant of $1,000 from the Film Fund. The film only cost about $13,000. We are not talking about a lot of money.

K. At one point we also showed the film to socially concerned people and got small loans up to about $2,000.

R. The distribution cost more than the making of the film and that again we paid for out of money we had saved.

Q. This film is made with very specific purposes in mind. Can you tell me something about those purposes?

R. Well, it has both specific and general purposes. Specifically we had two main audiences in mind. One is the unions today, and in particular, rank and file caucuses who are trying to make the unions more democratic and want to go back to some of the union goals we are talking about in the film. So that's the audience. Another is unorganized working people—to urge them to organize. We also tried to raise the question of women as potential leaders in unions today as they were then. And that's one of the real impacts it's had on the unions.

The other audience we had in mind was the women's movement which in the United States today is the largest mass movement that exists. And here we wanted to do two things. We wanted to explore another aspect of women's history and point people in the direction of looking at working-class women and their experiences.

K. We didn't start out making the film knowing specifically what we were going to cover. One value of the film which wasn't clear to us when we started making it, and which we only learnt about as we went on, was the connection of the past radical history of this country with people today, particularly people coming out of the antiwar movement and people who were radicalized in the sixties who have gone on to try and change the nature of this society. We, as part of that movement, didn't have any knowledge that there was any historical tradition of radical movements all the way through American history. And the reason we don't know it is because of the effect of the McCarthy period and the destruction of the lives of most of the people who made that past history. The McCarthy period prevented people from talking about their past if they wanted to survive. So we didn't get these stories.

R. There's a whole radical tradition in American history if you look into it and then there's a gap in that history starting in the late forties and going on through the McCarthy period. Only now is it starting to be reviewed and connected.

Q. You use some very strong songs with terrific emotional force. Songs like "Solidarity Forever" and "Union Maid." Do you think there is any danger of romanticizing the period and because of that, refusing to look where the unions are at today which seems to me a hundred and eighty degrees away from that film? At least that's how I see it in England.

R. I think there *is* a danger of using the stirring romantic music and all that militant footage of masses of people. The problem to me is that it all looks very easy. It looks as if it was easy to organize the CIO. It looks as if it was no particular trouble at all. And that's a lesson we don't want to teach people which maybe the film does to a degree.

We also tried, two or three times, at the end of some of the songs which are very high and where everybody looks great to make a fade to black and then a very serious question comes on like, "Well, how long did it really take you to organize?" And the answer is "A long, long time," so hopefully you don't get the sense that it was too easy. After "Solidarity Forever," a real high moment of the film, we come in with a question, "What about the union movement today?" We tried deliberately at times to undercut or balance that super-emotional feeling.

Q. At some stage you called yourselves "radical film makers." What does that mean? What do you see as the role of the film maker outside of the network organizations in America today?

R. There's a long answer to that question but one aspect of it is that we see ourselves as part of and wanting to (on some levels) serve the left in the U.S. today. We want to help the organizations that are trying to create social change. I don't mean just Marxist left or just revolutionary left but people who are doing community organizing, people who are organizing on their jobs for better conditions. We want to make films that organizers can use to reach large audiences. So, on one level, as radicals, we are trying to help enlarge the radical movement through the films we do and all the films that we've done have had purposes in that direction. That's one thing.

Another thing is it's obviously very important, if we are going to create radical change in this country, to change people's perception of themselves, of other people, and of the world around. I'll give an example. People are trained and encouraged to be competitive, to think you need hierarchies. That you need a leader, followers and people up and down the ladder for society to operate. People are taught to be sexist and racist. Those are the values in the society. Now it's very important in making radical film to counteract those values in every aspect of the film, not only in content but also in approach and style.

One example of how we do that in *Union Maids* is the idea of having three women tell their story as opposed to one woman. If we had only taken one you could easily have seen that woman as a heroine, as someone who is unique. And that was the attitude we *didn't* want people to have. We don't want you to think that there are a few people who are unique and unusual and the rest of us are just sheep, which is a tendency people have. And we cut their stories so that one blends in with another so that you get a sense that there is a collectiveness and it's not just isolated people who are written up in history books and credited with having created history.

K. One more important thing is I don't think we define ourselves as film makers who have political ideas. We are political people, political activists who are trying to use film in a way that will help make changes in society. We have a lot of respect for the film medium, for our craft, and want to make films that are popular and experiment with a lot of styles but the most important thing is doing work that helps bring about change.

R. We did start out as people in the Movement and then later decided that we wanted to make films. It wasn't that we decided to be film makers and then thought, well, what shall we make films about? It was the other way around.

Q. Do you ever feel yourselves as preaching to the converted? How can you get to the widest audience with your films?

K. I think the way you try to avoid that is not lead your life just in contact with people like yourself. We try to work with people who have very different views from us. I always think of these different people when I make a film. Julia says she thinks of her mother.

R. She was a Goldwater Republican, a working-class woman and in no way a political person. But when I'm thinking about a film I can picture my mother and how she thinks. And it really does help me to figure out what to say in a film. Or we can picture friends of ours who live on the block, who are not involved politically. And we think, how would we speak to them?

K. We are in danger of making films that are much more acceptable to younger people than older people because we don't have that much contact with people over thirty-five. We don't have that much sense of what people over thirty-five think and how their values are structured, and that's a problem.

R. The other thing about how you reach out to people beyond the committed, at least for us, has been through doing our own distribution. We try very consciously with the distribution to get the film out to all ranges of society. Catholic schools, high schools, YMCAs, unions, everywhere.

Q. You started film making about seven years ago. What have you learned in terms of distribution problems and methods since then?

K. When you do your own distribution you see the letters that come back about the film, negative or positive. We know everyone who's seen the film and how different kinds of people respond to it. As a film maker you make a lot of assumptions. You assume people understand this and don't understand that in your films. And you can use certain styles and it will make sense to this bunch but not to the other. Through being involved in distribution and having a lot of contact with the audience we've just learned invaluable lessons about film making. Like how much sarcasm or ironic humor to use within a film.

R. We also learn how far we can go politically and I think in general we have always underestimated this.

Q. One of the questions which has been bounding around recently is that it's no use just changing the content of the film but the committed film maker has also got to change the structure and form of the film in order to get a real participation and acceptance by the audience, to get them to think, to get them involved in the dialogue, to get them to move.

R. I agree with that notion in general but I think it's a long way from being fleshed out so that I can really understand what it would mean in practice. We have occasionally employed ideas like that. One example was the methadone film which we specifically made in two parts with a break for discussion in the middle. The words "break for discussion here" appear on the screen. It's almost like two separate films. The first poses a problem, and you have discussion, and the other poses an alternative. We give out a list of suggested questions with the film.

K. As film makers we've only made a few films and we are learning a lot all the time. Actually the element of form in a film is something that till now we didn't think a lot about but we've now begun thinking about it more and more. It's no good to simply make a film that has a very radical way-out form and nobody can understand what the hell it's talking about and therefore no one watches it. On the other hand I really agree that if you use all the same techniques then very little is demanded of your audience and you are working against your content. The trick is to grab your audience and get them to look at some new ideas without pushing them out of the cinema or turning them off.

Q. Up to now you've made four films. Do you see any general trends in your development?

K. When we made *Growing Up Female* the film really spoke to a problem. It spoke to the socialization of women and how people are getting damaged by the process of growing up in America. It's in that sense a very negative film. It shows no solution. No way out for women. It just points to a problem and shows it well.

As we've moved along through film making our style has changed, but when we started out we were really coming out of the radical generation of the sixties. A lot of rebelliousness, a lot of rage at the society and at the way we were raised and what we didn't like about that and what we felt really mad about. And to me it seems that our early films are really kind of crying out "Stop this!" There was an energy there attacking a system that exists. So in *Growing Up Female* there is no solution given at all. *Men's Lives*, which we helped edit, is very similar to that though at the end there is a certain sense of where it all comes from and a bit of social analysis.

328

It was really in *Methadone* that our ideas began to change, about what political film making is. We started out to make that film completely as an exposé on methadone. And we shot the whole first section on the methadone clinic thinking that was the whole film. As we edited that and came out with this indictment of how the government was dealing with drug addiction we realized we couldn't just present that as a film. It was so negative. It really showed people in a very bad light and implied that people can't change. The first structure of the film didn't lead people in any direction that would help improve things. In realizing this we made what I think was a break for us. The second half of the film, while not as analytical as the first part, begins to show some hope and some direction for people to go in order to change their lives and change their society, and change social relations between the different groups in the society. We are moving on to positive role models at that point. *Union Maids* takes that trend and completely follows that in the sense that the film is totally about positive role models and positive action to change society, to make it more what we want it to be.

So we see our development as having gone from simply crying out in protest against what was and is wrong with society to a point where we are now trying to influence people's thinking in a direction where they will take action to make improvements and change our society in a positive direction. And we see that direction in the shape of a more collective society or a more socialist society. One without hierarchies, and one without a competitive nature to it. One where people work cooperatively together to accomplish what is necessary.

R. What Jim is describing in another sense is that our first three films are about how capitalism controls people and shapes people to play the roles that this particular society and system want. And we tried to explore what kind of people they were and why this is true and the social processes and so forth.

What didn't really start occurring to us till later on in the methadone film and then in *Union Maids* is that it was also important not just to describe how society shapes people but how people have shaped the world and how people have shaped history. If we don't do this then in a sense we are making very pessimistic films. While they may show to the core how capitalism works they don't necessarily show people how to change things. And that's really what we want to do.

*20*

# *Hurry Tomorrow*
## *Richard Cohen*

An agonizing involving spectacle to watch . . . with more bitterness and outrage in any three-minute sequence than in all of *One Flew Over the Cuckoo's Nest*.

VINCENT CANBY, *New York Times*

Hurry Tomorrow *(1974) is a documentary exposure of forced drugging of mental patients as currently practiced in many state hospitals and psychiatric institutions in the U.S. Shot over a five-week period in a locked psychiatric ward at Metropolitan State Hospital in Los Angeles, the film concentrates on the forced drugging of patients which turns them into walking zombies. We are given an insider's view of inmates being physically tied down to enforce conformity. And we are also given occasional moments of warmth between inmates trying to keep some dignity in a dehumanized environment.*

*One of the main points of the film is the difference in treatment between inmates in a psychiatric ward and convicted criminals: the criminal comes out better because the psychiatric inmate is denied due process of law in the name of therapy and help. Thus after seeing* Hurry Tomorrow *William Bates wrote in the University of California at Berkeley's* Daily Californian: *"The irony of the liberal tradition is to have created, next to the criminal justice system— in which the individual is increasingly protected from arbitrary actions of the state—a parallel system of denunciation and imprisonment that recreates, with the added terrors of modern technology, the full horrors of the old."*

*Another main topic of the film is an exploration of the nature of voluntary commitment. A lot of the voluntariness is shown to be myth, with patients and their families being coerced into signing away their freedom. Once inside the ward the psychiatrist, dressed like a rather elegant hippie, subjects the inmate to the ultimate Catch 22: no release until you don't want it.*

*The film exposes brutal behavior. Bullying aides and guards treat the inmates like misbehaving schoolboys, applying punishments for every breach of the rules. Again and again we witness what is in effect psychiatric rape and chemical straitjacketing. Yet this film was shot in a "model ward." As the chief psychiatrist says, "You ought to see what it's like on the other wards of other hospitals."*

*Metropolitan is a public institution. Its wards are filled with working people, blacks, and the marginally unemployed. Few of its inmates can afford to stay in private hospitals and here the two-class system of general medical care is clearly illustrated.*

Hurry Tomorrow *was directed and edited by Richard Cohen and shot by Kevin Rafferty. Cohen's first film,* Two Days in a Halfway House, *dealt with the problem of people just released from mental institutions. While working on* Halfway House *Cohen kept hearing horror stories related by former hospital inmates. These stories, and the desire to investigate them, provided the genesis of* Hurry Tomorrow.

*I met Cohen in Boston, almost literally between trains. I was coming from New York and he was heading west. I'd seen his film in an Australian film festival in 1976, had been overwhelmed by it and then saw it again in New York. We'd spent a year writing and phoning and trying to get together and finally did the three-hour interview sitting on the steps of a Boston church and over coffee at a local café.*

*I wanted Cohen to tell me about his background but he was extremely reluctant. Enough that he was a graduate student in his mid-twenties, worked as a film maker in L.A. and was searching for funds about a film on the police, tentatively entitled* Deadly Force. *All the rest was irrelevant. The only thing that mattered was the film, which he spoke about with a passion that was deeply moving.*

*My own reaction is that* Hurry Tomorrow *is the most important film on hospital life to emerge in the last ten years and goes way beyond* Titicut Follies *or* One Flew Over the Cuckoo's Nest *in its indictment of mental hospital conditions. Given the difficulties of the filming it is beautifully made and at times almost brings one to tears.*

*Like* Union Maids *and* Men's Lives, Hurry Tomorrow *is made to evoke discussion and action on the part of its audiences. It was also made to evoke political action. When it came out it caused a furor in California and considerable interest on the part of Governor Brown. But did it achieve the action it hoped for?*

*When I talked to Cohen in the summer of 1977 he was extremely dubious about the amount of change in the system. However in November 1977 he sent me a cutting from the* L.A. *Times, which stated that the County Board of Supervisors had voted to sue the state to compel the correction of substandard patient care at a local hospital. A further note mentioned an investigation by the district attorney into the presigning of blank conservatorship requests. So though the change may be small it does appear to be taking place.*

Q. How did you get into the subject of *Hurry Tomorrow?*

A. I was doing a short film about Steve and Linda who lived in a large halfway house in Los Angeles. The halfway house was a 36-unit apartment building, with a swimming pool, that acted as a kind of refugee camp for people just released from mental hospitals. While we were filming we did a sequence about a man who had swallowed a bad mixture of Thorazine and Gallo wine. He was crying and very frightened, and some friends tried to guide him through the crisis. The next day his mother showed up and she and an administrator of the halfway house held a private meeting. Behind closed doors they decided to ship this twenty-five-year-old man back to Camarillo State Hospital, some fifty miles north of L.A. He refused to go and really broke down with fear. Nevertheless he was carted off, crying and weeping.

After this incident other horror stories began to emerge about the state mental hospitals. I started hearing about involuntary shock treatments and about death-simulating drugs. And there was this absolute terror of going back to the hospitals which was common to all the people who told me these stories. I heard all this and I watched the involuntary returns and gradually started thinking about a longer film on the subject of mental hospitals and psychiatric care.

q. Did you use this short film, *Halfway House*, as a fund raiser?

a. Yes. *Two Days in a Halfway House* was made as a student film for a few hundred dollars, and shot in five days. When it was screened in a lineup of student films it got pretty good reviews. Anyway, the whole of the next year I hiked around Hollywood with the film and a bunch of reviews under one arm and started begging. My pal and partner Kevin Rafferty joined me and we sent out several thousand letters to anyone we thought might have money to give to the larger film.

We'd formed a limited partnership with the aim of raising $30-$60,000, but by the first day of the shoot we had only $15,000. That seemed enough to start with. We decided to shoot black-and-white negative, double X, which gave a fast cheap stock. Consolidated Film Industries gave us an across-the-board 30 percent discount. Kevin owned his own camera and sound and a neighbor, Dick Davis, came on as camera assistant. Some friends moved in and did sound and all the salaries were deferred. So we started making a movie.

q. I understand you were originally going to do the longer film as a follow-up on Steve at Camarillo. What changed your plans and led you to eventually shoot at Metropolitan State Hospital?

a. What we wanted to do in the longer film was show what it was like to be a patient in a state hospital, and to show it all from the patient's point of view. I thought of following Steve who'd been in the first film, and after some difficulty (mainly bureaucratic tie-ups) finally tracked him down in Camarillo Hospital to which he had been shipped back after suffering from a severe reaction to a prescribed drug. He wanted to do the film and Sacramento gave the OK for filming.

q. I gather that your fund-raising letter mentioned looking into forced treatment. If I had been a hospital I doubt I would have given you permission if I read things like that, or at least I would have reacted very badly. How did you get entry to the hospital?

A. Well, as it turned out we didn't get to film at Camarillo. We were allowed in to observe and spent a week on a locked ward. However, at the last minute, just as we were about to start filming, the hospital director added a new stipulation. He felt that the hospital had to have the right to monitor the content. To me that meant editorial censorship and I couldn't agree, so we left Camarillo.

A little while earlier, while raising money, Kevin and I had shown the pilot to a group of psychiatrists which included a Dr. Ellerbroek. During the discussion afterwards Ellerbroek gave me his card and said, "If you want to film in my ward at the state hospital just give me a call." So when Camarillo fell through we switched locations.

Q. Did Dr. Ellerbroek set any preconditions for you?

A. No. He was very open to the idea. His staff, however, were a little more reluctant. They didn't really want to be in the film. Finally we came to a sort of verbal agreement with them that at any time they could come up to the camera and give an explanation of anything that seemed controversial or which might be misunderstood. They could do this at the time or after. In practice not once did any of them do this.

Q. Can you explain a little more what you had in mind about "from the view of the patient."

A. I think you can see many films on mental hospitals made by professionals. They are made by psychiatrists about mental diseases, about schizophrenia and so on, and there is little understanding of where the patient stands. I wanted to make a film about how patients experience and regard their treatment. I didn't want to show it all in an isolated context by following a psychiatrist around from patient to patient, but to be right on the dayroom floor with the inmates as the psychiatrist pops in and out on them. I wanted to see what the patients were like with each other while the staff is off in the other booth or preparing the medication.

Q. What background information did you have before you started to film? Had you talked to many psychiatrists? Had you seen *Warrendale?* Or did you just decide to go straight in and film?

A. I had seen a bit of *Warrendale.* During the year of raising funds I talked to a lot of mental health professionals and politicians, read through the recent history of state legislation, visited halfway houses, and talked with some members of the Network Against Psychiatric Assault (NAPA). But when it came to the first day of filming it was a new world.

Q. Did you spend any preliminary time in the hospital just observing or did you just go straight in and shoot it?

A. I spent about two weeks at Metropolitan, without the crew, watching drugged-out patients sleep or stare at the TV, play pool or ping pong, line up for drugs, line up for meals. One day I was perched on the radiator near the pool table when a group of psychiatric technician students fresh out of high school wandered in for their first exposure to what they had been told was the toughest, craziest ward in the city. Several nervous young women came and sat around me. I guess I looked like the craziest or the most harmless patient. There were a few minutes of silence broken only by crackling pool balls. Then one shyly turned to me and asked, "How long you been here?" I answered, "About half an hour." She turned away. There was another long pause, then she asked, "Why are you here?" I answered, "I'm making a movie." There was another momentary pause, then she and the other students got up and quickly moved out of the dayroom, probably to analyze my delusions. This experience clued me in to a problem of the attitudes of staff and the way they are going to treat patients. First it appears that most of the staff are afraid of the patients. The second thing is they don't respect what the patient says.

Q. Were you aware of any traps when you started, filmic or otherwise? Did you see dangers of misinterpreting or. misunderstanding a situation? What were the most important things you had to do and what were the things you had to avoid?

A. The main difficulty was trying to get the trust of the patients, real trust, and at the same time keep a relationship going with the staff so that we could continue to film in the ward. Most of the patients are there against their will. They don't want to be in a hospital and they know that we, the film crew, can walk in in the morning and leave at night. So there was that envy and distrust to overcome.

In a way we were like those students I mentioned. We were fresh to the experience. We had keys and could leave the locked ward. We needed space to eat lunch, store equipment and generally retreat from the oppressive atmosphere of the dayroom, so often we shared the observation room with staff or were in their coffee room. I'd be sitting there eating a chicken sandwich listening to their frightening stories of wild mental patients. I would actually tremble while returning to the dayroom wondering when some person would leap out from the deep end.

Favorite legends among the staff were the longtime lobotomy victims. From the first day we were warned not to go near one man because he would rip the camera away and smash it. The guy looked like Eugene O'Neill. He had been hospitalized for twenty years, had a lot of shock treatments and a lobotomy. I asked him about the operation, but all he could remember was that they told him he was going to the dentist to have a tooth pulled . . . then as he tried to remember more he became muddled and anguished. A day later, he refused to get up from his chair for medication so two technicians grabbed him. We followed them up the hall to the medication room, where they shut the door on us. A technician stuck his head out and said, "I don't mind losing my job but if you film what goes on inside here I might lose my license to practice." The door was left slightly ajar and we tried to film the scene through a mirror inside, but it didn't work. They were forcing him to take his drugs.

This scene was repeated a few days later with the same inmate. A psych-tech student tore into the technicians, berating them for mistreating the patient. One technician said, "I used to be like you when I started, but you'll learn." She was being trained and a few weeks later she got along well with the older technician. She had bought her role.

We could have reacted the same way as the student. A belief in psychiatry and mental illness or having a job at stake could have trapped us. Even the deadly state of the dayroom, the sluggish atmosphere, unbearable boredom could have forced us back into the staff's energy as a source for the film, as a source for understanding the hospital process. We could have viewed the film as a technician and sat back in the booth looking for any piece of behavior that was visible, didn't conform to the pattern of sleeping bodies, then gone out and filmed the incident. But it wouldn't have been the same. I was determined to search out the patient's experience. Given the inmates' hostility toward some staff, given our power to exit at will, inmates were remarkably open to our film making. Our key characters turned out to be great choices. They trusted us.

Q. What do you think was the impact of the camera on the situation? Do you think that certain things that were going on were being deliberately played up for your film making?

A. Before filming *Hurry Tomorrow* I thought the camera was a catalyst and sped up inevitable situations. But in *Hurry Tomorrow* I don't think the patients acted out their anger for the cameras. It was there. Their anger was their own, it was a question of survival. It was their indignation at being treated so poorly and their strength to resist. On the other hand, the staff controlled their actions a bit. As one top-level health department official remarked after viewing the film, "If this is what our staff is like on their best behavior, for the cameras, you can imagine what they are like when there are no cameras around."

Restraints were used more frequently and violently before the camera crew was around. I'll never forget one patient who spent most of his day reading to other patients and trying to set up classroom activities to pass the time. He was a Vietnam vet, as were many patients. He hated Thorazine, he hated psychiatric drugs. One day he felt like he might freak out. He went up to some staff and asked them to put him in restraints. "I'm gonna freak out . . . don't give me any drugs, just tie me down." They responded, "Sure. Okay." Then they grabbed him and the way they took him in there was very brutal and forceful. They threw him down on the bed, tied him real tight, then they came back in and gave him a shot of Thorazine. The appearance of the hypodermic freaked him out; he was helplessly restrained. Two days later he escaped and I heard that he committed himself to an open ward at Veterans Administration hospital.

Q. You say that the staff were more restrained because you were filming, but there's one scene near the end of the film where a fellow is put under restraints and the staff member is absolutely brutal and tells him to keep quiet and refuses to loosen things up. Was that done towards the end of your filming when they had already become relaxed and accustomed to your cameras?

A. That particular scene was filmed toward the fifth or sixth week. Yes, I think some of the technicians had relaxed a bit. Plus we melted in so well and had become just part of the wide-angle landscape. By that point too, as a crew, we acted tightly while filming. Kevin was quick and silent with the camera. After that incident I wanted to interview the technician, but he disappeared. At first they claimed he was shifted to another ward, then a nurse told me he had suffered a nervous breakdown.

Q. The film centers on the experience of four patients. Did you shoot many patients and then cut it all down? Did you focus on these from the start?

A. We would film a lot of intakes, where the patient first meets the staff. If it wasn't interesting then we'd cut the camera and not process the film. I threw out about one-third as much unprocessed film as was developed. In the end each person was selected because he represented some kind of rebellion at the beginning. You could just sense it when they came into the ward. Each morning ten or fifteen patients would be brought in. The process is they would come in and wait around for half an hour to an hour. We filmed Craig from the beginning, from his first day. We had John, whom you mentioned being tied down, at the end. He had been there before we arrived and he was still there when we left. Most patients only stay in the hospital for seven to fourteen days unless they end up in a conservatorship and the state takes over control.

Q. This is actually one of the points *not* made in your film. We have no idea how long people actually stay there. Were you aware of this?

A.  It is part of the experience of being locked up in a mental hospital not to know when you or the person you ate breakfast with might be released, or as it might seem, disappear. The Latino kid, Alan, was gone by 6:00 A.M. the day after we filmed that sequence. I met up with a few of the inmates on the outside, but it just didn't seem important to resolve those questions. While editing we considered using the title *Suspended*. The film was edited to bring the viewer in; that's where the scaring process occurs. The young black man was alert and thoughtful when he starts out at the beginning of the film and shortly he's transformed into a zombie, sleeping in a chair. Bodies may get out, but the humans are traumatized, stigmatized, and caught in a system. They may be out one day and back in the next. Stories aren't tied up neatly.

Q.  In terms of treatment one only sees two kinds of therapy. One sees patients being tied down and patients being given drugs. Is that the total treatment at these hospitals? Is there any kind of therapy besides those two things?

A.  The state has promoted "milieu therapy" as its chief therapy—just letting people hang out and interact with each other and that's prominent in the film. There was a group therapy session that met briefly each week for a few hours. Time-wise it didn't seem significant. Also it wasn't forced. The film centered around forced treatment and that was the real question for me, whether citizens can have their human and legal rights arbitrarily suspended by the state for the questionable "crimes" of paranoia and depression. Can people be denied due process of law in the name of psychiatric care? Most people in mental institutions in this country have not committed any crime, nor have they been a violent threat to anyone.

Q.  One of the criticisms that was made of *Titicut Follies* was that Wiseman was exploiting the position of the inmates of the mental institutions where he filmed, who didn't realize what was going on. Does this criticism seem just and in any way valid in relation to your own film?

A.  That's screwed up because *Titicut Follies* has done much more for patients than if it had not been made. That seems to be the position of some staff and relatives of patients who were committed, and politicians. One family of a patient in *Hurry Tomorrow* threatened to sue us because the father was upset. He had committed his son. That particular patient had been close to some of the crew during the filming, hung around a lot and talked. He was on a conservatorship which meant that his family had become his legal guardians. The family had said he would have to live with this stigma of being a mentally ill person now that the film had been shot. Now the stigma is one of the real problems for people leaving a mental hospital. But the film didn't portray him as a crazy sick person. Instead it portrayed him as a person being inhumanely treated by a technician.

Q. To go on with this issue of "fairness." The chief psychiatrist in your film says something like, "If you think these wards are bad you should see some of the other wards. They are really wild." While you were there did you see cases where this tying down might have been justified? I'm obviously asking this of you as a layman working from your instincts.

A. What he was referring to here was that on other wards people were much more severely overdrugged. He might have been right. His ward has been called one of the best, the cleanest and mild by comparative standards.

As far as the use of restraint being justified, I don't think so. In six weeks of filming I didn't see one instance of violence between patients. The only situation where a person had to be tied down was when he tried to resist treatment or tried to escape. John, the fellow who gets tied down in the end of the film, had tried to escape. It was his third attempt that weekend and he ended up being put in restraints. The explanation for putting the black kid in restraints is because he cursed and assaulted the staff and refused to take his medication. They tied him down on the bed and gave him an injection of Thorazine, which is a kind of instant lobotomy.

Then there's the opening sequence with the old man tied down. He hadn't done anything. He'd just fallen down. They picked him up, roughed him up, and brought him to the seclusion room. Later the psychiatrist tried to defend himself and his position by saying we didn't show that the patient had smashed five windows prior to the moment when they picked him off the floor and put him in the room. He said he'd attacked various technicians and that's why he had to be tied down to the bed. This was wrong. All that had happened was that the man had fallen down on the floor. I didn't see any violence from him the whole period we were there.

That's not to say people don't punch technicians and that technicians don't get smashed and get black eyes and fractured skulls. But you have to understand that most patients are locked up against their will and many are subjected to the most incredible modern experimental treatments. What you see in this film is mild and standard psychiatric practice. It's the tip of the iceberg, as far as mind control and behavior control go. Prolixin is a long-lasting drug with all kinds of strange and seemingly devastating side-effects. The way people walk in the film, like zombies, it makes you angry. At times patients might try to fight their way out—I would certainly try to escape if I were there.

338

Q. The image and parallel that keeps coming through the film is prison. This is set up right from the beginning where a psychiatrist says, "We educate them by one trip through the mill. Then hopefully they'll learn enough and never come back again." I can't remember if those are the exact words, but something like that. In your interviews with Dr. Ellerbroek did you put this prison image to him for discussion?

A. No, it wasn't put to him as a prison. Our questions were more, "How and why are people brought here and how do they get out?" The psychiatrist conjured up the image of "never again" which brings to mind Jewish people referring to the concentration camps.

Q. How loose and open was Ellerbroek with you in the interviews?

A. He gave a pretty interesting interview. He was willing to talk about anything in a very open way. I thought sometimes his examples were a bit exaggerated and defensive. This was particularly true of his descriptions of violent patients. Often they were patients I knew and it didn't fit quite with what I saw. However when we cut the interviews it was really because they were sometimes too long rather than that we disagreed (which we did) with a lot that he said.

Q. What was the most painful thing for you and your crew while you were filming?

A. Our sound man was an ex-patient. He just wanted to leave the room at times because he got so angry with the staff. For me, I found I was becoming numb to a lot of the violence happening around me because you just get so bored there and so depressed. It's one room and hours go by and nothing happens. You get lethargic and sleepy even without the drugs. And it was difficult and painful to even exist in that environment. Then once I became close to some of the people who were being filmed it became very hard to film them in those painful situations, when they were being put in restraints. We didn't know how to deal with it. To interfere with the restraints being put on people, to go on filming, just to stand by—?

Q. You have a very effective ending with a black strolling up and down and extemporizing a kind of blues song. How did that arise? Had you seen him singing at other times?

A. Yes, he was singing while waxing the floors in the hallway. Patients did those chores to gain favor or cigarettes from the staff. My first encounter with him was after I had broken my foot during the first few days of the shoot and was on crutches. He walked up and said, "It's 9:00 A.M. At 10:00 A.M., brother, you're gonna be able to throw down those crutches and walk." I said, "If I can throw down my crutches at ten then I'll give you my key to the door even if they do throw us all out." We were joking around because it was relatively easy for a person to escape from the hospital, especially if he was black. A few days later, I asked him to sing a song for the film. He walked over to the bars looking out over the grounds and let loose a medley. Then I asked him if he would move around and sing a song that expressed the feeling of the ward? He said "Sure." So we followed him around. But the song just wasn't right. Kevin repeated to him, "a song that gets into the feeling of the ward." The next tune from his lips was "Hurry Tomorrow," improvised as he moved.

He was an amazing person. He was in there because his wife had had a baby and he went out onto the streets where I imagine he was singing in the same fashion. Well, his aunt freaked out and called the police down on him and they said, "Why don't you cool it?" It was down in the ghetto in Los Angeles. Anyway he said, "Unless you cops stop hassling me I'm going to turn you into pillars of salt." And because he was giving them this lip (and they couldn't bust him for any crime because he hadn't committed any), they brought him in on a 5150 and said, "This guy says he can turn people into pillars of salt." So he came into the hospital. We got it on film but it didn't come out well enough to use.

They asked him what he was doing there. Did he think he was God? And he said, "My name is Joe Rudd." And they said, "Can you perform any miracles, like turn people into pillars of salt?" And he said, "I can throw my hat straight up into the air and make it come straight down and stop. And I can do this with any object at all." And the doctor said, "Okay. We'll get you a pool ball. Do you think you can make that stop when it comes down?" So they got him for thinking he could perform miracles.

The film was going to end with his escape. He was planning the great escape but actually our entire crew came down with a 103° temperature. That was our way of getting into the mood of the ward. We all got feverish and had to leave the day after we shot that song.

Q. Did you permit the staff or any of the inmates to look at the film before you completed it?

A. Yes. Craig, the young black inmate in the opening of the film, saw it in San Francisco while I was editing and he liked it. He particularly enjoyed seeing the staff alone or talking about him.

A few months after finishing the ward shoot, we interviewed the psychiatrist. I invited him to come up to San Francisco, visit the editing studio, and take a look. He never did. Then prior to the first public screening we called him again and offered to bring the film down to L.A. We also told him if he wanted to invite some staff he should. He was our liaison at the time. I'd called the hospital once but no one wanted to talk with me. The psychiatric nurse wasn't interested. Dr. Ellerbroek didn't invite anyone else so Kevin and I showed him the film alone. His first reaction was he thought it was "great" and "an accurate picture of his ward." A few weeks later he joined with ten staff members asking that the state ban the film.

Q. This situation in the hospital of tie-downs and forced drugging, was this fairly widely known or was it just publicized through your film? I'm interested here in what a film can do to spread a story as opposed to general journalism.

A. Certainly the government knew about it and patients and interested mental health groups knew that these so-called forms of therapy were definitely used for punishment. But unless you truly experience what it's like to be a patient, unless you emotionally identify, perhaps the psychiatric brainwashing works. As far as the difference between what journalism can do and film, I don't know how to answer that.

Q. You must have thought about the differences between your film and *One Flew Over the Cuckoo's Nest*. What do you feel is false in the latter, if anything?

A. *Cuckoo's Nest* was a powerful film that demonstrated to many people the horrors of shock, psychosurgery and psychiatric authority. But it left the impression that many patients like it in the hospital. That they were a voluntary ensemble of clowns having a good time. McMurphy was sacrificed by them. The fact is most patients are not voluntary. They may have volunteered in, but it's much harder to volunteer out.

Q. Were there any scenes in the film where your own internal sensitivity would say, "Leave this scene alone" and yet your film sense would know the material was very dynamic and powerful and would really make the film work?

A. There's the scene with Alan, the Guatemalan kid, and his father. They are both in the long corridor leading from the dayroom to the visiting room and it's very painful for the father to be there with his son who is in such a pitiful state. He had put his son voluntarily into the hospital and now he couldn't get him out. And he saw the privacy and integrity and morale of his son being totally destroyed by the institution. It was very painful. So it was a question of either filming it and showing how that happened in a real way or retreating from it. But we filmed it and I think it turned out to be the most moving sequence in the film.

That kind of question didn't occur with the restraints, like in the end where the kid is put in restraints and he's crying. He's pleading for someone to help him. That kind of filming dilemma didn't happen

341

there because the clear thing was to film this straight violent intrusion into the patient's world by the institution. With the father and the son together it was a lot more subtle because it was the father's pain more than the son's which was so evident there.

Q. Did you think of filming on an admission section or on a women's ward?

A. I initially wanted to film an admissions ward but the psychiatrist just didn't want us to film there. He was frightened of what might happen. I thought it would be good to get someone in admissions. They're brought in by the police in manacles. Incidentally, since the film has been out they've stopped handcuffing patients coming in. The patients are then systematically drugged as soon as they get in and it's only a question of their word versus the word of the person who's having them committed. It could be the husband, the wife, or the parent. It's often the parent these days because so many kids are committed. Youths, adolescents. Everyone is given mass drugs whether they need it or not. It's just a way to control their anger and subdue them. Then they're questioned, just as you see in the film, by a psychiatrist, a social worker, and so on. And if they refuse to answer questions then they are said to be hostile or paranoid or catatonic because they don't want to talk. And if they talk, and their words are contrary to what the police or their parents have said, that's used against them too. Basically mental patients don't have any of the rights that convicted felons have. They don't have the right to due process of law in this country.

Q. What about the possibility of filming in a women's ward?

A. There was a women's ward across the hall and I wanted to film there because the conditions were far worse. The ward that we filmed on was like paradise. It was sparkling and clean. In the women's ward their clothes were ripped. The women's breasts were hanging out. It was more like the image one has for bedlam from centuries ago. They are probably subjected to more inside the wards. Maybe because the technicians are men. One young girl told me and the assistant cameraman how she had been raped by a technician on her ward. We were going to talk to her about it on film a few days later but she didn't show up. But the story was repeated over and over again. In state hospitals about seventy percent of the inmates are women—committed by their husbands after childbirth, or if they are about to leave their husbands. Among the men it's more winos and people who have been in hostile confrontations with the police.

We very much wanted to film in a women's ward but we couldn't get permission. In fact Dr. Ellerbroek was the only one who would let

342

us film anywhere. We went off Ellerbroek's ward once to film the grounds—so they busted us. The only other time we were allowed off the ward was for the "medicine show." That was the monthly meeting between the drug salesmen and the physicians and psychiatrists. This is where the drug salesmen sell their drugs to the doctors, explain them, and give them free samples. They also give away scratch pads and hand lotion and even bigger things to help push their drugs. So that was the only time we were allowed off the ward.

Q. What was your involvement with NAPA after the film was completed?

A. When I was researching the film I went to the American Psychiatric Assocation to see about some research in San Francisco and there was a group of ex-patients handing out literature in the lobby of the psychiatric conference and I talked with them. They were just beginning. So I went to the first meeting of NAPA. It was just part of my research. Then, when the film was near completion I moved to San Francisco to edit the film and needed help moving into a studio. I called up High Energy Movers and the people who arrived turned out to be these ex-patients and they moved the Steenbeck editing table into my studio. They were really nice people and we became good friends and I called them in much later when I'd finished editing to look at the film. They really liked it, so I had the first showing of the film as a benefit for them.

Kevin and I rented the Clay Theater in San Francisco for one night. The theater was jam packed for two shows; you couldn't even walk up the aisle for popcorn. It was a terrific première; Malvina Reynolds sang between shows and the Beggars Theater did street theater outside for the waiting lines. After that Kevin returned to Boston and did a benefit with the Mental Patients Liberation Front at the Orson Welles Cinema. I set up several showings in San Francisco and towns north of there. I was coordinating much of the distribution work with NAPA. The film was a good organizing tool and speakers could follow each showing.

I think the most important showing was in Los Angeles where the film was made. Max and Bob Laemmle were running an independent documentary showcase on Sunday mornings at their Royal Theater in Westwood. It was a good deal, especially when you had no money. They would front the theater costs, some advertisement, help get out a specialized mailing to interested groups, make the theater available for press screenings, and they would give the film maker a scaling gross of the gate, 25-50 percent. We showed the film for three consecutive Sundays, two shows daily. There was a lot of good press. The film was not a great financial success there, but the discussions held in the theater after each show led to the organizing of a NAPA chapter in L.A.

Meanwhile, the hospital was pressing hard to have the film banned in California. News stories would break on TV and in the papers on how the state hospital system was torn with "inner strife" and was about to crack open because of the film and the issues it raised. Jerry Brown had just become governor and appointed Dr. Lackner as director of health. Lackner seemed to support an end to forced drugging of mental patients and was disturbed by the conditions in the hospitals. He refused to act on behalf of the staff to ban the film. Next the CSEA (the state employees union) allied themselves with the hospital and asked Mario Obledo, secretary of health and welfare, to stop the public showings of the film. He screened it and also refused to do anything to prevent it from being shown publicly.

Q. Why did they want it banned?

A. A social worker interviewed in the *L.A. Times* said he felt the film presented a "negative view" and that the public would not understand—they would be "shocked." He also felt one patient who signed an image release was too mentally ill at the time, and that if he'd known the film was to be shown publicly he would not have consented. As to that last remark, the image release he signed stated clearly the film was for the public. He also used to joke about the film becoming another *Godfather*.

Q. Can we return to the distribution of the film and its effect on the general situation?

A. NAPA held a month-long sleep-in at Governor Brown's office demanding an end to forced treatment and slave labor in the state hospitals. This was June 30–July 30, 1976. The film was shown several times in the Capitol building in Sacramento for legislators, aides, secretaries and so on. Then on the 4th of July Dr. Lackner invited the demonstrators to come over in groups to his house for food and a swim. That night Governor Brown showed up and screened *Hurry Tomorrow*. Afterward there was a discussion between him and a few NAPA people, including myself. He promised to investigate the state hospitals, and to make a surprise visit to Metropolitan.

A few months later a major investigation into the state hospitals occurred. There was an enormous amount of good press coverage, particularly in L.A. The investigation turned up several things about wrongful use of drugs, restraints, and denial of patient rights. Most shocking was that in the last three years more than 1,139 patients had died in the 11 California State Hospitals. The investigation finally reduced it to 139 very questionable deaths like drug overdoses. One technician had strangled a patient. Another technician had killed a patient with a blow to the head. The L.A. Coroner's Jury turned in a few verdicts of "death at the hands of another by reasons other than accident," but there have never been any prosecutions.

Governor Brown fired most of the hospital directors and there was a move towards restricting the use of drugs. But so far there has been no evidence of a significant change. Rather than trying to establish rights for the patients, the government has been adding millions to the towering budget for more staff. But all the media stories of the investigation have sown enough seeds. Many legal organizations are taking on court cases now to eliminate involuntary psychiatric treatment.

Q. Did the film get on TV?

A. The major networks didn't seem interested because the film was in black and white. When the investigation broke, the CBS evening news bought two minutes of *Hurry Tomorrow* for a national story. I held back on TV the first year hoping to play the film more in theaters and use it for organizing audiences. Then this year PBS broadcast a 60-minute version of the 80-minute film.

Q. I assume that psychiatrists as well as patients were present at many of the screenings. Can you tell me about the reaction between the two?

A. We showed it many times to NAPA groups and sometimes the discussions got very heated with psychiatrists coming in and talking and arguing. At one time a woman got up and had to be held back from attacking a psychiatrist who was saying these things just aren't true. That happened up at Stanford, at a theater in Palo Alto. A psychiatrist got up and said, "The patients just lie. They say they are having these side-effects from the drugs but it's my experience that they are liars and they don't. You can't believe what they say. You just have to understand that. They're crazy." He didn't know it but one of his patients was down at the other end of the row and stood up and said, "You told me these drugs were safe and that these side-effects I was having were just what I was thinking. Now I see by this film that they are caused by the drugs and other people have them." Then they started yelling at each other and eventually the psychiatrist just walked out of the theater. That sort of thing happened over and over during the discussions.

Q. How much time, altogether, have you devoted to *Hurry Tomorrow* including researching, making, talking, campaigning?

A. Including doing the pilot on *Halfway House*, I suppose three to four years. A year of raising money, a year of making the film and a year of distributing it and talking about it.

# 21

# You Are on Indian Land
## George Stoney

> People should do their own filming, or at least feel they
> control the content. I've spent much of my life making
> films about doctors or teachers or preachers that these
> people ought to have made themselves.
>
> GEORGE STONEY

*The essence of George Stoney's thinking is that film can and should be used
as one of the prime tools for social change. This was the key to his role in the
NFB's "Challenge for Change" program, and is the core of his continuing work
in New York.*

*But what are the responsibilities of the film maker in this task? Where does
one place oneself? Is one's main responsibility to society in general, to the people
being filmed, to the network, or somewhere else entirely? And how and when
should the film maker, if ever, yield up control? These are the questions to which
Stoney has been addressing himself over the last decade and which I tried to
cover in our talk.*

*I met George Stoney in 1961 when he gave me my first real film job. Since
then his ideas have very much influenced my thinking as well as the thinking
of dozens of his students in California, where he taught for a while, and at New
York University. Stoney is not just a film maker but also a passionately concerned thinker, doer, and mover who seems miraculously to have time for
everyone.*

*Most of Stoney's time is now devoted to teaching but he is in fact one of the
most successful producer-directors in the U.S. in the field of sponsored documentaries. One of his main approaches is to develop a fictitious drama to illustrate the way to deal with a certain situation. This method was used to good
effect in* All My Babies, *the best known of Stoney's films, and in* A Cry for
Help *(1962) which was a training film for police dealing with suicide cases.*

*Stoney was born in 1916 and minored in journalism at the University of
North Carolina. Later he worked as a free-lance writer dealing with socially
relevant topics, and contributed to Gunnar Myrdal's 1944 study of blacks in
America,* The American Dilemma.

*In 1946 he joined the Southern Educational Film Service as writer-director
but in 1950 branched out to form his own company. Since then he has made
films on topics ranging from birth control, insurance, and the mentally ill to
the nature of the Baha'i faith and* How the Myth Was Made, *a new look
at the making of Flaherty's* Man of Aran.

*In 1968 his independent film making was suspended for a while when he
moved to Montreal to become Executive Producer of the NFB's "Challenge for*

*Change" series. "Challenge" dealt with a variety of Canadian problems—from the urban poor, to the stricken farmer, to the situation of Canada's Indians. What was fresh about it as a series was its ability to confront and examine the policies of the same government departments which helped fund the program. But the confrontation was done in the spirit of "let's all learn and understand."*

You Are on Indian Land *is one of the "Challenge" films and deals with the problems of the Indians on Cornwall Island whose land is split between the U.S. and Canada. Its specific coverage is that of the one-day blocking of the international bridge across the St. Lawrence by Indians protesting unfair customs charges.*

*Among other things, the film pinpoints the crucial difference between the usual media coverage of certain political events, where a small amount of violence is given a distorting titillating coverage, and the reality of the events themselves.* \**

*Another vital point in the film is that it was used by the Indians to examine their situation and actions while the confrontation with the government was still going on. And it is this sort of element that is at the core of Stoney's thinking: that film should be used by different social groups to examine their stands, their actions, and their images. This kind of film making, according to Stoney, is as necessary as ordinary film making for the general public.*

Q. In the late sixties you were living in New York. You then got involved in the Canadian Film Board's "Challenge for Change," and later became chairman of NYU's undergraduate film division. How did all that happen?

A. Frank Spiller, the NFB's director of English programming, invited me to come to Canada to look at the "Challenge for Change" program with the idea that I might be its executive producer for a couple of years. The Film Board doesn't customarily take people from outside Canada, so this was quite an exceptional experience. I was there for two years, and then I was asked to join NYU. That was in 1970. I really came back home to the U.S. because I thought "Challenge for Change" was a very important concept and I'd like to see it work in my own country. Knowing that it would be almost impossible to do what we were doing in Canada through the U.S. government, I thought maybe a university base might work. So in effect New York University gave me a salary, a place to work, and a license to hunt for money. Soon I met Red Burns and together we found a large grant to start the Alternate Media Center.

*In this context see also* Sunday *by Dan Drasin, which strangely enough shows some of the same police officers from* Indian Land *trying to quell a folk music demonstration.*

347

Our mandate from the foundation was to devote ourselves to experiments in the use of cable television, for local programming, particularly public access programming. My own hope was that this would be one small part of a whole "Challenge for Change" approach, using film, videotape, closed circuit, the whole works. But you know how it is with foundations. They have an idea and you have to fit into their idea in order to get the money.

We started working in cable in New York City, and it was a good time because the city franchises were just opening up. For about two years we helped people here in New York and then in a number of other places to get public access centers going. Red, who has, and had, very strong connections with people in the industry, persuaded some cable companies to put up money for these centers at the beginning, and we worked very hard to help the centers raise their own money to match.

Q. When you came to the National Film Board what was "Challenge for Change" doing? What did you yourself do there and how did the experience of "Challenge for Change" affect your own thinking as to what film could or should be doing?

A. When I arrived they were making films about a number of things—housing, health, Indian affairs. These were made in response to government requests. There were six government departments subscribing to the "Challenge for Change" program. They would put up half the money and the Board would put up the other half. And these films were supposed to elucidate public problems.

This followed the big Fogo Island experiment. *Fogo* was the first of the big film projects done for "Challenge for Change." Colin Low was in charge of that one. His idea was to work with people on a remote island off the coast of Newfoundland. Most of the people were on relief because the in-shore fishing was dying. It was costing the government a great deal to give them public services—education and so forth—so the government was proposing that they move: just clear off the island after being there 300 years. And the government had suggested that Colin and the crew go in and see if they could make films to encourage the people to move.

What they found was that a great many of the people didn't want to move and were willing to make changes in their lives and their ways of doing business in order to stay. So a very useful exchange took place between the people of Fogo and the government through this series of twenty-odd films. From that Fogo experience grew a whole theory of "Challenge for Change."

348

When I arrived the government wanted to do similar films in a number of other places, or I should say, wanted to make similar efforts to use film to promote social change. We soon realized the film crews were too big, the turn-around time too slow, and the costs too high. So Dorothy Henaut and Bonnie Klein suggested that we use videotape.

Q. How would you characterize this new approach? What did you want to do?

A. We wanted to film ordinary people and get them to state their positions. Then we wanted them to reexamine their positions as they play the films back, so strengthening themselves in talking with officials. It gives the officials a clearer view of what people think and what people experience than they would get from the usual official visit. This is a beginning. You usually go through this and then the officials and the people get together.

Q. Probably your most well-known film from your time at the Board is *You Are on Indian Land*. How was that film set up? What had you hoped to do with it?

A. The way it came about was interesting. I'd only been at the Board a short time. We were working with the Indian film crew which had been unfortunately badly set up according to requirements of the Department of Indian Affairs. There were at first eight members, then six as the Indians dropped out. Indian Affairs insisted that they each come from a different tribe—Mikmac on the East Coast to Haida on the West Coast. The only thing that they had in common was that we called them Indians. They came into the Board, were given this very heavy training, and most of them collapsed under it.

One of the few who did well was Mike Mitchell, whose home was close enough that he could live on his own reservation. Mike was one of the young chiefs of the tribe on Cornwall Island in the St. Lawrence River. They had been having a lot of trouble down there with the government because their land is all split up between the U.S. and Canada, and the Indians were being charged duty for bringing their groceries back and forth across the border. So there was a mood to strike. A delegation of Indians went to Ottawa to protest. Mike called me up and said, "If we don't get satisfaction, which I doubt, we're coming back and we're going to block the international bridge." I said, "Well, what do you want me to do?" He said, "If we block the bridge I want a film crew down there."

That was on Friday. Mike would be back the next day, so I immediately went up to the cafeteria and started looking for a crew. Well, this was very unusual at the Board, moving into production so rapidly.

That kind of thing is just not supposed to happen. Fortunately I was an outsider. I didn't know the customs yet, so we were able to get a crew down that night. They were with the Indians the next day so that the situation could be recorded from the Indian viewpoint. And it was. They recorded the happenings and they came back after just a few hours of shooting.

Two days later the Indians came up and said, "We need that film." I said, "Don't be foolish, it's in the lab. It's Christmas holidays and we won't even be able to get it synched up till after New Year." And they said, "We can't wait. The tribe is falling apart. The people who got arrested first are accusing the people who got arrested second of not fighting hard enough. The people who got arrested second are saying that Ernie Benedict sold them out when he finally called off the demonstration."

Q. They wanted to use the film to review their own situation while it was happening?

A. That's right. They said, "We need to see what actually happened." So with the help of the Indians who came up, we were able to put it in synch, and then took it back down unedited, just spliced in chronological order. In the next two weeks it was screened at least ten times, all around the reservation. This clarified what happened for the Indians. Then we said, "All right, now we want to show this to the Royal Canadian Mounted Police and to the other white officials who were involved." The Indians were quite angry about this. They said, "We thought this was *our* film!" I said, "Well, what good is it if you aren't using it with these other people?" So with their cooperation we set up a series of screenings with the RCMP, the local police, and other government officials.

Q. You said before that Mike wanted a crew so that it then could be filmed from the participants' point of view. Now, I seem to recall that this event was also covered by the media. What was the difference between your coverage and the media's coverage in looking at the event?

A. An absolutely fascinating difference, and it's illustrated by an hour-long film put together by the local TV station, called *A Treaty Spurned*. They had gone out there to record the event for quick news coverage. So they had a whole bunch of two-minute clips of violence. They tied all these together with some interviews for the long film after the event with the principals. We, on the other hand, did a recording of the full event, and not just the violent moments. So when you see *You Are on Indian Land* you notice there are long passages of talk be-

350

tween the moments of violence. You begin to see how the violence happens; you begin to see the nature of the violence, and you see the violence tapering off and some more palaver following. You see what a good job the RCMP did, for example; you see what a wretched job the local police did. Because ours was a more open view, this was even more apparent in the three hours of rushes than it is in the 45-minute edited version.

Q. When you came to New York how did you start using the ideas that had been developing at the Film Board, and where did those ideas differ from standard conventional documentary film making?

A. Our fundamental tenet was that people do their own recording. In effect *they* become the film makers. We gave them training here on half-inch video, and they went out and did their thing, although we had some facilitators to do some basic teaching of editing. The idea was that people should do *their own* filming, which is the opposite of always doing films *for* people. I realized that I had spent much of my life making films that doctors ought to have made themselves, that teachers ought to have made themselves, films that preachers ought to have made themselves. And so this gave us a chance to see what it was like when people took a major hand in production. I've since tempered that a bit. I see now that it doesn't matter so much who's handling the camera if the people in front of the camera are controlling the content and *feel* they're controlling the content.

Q. Can you give me any instances of the films made by you or your students in New York where the film maker has been caught between his responsibilities to his own group and his desire to make a conventional documentary?

A. The most obvious case I think is the film called *Godfather Comes to Sixth Street,* a very fine film made by a group from my documentary production workshop lead by Mark Kitchell. Mark was a member of the block association on East Sixth Street when Coppola appeared wanting to use their turf for *Godfather Two,* and Mark proposed to make a film from the point of view of the block association. They had the usual hassles with Paramount and the police and the neighbors and so forth, but they managed to get a lot of good stuff on the screen. They got the change in the neighborhood. They got a beautiful story (and you see it in the finished film) of the neighborhood's response to the whole mystique of film making.

They also got a parallel story which you do not see in the film. That is, that this was an old neighborhood, deteriorating. It used to be "Little Russia." Then it became "Little Italy" with some of the Russians still in there, and then some Puerto Ricans started moving in and American blacks. At the time of the filming the block was about half Puerto Rican.

Everyone wanted to be in the movie. Coppola and his cohorts said, "Yes, we're going to hire people, but they have to look Italian." This seemed to imply very quickly—if you don't look Italian, you're second-rate. And it made a serious breach between the Italians and the Puerto Ricans on the block who had been struggling to find some common ground on which to work together. When the filming began, this division was pointed up by the fact that the Italians were getting the film jobs and the others weren't.

Finally, violence broke out one night when the young Puerto Ricans did about $20,000 worth of damage to the set. We got a little footage of that and put it in the first rough cut.

Then Mark realized that he was going to have trouble with Paramount getting permission to release this film anyway and he saw that he had a film that might get a television release—a film that might get him professional notice. He began to see that he had a more general metaphor in his film beyond the happening on East Sixth Street. What had occurred there happens any time a movie crew moves into a neighborhood. If you put in the fight between the Puerto Ricans and the Italians, it would make it a very *special* case. So he decided that he would leave it out. He wanted to make a half-hour film anyway and his rough cut was very long. I think that when Mark cut out the sequence he weakened his film, although it's still a very good film.

Q. Where would the responsibilities of a film maker lie today?

A. Well I think there is the conventional road for the documentary, informing the general public; and thanks to television the documentary can get to a wide public. However, my feeling is that the documentary approach is being exploited for entertainment purposes by a great many people, especially on TV. Very often the subject matter is chosen for sensational reasons. It's edited for sensational reasons. It's edited to hold an audience before anything else, though there are many exceptions.

I think that there are other roles for the documentarian. For example, we can go back to Grierson's idea, which was that your first duty was to educate the opinion makers—not so much the opinion makers as the policy makers. He said many times that if he could get the right dozen people into a screening room to see a film, he was happy.

My own feeling is that we have another duty, and that is to help people to realize the possibilities of changing their own lives, their situations, and to get them to do something about it. And when they get involved in making media (films, videotapes, audio tapes, whatever) about those problems, or those possibilities, they're more motivated to do so.

Q. You told me once, George, that you'd made fifty documentaries. What have been some of the key ethical problems for you as a film maker that have come up during these films—situations where you've had to examine yourself internally and not just say "is this one going to work filmically?"

A. Well, always there is the question: "Is this scene right for the film, or are you doing this because it's going to make you look good?" I think this is the question that always arises. The next thing is always the exploitation of the individual. They perceive it in one way and the viewers perceive it in another way.

Q. Can you give me specific examples here?

A. Yes. A very early documentary which I think you've seen is called *Palmer Street*. The mother in that film was a marvelous black woman in Gainesville, Georgia. We were an all-white crew, so this was a very strange relationship at the time (1949) but we got to be friendly. Now she insisted on speaking very correct English during the first scenes we were recording, because that's the way she wanted to be perceived at the time. I knew this was going to come across as un- natural, and I was worried about it. I didn't know how to handle the situation—to say, look, you're not talking naturally. I knew it would hurt her. What was I to do? Fortunately her husband got me off the hot seat there, because he came in one day when we were shooting a scene and started making fun of her. And finally she then relaxed and we got much more natural dialogue out of her. But I think you con- stantly have to be aware of how people want to be seen, and help them feel comfortable with themselves. That was long before Black is Beau- tiful was recognized, before black talk was the way people liked to speak.

Q. Have there been occasions where you knew the fact of filming a certain situation was going to make life extremely difficult for the participant long after you'd gone? That when the film would come up, and the people would be seen in the context of their community, they might be ridiculed or laughed at? Has this happened? If so, did you think that the general good coming from the film was worth the in- dividual problems of that scene?

A. A good example of what you're describing came out of a very early "Challenge for Change" experience. I was not there at the time but a beautiful, very moving film called *Things I Cannot Change* was made about a poor family in Montreal—people with nine children. The

353

film recorded the last weeks before they were going to have a tenth child. You realize when that film starts that the last thing that family needs is another child. By the time that child comes you wouldn't, however, want to do away with it. You realize that somehow that family needed this reassurance of itself.

Well, the film was made with great care and was also made the way we ought to make films, by winning the confidence of the people. Any good documentary director sets a climate in which his cast can behave normally. However, often they don't realize what this is going to mean to their futures. And there is no way that you can explain that to them. So *you* have to make the judgments if they're going to expose themselves. And you have this to wrestle with in the editing room.

The young lady who made *Things I Cannot Change*, which was her first film, didn't do that. These people gave her their souls, in effect. She put their souls on the screen. And as I say, it's a very moving film. The first time that family saw that film was on TV, and their neighbors saw it at the same time. The children became the butts of jokes. The family began to see themselves as other people saw them—as poor people without dignity. That's the way the neighbors perceived them anyway, and they literally had to move.

It was a family on the brink of breakup anyway. The father was an alcoholic, mostly unemployed, a kind of bragger. All of this came across in the film. Most of those who saw the film outside the neighborhood had a very warm reaction to it. Yet the family was deeply hurt by it. Now, my own hunch is that this came about, not because the film was made as it was, but because the film was not introduced properly. The way I would have handled that film (and the way I do handle my films) would have been to show the film to the family in rough cut, and get their reactions and talk to them about it. Help them learn to deal with it. Then I would have set up screenings where they brought in their neighbors and friends and we could have talked about why the film was made. This way they might have begun to see the film in context so that by the time the film was actually seen by the general public they would know what's there, and would have been proud of what they had done, rather than ashamed or betrayed. Because it's usually two sides of the coin.

It's like the Loud family in *An American Family*. You remember, Craig Gilbert who produced that series said the Loud family saw every foot of film and approved it. Of course they did, because they were seeing it completely out of context. They didn't know what the public's response was going to be and they weren't prepared for that.

Now I have a method of preparing myself and other people for films which I've used since 1960. Any time we make a film we do a trial mix of the sound and we take it out in double system and we show it to a lot of representative audiences. We do this first to see what we've got, and to feel an audience response. We know if things are misinterpreted then. And at that stage we can always go back and change it. I found that when I take people along in this way, we don't have that kind of problem.

Q. What have you been doing recently on videotape?

A. Well, I do a lot of videotaping. It's the thing I get the most pleasure out of, because now that I own my own portapack, I can do pretty much what I damn please. I've never been able to do that with film because of the cost.

What I like about the portapack is that it's a marvelous way of bridging the gap that develops in the modern world between people. Playback is of course a vital part of this and I always carry along a monitor. I was in Nigeria, for example, and I would go into a remote village, do a little taping and then hook the monitor up to a battery, take my belt off and hang the monitor in a tree and play it back. People would recognize themselves and usually I could tape anything in the village after that.

But I have found that a great many people are disturbed by their own image. This is not easy to perceive because people *seem* so anxious to see themselves and when they see themselves they always smile. But to say that they enjoy it is very often incorrect. You can't deny your own image. It's there. So you're not going to say you don't like it, though you might say "I look awful." But very often you dread to see it.

For years I used to see myself on film at the end of shots, catching the baby or holding the slate and frowning into the sun, so I always had an excuse for the way I look. But on videotape I began to see myself more and more and there was no escaping it. I am as old as I am. I'm skinny and bald and kind of funny-looking. But then after a long time I realized that nobody seems to mind. They just accepted me anyway. So I've begun to accept myself. But this takes time, and I think that people often need help to do that.

When I go into a place to shoot I try and put myself or my companions on tape first so they can see that the gun can shoot both ways— that we're not afraid to be on view ourselves. And then I do my best to see how people *like* to be seen. What are they proud of? Perhaps it's a homemade gun like the one I saw in an African village. Or it may be their hairdo or their garden or whatever. And after you tape that then you come to other things—but what you've done before makes them feel at ease.

It's a trick in a way but also I think it shows a certain amount of respect. What you do is get people coming across more fully themselves. This is quite different from the usual TV reporter's idea of cutting people down, exposing people, catching people off guard—what Geraldo Rivera once described to me as those "golden moments" when politicians' false teeth fall out. This I abhor, whereas the first method is what filming is all about.

*Liberation Calls*

# 22
## *Antonia*
### *Jill Godmilow*

*When I first met Jill Godmilow there was a certain shyness and wariness, but this soon melted into an openness, and an obvious desire to make contact. One quickly senses both her warmth and her strength. I suppose "direct" may be one of the best words to describe her. So we chatted about* Antonia *but also got onto the state of the nation, the joys of Balkan singing, and jeep riding in the Israeli deserts.*

*Although Godmilow's name came to the fore in 1974 with the success of* Antonia *she had already, at that time, been working in film for seven years. Her first film* La Nueva Vida *was made in 1967 with her Puerto Rican boyfriend for $2,000. The genesis of this film, full of beautiful blondes and handsome dark men in night clubs, is amusingly described in Sharon Smith's* Women Who Make Movies.* *The film was never finished and according to Godmilow "still sits in a closet somewhere unmixed and unloved." After* La Nueva Vida *Godmilow moved into cutting commercials and editing documentaries for KQED in San Francisco.*

*For a while Godmilow was involved in a film commune in California but evidently few of the projects ever came to fruition. Godmilow got work as an assistant editor on* The Godfather *and then on* The Candidate *which featured Robert Redford.*

*Disliking the Hollywood set-up, she returned to New York to work on* Tales. *The film concerns itself with women's attitudes to their own sexuality and was made with Cassandra Gerstein.*

*The original impetus for* Antonia *came from Judy Collins, the folk singer. Collins had been one of Dr. Antonia Brico's students and had stayed close to her teacher through the years. However, what was seen originally as a meeting and study for a magazine article somehow slipped into a concept for a film.*

*Antonia is a portrait of a few months in the life of Dr. Brico, a symphony conductor in her early seventies. For an hour the film follows her through her*

*Sharon Smith, *Women Who Make Movies* (London: Hopkinson and Blake, 1975).

*daily activities, including music classes and performances with the Denver Symphony Orchestra. Interwoven are memories of past friends such as Dr. Albert Schweitzer, and the sheer trials and tribulations of being a woman conductor trying to succeed in the musical scene.*

Antonia *got rave reviews with a great deal of emphasis being placed on it as a tract for female emancipation. According to Grace Lichtenstein in* The New York Times *it was "a feminist documentary about the still overwhelmingly male chauvinist world of music, made by women working in the male chauvinist world of film."*

*In many ways I think this emphasis is wrong, though it certainly helped sell the film.* Antonia *is a fine, well-made film but not really a piece of women's propaganda. However its timing was fortuitous. In 1974 there were few films by, for, or about women and a gentle film like* Antonia *not only fitted the role, but could easily be accepted by men without really challenging their beliefs as other women's films were to do.*

*Both the strength and clarity of Godmilow as a film maker emerge clearly from the discussion. One sees all this particularly in her analysis of the relationship with Judy Collins and her very forthright remarks on objectivity. About the latter she says, and I think she's right, that the main task may not be to understand "objective facts" but rather to understand where a subject is speaking from. This seems to me one of the most important things in her interview, along with her description of trying to take on independent distribution.*

*After finishing* Antonia, *Godmilow directed* Where Do All the Mentally Ill Go? *for WNBC and* Louise Nevelson, *a portrait of the artist, for WNET. The latter was co-produced and co-directed by Susan Fanshel, another very talented New York film maker.*

*Two of the most important elements in Godmilow's life appear to be music and Eastern European culture (the latter a partial result of a B.A. in Russian literature). Both elements came together in* The Popovich Brothers of South Chicago *(1978). On the surface it's a celebration of the brothers, their friend Pete Mistovich, and their Serbian music group. On a deeper level it's a warm exploration of a folk heritage and tradition.* The Popovich Brothers *is very much a labor of love. As Godmilow says, "I'm sensitive to women in any situation but it's not my main theme. My strongest direction is music. That's what I really love and want to keep making my films about."*

Q. What did you see as the options for your career when you'd finished work on *The Candidate?*

A. I'd very much enjoyed working on *The Candidate*, had enjoyed working with Redford, and ended up down in L.A. with the feeling that if I wanted to stay and become a big feature editor, I could do it. I had done a good job and had an entree to various producers. But I took a good hard look at everything and decided to come back to New York and make my own films instead.

Q. What kind of projects were bubbling through your mind then?

A. No projects. I just knew that I wouldn't survive that Hollywood life. It was a total turnoff to me. There were too many absurdities that entered into the actual film process and that made me crazy. Too many egos that insisted that it be cut another way or mixed again for political reasons or for ego reasons or money reasons. It was too far removed from what film making was supposed to be for me. Generally it had been an enormous disappointment to work on features and I had no desire to continue. Now I have vague dreams that someday I'll write a script and I'll direct one of those, but I would have to do it in a different way.

So I came back to New York to think. I'd already made a few films before California including a film called *Tales*, with four or five other women, which was extremely experimental. It was about sex, really, way before the feminist revolution and it was scandalous at the time and very few people understood it. It was about people telling sex stories but telling them as they tell them in a social situation, the way a man tells another guy all about "last night with the most beautiful chick he ever had and how they fucked all night." It was about the language men use and about women and the kind of stories women tell and the language *they* use. It was in the Whitney's First Young American Film Makers Series and nobody knew what to make of it. It was way-out.

The strangest thing about that film is that it's still circulating around a little bit now and because *Tales* was produced by women, it gets programmed by people who haven't ever seen it, with lots of very strong feminist films. *Tales* was made before any kind of feminist consciousness and the content of the film is, on one level, quite sexist, and I am constantly running into people who attack me for it—with "What kind of feminist are you?" Various radical feminists have attacked me for this film because it lacks a clear feminist consciousness, which is true. But it was made "before the revolution," and before many of us had a clear feminist consciousness, including my attackers. In the end I do think it takes on, pretty seriously, the question of male-female sexual attitudes, which no one else was doing at the time.

Q. How did you start working with Judy Collins, and how did *Antonia* begin?

361

A. Judy had grown up in Denver and Antonia Brico had been her piano teacher. *Ms.* magazine had asked Judy to do an article about a strong female influence on her life and she chose Antonia. She also decided to film the interview. Judy had seen some of my work, found my number, and called me up out of the blue to come and help her and show her how to use a camera. I told her I was not a camera-woman, I was a director-editor, but I would go with her, and maybe, if she was serious about film making, instead of messing around with a nonprofessional camera and trying to interview and direct and shoot at the same time, we could put a small professional crew together with good 16mm equipment and shoot the interview seriously. Then she could look at the footage and decide whether she wanted to get any further involved in film making.

Q. At that time it was only going to be a simple interview?

A. Yes. I asked a friend of mine, Coulter Watt, if he'd shoot it for nothing, I did the sound, and then the two of us and Judy went out to Denver and filmed what now constitutes the major interview in the film.

Q. The interview at breakfast?

A. That's right. At the kitchen table. On that trip we also shot, just because it was happening, a rehearsal of her community orchestra. That's the first rehearsal in the film.

Q. When you interviewed was there any particular line that you wanted to pursue?

A. I was working blind. Now I struggle with such consciousness of what's right and what's wrong to do. I knew nothing more about Antonia than what Judy told me on the plane out there. I was just free-wheeling in some crazy way and not worried at all. I guess I had some idea that it would be biographical for starters but what became apparent almost immediately was that Antonia was a wonderful storyteller and engaging speaker, and would tell her own story without my questions and answers. So there I was, turning on and off the camera when I felt it was relevant. I was extremely lucky that she was so vital and so ready to talk because I was quite unprepared otherwise. I was really innocent, but could only work that way once.

One of the great things about that interview, and it was throughout the whole film, is that Antonia is such a non-media person. She doesn't go to the movies or watch television, *ever*, so that she had no conception that she was "on" or anything. She thought it was just Judy and a couple of friends making home movies so there was never that tension which you almost always get in other situations. Anyway, back in New

York, I synched it all up for Judy, talked to her about how it could become a film, what else I would shoot and approximate cost. Judy was interested and decided to go ahead and put her money down.

Q. How were you thinking about the film at that stage?

A. I picked up the themes that I thought were most important, the woman theme, the teacher—what a teacher is, what teaching really should be—and there was Antonia talking about her teachers in a way that was overwhelming to hear. And then there was that situation where she was teaching. So it seemed that that was one place to focus.

Q. Where did you go for the money?

A. Judy put up all the money. I couldn't believe it. In fact, I tried to talk her out of doing that because I think there's always a conflict between creative production and financial control on a film. For instance, if you go over budget you tend to suddenly not want to spend more money if it's yours. Whereas if it's someone else's, you're totally involved in the film's point of view and you say, we *have* to do this and you find the money somehow.

So I was very worried about it. At one point, some investors were found who were interested and ready to contribute (I think that was only because of Judy's name), but in the end she decided that she didn't want to share the producer role and wanted to put up all the money herself, so she did, very generously.

Q. How did you work out the different functions of Judy and yourself: were there any problems or difficulties as to defining your different roles?

A. Judy was quite unhappy about it at first but I insisted, upon threat of not working on the film, that there be an equal collaboration and parallel credit. Judy put up all the money for the film so she took the producer's credit. I did all the editing, so I took that credit. And then we split the director's credit. Once we'd agreed to these terms we managed to get through all those moments of violent disagreement when either of us was absolutely certain the other was wrong. This equality of status was essential in an understanding like this. It was what held our partnership together when either of us made a move for "control." Without that equal status that guarantees those differences *must* be resolved, someone always wins and someone always loses.

All the ideas about what, where, when, how, and why to shoot were mine but were discussed fully with Judy beforehand as much as possible. Obviously the film could not have been made without her, her money, her relationship to Antonia, and her commitment to the project. But I was the film maker, and as cool as I would like to appear about this issue I really resent it when the press and others who should know better speak or write about "Judy Collins's film."

Q. When you went back to Antonia and explained the idea of a full film about her, what was her reaction? Where did she think the film ought to go?

A. Antonia never put forth what she thought. She was a wonderful subject in that way. I think she expected that in some general way the film would help her career. But she was incapable of conceiving what that film would be, or of verbalizing any boundaries. In fact I felt that if she had, there would have been trouble. I feel very, very strongly about the subject of the documentary film having no "editing rights" and I wouldn't start a film if that wasn't absolutely clear.

Q. Did you at any stage show Antonia anything you'd shot?

A. I showed her a couple of rolls of that first rehearsal that we shot. She was very unresponsive to it. Didn't say much. She was trusting Judy I think, totally trusting Judy. It was rare. I don't find that common.

Q. Were there any sections that you cut out of the film? Basic elements that you thought about or developed but then in the final editing didn't use?

A. I shot one scene that was stupid, which I shot out of a paranoia about how limited the film was going to be in terms of location and texture. I was desperately searching for some other activity of Antonia's, some location which could provide space and tone, other than rehearsal and interviews for the film. Antonia was going out to some elementary school to speak about Holland (her birthplace) to a second-grade class and I actually tracked out there with my crew and filmed it. It was very charming and she was wonderful with the children and it had nothing whatsoever to do with the film I was making so I never even processed the negative. Other than that, the film was shot about 10 to 1—extremely tight.

Q. There seems to be in the film almost a kind of parallel. You have a very sweet young woman who is a pianist who obviously has talent, who's very warm and very affectionate and you have the older woman Antonia. I find myself thinking what's going to happen to this young woman as a pianist? Were you thinking about these parallels?

A. Yes, I was very aware of it. Just raising that question of, all right, here's a sixteen-year-old pianist who's just determined to go on, in fact, she's at Juilliard now. What kind of limitations will happen to her? You know, where will she get stopped, if at all, because she's a woman?

Q. About a third of the way through the film really takes off on, I won't say feminist tracks, but it gets into the meat of the film and how unjustly Antonia's career has been treated. And the basic issue is put forth that she is an extremely talented conductor but as a woman she can't succeed. Did you in terms of objectivity or any other words you want to use like that, did you think of investigating how many men conductors were out of work at that time? Whether it was a general situation or whether it's a situation very specific to Antonia as a woman?

A. No, because I am not interested in establishing the facts and the quote "objective truth" about a situation. I am not interested in that in a documentary. I am interested in people and how they relate their story. At one point Judy and I were very paranoid about that issue. How could we make this film about a woman who says, in her own words, that she never had a chance, without providing a scene in the film where, in fact, she has the opportunity to prove that she's a fantastic conductor?

We considered, in very paranoid moments, getting some famous conductor to say on camera, "Yes, she's very good," proving in other words that yes, she could have been great if she'd had a chance. And then I thought that was not the film's duty and it is not my duty to prove that. I'm presenting a human being who has a story to tell and I don't have anything to prove. I guess it really influenced my whole way of thinking about documentaries. I don't believe in that "objective truth."

It's hard sometimes because you get fearful that an audience won't stay with you without the facts but I want the audience to believe the person who's speaking—not believe that they're right, but understand where they're speaking from and why and, if I "proved," if I brought in some objective reality or expert to talk about the subject, to prove that yes it's true, I think I would lose something.

Q. There's a very sweet moment at the end where Antonia loosens up and she's playing pop music on the piano. Is that your suggestion or is that something she would generally do?

A. No. She was extremely worried about it which is why I leave in that line about, "I'm not sure I want this public, my dear," so that I can use it in the film. I wanted her to at least make that statement about being very nervous about showing it. In fact, when she saw the finished film, it's the only thing she felt negative about. I tried to explain to her why it was important that it be there. She does mess around like that in loose moments, very rare loose moments. Judy had told me that she plays old barrelhouse stuff and I pushed that she play for us that night. I always feel that it's important at the end of a film not to leave an audience feeling that the world is screwed up, that

365

there's no way to win. I thought that one of the strongest things that you could take from Antonia was her energy and her spirit and I wanted that to be the last impression of her.

I should add that her objections were based on very real issues. She's a woman who has essentially struggled with an image problem all her life—that of being a woman. Her fear was that if the world out there saw her being so loose and messing around, she wouldn't be taken seriously as an artist.

She was also terribly concerned that her age not be revealed in the film, because age is another image problem for a conductor these days. There's a heavy youth cult on now. Ozawa conducts three major orchestras and old people are kind of being retired earlier, so someone who's struggled with those kind of problems all her life is very nervous about being silly and "too old" on camera.

Q. Did you find any point of struggle between things that you realized you needed for the film and a sense of privacy that had to be maintained for Antonia? You mentioned her playing the pop songs. Was there anything else like that?

A. Yes, the big kitchen scene where she blows up had to be provoked.

Q. That is where she starts talking about her problems of being a woman conductor.

A. She gets very, very angry.

Q. How did you provoke that?

A. I had Judy ask a very stupid question to which she already knew the answer, and to which I knew Antonia knew she knew the answer. Antonia refused to bite for the first few times and Judy kept asking her, "But Antonia, you have this wonderful community orchestra and you have your marvelous studio and you have these wonderful students and you were a pioneer. Really now Antonia, what more do you want?" And she looked at Judy with disbelief the first few times and finally she stood up at the table and I signaled the cameraman, "Let's go." And she's staring down at Judy and she just hammered away about, "Do you know what it's like to have five concerts a year instead of five concerts a month?" The kitchen was tiny and there was no way to get back from Antonia, so I told the cameraman to just keep moving around there and hand-hold; I wanted it rough and I wanted it strong.

I considered the issue very seriously before I provoked her like that. I knew it was going to take her "out there" and it did. She was very shook up when she finished and she was angry at us for having done it. We had to live with that for a while. She said, "It's all very fine for you to bring these feelings out and then leave with it on your film, but I have to live with them." And that's why I leave in that line where she says, "I don't discuss my heartbreak every day."

Q. Despite the intimacy of the film, there is very little discussion of Antonia's feelings about being a woman, only her feelings about her music. Did you purposely avoid this part of her life?

A. I think that's just a technique I favor when interviewing. If you get someone talking about something that really interests them, they reveal themselves by their body movements, their gestures, their language. You can read how they feel about themselves. I never go head on, besides which, I think I would have gotten a kind of stock answer to questions like that, which don't reveal much and which everyone's heard a thousand times. I wanted to allow her to present herself as a person—not only as a frustrated woman.

Q. Had you come to any arrangement with Antonia on censorship? If there were certain scenes which offended her, would you have been willing to take them out? Or did she give you *carte blanche*?

A. It was just not discussed and I would have argued strongly against making any kind of arrangement other than total control. The biggest problems were really between Judy and myself. Judy had a much more protective instinct toward Antonia. Judy kept asking people that she trusted (some of her music teachers and friends) about certain things. Someone told her, "Oh, you can't use that Schweitzer scene because there are a lot of people in the music business who think Schweitzer is a phony, not a great expert on Bach, so that has to come out." And I had to say, (and it was a long battle, believe me), "It's terribly important to hear Antonia talk about him in that way—to talk about what teachers have meant to her and to get a sense of what kind of romantic father-figure he was. It's emotionally so important for the film." Judy felt she had to protect Antonia from saying things that might be embarrassing, or from being too emotional, and my sense was that this kind of thing was the meat of the film.

Q. Were you and Judy in basic agreement on the lines of the editing?

A. We had major battles but I think we worked them out in a true, very true collaboration. It is very difficult, I think, collaborating with someone on a really equal basis. I've done it once since and it's valuable and I'll try it again but it's hard. And it was interesting where the struggle was coming from. I was coming from, "It has to be *my* way because I am the film professional and I am going to look like an ass if it's not exactly how I want it." Judy was coming from, "I'm the public person and the famous person so it has to be as I see it because look how much I have at stake." But we got those things out front early in the editing process so that later discussions were about real issues. We worked out almost everything.

Q. What was the cost for it?

A. The cost didn't work out that high: $60,000, which I consider a very moderate budget. Judy would have gone higher, if it had taken more.

Q. Where did you go with the film once it was finished?

A. We were fabulously naive. I had not really been through that kind of process before, and somehow we had expected that we could sell it to commercial television. It was essentially inoffensive material. It wasn't a particularly political film. It was a loving film and it was a cultural film. We blindly imagined that it was also a good film. That we could sell it to CBS or ABC.

And that's where we started. Judy had enough contacts to get us in to all of the vice-presidents in charge of programming. They loved the film and asked to borrow the print and take it home because they thought their wives would like to see it. At the same time they said (and this is a line I've heard many times since), "We have no way to program it." At that point Judy was negotiating some kind of concert arrangement with the William Morris Agency here in New York, one of the biggest, and she asked them if they would take it on. They were being very nice to her, so they "took it on." It took them three months to show it to their television experts who evaluated it and came back with the conclusion, "No, we cannot sell it to commercial television."

I was stumped. I thought, well what do you do with one of these films? That had not been a question either of us had really addressed all the time we were making the film. I started to go to the nontheatrical distributors. The almost universal response was, "If you'll cut it down to 29 minutes we might take it on." I couldn't believe it.

I know a lot now about that market and they say that because they are for the most part only interested in and capable of selling films that easily fit the narrow "educational film form." A film has to be 29 minutes because it has to be "classroom length." They want a short film so that they can have time for a 20-minute discussion afterwards. Distributors only want to sell exactly what they think teachers want, and they have no energy nor desire to make any special effort for a film that is, quote, "educational in some other way." So the basic response was, "It's very lovely but we don't want to take it on." Again I was in disbelief.

368

About the same time, I was beginning to enter *Antonia* in festivals and getting unbelievable positive feedback from audiences. Ann Arbor was a huge success and then we had it at the Flaherty seminar and a hundred film makers stood up and applauded. I was getting angrier and angrier about the kind of responses I was getting from the official world of film distribution in the face of such hearty audience approval, and then I met a man named Jerry Brock. He is the film maker who made *I. F. Stone's Weekly* and he had distributed it himself. He got hold of me and said, "You have to distribute *Antonia* yourself and I will help you."

He is an extremely generous guy and he had been amazingly successful distributing his own film. He had already done about 15 strong, successful theatrical runs with his 68-minute black-and-white documentary and was also doing a brisk business in library sales and university rentals. He told me, "You have to do it for political reasons because you have the opportunity to open up actual theatrical situations for documentaries and you have to do it for your own career." And somehow he convinced me to take it on. I had a sense of myself (as a woman) of being incapable in financial and business matters, but he promised to help and he did.

Then I had to convince Judy and her lawyers and accountants who were beginning to be financially interested in this film (which had previously been "Judy's folly"—for throwing $60,000 away "on this idiocy"). These advisors of hers were beginning to talk to people in the film business and suddenly they began to understand that they had a modest commodity on their hands. It was all very complicated but in the end Rocky Mountain Productions, Judy's own company, retained the rights and I distributed it for them for a year and a half.

Q. How do you go about this kind of distributing?

A. I followed Jerry Brock's lead almost entirely. First I tried to get the major film critics to write about it, which is an almost impossible task. They don't review these films. You have to drag them to screenings, which means finding some kind of showcase to start with in New York. New York is the key, and fortunately I was here. So I did all that: made posters, press releases, called every critic in town—and they came and they liked it and they wrote wonderful zappy reviews on the film. Jay Cocks and *Time* said it was one of the best ten films of the year. We were lucky.

We got very good responses. I had the opening slot at the Whitney which is a wonderful showcase in New York because it's a real run. It's not like an afternoon screening at the Museum of Modern Art—

it's two solid weeks of screenings. It was packed every night. Suddenly somewhere on the Upper East Side there was this new film that everyone was talking about.

The idea was to move it, very quickly, from the Whitney into a theatrical situation, which we did. We ran ten weeks at a downtown theater in the Village, then transferred it to an upper west-side theater. As soon as that was going I started negotiating for a Boston run. I went everywhere myself and in the end, I did twenty cities. I went to every one of them, never making enormous amounts of money but establishing what Jerry calls "a pedigree" for the film by having it play in real theaters and getting it constantly reviewed and getting people to talk about it. Now all this made it an extremely desirable film in the nontheatrical market—a film that, even though it was an hour, a teacher of women's studies is going to rent and feel that she had to have it.

Q. Do you think there's anything about a right sense of timing? That the critics or the public were waiting for a major women's film breakthrough?

A. Timing was crucial. We were three quarters into the women's movement and there was a woman's audience out there ready to go, ready to try new things like this. That was part of my nontheatrical technique. In cities where I couldn't be until the day before the theatrical opening, I would hook up with a women's group that was, for instance, trying to raise money for a health clinic, and offer them a benefit for opening night. Since they were there and they had numbers, they could plaster the town with posters and set up TV and radio interviews for me so that by the time I got there the night before the opening, a lot of work had been done. I would come into town with a big bang. This is all small potatoes in the big world but for a documentary film it was big stuff. The women's group would make some money and I would have a great first night. And if that movement hadn't been there I would have had very little success, I think, no matter what.

Q. Do you think the film could have been done by a man or was there a certain sympathy between yourself and Judy and Antonia which wouldn't have been possible with a male director?

A. I think in general, Antonia would have related differently to a man. I don't think a man would have gotten the same kind of stories about her childhood. She would have presented a different front, much less vulnerable. But who am I to say there isn't a male film maker who could have gained her trust and gotten that intimacy.

370

Q. There are a number of women film makers now who are very intimately tied up in doing films about the women's situation in America and women's problems. Do you find yourself within that orbit or on the sides?

A. For a while I did feel obliged to be compulsive about being a "feminist film maker," and I was driving myself crazy, trying to come up with women's subjects. But my strongest direction is music and in fact I have embarked on a heavy music film. That's really where I live and love and I want to keep making music films. I think I'm sensitive to women in any situation, but it's not my main theme.

Q. *Antonia* comes out as what one might loosely call a feminist film, and yet it seems to me a very subtle, loose, soft, gentle feminist film. How do you think this works as against the more radical, more committed women's film?

A. Well, I don't think it was a completely conscious decision, but somehow I found out a lot about myself and film concepts on that issue. I avoided consciously and unconsciously making a radical statement about Antonia. As a film maker, I never wanted to say, "Women don't get a chance and men are pigs for doing this to them." That's why I let Antonia's voice be the only voice in the film. I think I have a much, much larger audience in this way than if I had made a film that had a lot of political statements in it about what happens to women and what happens to men and who's doing what to whom.

Audiences for the film, theatrically and nontheatrically, have been consistently mixed equally. Women brought their boyfriends and some men came along because it was considered a good film that you could learn something from and that wasn't an anti-male film. I thought that was fantastically important to the success of the film, and I don't think I'll ever take a hard line. I think if you take a hard line, you don't "see." I think if the film has something to prove, then the film isn't open, can't investigate, and the pressure on the film maker to edit the material so that it effectively proves some line is a limitation that I don't ever want to work with.

I come back with footage. I look at it again and again and again. I find out how it makes me feel. I take those feelings and I try to amplify them in a form that will communicate to an audience. I use myself as a vehicle for the way I responded in a certain place with a certain person and I work very hard to keep my "ideas" out of the film. Now that only works for a certain kind of film but that's the kind of film I want to make.

371

# 23

# *Grey Gardens*
## *Ellen Hovde*

*The dynamics of cutting a* vérité *film can be murderous. Sixty to ninety hours of film may be dumped in an editor's lap, who is then told to go ahead, often without any guide from the director or producer. Often it is up to the editor to "find" the film, to sort out the threads, to see if there is indeed any main story. The problem is how to make shape and sense out of this ungodly mess.*

*I chose to speak to Ellen Hovde about this for two reasons. First, she is one of the most gifted, articulate, and intelligent* vérité *editors around. In addition, she had just finished work on* Grey Gardens *which seemed to me one of the best* vérité *films of recent years, and one which I wanted to explore in detail, particularly in regard to the editing process.*

*Though now well-known as a film maker Hovde started as a drama student at the Carnegie Mellon Institute in Pittsburgh. After a short period in the theater as an actress and electrician she turned to film, where she has been working ever since as editor, director, and producer.*

*Her credits include a number of films made for NET, among them* Head Start in Mississippi *(producer) and Margaret Mead's* New Guinea Journal *(editor). She has also worked for CBS, and in 1969 edited* Songs of America, *a CBS special with Simon and Garfunkel.*

*Though an excellent director in her own right, Hovde is probably best known through her association with the Maysles brothers. Her earliest work with the Maysles was as co-editor with Charlotte Zwerin on* Salesman *(1966). In 1970 she again collaborated with them and Zwerin as co-editor on* Gimme Shelter, *a nonfiction feature about the Rolling Stones. On both* Christo's Valley Curtain *(1974) and* Grey Gardens *(1975) she is credited as co-director along with David and Albert Maysles, with Muffie Meyer making up the fourth director in the latter film.*

Grey Gardens *provides a portrait of two unusual women—Edith Bouvier Beale (Big Edie) and her 55-year-old unmarried daughter Edie (Little Edie). They are respectively Jacqueline Onassis's aged aunt and first cousin, and lead a squalid hermit-like existence in a crumbling East Hampton mansion on Long Island. This house—the Grey Gardens of the title—was in the news some years ago when its decay and neglect brought it to the attention of the local authorities.*

*The film reveals the intimate details of the lives of the two women. There is constant bickering between mother and daughter in messy cluttered rooms full of masses of cats and unwashed plates. The mother sings "Tea for Two" from the bed; downstairs Little Edie dances for the film makers. Their strengths and their vanities are there for all to see. And so are the dreams and memories of riches and social glory, and the romance and despair of marriage hopes that never came to fulfillment.*

*It is a beautifully wrought film revealing more about human relationships than almost any film I can remember. When it was first shown, though its artistry was praised, it was subject to violent criticism in regard to its ethics, revelations, and general approach. What right do the film makers have—so ran the comments—to invade the privacy of the women and to put their troubles and flaws in front of the masses? And even if permission was granted—the comments continue—the women obviously could never have understood what they were letting themselves in for.*

*These are pertinent and important questions in documentary, particularly because film making ethics are so rarely discussed. In this situation, however, I think the critics were wrong and I totally agree with Hovde when she talks about these points.*

*Since completing* Grey Gardens *Hovde has produced and directed* Middle Age, *a film shown as part of the "Woman Alive" series on educational TV. She directed (again with the Maysles and Muffie Meyer)* The Burk Family, *and produced and directed several films for "Sesame Street." She has also received a grant from the National Endowment of the Arts to produce and direct a dramatic film with Mirra Banks based on a story by Grace Paley.*

Q. The last few years you have been associated with the Maysles brothers on various films. What were you doing before that—how did you come into films?

A. Well, I came into films years ago, through editing. I had originally gone to drama school to be a stage director, and didn't find enough work to keep me together. I then found a job in a film school as an administrative assistant, got interested in film, and soon apprenticed myself to a film editor who taught at the school.

I felt that, at least in documentary film (I haven't had much experience in theatrical film, though I'm producing and directing one now), the person who is doing the editing is doing something very like a mix of writing and stage directing: that person is shaping, forming and structuring the material, and making the decisions about what is really going to be there on the screen—what the ideas are, what the order of events will be, where the emphasis will be.

These responsibilities very often rest almost entirely with the editor.

373

Some documentary directors do sit in the cutting room and take part in these decisions, but many do not. Many simply give the editor the footage and say, "When you have a cut, let me know . . . ," and they go away. So the editor, alone, makes absolutely basic decisions—the sort of decisions that the director and producer, when they come back, have to base their decisions *upon*. They may have photographic memories or may have taken detailed notes about the material. They will say, "Look, there must be a better shot than that," or "We must somehow make the point how poor these people are" and so on—all valuable criticisms. But the way things are structured, and whether the film is "working" to make the desired points—that is really done in the cutting room.

Q. Are you talking basically about *cinéma vérité* or have you worked with the old prestructured, pre-scripted films? How do you get the balance between the director's responsibility and yours?

A. I've worked with all those systems. There are documentaries that are prestructured—some people even record a narration first and then have you go out and shoot pictures to fit it. Quite boring. Yes, I've done that. And then there are those montages that everyone used to do, usually to music—commercials still use that technique. It's difficult to do well, and it's certainly the editor who makes it work if it's going to. But it's in *cinéma vérité* that the editing takes on the same importance as the camera work—and camera work and editing combined *are* directing, in *cinéma vérité*.

Q. What was the first *vérité* film that you cut?

A. Oh, boy! I suppose it was at a company called "Filmmakers," with Bob Drew and Ricky Leacock and Don Pennebaker; and the Maysles were there as well. We did many films—in fact, we all learned how to do this as we went along, by working on films like *Susan Starr*. Then there was a film about the Aga Khan, then a film called *The Chair*, about a man who is about to electrocuted, Paul Crump. And there were films with the Kennedys and so on.

Q. What did you learn during that time about that new style of editing totally nonscripted films?

A. Well, first of all, speaking technically, we had to develop a whole new attitude toward how the film would *look*. The camera wasn't on a tripod anymore and was swooping around all over the place, zooming in to find focus and zooming out again (often in the middle of something very important!), running out of film at the worst possible moments—and of course nothing was repeatable, it was real life. So we would cut and patch and discard old conventions and invent new ones.

374

On the good side the films had a kind of new vitality and energy that was very exciting; on the bad, we all sometimes tried to push footage around and convince ourselves we *had* something on film, that we didn't.

But I guess the most important thing we learned was that you have to take an enormous amount of material, shot in real time, and sift it and sort it and condense it into a "dramatically told" story. People who shoot this kind of film shoot a lot, because if you are shooting an event that doesn't have those predetermined beginnings, middles, and ends, you don't *know* where the critical moment is going to be—often you don't even know what the *story* is going to be. You think you do, because you've got to have something to hold on to when you're shooting, but unless it's a film like *On The Pole*, which was another of those Filmmakers films—a film about the Indianapolis 500, and you know there is going to be a race and there's going to be a finish to the race—unless it's like that, you don't actually know in a lot of these films what the outcome is going to be, or who the important character will be.

The first person who has to contribute to those decisions is the person who decides to film that particular situation; and then the cameraperson, whoever that is, has to make a constant, running series of split-second decisions about what's happening and what will happen next and how important it is. The person who is taking sound is often the so-called journalist or reporter, and he or she is often nudging the cameraperson, saying oh, do that, do that, while the cameraperson is doing this, and this. (If they have a good rapport they work it out between them; if not, well, cameramen have been known not to shoot any close-ups simply because they didn't like the person they were filming, or to shoot very badly a scene they didn't want to shoot. Editors of course also do such things by making a poor cut of a sequence they don't believe in.) Anyway, I would never minimize the decisions that are made like that in the field; it is extremely difficult to know whether you "have something" or you do not. Generally speaking, people I've worked with have tried to keep shooting until they have some sense in their gut that there is a film there . . . that there was some critical scene in which something "happened."

In *Grey Gardens* that critical scene was what we called "the pink room." The scene that is placed very near the end of the film, although it happened very near the beginning of the shooting. That's the scene where Edie Beale tells a story about a man who wanted to marry her, and her mother sent him away in 15 minutes. Now Edie told that story, during those five weeks of shooting, at least three or four times on film,

375

but the *particular* time she told it in the pink room—for some reason, it had a lot of pain in it, in fact she cried when she told her story. And when we saw that, it moved us, we thought we had something. We didn't really know what we had; we thought it gave us some kind of insight into the relationship between these two women, and what kind of pain they could cause each other.

Q. Can we just go back to how you started working in close cooperation with the Maysles. You said that you had been working on a few films, but during the last few years you seem to have been working almost exclusively with them?

A. Yes. I used to have a company with my ex-husband, Adam Giffard. We made films, particularly in Mississippi during the Movement, but Adam hated producing and our company more or less dissolved. I then began working more and more with David and Albert, and Charlotte Zwerin as well. I cannot really say why we kept on working together, except that we are all fond of each other and seem to get on very well, and the films that we have worked on together have been things we all like and they've been fairly successful. I still do independent productions. I make films for "Sesame Street." I'm making right now a dramatic fiction film on a grant from the National Endowment for the Arts. I'm involved in a possible feature deal, and so on—and none of these are Maysles productions.

Q. What was the first you heard of *Grey Gardens*—of the idea, of the concept? Do you remember its very first moments?

A. Yes. While I was working on *Christo's Valley Curtain*, David and Al were starting to shoot a film with Lee Radziwill about her childhood in East Hampton. The idea of the film was that they would go out with Lee and photograph her talking to a lot of people who had known her parents, had known her and Jackie, and so on. And one of the people she wanted to interview was her aunt, Mrs. Beale, because obviously she knew a lot about Lee's parents and their early life, and Lee liked her a lot, I think. And it was at that time that the Suffolk County Board of Health raided the Beales' house and tried to evict them because of "unsanitary living conditions." Lee was put in charge of renovating the house by the Bouvier family, who of course got involved in the publicity. And so, partly because Lee wanted to talk to her aunt about the past, and partly because she had business to do there, she and the Maysles spent a fair amount of their time at that house, more than Lee would have done ordinarily.

David and Al then began to shoot what was going on, which was of course amazing. Here were these two women who were very flamboyant, very theatrical, very funny, in the midst of a crisis. They were trying to save their house and their way of life. The footage began to come back, and David and I looked at that footage and he said, "Come on, let's just put it together very roughly and see if we can't talk Lee into making a film mainly about the Beales."

So in a week and a half we put together a very rough hour and a half film, and showed it to Lee, and she hated it. It wasn't at all what she had in mind, and she said, "Please, I do not want to do this at all, I want to go back to my original idea." And David and Al said they didn't want to go back to that, because this was obviously much more interesting, and she said, "Please give me the negative and let's quit." So they had to do that, because they didn't own it. She took the negative and went away, and we all went on to other things and thought that would be the end of it.

But no one was able to forget this incredible couple who had dominated that film; we all felt that if there was ever going to be an opportunity to make a film about these two people, we would like to do it. David, especially, felt close to Little Edie, and since he had a summer place out there near the Beale house he stayed in touch with her and talked to her frequently about making a film. And then, when a year had gone by and Lee had done nothing about the footage we had given up, the Maysles decided to go ahead and venture making a film about these two women. Big Edie didn't really want to do it, at first. Little Edie did.

Q. At that point, did David and Al say to you what they thought they had been looking for in this film, what might come out?

A. No, never, they had no idea.

Q. Just a sense that the material was there?

A. Just a sense of two charismatic people; that there must be a story there. They have a sublime confidence in sensing that there are people who are interesting people and leading interesting lives—but what the film would be "about", they had no concept. In fact, Muffie (Muffie Meyer, a co-director and co-editor on the film) and I once, during the editing, sat them down with a tape recorder and tried to get them to put into words what they thought they were doing, and they were unable to say. They really had no idea even why they were interested in these people.

Finally we suggested to Al that he was interested in Big Edie because she was rather like his mother, and that struck a chord in him. He was very involved with his mother, who had recently died. David said that it was maybe because he identified with Little Edie because he too was afraid of getting married, and was very attached to family. But that was as far as they could come with any reasons for making the film.

The big reason was just that they wanted to do it, and so did Muffie and I.

Q. You and Muffie are listed as co-directors of this film. What exactly does that mean? When material started coming in, what was your function; how did you work on the material?

A. Well, I started before Muffie did. When the material came in, I and David and Susan Froemke (who was then the assistant), looked at it together, and usually Al did too. And we just let it wash over us. We all made notes about what appealed to us, but what I did when I first started working on it was to go for that scene in the pink room, to see whether that was going to be the strong, pivotal scene we all hoped it would be.

The material in general was very strange; you almost couldn't tell if you had anything until you cut it, because it was very free-flowing, very repetitive—it didn't have obvious structure. There were no events, there was nothing around which a conversation was going to wheel, there were no other people in and out of the house except for Jerry, and Lois Wright. It was all kind of the same in a gross way, and you had to dig into it, try to find motivations, condense the material to bring out psychological tones.

Q. Did you start editing before you had all the material, or did you have all the material available and then start to look at it?

A. I didn't start cutting until we had all the material, and I then started on scenes that simply appealed to me. I was not examining myself too closely about that either. I was always, I guess, looking for relationship, because I felt there was no question that the film would turn around a dependency relationship in a family, and that interested me very much. When Muffie came, David and I had already cut a few scenes, and we all went over what we had, and decided which scenes we would cut next. I think we were pushing in film terms towards a novel of sensibility rather than a novel of plot.

We were still pretty much cutting things that we liked—that were funny, or had emotional outbursts from Edie, or songs from Mrs. Beale. Because the "raid" by the Board of Health had been such a traumatic experience for the Beales, they talked about it constantly, and we felt we had to deal with that and we cut a lot of material relating to it.

Q. Sometimes when you are doing a *vérité* film, the difficulty is defining what the film is about. You are going off in seven different directions till you find what it's all about. Was there that problem with this film, or were you pretty clear which direction you wanted from the start?

A. No, I don't think we were clear at all. I think we all knew there was nothing in terms of "action," but what was really going on was not clear. David thought in the beginning that the issue was, would Edie leave or not. Well, for Muffie and me that was never an issue. We felt absolutely certain that Edie had no intention of leaving, and that her *talk* about leaving—which she did all the time—was simply one of the devices that she and her mother used as a kind of conveyance of feeling . . . that neither had the slightest intention of changing the balance of power, or the situation. In fact, we felt that each knew exactly how far the other could be teased or goaded or pushed, before causing an action which might actually change the situation. And then each withdrew, because it was the battle and not changes that interested them.

The main themes that Muffie and I decided to go with were the questions around "why were mother and daughter *together*—so together that they almost totally excluded the rest of the world?" And in order to build audience interest, we began to structure the material so that first, it would be possible for the audience to believe that the mother was strong, witty, and charming, and was taking care of Little Edie, her daughter, who was too weak and fearful ever to have gone and lived a life of her own by herself.

Our second theme was that it was possible that Edie was there to take care of her *mother*, and that her mother was very demanding, manipulative—it was she who arranged that her daughter couldn't leave, because she needed someone to wait on her and didn't want to be left alone. Our third theme, the resolution of the other two, was that we wanted the audience to feel finally that the relationship was a symbiotic one, and that on both sides, the need to care and be cared for was equal—it was a balanced situation of dependency and strength, love and hate.

Q. Did Al and David come in on the structuring, or was it left to you and Muffie?

A. Al never comes in on structure; he has never, to my knowledge, been in on the structuring of a film. David wasn't involved in the structure of this one very much, though he often is. For one thing, the editing process was very long, and they had to go and make some money to keep everything going, so they were out doing commercials, that sort of thing. Muffie and I structured the film. David came in when he could. David is always very interested in the editing process and sometimes takes part, but here the main work we did together, except at the very beginning, was at the end. Then, there were certain scenes that Muffie and I wanted to have in, that he didn't want; there were some that he wanted and we didn't want. We traded off on those. David, of course, is the producer, and if he really puts his foot down and you are unable to convince him, you give in. I would say nothing was ever done without David's agreement.

Q. You mentioned those scenes that you traded off, scenes you wanted and David didn't. Can you tell me about these scenes? And why you wanted them in or out?

A. Muffie and I wanted a scene in, which first of all was very nice in terms of photographic variety. It was shot from the garden, looking up at Little Edie in a window—she was shouting down, talking about politics, and was complaining bitterly about local Republican politics. And then she went into a general statement, quite a funny one, about politics in general and Republican politics in particular. It was very witty and always got a laugh, and was a lovely change from always being in that bedroom.

But the real reason why we wanted it was that it showed Edie in a moment that was not narcissistic. She was showing that she did read, that she was aware of public events, that she thought about them and that she had very strong opinions about them. We felt that it was a very strong card to play in presenting her character, because she does come off so easily as a completely narcissistic and dependent person who is unaware of anything outside her mirror. She is *not* like that, and so we did feel strongly that the scene should be in. In fact, we were constantly putting it in, and David was constantly taking it out.

Q. Why did he want it out?

A. David was never able to explain to us satisfactorily why he wanted it out. He said that it was self-serving, that he simply didn't like it, that he didn't want Edie talking about politics. I think it had something to do with the fact that he thought it was some kind of cheap shot for a Kennedy-related person to talk about Republican politics. That's about as close as I could get to his reason, and he finally said "It just has to go, I will not have it."

Q. What are the scenes that he wanted in and you didn't want?

A. Let's see. The beginning, I'm not fond of . . . the way the newspaper scene worked. I wanted to start the film (and Muffie did too) with a dolly shot down Lily Pond Lane where the Beales live. On that road are enormous houses with espaliered trees, and fancy gravelled driveways—they are very elegant. And we thought it would be wonderful to just go right past those houses and come to the Beales' house. You would be immediately saying a lot. You would be putting them in a context. Now both David and Al were adamant about that they would never do that shot. Al said, "I don't care where this house is,

it could be in the middle of Harlem, and the story would be the same."
Muffie and I don't agree at all; we think the story has very much to
do with the society, and the place, and the contrast of the way they
live with the way people live around them, the class they come from
and how they deviated from that. We think it's critical.

Q. And Al did not?

A. He refused to shoot it. He did do some still shots of other houses
and scenes in East Hampton, and we used those, which helped a lot.

Q. Was there any material that you felt was too painful or too private
to include? I want to get on to that question because many people have
criticized the film for being too exposing of the women. They say that
it should not have been made, and so on. What were the judgments
or the self-censorship, if at all, that you used on the film?

A. I don't think there were any too painful or private events that
they talked about. I don't think we eliminated anything because it was
too private, except certain physical scenes of Edie's partial nudity. She
wore very odd, wonderful, make-shift costumes, and sometimes they
were really very revealing. We always eliminated those.

I think we felt in the footage that there was a certain need to balance
out the two women, and it was hard to do. Mrs. Beale, who was a very
strong personality, often came off as extremely cruel and bitchy and
ruthless; and in a way we almost wanted to protect her from making
that kind of impression too strongly. It was partly true but it wasn't
the whole story. For one thing, Edie's ways of getting back at her
mother were cruel too—she handled her mother by withholding, by
delaying information, food, whatever. She was just as involved, just
as manipulative in her way. But her way was much harder to present
on film, because Mrs. Beale's way was with wit and charm, which
always attracts people. It was one of the things we really struggled
with.

As for exploitation, Muffie and I worried a great deal during the
cutting about exploiting them, and exposing them to ridicule from people who wouldn't understand them, and so on. David and Al never
did. They felt that everything that had gone on was all right, and that
if the Beales revealed themselves completely, fine. And I think that
they were absolutely right.

I think that really what happens in that film is that an audience is
amazed and identifies with them, and is frightened, maybe repelled.
But when people say that those women were exploited, I think what
they are really thinking about is themselves.

I think basically all *vérité* films are criticized on that ground, that
you are invading someone's privacy, just by pointing a camera at them.

On the other hand I think that people are aware in our society of what a camera is, and very aware of what they ought to be doing in front of it, so unless a person is really *non compos mentis* it is pretty hard to put someone in a film with their own knowledge and consent, without them having a very good idea of what is going on.

Now the criticism in this film is that they did not have any knowledge of what was going on, but *I* think that they *did*. At the time of cutting it, I was not sure that they did, but since it was made, it is clear to me that they knew and accepted a great deal about themselves, that other people had no idea of.

The Beales themselves were the ones who really defended the film more than anyone. They saw the film at their house and loved it. I thought—fine. That just means that they recognize themselves, but when they see it with an audience, and the audience begins to pick up on certain things, and to laugh at certain things, their reaction may change. I sat with Edie at Lincoln Center when she saw it for the first time with an audience. She laughed, she cried, she enjoyed it. She treated it almost as if it were someone else, and yet she realized very well that it was herself and her mother.

And then, in the months when there was a lot of controversy about it, it was Mrs. Beale and Edie who called us and said, "You know there has been this criticism—don't worry. It's all right. We know that it is an honest picture. We believe in it. We don't want you to feel upset." That was their attitude and they never wavered from that.

Some of the things that people have said to me when I go around and speak about the film are, "Well you know, those two are not quite right in the head, and therefore they are not responsible for themselves, and therefore you had no right to expose them in this way. They had no idea of what they were revealing." Actually I've mostly heard that in New York. However, no one stops to remember they managed their own affairs all their lives. No one tried to institutionalize them, and it is presumptuous to make decisions for other people about what they do or do not understand unless they are really incompetent, and I do not think that they are incompetent. You get into the issue, well does a person *really* know what they are revealing, and I don't think that it is possible for anyone to really know what they are revealing. That is a risk that you take, but they took it gladly, and I think that they were very courageous to do it.

Q. At what point did you know, "That's it, the film is finished." That you had it completely, when there must be a tendency to go on, to change or to play around?

A. Well, Muffie and I worked it into a form where we thought we had something basically along those lines that I described, "Did Edie stay to care for mother, did her mother keep Edie to protect her, or were they both involved and were both fulfilling needs of their own." That was our base line. When we had that, we had been working a long time, and we began to screen the film for just a few very close friends, to see whether *they* were getting what we thought *we* had gotten out of it, not knowing anything about the Beales.

There were confusions, and certain people were upset about certain things. The most interesting thing that happened (I think it happens always for people who edit film) is that if you invite someone to see a film that you've never shown to anyone, they don't have to say a word. Just the fact that a stranger to the film is *sitting* with you throws you into the audience yourself. Your own perceptions of the film change completely, and you begin to see it for the first time as an audience yourself.

That is what we tried to do and it was very successful for us. We saw the film in new ways and began to really hone it down. We had a blackboard thing with three-by-five white cards with scene numbers on them, and we really spent a lot of time shoving them around, saying, "Let's take this scene where Edie shows that she can swim (which means that she has a kind of style and confidence) and put it ahead of the little bit here. What will that do?" We played with that until we were almost blind. And once it settled down, it began to lock down almost like a crystal formation, and began to be impossible to move whole blocks of scenes apart. They just seemed inevitable, and the film (quite rapidly, I think) finally got locked down.

Q. You said that all the material had been finished before you started editing it, but did you find there were still things you would really have liked to talk to David and Al about, saying, "We need you to film this—to do some more filming—to help us with the structure and the form."

A. Well, we did do that, and they did go back and do more filming.

Q. Do you remember the things you asked them to shoot?

A. We never asked them to go back and ask the Beales to talk about anything. That is a cardinal rule with all of us. It is something you don't do. But we needed a few things technically to smooth a few transitions. Cutting around two characters in one location, changing costumes every day, really is a terrible problem, so you are always trying to think of ways to cut, and things to use as cutaways. There were certain scenic things that we wanted—certain things that Al had done but weren't quite right, like the shot of the moon at night over the house. We said, "Do that again, Al, and do it better." There was also the tracking shot we wanted of the other houses in East Hampton. Al finally compromised. He didn't give us the track but he gave us a number of individual shots. They weren't quite as elegant as the simple shot, but they did the trick.

One of the other problems with the cutting was that these women talked on top of each other all the time, and there was almost no room tone—no silences. As one conversation finished and you wanted to say, bam that's the end of the scene, the other voice would begin. This made for certain unsolvable problems. So we said, "Go back and try and get Edie to repeat this sentence." Edie was a pro. She could hear the original recording and then repeat it with the same emotional tone. We never asked her to say something that she had not said, but both she and her mother were able to give you a new line that was clean.

Q. How did working on *Grey Gardens* affect your general feelings about what *vérité* could and couldn't do?

A. I guess it changed my feelings very much about *cinéma vérité*. I felt we were pushing it in a new direction, and so did Muffie. You know the kind of axiom of the people who invented *vérité*. They were all cameramen, and they had really objected to tampering with reality. Reality to them really means you photograph it as it happened and you do not cut it. It is just happening. You hear Pennebaker say this, and Leacock will say it, and I am sure Al will say it too.

It is just patently untrue, you know; all those films were *always* cut. The difficulty in condensing reality is that it is not written as well as O'Neill. It is not as economical. And when you try and condense it into film time, you very often find that the whole scene is falling apart. If the audience could sit there and watch for 30 hours the material would be wonderful. But they won't. So you have to condense, and it falls apart.

So the first real problem is to condense "real time" into "film time" without it losing the very quality that you liked so much about it. It was also very difficult in this film but it was the interesting thing about it, how to make a film about *process*, rather than *events*. We were really trying to take real people's lives, and the interactions between people, and make *that* interesting because it is psychologically interesting, and not because something is going to happen that you are waiting for.

It is, as I said, a novel of sensibility, and in the end slightly Proustian, though I don't mean to be arrogant about it. What I mean is that if you can interest an audience and hold them, because you are trying to do something psychologically revealing, that is a *new way* to think about *vérité*. One of the things we did like that, for instance, was the story that I talked to you about, in the pink room. That was one of the critical scenes where Little Edie cries about the fact that her mother sent away the man who might have married her.

Edie told that story several times. We used it twice in the film; she tells the entire story earlier in the film and she *laughs* about it, and then she repeats almost word for word the dialogue, and *cries* about it. There were many other smaller instances in the film where we did repeat information, because we were making a film about an obsessive, repetitive relationship, and what we wanted to show our audience were not the words but the emotional effect and the tone. The words were simply like Pavlov reactions. The story would just roll out, and the responses would be there automatically. But what was *really* going on, was that their relationship had different emotional tones at different times, and they were expressing their needs that way rather than by events or by varying their conversation. And they did not have to have very much conversation, a couple of topics would do.

Now all this is very risky for the film maker because you hope an audience will understand that and will go with it and will bear with it, even at times when it might seem boring. But your hope is that they are hooked enough that they will stick with you and come out the other end and not feel that they have been bored.

Q. How did you work with Muffie? I find it very unusual to have two editors. Are your tastes very similar?

A. Yes. First of all I like very much working with other people. I have worked frequently with Charlotte Zwerin; and Charlotte, Muffie and I edited many of the Maysles' films. Charlotte and I feel, and I think Muffie does too, that there is an advantage in several editors. There is so much footage coming in; for example in *Grey Gardens* we had a minimum of eighty hours of sync footage, and then seventy reels of wild track, and thirty or forty reels of other stuff. One person cannot really hold all of that inside without help. If you can share that burden with someone who has sensibilities close to your own, it is just so much easier.

Then sometimes you just get tired, and you cannot think about an alternate way of doing something—you are locked into it—and then your friend says, "Well, give me that scene, and I'll try something slightly different." And we would just trade scenes, sometimes in the middle, if we were stuck, or we would do complementary scenes. We always discussed the film in the morning and tried to be pretty sure that we had the same ultimate goal. But then it is just gravy after that, delightful to have someone to bounce ideas with.

It is unusual, but not, I think, all that strange. Musicians do it a lot—Rodgers and Hammerstein, Gilbert and Sullivan. And film is a kind of communal thing anyway. I have never believed in the *auteur* theory of film, with certain very few exceptions. In *vérité* I do not know of anyone who really creates the whole thing by himself, and I think it is nonsense to say that it is done by one person. All of this started, I think, because we had four directors on the film. The reason we have is that there *were* four directors on the film, and the responsibility and the creativity was shared equally. The word is a little misleading. Al hates the word "director" because he feels that it implies that he told people what to do, which is not the meaning at all. It means that we made the film, and that it would have been a different film had any of us not been there.

Q. If the root of politics is power transactions then this is a very political film, wouldn't you say?

A. Very much so. It is political in the sense that it is dealing with human relationships, a very modern situation, where people were living in intimate contact with maybe only one other person. Today, living in nuclear families, we expect the other person to fill all our needs, and we to fill all theirs, and people get into very bizarre situations, even in quite ordinary-looking homes. When people see *Grey Gardens* sometimes they think, oh my God, are they crazy! That may be your first reaction, but I think most of us feel that there is a lot that goes on between those two people with which we can identify. Intimate relationships are very complicated that way, they *are* power transactions. You are dependent on each other, you are trying to manipulate each other, you love each other, you hate each other. All of those things are happening on top of each other.

Now in America, which is such an open society, we claim that we admit everything, but the fact is that we admit very little. People are frightened to see another person reveal that much about themselves, apparently without shame. It is very upsetting for some people to think that Mrs. Beale does not mind having her sagging flesh out there on the screen. I have heard older women say that it is not decent, and how could you be so cruel to show the flesh hanging off her arm. Well, as a matter of fact, the flesh *is* hanging off her arm, and Little Edie's reaction to remarks like that was, "Well if you are fifty-eight and your thighs are going flabby, too, that is how it is."

It is hard for people to accept that you can say something that was really deeply cruel to someone, and then say, "By the way, please, pass the sugar." The sugar is passed and life goes on. And if in *vérité* you can really begin to show people that that *is* how life is lived and that people *survive* that experience, I think that is a very political thing to do, a very important thing to do.

# 24
## *Men's Lives*
### *Will Roberts*

*It was no trick finding Will Roberts among the crowd at Chicago's O'Hare Airport. He looks exactly like one of the overgrown, high-school basketball players in his film* Men's Lives.

*Will was born in 1950 and grew up in Springfield, Ohio. He attended Antioch College on a partial scholarship where, he states, "I was their token working-class student." During his junior year he met Josh Hanig in a class on "Media for Political Change," conducted by Julia Reichert and Jim Klein. Josh was from Kokomo, Indiana, where both his parents taught college. Influenced by the work of Reichert and Klein, who had made* Growing Up Female, *Will and Josh set about to document the relatively unexplored terrain of male concepts of masculinity in the United States. Their investigations led to the making of* Men's Lives. *It was their first film and Will readily admits they learned as they went.*

Men's Lives *takes a look back at the major influences which affect men, especially during the formative years— the classroom, the sports field, teachers, the media and the contact with other classmates, both male and female. Later sections focus on the workplace. Interweaving informal interviews with vignettes from the lives of males from boyhood and adolescence through young adulthood and marriage, the film asks the questions: What does it mean to be male in America today? How did we get there?*

*Shunning authorities, the directors allow men to speak for themselves and in so doing certain themes arise, especially the stress placed upon the need to prove one's masculinity, to compete, to get ahead. But with great sensitivity, the directors also reveal the cost of adhering to such standards —the price paid in uncertainty, discontent, and the suppression of human values.*

*If the film has one major fault, it is a failure to indicate how men might live more meaningful lives, for as Will states at the end of the film, "I know that changing personally is not enough." The film ends with a challenge—the need to rethink priorities and to restructure society. How this is to come about isn't spelled out. But perhaps first things first, and certainly* Men's Lives *has forcefully taken the initial step by intelligently posing the problems. It asks the questions and thus serves as a major document in the broader feminist struggle to change all sexually limiting roles which presently define our social condition.*

*For their premier work Will and Josh received an Academy Award for the best student documentary of 1975. Since 1975, the two film makers have each taken on separate projects. Will is now living in Athens, Ohio, and raising two young daughters as a single parent. He is completing a new film,* Between Men, *a work which deals with masculinity and the military in the United States. Josh is living in San Francisco and working on* Song of the Canary, *a film about occupational health and safety hazards.*

Q. What was the motivation for making a film on men's lives?

A. Josh Hanig and I both had a lot of friends who were involved in feminism and we felt that there was nothing for men to grab on to in order to ask the kind of questions they needed to be asking about their roles. As women were going through changes many men found themselves very alienated or very defensive about their roles and where they stood.

Q. What kinds of questions did you feel that men needed to be asking?

A. There were questions that men weren't asking about their socialization. Many men, who were trying to relate to women who were involved in the women's movement, found themselves unable to call them "girl friends." They found that the ways they had learned to relate to women were no longer effective. They weren't asking themselves what their socialization as men had to do with their relationships, with their futures, with the way they perceived work, success, or how it affected them emotionally and physically. They weren't examining that, and at the same time they were rejecting the ways women were examining themselves. Or if they weren't rejecting, they became confused, somewhat defensive. So we made the film to deal with the issues of being a male and how socialization affects us. We were also curious to see where it would lead.

Q. How much influence do you feel the women's movement has had on men's attitudes towards themselves and towards women?

A. The men's movement and the present male examination of socialization owes its roots to the women's movement. If women had not done it, men would not today be questioning their roles in the socialization process. As men we tend to assume that we have a privilege because of our maleness and we don't realize that many men are in oppressed positions. They are directed by men in the same way as women are generally directed by men in this society.

Q. How did you raise the money to do the film?

A. Josh and I had never made a film before *Men's Lives*. We didn't really have much of an idea of the work involved or the money it would take. We thought it would take about three months and maybe $4,000. It ended up taking a year and three quarters and $14,000, which is very inexpensive for a film like that. The original money for starting the project came as tuition rebates from Antioch College and then we had a series of loans and investments and help from friends. A lot of the equipment was free from the university and from people. But it wasn't easy.

Q. I understand that *Men's Lives* started out as a slide presentation. What made you decide to turn it into a film?

A. Josh and I had made a 25 minute slide tape with another man, Peter Sonnenthal, which was called *A Male Condition*. We went around showing it to high school classes, community organizations, and colleges. There was an incredible response from both men and women about the material, and we became aware of the need for that kind of film. There was nothing around at that time that supported men for asking the kind of questions that needed to be asked about their changing roles.

Q. What ideas changed in reworking the slide presentation into a film?

A. I think that we gained a sensitivity to some of the problems that men have. The slide tape was much harder on men. It saw men as the villains and women, more or less, as the victims. It didn't look at the relative victimization of men in this society, men as controlled by other men, exploited by other men.

Q. As you worked on the project what did you discover were the dominant roles that men were being encouraged to assume in our society?

A. Just as many women in the women's movement reacted against being viewed as sex objects, as being seen for their beauty rather than any other qualities, men were in the position of being viewed as success objects. That is, men felt their work and physical appearance reflected their manhood. Also, men felt physical strength was very important, although women felt less so. There are a lot of ways of competing and being on top—if you win at playing games, if you're the sports hero. Some of it involves intellectual competition, other times it's physical competition, and there is a lot of economic competition. The barber in *Men's Lives* used to talk about how economics shows up in the bedroom, which I think is true in our social structure.

Q. Were there other areas that you felt needed further exploration when you conceived of making a film?

A. The film became an exploration in itself. When we approached the film there were many questions we wanted to ask. We had preconceived notions of what we would find and we would go out and shoot material and come back and it would not be what we wanted. The material said something very important—but different. So it was

390

like a process of discovery. Our preconceived ideas expanded as the material raised our consciousness.

Q. What were some of the preconceived ideas that you had?

A. One of them was not recognizing the complexity of the male role. There was an interview with the factory worker who obviously shows political consciousness on one level, but does not want his wife to work, which is a contradiction in his consciousness. And I don't think, at that point, I understood the problems of the man changing. If Gerald, the factory worker, was to decide to change his life, the alternatives for him were very limited—almost nonexistent. He could quit his job and perhaps go on welfare, but that would destroy his sense of manhood. He saw work as literally "shit" and to think of Beverly, his wife, going out and getting a job was more than he could accept. He wanted to protect her from that. It wasn't that he wanted to prevent her from having a career or prevent her from having something to do outside of the home, but he saw his work as something that was demoralizing, dehumanizing, and he wanted to protect her from that.

Q. What decisions did you make concerning the kinds of people that you wanted to interview?

A. We made a conscious decision at the beginning not to go to the experts. We wanted to talk to the men who were in the positions. We wanted to talk to the factory worker, to the children, to the barber. We didn't want to talk to the psychiatrist who would analyze them and say these men out there in society have problems with their feelings, have problems with their work, have problems with their family relationships. We wanted to talk with the men directly.

Q. How did you find the people that you wanted to interview?

A. We did a lot of preliminary interviews. It was a process of elimination. Part of the problem was that a lot of people didn't have media consciousness. We looked for people who could express themselves, but were not overeducated.

Q. How many interviews did you do?

A. We talked to literally hundreds of people. We must have interviewed thirty black adolescent males before meeting with Jeff and André who talked about a pretty blue Cadillac and keeping it clean all the time and being seen in it.

Q. What was the reaction of people when you approached them for an interview?

A. Most of the people in the film were happy and surprised that we wanted to talk with them. The two people we had the hardest time convincing to be in the film were Gerald, the factory worker, who had such a low opinion of himself that he didn't believe that he had anything important to say, and Joe, the male dancer, who worried that we were going to make fun of him. He cried to me over the telephone because he was afraid that we were going to mock him. So it became necessary to support the people in their positions and not to attack or threaten where they were.

Q. The footage of Joe, performing his gymnastics with such skill and control, is one of the most moving pieces in the film. How were you able to convince him to open up, to dance?

A. We had gone to my old high school, and were looking around for males who were sensitive and in the position of being suppressed or ridiculed because of their sensitivity. Joe was such a young man. The problem was that after we had done the initial interviewing and had asked him to deal with his feelings and how other people related to him, how they responded when they saw him dance, he became frightened about the second interview, the actual filmed interview. He was afraid we would exploit him because he still had guilt that he was "abnormal." He wasn't sure that we were supporting him in what he was trying to do and who he was. There's a line in the film where Joe says, "I think a man is someone who stands up for what he believes is right, regardless of what other people think." We reminded him of that line and that's one of the reasons that I think he decided to continue with it. It was necessary for him to stand up.

Q. Besides Gerald and Joe, were there any other kinds of problems that made men reluctant to talk about themselves?

A. In doing the interviews we wanted an executive to show one type of white-collar position. I think that the problem with the executives was that when I went around trying to do the preliminary interviews, they were always very busy or would just say, "I'm very happy." They had all this facade of satisfaction. It became very difficult to get through to these people.

Q. Another aspect I was curious about is that there are no interviews with college students like yourselves who are examining their roles as men. Why did you not include someone like yourself in the film?

A. Well, I think we were included. We were included as college males who were examining our roles even though we didn't identify ourselves as undergraduate students at that point. Also there was the fraternity party. But when you are going to college the types of adults you normally deal with are the professionals, the experts, and people like yourself. And we wanted to reach out into the community and deal with the other people. Because if you're in college most of the time you don't see the factory worker. You never have contact with him. You ignore certain sections of society. And you get lost in your books and your research and academia.

It is funny because Josh and I considered Antioch this oasis of liberal thought, then we'd go outside and the real world was totally different. We'd come back and discover that the questions the college students were asking weren't relevant to what was really going on outside the oasis. There are a lot of assumptions that college students make about where the working class is, but they don't ask the working class. Students talk about social change and social organization, but they aren't really aware of where working-class people are and what their problems are. It's a difficult situation.

Q. For me the most interesting interviews were with Gerald and Joe because they were questioning their roles as men. Do you feel this was a result of the film making process or were these men thinking in these directions already?

A. I think part of the problem was that they hadn't thought about it. They had experienced it, but no one had ever asked them how they felt about things. I think that's one of the reasons they were willing to open up. Joe became difficult because he was frightened and in a sensitive position. I found that interview very difficult to do, because he was in my old high school. I felt the tension coming back that I had felt when I was in his position. So that made me uncomfortable. But I think for Joe, it was very supportive. For Gerald I was trying to be very supportive and not threatening.

Q. You said you did several interviews with Gerald. Did you see changes as you continued that relationship?

A. Well, interestingly enough after the first interview with Gerald, we thought we didn't get anything. But we had gotten some of the best material, the most personal material.

The problem was it wasn't what we were looking for. It was the example I was talking about earlier where you go out hoping to get something and the person doesn't say what you want. He says something entirely different. Later as we began to work with the material we began to realize how valuable those things he said originally were. So that was one of the consciousness-raising experiences for Josh and me.

It became very difficult to finally put the narration in to include ourselves personally. This decision came as a result of feedback from some friends. They felt we were examining masculinity and not participating. But I think that both of us were frightened about putting our ego into the film. It seemed somehow self-indulgent. There is a very fine line between what is self-indulgent and what becomes personally connected.

Q. What were your fears about incorporating yourself into the film as narrator or in other ways?

A. It's just normally not done in film. It's very seldom that a film maker comes out and says, "This is what we're trying to do," and not only that but, "We're men too and this affects us." Most of the time films seem as though they come from God. The film maker is absolutely behind it or above it and the film presents itself, so to speak. There is no personal involvement or personal commitment in that. Josh and I were both frightened about bringing that personal element into the film.

Q. Had you seen any films by women? Many of those films deal specifically with the woman film maker, either as central character or as narrator.

A. I think some of the women's films become a little self-indulgent. When I talked with European women, especially in England, they were appalled at the self-indulgence of American women film makers. Even *Men's Lives,* when it played in England, was criticized because the film maker came into it.

Q. How do you define self-indulgence?

A. When what is happening relates more to the person than to society, when the film becomes relevant for examining a personal life, but not relevant for examining that personal life in the light of the social structure. Many of the women's films involve personal feelings, but frequently they don't look at the social context. I think that was one of the reasons why it was harder for us to incorporate the personal element.

But also as males there is a tendency not to want to deal with something too personal, especially if it makes you vulnerable. Males are taught not to have vulnerability, or if they do, not to let it show.

Q. What do you feel was the greatest area of change in your thinking about men's lives from the time you started the project to the time you finished the film?

A. There were a lot of changes that took place. There were changes that happened in the relationship between Josh and me—two males working together and dealing with our male egos, being vulnerable, sharing creatively, and examining our own myth of manhood.

Q. From a practical standpoint, how did you and Josh split up the responsibilities?

A. At the beginning of the project we decided that Josh would do the photography and I would do the interviewing. In the preproduction stages we worked closely on what questions to ask of people and how to approach the material. We did the preliminary interviewing together and chose people together.

Normally I worked on the access to institutions and individuals before production. In actual production I dealt with people and Josh dealt with the equipment and technical aspects. In postproduction we both worked together in arranging and editing the content of the material.

Q. Was there a difference in perspective between your thinking and Josh's?

A. Definitely, but I think that frequently differences can complement one another. Josh and I come from different backgrounds. We have had different experiences, but there was a lot in common too.

Q. How did that affect the film?

A. Both of our backgrounds were working-class. Josh's parents are both college instructors, but they had always had to struggle very hard for the income they had. So in growing up and going through school, his life, like mine, did not seem to have many options. When I was growing, my mother worked in a factory and my father was a roofer. Thus in making the film we looked more to the working class. We looked more to men who were struggling, rather than to the professional classes to find answers to problems.

Q. Several women in the film comment on what it means to be a man. To what degree do you feel that women reinforce male stereotypes?

A. In some of the outtakes that we consciously did not want to show, women did reinforce male stereotypes. We excluded all that because we felt that men would say, "I told you so" and that it would make some women quite angry.

There are ways that women can tease men. We had done interviews with some high school women. I asked a woman what she was looking for in a man and she said (she was chewing gum), "I like tall men with muscles." I asked her what kind of a husband she was looking for and she answered, "Well, I want someone who will support me so I don't have to work or do anything." I think that frequently women expect this from men.

Sometimes there is reinforcement from women who are in the homes or women in the dating situation and it's very hard to go beyond it. It's hard for men to go beyond trying to be successful in the same way as it is for women to go beyond expecting success of males, or finding success as a focal point of attraction.

Q. The scene in which the coach talks about men not being emotional seems subtly provoked. He gets very embarrassed and you hold the camera on him for quite a while. To what degree did you intend to undercut his statement?

A. What happened was that when he first responded, there was a question that was later taken out. When he initially responded, he said that men should be able to open up. If you remember, he begins, "I think men hide their emotions, don't cry. Kids learn this when they're growing up." I had asked how he felt personally about that and he said, "I'm not an emotional person," which was like saying, "It's okay, but for other men. It's not a bad or negative thing, but I personally didn't show emotion." There's a contradiction between the way he could objectively look at the male situation and the way he personally viewed his manhood.

Q. Much of the film concentrates on Jim, the barber. Why was he singled out for so much attention?

A. Actually not that much time is spent with Jim, but I think that he has a value for people who see the film. Everyone says, "Wow, where did you get that barber?" I had an interesting reaction from a friend of mine who worked in Hollywood. He said, "That barber, his enunciation, his pausing—why he's so good, he's *real* enough to be an actor." Which shows the state of documentary reality. But the barber sticks in people's minds. I think part of his weight is that he's not a professional figure. He is not a psychoanalyst or a therapist who is objectively analyzing the problems of other men, but someone who has come to his understanding through experience.

Q. At what point in the planning did you decide to put yourself into the barber's chair?

A. That seemed the most practical way of interviewing him. Josh and I had agreed at the outset that the best way to interview the barber would be to have him working.

Q. The young black boys in the film seem very caught up on material success, sports and keeping clean. What did you find were the differences between black and white males and their attitudes towards masculinity?

A. We interviewed some thirty black adolescents and when I asked them what they wanted to do when they finished school, they had three responses: be a sports star, be a rock star, or join the military. All three are ways of getting out of the ghetto, getting out of the traps that they're in.

For the black male growing up, success has always been defined in white male terms and a black male can never be a white male. Therefore, he can never actually achieve success in the American structure. The black woman has always been able to get a job, and frequently has when the black male could not. I think in many ways this has tended to emasculate the black male and put him in the position where he could not satisfy the economic needs of the family in the same way the white male could.

However, the white male is also oppressed by other white men. Not that many men actually achieve the position of being on top. Many strive for it, and end up with the ulcers and perhaps the money, but is money really a satisfying part of humanity? The American male tends to think of satisfaction in monetary terms rather than in emotional terms, in personal relationships.

Q. You mentioned that it was hard to get to businessmen because they were smug or busy. But there were no interviews with men who represent the American success story. Was this a conscious decision?

A. Well, how many success stories are there? I mean the success story is a stereotype. It's the exception that most men strive for. But most men don't feel that successful, and if they do, it has limitations.

Q. Yet a great portion of your film deals with the importance of competition in the lives of American men. Do you feel this is a negative value in our society?

A. The educational system in America promotes competition on a level that goes well beyond friendship. I think this is true for women as well as for men. It's true in the economic arena. Success has to do with the existence of failure and if you compete and you win, then you are successful. But there are far more failures in this society than there are winners, successful men. I think that competition is something that other cultures don't emphasize as strongly.

Q. Your film seems very one-sided to me. You show very few satisfied men, very little comradeship among men, no warm relationships between the sexes except for Gerald and his wife.

A. Most of the positive relationships between men happen in youth. By the time you have a family, by the time you have responsibilities to a job, these relationships often vanish. Jim Koehler has a line in the film, "I don't think men are friends with men they have worked beside for fifty-five years."

Q. What were some of the sequences that you eliminated as you edited the film?

A. We had interviewed some men in a place called Harmony, Ohio, called the Freedom Seekers. They were a young, white, factory-working, motorcycle gang, who earned their money and then went out and bought the Harley-Davidson—what's called "The Great American Freedom Machine." So now it seems that freedom is something you buy. Many products are sold to men because they are associated with freedom. That was one of the things we had to eliminate. We even filmed a sequence where they were stopped by the police, ticketed and measured for the way their choppers were chopped. But it didn't fit into the structure of the film because it was an exception, rather than something that all men could relate to. It was almost a bit of a freak show.

Q. What else was cut out?

A. We had a 20-minute section on black masculinity, but when we decided to make the film the present 43-minute length, we had to take it out. It could be a film in itself. The problem with leaving it that long was that it took you on a tangent and tended to polarize the differences between black and white masculinity. Josh and I both felt that there was enough divisiveness in the system already. Furthermore, we didn't want to concentrate on just one segment of society. That's also why we cut a sequence dealing with men in the military.

We had extended energy in so many directions. We had talked with literally hundreds of people. There were so many people in the film that we were trying to connect together. Josh and I had spent all of our energy, all of our time, all of the money we had, and a lot of money we didn't have. We set up incredible credit lines that didn't exist because we had a box at the Antioch faculty mailroom and that sounded like a credential, although it wasn't a credential. It was just something that helped.

But there was a limitation which we constantly felt. I think we could have made a film on any one of the individuals. But it's just one film, 43 minutes long. And there came a point where we had to recognize the limitations, although originally we didn't.

Q. What was in your mind as you came close to the final edit?

A. Josh and I used to talk about what student films are usually like. We had nightmares of having a deformed baby. Richard Lester once said that making a film is like having an hysterical pregnancy. Well, we didn't know anything. Josh had never shot before we took up the cameras to make this film. I had never done interviewing, never raised money. And every step along the process we would stop and read something to learn how to do it, talk with friends, talk to people about the methodology of doing things. And we had gone to so many different places—football games, the high school—seen so many different people. And we had to tie it all together. We felt we had a monster on our hands.

Q. Jim Klein is given editing credit on *Men's Lives*. What was his contribution?

A. The final editing process became very hard, making the cuts, doing the timing. Jim has a real talent for that, a talent for making things work, making things flow so that it comes in at the right moment and goes from there. He's a true musician with timing and content. Josh and I needed that kind of professional help on our first film.

Q. What was the response to *Men's Lives* among different groups?

A. The response was and continues to be somewhat incredible in the range of groups who have responded positively and found the film useful. I've been told by many women who were not sympathetic or

interested in feminism that *Men's Lives* opened them to considering their
own socialization. It brings a lot of men into feminism in much the
same way, I think. While Josh and I were not surprised that the film
had wide educational usage we have been shocked that organizations
like General Foods, NASA, and the Naval Weapons Academy have
purchased it for their collections.

Q. What has been the major criticism of the film?

A. I think that one of the major ones I've heard is that it is hetero-
sexually biased. This criticism has come from gay men. They did not
feel that it dealt enough with the issues of men's relationships with
other men. While this is a limitation, it was a conscious decision on the
part of Josh and myself. We felt we didn't want to deal with something
that would alienate a lot of instructors or students who might find the
film useful. We thought that the sensitivities dealt with in the film
would open up other sensitivities which could then lead to the issue
of homosexuality.

Another criticism of the film has been that it doesn't deal with the
relative privilege of men in the society in comparison with women.

Q. At the end of *Men's Lives* you say that personal change is not
enough. What do you feel are the steps necessary in order to accomplish real change?

A. Part of the way to answer that question would be to reflect back
on Joe, the dancer. Personally he has accepted, or tried to accept the
feelings that he has, the sensitivity he has, and what it means to be a
dancer. Society on the other hand comes back to him with this guilt,
and although he may not personally feel it, it is imposed on him socially
from other men, from other people.

If we are only talking about personal change, I could perhaps go off
to the woods and solve all my problems. But it would not help men
growing up in the future. It would not help create the kind of structure
in which men would have other alternatives and the freedom to develop
new sensitivities. If you just keep taking care of yourself personally,
and the structure keeps producing the same kind of problems, that's
not really sufficient.

I received a letter from a woman in Sweden when *Men's Lives* was
on television there. Having lived both in America and Sweden, she
made the observation that Americans felt if you changed your life personally you solved your problems, whereas in Sweden they believed
it was necessary to change the government or the social system. One
country tends not to look at the social structure and the other tends
not to look at the personal problem.

Q. Since making *Men's Lives* do you feel that the options for males
have increased or are we just standing still?

A. I think the options for some men are greater. Generally, however, it would be dangerous to say that things are really on the road to change. I think that while some things have changed, there are far more changes to be made, far more re-examination of the structure necessary. Women have been doing it for a fairly long time, longer than men, and in that respect I think the women's movement is far ahead of the men's movement. Now it's the time for men to get organized.

NOTE: This interview conducted by Patricia Erens.

# 25

# The Chicago Maternity Center Story
## and
## The Kartemquin Collective
### Jerry Blumenthal and
### Jennifer Rohrer

*The interview with two members of the Kartemquin Collective took place on a snowy Chicago afternoon. Their cozy studio on the Near West Side, the upper floor of a converted apartment building, was a welcome refuge from the subzero weather outside.*

*The history of Kartemquin is typical of many small collectives throughout the United States which have sprung up during the seventies. Kartemquin began in 1966 as a partnership. Two film makers, Gerald Temaner and Gordon Quinn, come together to make socially committed documentaries, which in the mid-sixties meant* cinéma-vérité *style films. Their names, plus that of a third member Stanley Karter, make up the word "Kartemquin," which also playfully rhymes with Potemkin.*

*Working individually and together with other film makers who joined the group, Kartemquin members turned out several feature-length documentaries:* Home for Life *(1968), an interview film where two nuns ask people, "Are you happy?";* Red Squares *(1970), about a student strike over Cambodia; and* Marco *(1971), a film about natural childbirth. To support these projects and their own families, the group also worked on commercials, educational films, and did free-lance work for television.*

*The transition from a loose association to a true collective occurred in 1972–1973 with the addition of twelve new members, eight of whom were female. It was at this point that the need arose to define priorities and to hammer out policy. Problems of skill sharing, sexism within the group, and political commitments had to be worked out.*

*Over the next several years the collective produced several short documentaries focusing on community problems in Chicago and the urban scene. These include:* Now We Live on Clifton *(1974),* Winnie Wright, Age 11 *(1974),* Viva la Causa *(1974),* Trickbag *(1975),* All of Us Stronger *(1975), and* The Chicago Maternity Center Story *(1976), the major work to come out of the collective. In addition, the group also made several political videotapes in-*

*cluding* Where's I. W. Abel? *(1974)*, It Can Be Done *(1974) and* What's Happening at Local Office 70? *(1975)*.

*Jerry Blumenthal has been a member of Kartemquin since 1967. Before that he taught and wrote about film. A product of the Midwest, he was born in Chicago in 1936, and received his M.A. in humanities from the University of Chicago. At Kartemquin Jerry worked on* Red Squares, Now We Live on Clifton, Trickbag, *and* The Chicago Maternity Center Story. *Presently he is finishing a film with Gordon Quinn about a strike at a steel fabricating plant in Gary, Indiana.*

*Jenny Rohrer was born in 1949 and has spent the last eight years as a community organizer. From 1973–1975 she served as co-chair for the Chicago Women's Liberation Union. Her film background includes one year at Columbia College in Chicago, followed by work with Chicago Newsreel. Having completed* The Chicago Maternity Center Story, *Jenny returned to office work and union organizing.*

The Chicago Maternity Center Story *was begun in 1972 and finished in 1976. Five members of the collective worked on the film. The project was brought to Kartemquin by Jenny and Suzanne Davenport who wanted to make a short film about the work of this local social service organization which offered home birth to mothers who chose not to deliver their babies in a hospital. During the process of shooting, the Maternity Center was threatened by a decision from Northwestern University Hospital to close its doors. The film makers immediately saw the possibility of documenting a dynamic and important story—the struggle of a small, nonprofit community organization to remain viable. And so they stayed with the story, restructuring the film and following the citizens' fight against a large institution. The fight was lost, but the film remains as an invaluable tool for organizing in similar struggles, as well as a thorough analysis of health care in America.*

*After the completion of* The Chicago Maternity Center Story, *Kartemquin slowly decreased in size and eventually disbanded as a functioning collective. Attrition was due to a combination of factors which included changing priorities, financial stresses, and personal problems among the various members of the group. Kartemquin now comprises Jerry Blumenthal and Gordon Quinn, plus Judy Hoffman and a few film makers who work with them on a part-time basis. Jenny Rohrer has stayed on to oversee the distribution of the Maternity Center film.*

Q. Could you give me some background on the formation of the Kartemquin collective?

BLUMENTHAL. The collective was founded in 1972. It was a time when Gordon Quinn and I were working almost exclusively on a series of sports documentaries for television. We were making a lot of money and buying a lot of equipment, but we weren't happy with what we were doing. We knew that we needed to do more. We wanted to get in touch with people in Chicago who thought the same way that we did about film—who had the same political ideas that we did about film. We began poking around and talking to different kinds of people, not only to film makers, but to people who did political work of one kind or another, people who worked with unions, people who worked with community groups and teachers.

The first people who really were concrete possibilities were Jenny Rohrer and Suzanne Davenport. At the time they were students at Columbia College and were doing a student film about the Chicago Maternity Center. They came to us knowing that we were interested in that kind of subject, that we were experienced documentary film makers and that we were eager to find other people to work with. They showed us a script, which we went over with them. Both Gordon and I were very interested in the subject and thought that it was a possibility for a film that would be more than just a student documentary.

Q. You mentioned looking for people with the same political ideas. What were your politics?

B. Our politics were left politics, but independent left and nonsectarian. We were not tied to any particular line in any particular left group, but we were very interested in making films that could be used in organizing and teaching. We may not have agreed with one another specifically on a given Marxist line, but we all felt that a film had to have basically a left or socialist analysis of what the problems were in American society and how those problems were to be solved.

Whenever anybody had an idea for a film, the first questions that we always asked were, "What's it for and who's going to use it?" We didn't start out from the premise that film makers have traditionally used in America, which is "What do I want or need to express?" That became a secondary question and at times became an irrelevant question.

Q. What were some of the films that you decided to get involved in based on those politics?

ROHRER. We tried to pick subjects that showed organizing situations. The Maternity Center film was a work that started around an effort to keep the Center open. It grew out of our desire to do a film about issues raised by the Women's Liberation Movement. We also did a 20-minute film called *Trickbag* about racism as expressed by people who live in a variety of Chicago neighborhoods. The film revealed how they saw themselves being put into racist situations, whether in the army or on the job, and how they responded to it.

Q. What happened in your growth the first year of the collective?

R. We grew from two members to about twelve, and our group consisted of two types of people. There were those who came with film skills—camera, editing, etc.—who had a share of politics and had already worked in the industry in some way. They were the experienced film makers. Others came in with very little film experience. Sue and I had had some experience. I'd been in Chicago Newsreel and in film school for a year where I learned some level of production skills. But basically I learned about everything I know at Kartemquin in the process of making a film. That was also true of a few other people. So we had people of a real varied skill level.

Q. How did you handle the differences between the levels in skill?

R. We recognized that people brought different things and everything was valuable. Some people came in as experienced organizers with a lot of connections with the groups and organizations that we intended to use in our films, and also a good outlook on how to communicate information in a film. This was seen as a very valuable skill. But everyone wanted to participate in the film making process, so we made quite an effort to do skill sharing.

The story of how we tried to share skills is much the story of the whole history of our group. In fact, one problem clearly reflects society, just as much as who we were as individuals. By and large, the men had the film skills and the women didn't, because the men had been working for years in the film business. So a real emphasis was to teach people skills. At a very early point we decided that to a great extent people had to specialize in certain skills. Originally Suzanne and I thought that we could both shoot and take sound and we did learn each skill to some extent, but it was a naive idea not to have each of us specialize.

B. One way to look at it is that the collective was formed in a very clear and definite way to go against the grain of the culture and the society in which it existed and to achieve things that could not be achieved in the outside world. Skill sharing was one of the most concrete examples of how that kind of thing was attempted by the collective—to give women who wanted to be film makers a chance to gain the skills that they needed. To give them that opportunity in a working situation. We've often been asked, "Well, why didn't it work?" "Weren't the people talented?" "What happened?" Part of the reason it failed is that the forces arrayed against it were just too powerful.

Q. What were the reactions of your clients seeing women performing all sorts of technical jobs?

R. Well, often the people we were working for had never seen women as assistant camerapeople, or as grips. That's where I feel we did pretty well. I think that we had a certain limitation that was just a little overwhelming. When we went into commercial situations, a woman would perform a job and someone that we were working with, not a member of our collective, would constantly be trying to interrupt and say, "No, I'll take over that part. I'll put up that light." Also, one of our main clients, a woman, would specifically say when she called for a crew that she didn't want any women. That didn't stop us from sending women.

Q. You were basically supporting yourselves by making commercials to get money for the films that you wanted to make?

B. Yes, we did commercials or educational documentaries, sponsored documentaries, and set up a system of equipment rentals. By the time the collective was formed, we had amassed the equipment that we now have and often rented it out at good prices.

Q. Can you explain some more what you mean by "forces ranged against you"?

R. It was difficult getting work. We developed a kind of notoriety among film makers in Chicago. Kartemquin became the group you went to when you didn't care who it was you wanted to work for you. Some of us who had had contact with the commercial world and had developed clients of our own would continue that kind of work, just because we needed to make money to live on. However, it was a policy of the collective, which is unheard of in the commercial world, that people would take turns. The work that came into Kartemquin was divided equally among the people who were there. So that it was this person's turn, that person's turn and the next person's turn to go out on a job. No client could be sure that they would get the person they had developed a relationship with and that made it very difficult for Kartemquin to really succeed at getting an established clientele. To some extent one can understand that.

Q. Did you look for foundation grants for your films?

B. Yes, but it became very difficult. After a series of films that sort of established Kartemquin (films like *Home for Life, Thumbs Down, Marco,* and a few others) we thought that the foundation path was the way that Kartemquin would really survive in this society. We thought that by approaching liberal foundations with good ideas for useful social documentaries we would be funded and Kartemquin would make its way.

But that didn't turn out to be the case. For a two-year period in the late sixties and early seventies we found that we couldn't get any foundation money, because we didn't want to make films that were promotional films for programs already in existence. We wanted to do films that were much more a kind of inquiry and much more honest

405

and truthful, and it's very difficult to get money from foundations for films like that. That's when we turned to the commercial world and did the series of sports documentaries.

Q. In 1973 you had twelve members. How did you work as a group? Did you have weekly meetings? Did you discuss policy? Did you try to reach consensus, or did each person work individually?

R. We had group meetings, to discuss skill sharing, as well as our policy in taking certain types of commercial work. We felt because of our politics we would not accept any kind of commercial work, but in reality there have been only a few things that we've turned down. For instance, we were asked to a series of promotional films that would have made a lot of money for us on the new reforms in the North Carolina prison system. We did a little research into that and knew that we wouldn't feel comfortable making propaganda films on the North Carolina prison system, when we knew it was the worst in the country!

Q. What were the major problems of keeping the collective afloat?

R. Well, one source of conflict was the demands film making puts on people's time and their real need to support themselves. People were working on particular films, putting in a lot of time but without any financial return. Yet people had to support themselves, and that's why there was so much tension around skill sharing. Some people wanted to be able to see the commercial film business as their primary source of income and for people who had spent five or ten years in the business, they had the ability to generate an income. But at least half of the collective, again primarily the women, had to go outside the film industry to find jobs, often pretty bad jobs as waitresses or in some cases as part-time teachers. So there was a real tension about time and money. That problem was never really solved despite our desire to equalize the work.

Q. What has been the major reason that people dropped out? Where have most of the former members gone?

B. They go into one of two places, I would say. A couple of people have gone into film making, joined the union, and become skilled technicians, who are very secure in the kind of work that they do and the jobs that they get. Another direction in which we've taken a loss is that people have gone back to do the kind of political work that they did— organizing, teaching—before they joined the collective.

These changes can't be seen simply as economic decisions, although they clearly have a material basis. Everything that happened to the collective, although it was often discussed in very ideological and political terms, has the material basis that is really very hard to get away

406

from when you look at the thing clearly. There were a lot of times when the collective would act as though it was a world unto itself and forget about the context, the social and economic context, in which it existed. It was unsuccessful partly because you can't forget about economics. It closes in on you eventually.

R. One characteristic of Kartemquin that was different from collectives I've seen in other cities is that a great number of the people were trying to be both film makers and organizers at the same time. So as a group we had a lot of fingers in work that people were doing around the city, yet at the same time we were trying to make films. It also meant that there was another tension that took people's attention away from full-time film making. Basically the people that came to the group with film skills are now still in the film business, and it's the people who came to the group without film skills that have left the group and are combining their political work with their full-time employment.

I would just like to mention another aspect of the collective which functioned for a period of over two years. We designed a series of film screenings that lasted most of the year. We showed films on certain themes: women, labor, strikes, foreign affairs, health care. We constructed a mailing list and contacted people who we felt should be using these films, but probably didn't know about them. In our role as film makers and film distributors, to some extent, we wanted to make these films available to the people that we felt should be using them and to talk about the films after the screenings as a way of encouraging people to use film more often in their organizing.

In terms of deciding what films we should make, it became a question of talking to people we really saw as the people who wanted to use the film. We always asked, "Is there another film which does the same thing, which would eliminate the need for us to make a film like this?" We also looked for gaping holes where there were groups that need a certain kind of film that hadn't been made yet.

B. I would just like to say one thing about the disintegration of the group. It shouldn't be seen as an isolated phenomenon, personal to our group.

R. We were a group of the left, and most groups of the left aren't around any more. In fact, most of the groups that we made films about and distributed films to aren't around any more. For awhile we were looking at our disintegration and wondering what the cause was. Part of what we saw was a process that was affecting all organizations.

Q. What was the origin of *The Chicago Maternity Center Story*?

R. I was a student at Columbia College and wanted to make a film about some struggle-oriented issue that was a women's issue. I was

407

involved in a women's organization at the time, the Chicago Women's Liberation Union. There was a broad-based coalition of women involved in a women's organization called Women Act To Control Health Care (WATCH) which was involved in trying to keep the Maternity Center open. It seemed like a good way to explore the women's issues behind the kind of care the Maternity Center had been providing for the last eighty years, as well as the reasons it was closed by Northwestern University. This meant that the film could express anticorporate politics which traditionally were not dealt with in the politics of the women's health movement. It started out as a modest ten-minute film and because we kept realizing its potential to explore certain issues, it kept expanding.

Q. Who did you think of as the potential audience for the film?

R. The most immediate audience was the women's health movement. It was at that time really growing and is the healthiest, most organized part of the women's movement, with over 2,000 women's clinics around the country. Also other women's groups, health groups, and in health community issue classes. We felt that any kind of group that was involved in an institutional struggle would find the film useful, because of the power structure research that we show in the film and because the group of people in the film were trying to keep a service-oriented institution open by attacking a large institution and corporate power.

Q. Why did it take five years to finish the film?

R. Well, one thing we forgot to mention was that in June 1973 our studio caught fire and that put us all into nine months of reconstruction. So that time was a nonproductive period.

We began the film as a modest project and gradually began to realize its political potential as we began to understand more about the health care industry. None of us were any kind of health care experts. We had to do a lot of self-education. We realized that we were going to start handling questions about the history and development of medical care in the United States, and why it changed from service-oriented care into making profit. We were helped by friends of ours who were writers and educated in the health care field. We were still shooting WATCH's fight to keep the Center open and that lasted through early 1975.

Q. How did the closing of the Maternity Center change the concept of the film?

B. It meant that the struggle that we had documented and the struggle that we believed in had in a sense failed. It then became a problem of what kind of analysis can the film provide and what kind of dramatic

408

context can it present which is honest in documenting the failure but which can also help people to see what was useful about the struggle and what makes that struggle, even though it failed, something that ought to be fought in other circumstances.

It was part of the larger problem that Jenny was just talking about before. We were trying to find an analysis that would underpin the film. Basically it was a question of what story it should tell. Is it just going to be a report on a struggle that failed? No, we wanted the struggle to be portrayed in a very favorable light. We wanted a certain analysis, but also dramatic material to support it. After all we were making a film, not writing an essay.

Q. The film is divided in two parts. What do you see as the function of each part?

R. Part one is titled "Healthcare Worth Fighting For." It takes you into the Maternity Center and shows how it operates. It includes interviews with women in the Center saying why they prefer home delivery: it shows the Center's commitment to prenatal care and a long home delivery sequence. We realized that we were going to be showing this film to many people who would be shocked at the idea of delivering babies in people's kitchens and dining rooms, and we had to make a case as to why the Maternity Center was a positive thing. Although most of our parents and grandparents were born at home, birth has been moved into the hospital. People view that as moving forward. Although the home birth movement is strengthening, we had to build a case for why home delivery was good.

We had to present the operation of the Maternity Center, showing how the Maternity Center runs and on what principles it runs. You pay on your ability to pay. They concentrate on preventive medicine. They give a tremendous amount of attention to the patient. The Maternity Center was one of the few institutions left in the States that actually practiced medicine and wasn't a two-year-old, community free-health clinic. It was an eighty-year-old, very successful institution that played quite a role in the development of maternal care in this country.

B. The second part of the film, "The Struggle for Control," is devoted to trying to understand the historical concepts out of which the Center developed and why the Center was in a sense doomed as an institution in our society. We wanted to show why service-oriented health care, as opposed to product-consumer-oriented health care, was losing its place in the American health care system. We felt that it was really important that a long section of the film be devoted to a thorough analysis tracing the origin of the Center, as a charitable institution,

409

owned and controlled by what later became the corporate forces that owned and controlled the health care industry. We wanted to show how the Center was doomed to be shunted aside when the interests of the Center's Board of Directors changed. In the second part we also document the struggle of WATCH to try to save the Center.

Q. The film is very didactic. You have a female narrator who presents information and interprets for us. Since your earlier Kartemquin films utilize *cinéma vérité* techniques, why did you change your approach on this project?

B. When Kartemquin began, the films that it made were very socially conscious. There was *Home for Life,* a film about the Drexel Home for the Aged, *Thumbs Down,* a film about an antiwar youth group; *Marco,* a film about natural childbirth. They were all films in the *cinéma vérité* style and were committed to not having any narration and allowing actions, people, scenes to speak for themselves.

As the political situation in America changed, it became clearer to us as film makers and people who the enemy was. It became important for us to try to find the way (and this goes back to the question of style), to communicate that kind of analytical grasp of the situation. One way that you can do that in a film is by narration. There are other ways, but narration is certainly one of the most useful tools for communicating information, detail, and background which people need to understand a situation. Narration also helped to structure or point out certain details which were in fact up on the screen, but which might go unnoticed otherwise.

There is always a strong contradiction between the tension of wanting to let the scene play well without narration, yet also wanting to give people information, so that they could in fact achieve the same kind of understanding of the situation that we felt we had. In the Maternity Center film, we decided that we had to combine the two methods of film making and that if certain scenes were not as dramatically satisfying as they might be without the narration, well then that's too bad, because the information and the analysis are in fact very important.

Q. Many left-wing film makers feel that in order to change consciousness you not only have to have a revolutionary or radical text, but you have to put it into a radical form. The Maternity Center film has a very traditional presentation. How do you feel about revolutionary forms of film making?

B. There were differences of opinion within the group on that question. Some people were more of the Godard school. They felt that you did have to change the form; that stylistically you had to find the form appropriate to the ideological thrust of the film. That, stated in general terms, is something that I think everybody would agree on. Yes, you have to find a form that is appropriate. But a lot of us, and I for one, felt that it didn't have to be a new form. The ideas that are being expressed are not that new. They're ideas that people have to understand and that's what's most important, not that the film maker be personally satisfied, because he's found some abstract, philosophical form that he feels appropriate to the ideas that he's expressing. What's important is to find a form that will communicate the ideas, and I think that that is what someone like Godard often forgets. He's not that interested in communicating ideas to the people who need the communication. He's more interested in satisfying himself and perhaps a few of his intellectual friends.

Q. There is no footage of women who have delivered babies in hospitals. What was your thinking behind that decision?

R. In some of the interviews the women talked about the bad experience they've had in County Hospital. That could have been a strong portion of the film if we could have gotten into a hospital situation and shown the use of leather straps on the woman's wrists and ankles, IV's, routine anaesthesia, episiotomy—all the things that women experience in hospitals. But we realized that we couldn't really present everything and that most of the people that we were showing this film to had had that experience for themselves. They knew all that. The film would only repeat it and it would only be helpful in the case of women who hadn't had children and men who hadn't been present at the birth of any children. It was something that the film could do without.

Q. How did you divide up responsibility on this film?

R. Jerry and Gordon did the camerawork and sound initially; they shot the birth which is a really beautiful section of the film. That was one of the first shoots, in fact. Gradually over a period of time during the next two years, Sue and I assumed those responsibilities. We all participated in the editing and would have a number of meetings where we would draw up and go over film outlines. We really grappled with some structural problems because the film does develop several main themes. It shows you the Maternity Center; it shows you an historical analysis of health care in America; it shows you an institutional struggle of a community group versus a large institution; and it shows you through the use of the 1940s footage (*Fight for Life*) some of the historical significance of the Maternity Center itself.

B. At the same time it also follows the history of a single individual going through the Center: Scharene, the mother who is seen from her prenatal visit all the way through to post-natal care. The film is doing

411

a lot of things at once and it tended to divide itself up into sections and into scenes. People would work on major scenes, take the primary responsibility for a major scene, but always come back to the larger group. There were two larger groups. One the one hand there was the group within Kartemquin that was primarily responsible for the film and that group changed from time to time. And that group in turn was responsible to the collective as a whole. It presented its footage to the collective and expressed its ideas. The collective would hold the smaller group responsible saying, "Well, you thought you were going to get this done by then, and you didn't. What's happening with the maternity film? How come that's not done yet?"

q. How much feedback was there from the Maternity Center and WATCH?

r. Sue and I had both been active participants in the women's movement and women's organizations in Chicago. We decided that in order to make the film, to earn the trust of the people in the group and also to understand the issues that we were filming, we would join WATCH as members and participate in the strategy formation that their group went through.

q. Is this what you refer to as the "activist film making approach"?

r. That's one part of it. We wanted to make a film that continued to be *responsible* to the people who were in it and who would recognize its form. We didn't want them to say, "That wasn't what we did." Also since they were the people who would be active in similar struggles in other ways and who were the type of people that were the intended audience, we wanted their continued input.

What we did was to make a videotape of our film. The film was still in double system and couldn't be projected. We wanted to know if we were on the right track. Was it working? Was it understandable? Was the birth too scary to people?

We chose about six situations. We showed that videotape to several nursing classes, to a part of the WATCH group, to the Intercommunity Clinic, and we showed it at a Puerto Rican community house. We showed it in the situations where we wanted the film to be useful and had discussions afterwards with people. We learned from that that we were on the right track and also learned some things that really needed to be changed.

q. How was the Maternity Center film received?

b. First it's been well received by the groups for which it was made in Chicago. There was a series of six screenings in Chicago, in Latin and mixed working-class communities. The film was received very well by the mothers and nurses and health care people from the neighborhoods who came to those screenings. The film is being used very widely by women's groups, nurses, medical institutions, all over the country and it's been well received particularly on a different level, that is, the film festival circuit.

R. Jerry and I went to a festival in Berlin this summer. We were surprised that a critical film showing the state of health care in the United States would be of interest in Europe where health care has such a different emphasis, structure, and orientation. In fact, they loved it. They loved the fact that it's analytical and they see very few independent films out of the States that are that analytical. They love, of course, the fact that it is critical of the U.S. health care system.

Q. At this point what is the future of the collective?

B. The collective doesn't exist.

R. It's back down to the original two.

B. It's back to me and Gordon and some people we were working with very closely, like Jenny and a few others.

R. There's two or three of us in addition to Jerry and Gordon, who work around here on a limited basis. I work here only on distribution of the Maternity Center film.

B. Kartemquin has to retrench in a way by making films that will make it some money if it's going to survive and rebuild its financial base. At the same time it does that, it has to really come to grips with the question of what films need to be made now. We feel that it's not so clear as it was three years ago. The question can only be answered by seeing what work is being done by people who use films. Now when we look we see a situation that is quite ambiguous. Many of the groups that we related to on the left no longer exist. Those are the groups that we depended on, not only to use the films that we made, but also to do the work about which we would make movies.

R. There are still plenty of issues though.

B. The issues are there, but what's being done about them and what stance one is going to take with them is not so clear as it had been during the period when the collective really flourished. Another thing about the collective that is kind of an outgrowth of this whole discussion is that what the collective tried to do was to become a total service agency—an arm of the state. But that state did not exist. It had not yet come into existence. The work that we did encompassed the full spectrum of what you would expect a film-producing unit in a society to accomplish, producing films, distributing them, and teaching organizers how to use films.

And teaching people film skills, and political skills, all at the same time. And, at the same time, be a home for those people or a base out

413

of which those people could operate and survive economically. We in fact had set ourselves up as an arm of the state, but as I said, that state did not exist. The state that existed was in fact a state that was hostile to what we were trying to do and did not support our work.

R. Now what we're really faced with is finding a suitable mechanism to distribute the films we've made—to reach our intended audience. There's just no film distribution organization that offers a wide variety of socially conscious, issue-oriented films. There's very little of that kind of support from either the government or from private funding. We're trying to create that, to do it well, but it needs money.

NOTE: This interview conducted by Patrician Erens.

# 26

## *It Happens to Us*
### and
## *Nana, Mom and Me*
### Amalie Rothschild

*Amalie Rothschild's name crops up almost inevitably in any discussion of film makers who are exploring ideas and issues relating to women in the seventies. An extremely intense woman, she is concerned not just with film making but is also very involved in improving the lot of the independent film maker.*

*Her first film* Woo Who? May Wilson *is a poignant disarming study of a 60-year-old artist whose husband just walks out on her one day after forty years of marriage. Wilson has never known independence and the film is a funny rather than a sad story of May Wilson's attempt to bring that side of herself to life. The film was made while Rothschild was an M.F.A. student at New York University and won her a 1970 Cine Eagle award.*

*After graduating from NYU, Rothschild worked for three years doing special effects cinematography for the Joshua Light Show at the Fillmore East theater. During the same period she worked very widely as a free-lance photographer publishing everywhere from Time-Life books and* Newsweek *to* Rolling Stone *and* The Village Voice.

*In 1971, while still working for the Light Show she began production on* It Happens to Us, *raising $21,000 of production money from five different foundations.* It Happens to Us *is a plea for legalized abortion. Unlike many "educational" documentaries which swamp one with statistics and facts, the film is content to let twelve women speak candidly and simply about their own experiences. The stories reveal the problems of illegal versus legal medically safe abortions and illustrate the quandaries of the personal situations underlying this emotion-packed issue.*

*In the same year Rothschild helped organize and found a distribution company New Day Films together with Julia Reichert, James Klein and Liane Brandon. The move was both an attempt to stop the rip-off of independent film makers by distributors, and a move to open up the market and audiences to a slightly different type of film.*

*Nana,* Mom and Me *(1974) brings together two key themes of Rothschild — women and independence, and the nature of the family. The film began almost as a home movie about Rothschild's grandmother. Gradually, and partly because of the reluctance of "Nana" to be filmed, the film shifts focus to involve Amalie herself, and to explore the relationships between Amalie, her mother, and her grandmother. The film is very sensitively done and one comes away wondering not just about Rothschild's family but also about all one's own relationships.*

*Other important films of Rothschild's are* The Centre *(1970) which was produced for the defense fund of a Black Panther, Robert Collier, tried and acquitted in New York in 1971, and* It's All Right To Be A Woman *(1972). On* It's All Right, *which was made for Channel 13's show "The Fifty-First State" Rothschild got credits for photography and editing. At present she teaches narrative film at NYU and is currently shooting a film on Willard Van Dyke, the celebrated documentary film pioneer.*

Q. Prior to going to film school what did you see yourself doing in film?

A. My background was graphic design and still photography and I saw myself getting involved in film work by using those skills. My hero was Saul Bass who did all kinds of fancy graphics and animated title sequences and that's how I saw myself. My idea of the ideal job at that time would have been to do animation and cinemagraphics for a commercial firm. However, after my first year in film school many things in my personal life began to coalesce and take shape to the point where I began to realize that I had ideas of my own that I wanted to express in film.

Q. I would like to go more into this because the body of your film work deals very much with women, their lives, their problems. How, in fact, did everything come together?

A. It has a lot to do with a very disturbing event in my personal life that catalyzed a lot of internal changes that allowed me to make the "leap in consciousness," and I use that phrase with quotes around it, to connect with ideas that I had of my own to express in film.

I had been engaged to a Rumanian film maker, my first real love, who died, and that experience knocked me way down. It was overcoming it that really got me in touch with my own needs and drives for the first time. Suddenly I began to see myself as a *separate* person and not as someone whose identity was tied to working with someone else. It was that experience, once I survived it and overcame it, which set me up on my feet independently and separately as a complete person.

Q. Your first film, *Woo Who? May Wilson*, was shot at film school. Was that film related to this searching you were going through at the time?

416

A. Very much. I had gotten to know May when I was in high school because she was an artist colleague of my mother's and they had exhibited together. I would see her at gallery openings and I became fascinated by her. When I began film school in New York I looked her up, and we became very close.

As you also know, the film really focuses on her overcoming a period of acute emotional crisis in her life and discovering her own independence for the first time. She had been a suburban housewife in Maryland. At sixty, her 40-year marriage breaks up, and she's forced to find a new life of her own. That whole experience of hers connected very closely with what I had just gone through and that's why I felt comfortable and close to her and really identified tremendously. I knew that what she had gone through was an important experience. It was a story that needed to be told and I connected with it because of my own personal involvement with those same issues. Of course, what turned out later on was that the film struck a responsive and important chord in many women.

Q. Can we take that further—how women responded to it in the late sixties?

A. Well, by the time the film was finished the women's movement was being publicly recognized at last, and these things were finally beginning to come out into the open and be acknowledged as valid areas of concern. So the film was really born of its time and it was the women's movement that enabled it to find an audience and a life of its own.

Q. I remember you doing various short films after that and then coming out with *It Happens to Us,* about abortion. Were you thinking about the subject a long time?

A. Well, yes. I understood the implications of the subject through my own experience of having an abortion and came to see that that was the next area that was burning me up to make a film about. It was made over a very long period of time. It was a stop-and-start production as I kept running out of money.

Q. Where were you going for money?

A. Well, I basically raised the money through five different foundations. I had three matching grants for $5,000 each and two matching grants for $3,000, a total of $21,000 in all. The actual production budget of the film was around $18,000 and I used the additional $3,000 to launch the distribution.

I started the film by putting in about $1,000 to begin shooting and I lucked onto the discovery that you have a much better chance of raising money for a film if you've already gone out on a limb with a

417

project and begun to shoot. People then begin to look at the material. They know that you're committed to the project and are not going to back out.

Q. When did you really commit yourself to the film?

A. There was a big demonstration for legalized abortion in Albany in March 1971 and I put together a crew at the last minute. I wavered and vacillated back and forth whether I should go to Albany and film or not and would it really make a difference. Then, two days before the rally, I decided that if I was going to do this thing I'd better put my ideas where my mouth was, so I went.

And then I seriously began looking for the means to finance the film. I made a lot of initial phone calls and one call led to another as people gave me different leads. I also recognized that I had to have an arrangement with a nonprofit tax-exempt organization that would sponsor the film and be the conduit for raising funds. So I started looking for someone who was connected with a group that would be interested in the subject.

Eventually, through the phone network, I heard of a woman doctor, Felicia Hance, who was then vice-president of the Medical Committee for Human Rights. The head of the organization was Dr. Quentin Young, who is a rather well-known and very outspoken physician and important supporter of radical changes in the American health care delivery system. We met, and they both agreed to get involved with the project and help me with the fund raising. We made contacts and wrote proposals for about four months and then one week in July I suddenly found myself with $10,000. The proposal had gotten through two places each of which said, "Well, if the other one puts up some money, we'll put up some money." So they both agreed and were willing, and we had a solid shooting amount.

Q. What did you want this film to do? What kind of audience were you aiming at?

A. I was aiming at a middle-class audience who probably had not had any personal experience with abortion in their lives. I felt, if they understood emotionally what was involved and the life circumstances of the women who find that abortion is the only solution to their unwanted pregnancies, they might view the whole situation more sympathetically. I wanted them to understand that women must have the choice to decide for themselves how they're going to deal with the circumstances. And I knew what this audience was probably thinking because of my own unrealized biases and prejudices. Until it happened to me I basically thought that any woman who found herself with an unwanted pregnancy was somehow personally responsible. I thought

418

that she was either careless, or stupid, or secretly wanted to be pregnant and that in any event, it was her problem and her fault. When I became pregnant myself I realized through my own circumstances that that certainly was not the case, and I had to confront my old unsuspected attitudes. And then it was a real blow to discover my own prejudices against other women.

Now, I considered myself pretty open-minded and unprejudiced and it finally sunk in that if I had felt that way without knowing it, God knows how many other people did as well, and maybe the best thing I could do would be to make a film that would lay out the arguments and information on the subject. I wanted to show the emotional and personal levels of the situation. I wanted to tell the stories of women who had been through this experience and share those stories and those things with other people in a very open and honest way so that perhaps they would come around to the same way of thinking and understanding.

Q. Were you working with an all-female crew?

A. Yes, and for a number of reasons, first of all because I knew many women who were working in film who were competent technicians and who clearly needed work. But the other reason, which was really the more important one, was that it was clear to me that there would be a much greater atmosphere of trust among the women I was interviewing about their abortion experiences if there were only women present. I thought a rapport and a feeling of sisterhood was absolutely necessary so that the women I was interviewing would feel free enough to share their very personal and very intense and in some cases painful abortion experiences with us in front of the camera.

Q. You must have had to make very difficult human judgments within the film. Were there any scenes which you shot, which in the end you thought were just too sensitive or too painful to put in the final film?

A. Well, that worked in a slightly different way. The interviews I eliminated were cut mostly because of aesthetic decisions about the way in which some of the women came across. Also in some cases there was repetition or one person told a similar story better than another.

I did preliminary interviews with between thirty-five and forty women from all walks of life. Black women, white women, poor, rich, old, young, and so on and so forth—seeking a real cross-section of what I discovered were the basic kinds of circumstances that people's abortion stories fell into. I then selected twelve women whom I actually filmed interviews with, and portions from ten of them appear in the film.

Q. You said you wanted to make a film for a fairly wide general audience. How did you go about selling it? What were the responses of the distribution companies you went to, with a film that handled such a controversial issue as abortion?

A. I never went to any distributors with it. I wouldn't have given it to anybody else for anything in the world. I wanted to distribute it myself because I felt I knew best for whom it was made.

When I say that I knew best, it's not to say that I knew very much about distribution in general but that I was committed to the subject from start to finish and that included getting it out to people. Anyway, while we were working on the film my sound woman kept telling me about some friends of hers she had gone to college with who were making a women's film called *Growing Up Female*. They were in Ohio and I really should see it and so on. She told me a fair amount about the people who made it, Julia Reichert and Jim Klein, and I ended up meeting them at the 1971 Flaherty Film Seminar.

At that point I had already been having some serious discussions with several other women who were interested in setting up their own distribution and we had gone fairly far in making a decision to do something. In the end it didn't work out but then I met Julia and Jim and they had already begun this process themselves with *Growing Up Female*. We hit it off right away and they said they were interested in joining up with someone else as well. As it happened I was still in the middle of production of *It Happens to Us*. I showed them what I'd cut so far and they got very excited. They were just moving to New York and came to stay with me for three months. They saw a lot of the rushes, and got very involved with the film. In fact, as a result of all that Julia opened up about her own abortion experience and I filmed an interview with her that became one of the more powerful stories. She is the woman who had the very devastating encounter with her father who blamed her for getting pregnant, and had a very awful, illegal abortion experience. So New Day, our distribution cooperative, was born out of all that.

Later that Fall, Julia and I were both on the screening committee for the First International Festival of Women's Films (the screenings were held in my loft twice a week) and during one of those screenings we saw a film, *Anything You Want to Be*, by Liane Brandon. We liked her film very much and on the basis of that, Julia went up to Boston to meet Liane, to talk to her, and to find out what she was doing, how her film was being distributed, and if she was perhaps interested in distributing it herself and getting involved. Essentially that's how we first got together with the three original New Day films, *Growing Up Female, Anything You Want to Be,* and *It Happens to Us.*

Q. How did you organize the distribution?

A. The backbone for distribution is mass mailings of catalogues and information about the films to people, mostly in education, who are likely to use them. We did a 10,000-piece mailing and it went, for example, to the head of the department of sociology and the head of the department of psychology, in every university and college in the entire United States. We sent the brochures to schools, libraries, universities, junior colleges, technical schools, vocational schools, and community groups and organizations. We sent the brochures to anyone we thought could use the films as tools for discussion and for the raising of the important issues that we felt people would want to know about. In fact the underlying concept of New Day is based on the idea that films are tools for social change and that one's concern as a social and political film maker is to start educating the public on a wider scale to the issues that one's films are designed to raise.

The perennial problem for all film makers is, once the film is made, what good does it do if people don't see it? How do I get people to see my film? We faced that problem directly because at the time none of the existing commercial educational film distributors were interested in films about women. It was a new area that was not yet proven financially viable. You have to understand that commercial distributors are not there to take risks on the creation of new audiences. They are there to make money from what they've already learned will work. However, our work with New Day proved that there was, in fact, this huge audience out there interested in the subject of women.

Of course, once it became clear that "women's films" were salable, the commercial distributors suddenly wanted to handle some and everybody suddenly had to have women's films—or at least a token women's film.

Q. When you go through a commercial distributor in the States what percentage of the profit do they keep and what do they pass on?

A. That's the bleak side of the picture. Film makers don't generally make a living from their films and that's because the distributors take anywhere from 75 percent to 80 percent of the profit. Today, in 1977, you know you've got a good deal if you can manage to get 25 percent. It used to be that 25 percent to 35 percent of the royalty would go to the film maker. Now 15 percent and 20 percent is what they generally offer and if you have a film they really want and if you're a hard negotiator or whatever, then you get 25 percent and that's not a whole lot. Of course, after having become a distributor myself, I also understand what costs and expenses are, but with the present system the idea of distributing the film oneself has become important for many film makers.

Q. In *May Wilson* and in the abortion film you were working with subjects which related to your life sometimes centrally, sometimes more peripherally. In *Nana, Mom and Me* you deal with your grandmother, mother and yourself. How did that film begin?

A. It began very simply as a film about my grandmother, and I didn't think it would be for any audience other than my family. Nana had had a very serious operation when she was 84, from which she had not expected to recover. In fact it took her a full year afterwards to accept the fact that she was still alive. She aged incredibly during that year and it was very shocking and alarming and disturbing to me to finally see my grandmother as an old woman and realize that she was mortal and that she simply wouldn't be in my life forever. I wanted to keep her alive and have a record and to catch her for my children when and if I had them, so that they would know who this woman was who had been so important to me and the family. And that's really how it started.

I just began by filming some family stories of one thing and another. Unfortunately Nana was not cooperative. She wasn't very enthusiastic about the project and the idea. It took me six months to get to film her for the first time. I would make plans to get down to Baltimore with the equipment, and then at the very last minute I'd get this panic phone call, "Nana doesn't feel well, don't come." At a certain point I caught on and just went down there with a Nagra and recorded her voice, some family stories, and people talking to her. And she seemed to go along with that.

And then, in October of 1972, my mother decided to take her on a trip to Virginia and invited me and my sister to come as well. I asked my mother about bringing the camera and she finally said, "Well, it's up to you, but if you do bring it, don't expect to be able to use it. If you want to have it there just in case, that's your business, but you don't know how she's going to react to it, so we won't tell her." So I didn't tell her. I just went and showed up with all the gear. I had to do the shooting because I couldn't bring anyone else and I taught my sister to take sound.

Q. Could you tell me more about your mother's attitude?

A. She was very cooperative, but at that stage wasn't part of the film herself. She recognized that if Nana had known in advance she probably would have gotten sick and not gone. Once, of course, I was there

422

I just used my chances and shot about 2,000 feet over the span of an entire week. It wasn't a lot, but it was a beginning. And then I went and put the material on a shelf because I didn't have any more money to sink into it and I was moving on to other projects.

Some months later I got a $10,000 film maker's grant from the American Film Institute for a project about women and mental health. It had a much larger budget, close to $50,000. To cut the story short, I couldn't raise the extra $40,000 for the mental health film but after some correspondence with AFI they agreed to let me put their money towards a film about my family. However, even at that time it was still a film about my grandmother.

Finally I had the funds to go ahead seriously with the project. In August of 1973 I went down to Maryland for four days and the first day we had a family crab feast, which is a real Maryland tradition. Nana was all excited because she'd invited a lot of members of the family and she was making her famous crab soup, and these were all things that I wanted to film because this feast was a real central event in our family life. But it was a very exhausting day for her. She was 86. She'd started at 6 A.M. working in the hot kitchen and continued right through the day preparing for a dinner that didn't end until nine o'clock at night. Of course she was exhausted, but she attributed her exhaustion to the fact that I had been making a film at the same time. Thereupon she decided that she would no longer have anything to do with my crazy film project because it had wiped her out.

So it was then I began turning to my mother, initially for information about Nana that I was no longer able to get from Nana herself. And it was only then that I began to discover my mother as a daughter for the first time—which was a revelation to me. I also began to understand that the film I had all along really wanted to make was more about *my mother* who has been *the* pivotal influence in my life. For years I hadn't really known how to get close to her and how to approach her. Now something was happening, and the film really began to grow and take off at that point. It suddenly became clear to me what I was really after. And the way the film is assembled is very much a reflection of the sequence of events that happened over the film making process— a sequence that I wanted to preserve as part of the odyssey of discovery.

Q. Was your mother totally open and totally cooperative with you? Was she keen on the project?

A. No, she wasn't. She was very ambivalent and I think that uncertainty is in many ways evident in the film. I felt that uncertainty while I was making the film but it was not entirely clear to me where it was coming from. I was upset by the fact my mother wouldn't trust me and was wary. Later I saw that it came out of her concern that she would not be presented in the film as an artist and as a professional person. She was afraid that all I was going to do was show her as Nana's daughter and my mother and not as the separate professional person that she was.

Now that was an astounding revelation for me. I hadn't realized that she was worried that I wouldn't show her as a professional because it was as a *professional* that she had been such an important force in my life. That was the real person that she had always been to me and that was the most crucial thing for me to deal with because it was what I admired most about her. Once she understood that, she began to loosen up. There was another dynamic that was operating also because of the fact that *I* was filming *her* and using my *professional and creative tools to reveal her*.

This was part of the subtext and undercurrent of the rivalry that in fact has long existed between us and which I attempt, as openly as I can under the circumstances, to deal with directly in the film. I also think it's probably one of the most important, crucial and controversial areas in the film; that whole discussion towards the end of the mother-daughter rivalry which comes about as a result of our names being the same. When we started discussing the fact that we had the same name that brought it all to the surface and made it possible to see the emotional terrain more directly.

Q. You've become known as one of the more prominent American film makers dealing with women's issues. Is this a mantle you gladly accept or is it something you want to throw off? Would you say that the whole subject of women has still not been treated well on film?

A. Of course it hasn't been explored adequately. The surface is just beginning to be scratched a little bit, and as you're probably well aware, the commercial cinema is light years behind. There have been very few commercial films that have dealt successfully and positively in any way with women as equal and full members of the human race. But the whole thing of "women's film" is a term that really needs to be defined. It's very vague. It has meant many different things at many different periods. In the thirties and forties, women's films were soap operas, tearjerkers, designed for what was at the time, derogatorily, seen as a women's market—you know, housewives who needed romantic fantasies. Women's films today, of course, mean something different, but while lip service has been paid to equality, I don't think things have changed as much as we've all been led to believe and would like to believe. There still is a negative connotation in the mass public's mind to women's films, and they see them as militant, radical, badly

424

made, strange documentary things that nobody understands, coming out of some radical fringe.

Q. Where would you like to see yourself going? Or what would you like to see yourself doing in the next few years?

A. I've recently been moving into and around fiction film making for a variety of reasons. One is directly connected to the experiences I had making *Nana, Mom and Me,* which is that I felt I had really pushed back barriers as far as I could in terms of delving into intensely personal and private matters in real people's lives. I think that documentary film makers have a very profound responsibility to the privacy and dignity of the individuals whom they're making films about and that there are limitations as to how far you can go without crossing that thin line beyond which you're exploiting someone else for your own art. For myself, I have certain personal ground rules that I won't break.

While making *Nana, Mom and Me* I found that there were certain thematic areas I was interested in exploring further, particularly mother-daughter relationships for example, that I couldn't possibly do in a documentary film with real people. And therefore it is a logical extension to turn to the freedom of fiction film making where you can express those ideas very directly. So I do see myself as eventually going on to feature film making, but I'm not in a hurry. I want to get there in steps. And I never intend to stop making documentaries.

435

| | |
|---|---|
| Compositor: | Chapman's Phototypesetting |
| Printer: | Murray Printing Co. |
| Binder: | Murray Printing Co. |
| Text: | VIP Janson |
| Display: | VIP Helvetica Italic |
| Cloth: | Holliston Roxite B 53603 |
| Paper: | 50 lb. Writers Offset |